International African Library 5
General Editors: David Parkin and J.D.Y. Peel

IDENTITIES ON THE MOVE

International African Library
General Editors

J. D. Y. Peel *and* David Parkin

The *International African Library* is a major monograph series from the International African Institute and complements its quarterly periodical *Africa*, the premier journal in the field of African studies. Theoretically informed ethnographies, studies of social relations 'on the ground' which are sensitive to local cultural forms, have long been central to the Institute's publications programme. The *IAL* maintains this strength but extends it into new areas of contemporary concern, both practical and intellectual. So it includes works focused on problems of development, especially on the linkages between the local and national levels of society; studies along the interface between the social and the environmental sciences; and historical studies, especially those of a social, cultural or interdisciplinary character.

★ Published in the USA by Indiana University Press

IDENTITIES ON THE MOVE

CLANSHIP AND PASTORALISM
IN NORTHERN KENYA

Günther Schlee

MANCHESTER UNIVERSITY PRESS
for the INTERNATIONAL AFRICAN INSTITUTE, London

MANCHESTER AND NEW YORK

Distributed exclusively in the USA and Canada by St. Martin's Press

Copyright © Günther Schlee 1989

Published by Manchester University Press
Oxford Road, Manchester M13 9PL, UK
and Room 400, 175 Fifth Avenue,
New York, NY 10010, USA

Distributed exclusively in the USA and Canada
by St. Martin's Press, Inc.,
175 Fifth Avenue, New York, NY 10010, USA

British Library cataloguing in publication data
Schlee, Günther
  Identities on the move: clanship and pastoralism
  in northern Kenya.—(International African
  library, 5).
  I. Kenya. Ethnic groups
  I. Title   II. International African Institute
  III. Series
  305.8′009676′2

Library of Congress cataloging in publication data applied for

ISBN 0-7190-3010-2 hardback

Typeset in Hong Kong by Best-set Typesetter Limited

Printed in Great Britain
by Biddles Ltd, Guildford and King's Lynn

CONTENTS

MAPS, DIAGRAMS AND TABLES

TABLES

FOREWORD

This study brings together, in an imaginative and innovative way, what have been separate modes of investigation. As old tribal designations have come to seem fuzzier and fuzzier we have all become increasingly interested in the interactions of culture and ethnicity. Some have looked to broader categories such as emergent classes, elites and new social and political formations, while others, especially those concerned with agricultural developments, have concentrated on analyses of social and productive relationships in and between homesteads which have decision-making autonomy about production and consumption. Professor Schlee's starting point has been with those relationships which traverse ethnic boundaries. Many Rendille pastoral homesteads maintain and utilise ritual and social relationships across ethnic boundaries and in hard times, such as the recent droughts, make use of them for assistance. Those relationships are rooted in shared clanship and are quite distinct from stock contracts or stock friendships, in that they are ascriptive and not contractual. Members of the same clan may belong to ethnic groups which are quite different culturally and speak distinct languages and, indeed, may well be hostile. In order to understand these links Professor Schlee was led to detailed studies of local clan histories.

This book documents such connections among the Rendille, Sakuye, Gabbra and Somali of northern Kenya, but such connections probably ramify across the Horn. As the markers of clan identities differ from those used to mark the broader ethnic identities, obviously language cannot be one. The markers are similar names, shared stock and property marks, similar ritual practices and avoidances, bodies of shared knowledge and rules of exogamy. These markers pre-date the formation of present ethnic groups. In order to reconstruct clan and ethnic identities Professor Schlee has drawn on insights derived from German ethnological and linguistic theorists. This particular blend of social anthropology, history, comparative linguistics and ethnology has, I think, been immensely productive. Certainly my own understanding of inter-ethnic relationships and of the cultures of the Cushitic-speaking peoples has been enlarged. The synthesis of methods is so productive because of the range and depth of Professor Schlee's field research, his fluent command of the Rendille, Boran and Somali languages, and his knowledge of neighbouring languages and cultures. Surely it is on such in-depth studies, rather than on short research visits, that African studies must depend if they are to have an intellectual future. The methods pioneered here, I am confident, could be applied elsewhere, and certainly to the Oromo peoples, the inter-lacustrine Bantu and the Nilotes.

I am honoured to be associated with this ethnographic voyage of discovery.

P. T. W. Baxter
University of Manchester
March 1989

ACKNOWLEDGEMENTS

A number of colleagues helped me, much beyond the usual exchange of ideas in organisational and practical matters, with advice and contacts. After lengthy deliberation I decided against listing them here because I did not know where to draw the line. Some of those who gave encouragement and practical help are also among those who contributed ideas and information and can therefore be found mentioned repeatedly in the bibliography and in the footnotes, in which our discussions are quoted.

The same applies to the informants in the field: I only quote the interviews with them below and do not list them here, although their help in many cases went far beyond the interview sessions. But again, I did not know where to draw the line.

One person, however, who is neither a colleague nor an informant must be mentioned here because his contributions are not cited below. Tony Troughear, an Australian teacher and journalist, showed me much of the less accessible literature, introduced me to helpful people and kept me informed about Kenya's social scene. He was permanently based in Kenya whereas I, because of various commitments, had to spend about half the last decade in Germany. That he now has gone back to Australia is a loss to many people.

My wife Isir went through the Somali, Boran and Rendille texts. Frau Gertraud Specht in Bayreuth did vast amounts of typing – earlier versions of the manuscript were much longer than the present work – and Frau Liisa Kurz in Bielefeld finished the remainder after I moved to Bielefeld.

In 1975–76 I spent eighteen months in Kenya with the financial help of the Studienstiftung des Deutschen Volkes. The results of this research have let to earlier publications but have also contributed directly and indirectly to the present work. From 1978 to 1980 and in 1984, 1985, 1986 and 1987 I received grants and travel funds from the DFG (German Research Board) to go to Kenya and Ethiopia, first individually (Schl/186/1) later in the framework of the Bayreuth 'Identity in Africa' project (SFB 214: A3, A4, A6). A shorter trip in 1981 was financed by the University of Bayreuth. I thank them all.

CHAPTER 1

INTRODUCTION

Social identities are subject to constant redefinition by their bearers and others. Groups can change their composition, or their status, or their name, or their affiliation, or even all these features. There is no reason to believe that the ethnic group, the preferred unit of study of social and cultural anthropologists, is exempt from such processes of remoulding. In fact, the recent and artificial nature of some ethnic identities – a number of which have apparently only formed in response to colonial rule – has repeatedly been stressed.

There are no theoretical grounds for giving the ethnic group precedence as the unit of study at the expense of other social units and networks, whether they be larger or smaller than the ethnic group or of a similar size but different in nature.

Why then are anthropological studies of poly-ethnic districts, international networks, trans-ethnic links, etc. so comparatively rare, while studies of ethnically and linguistically homogeneous and spatially contiguous groups still form the subject matter of the typical monograph? Apart from pragmatic reasons (such studies might involve learning more than one non-European language and necessitate much travelling),[1] some of the established patterns of social anthropology seem to generate 'units' and 'subunits' which reinforce the tradition of the mono-ethnic monograph.[2]

A theoretical concept widely used in monographical studies of African – and later also Melanesian – societies is that of the segmentary lineage system. Such systems necessarily comprise hierarchical taxonomies. A tribe is subdivided into major lineages, then into minor and finally into minimal lineages, or into phratries, clans, subclans, lineages and so on.

The segmentary model which shows the clan as a subunit of a tribe and/or an ethnic unit does not show the disposition of the same clan in different ethnic groups. Inter-ethnic clan relationships cannot easily be incorporated in the treelike diagrams which depict segmentary systems. From the perspective of a clan, its representations in different ethnic groups are subunits, while the clan as a whole might not be demographically smaller or sociologically less important than any single ethnic unit. This double hierarchy can be depicted by two tree diagrams (Diagram 1).

This book examines inter-ethnic clan relationships, clan by clan, between a number of Cushitic-speaking ethnic groups of northern Kenya and southern Ethiopia. Their linguistic, religious and other cultural differences are quite marked but, nevertheless, their cross-ethnic clan ties form a dense web.

The Rendille who live in the southern part of Marsabit District, between Lake Rudolf (Turkana) in the west and Marsabit in the east, are mostly camel nomads. The 1979 census (Republic of Kenya 1981) gives their number as 21,794. This number, which is based on self-classification, also comprises the Ariaal (see p. 9) and about 2000 migrant labourers

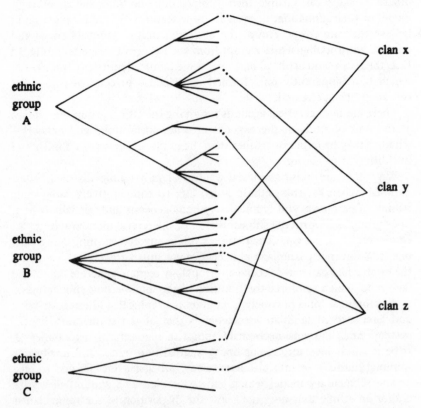

Diagram 1   Alternative forms of inclusion of clans into major units

who no longer participate in the pastoral economy but work as nightwatch-
men, soldiers or policemen in towns and garrisons throughout Kenya.
They speak a Somaloid language which, if it were spoken in Somalia,
could have been classified as a Somali dialect. Ethnically, quite clearly,
they are not Somali because they do not perceive themselves as such, and
because they are not Muslims – Islam is one of the main components of
Somali identity. The belief system of the Rendille is a traditional mono-
theism not unlike that of the Gabbra and the Boran (see Schlee, 1979, who
focuses on Rendille beliefs).

The northern neighbours of the Rendille are the Gabbra who extend to
and beyond the Ethiopian border in an area which is even drier and
harsher than Rendilleland and which largely consists of immense rugged
lava fields. One separate local subgroup is the 6000 or so Gabbra Miigo of
the northern part of Wajir District. Together the Kenyan Gabbra number
30,553 (1979 census).[3] Their language is the Boran dialect of Oromo. The
Gabbra Malbe adhere to their traditional beliefs. The Gabbra Miigo refer
to themselves as Muslims, at least in their contacts with outsiders.

The Sakuye live in two separate clusters, one around Dabel, in the
northern part of the Marsabit District not far from the Ethiopian border
on the Moyale–Wajir road, another in the Waso (river) area of Isiolo
District (i.e. along the Ewaso Nyiro).[4]

Today many Sakuye, formerly camel nomads very similar to the Gabbra, have been reduced to peri-urban pauperism because of the *shifta* war
of the sixties. (They have been regarded by the separatist Somali as Boran,
i.e. pro-Kenyan, and have been raided accordingly, while the government forces, mistrusting all nomads, suspected them of supplying the
separatists with food and therefore machine-gunned their camel herds.)
The number given by the 1979 census, 1824 persons, is far too low.
Because of their language and their interlocking settlements many southern
Sakuye must have said Boran when asked for their tribe. The Sakuye have
been weakened by recent events and to identify oneself as a Sakuye no
longer sounds attractive. The preceding census of 1969 gave their number
as 4369, and the decrease is not due to biological factors but rather to the
fact that the census was an official event on the national level and that
Sakuye as an ethnonym is losing some of its wider currency, even though
it may continue to be locally important. The Sakuye have converted from
traditional theism to Islam within the memory of some living elders.[5]

The Boran, whose language the originally unrelated Gabbra and Sakuye
have adopted, belong to the wider Oromo nation, of which they form the
subgroup which has had the most important influence on Kenyan history.
They do not form part of the inter-ethnic network of clan identities which
is the theme of this study but they have to be included because of the
hegemonical role they played in the area and because of the catalytic

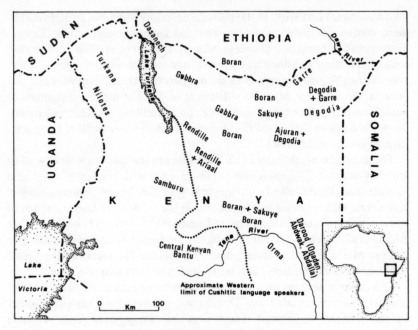

Map 1   Distribution of ethnic groups
Source: Schlee 1985b.

impulses they gave to the ethnogenetic processes of others. The main body
of the Boran live in Ethiopia. In Kenya they number 68,894: a large group
in comparison to others in the arid lowlands of northern Kenya but small
in comparison to their brethren in the higher and more fertile Ethiopian
cradleland.

The Kenyan Boran mostly practise their traditional cattle economy
rather than camel nomadism and therefore tend to concentrate in the
more favourable areas along the Ethiopian escarpment, on Mount Marsabit and along the Waso. They comprise both Islamised segments and
traditionalists.

The Somali groups which are most important for our study are the
Ajuran and the Garre.

The Ajuran can be found in many locations in the different states of the
Horn. In Kenya an important concentration lives in the northern part of
Wajir District. Like all Somali, they are Muslims. They number 22,006.
Some of them are Oromo monolinguals, while others are bilingual, and yet
others, who stem from later immigrants, speak only Somali.

The population of the Garre in Kenya is 83,083. They mainly live in the
districts of Wajir and Mandera. Many Garre also live in Ethiopia and

Somalia. Their linguistic situation is similar to that of the Ajuran. Their wide area of dispersal comprises both bovine and camel pastures. Like some of the Degodia Somali, who are numerous in Kenya (93,035),[6] some Ajuran are traders in the areas of other pastoralists. Trading is one of the many types of contact between the different groups.[7]

Although the linguistic differences are marked,[8] they are bridged by a high incidence of bilingualism. A negative aspect of inter-ethnic relationships is that they often consist of intensive mutual raiding and warfare, which, if it occurs between 'pagans' and Muslims, is often ideologised as 'holy war' by the latter. Consciousness of belonging to a single state and nation is weak.

Ethnic differences are also evident in dress, custom and attitudes. In the process of ethnic reaffiliation, for example, if a Rendille girl marries a Somali, she will have to exchange one standard of cleanliness, decency and beauty and all the habits associated with it for another standard and a different set of habits. She will have to abandon fat and red ochre for water, soap and perfume, skins for clothes, huge loads of glass beads, wire, and brass coils for a few grammes of gold. Ethnicity is thus very visible.

These ethnic differences have been thought of as quite stable over time. The ethnographers of Boran-speaking groups such as the Gabbra and the Sakuye (e.g. Torry 1973 and cursorily Haberland 1963: 141ff.) often describe these groups as subunits of the Boran or as being of Boran origin – but wrongly, as we shall see. The British colonial administration shared this view and drew a territorial boundary between the two broad categories of peoples they recognised in the area: 'Galla' and 'Somali'.[9] In fact, as we shall see, many of the so-called 'Galla' are more 'Somali' than anything else.[10] In spite of marked cultural differences which pervade almost all levels of culture and spheres of life (language, religion, political affiliation and organisation, habits, dress, ornaments, etc.) these Lowland Eastern Cushitic-speaking pastoralists share many clans. The Gabbra, the Rendille, the Sakuye and the Garre in particular can be shown to be composed of clans many of which occur in two or more of them. These inter-ethnic clan relationships will be analysed synchronically and diachronically (or sociologically and historically).

The historical question is how have these relationships come to be? This I attempt to answer by a combination of two methods: (a) the evaluation of verbal sources, including written sources, which are scarce in this area, and oral sources; and (b) cultural comparison. My conclusion is that the clan relationships between the Rendille, the Gabbra, the Sakuye and the Garre, i.e. the clan relationships on which this study concentrates, are due to a common origin, while other clan relationships, those between some of these groups and the Boran, stem from a political alliance which expresses itself in collective adoptions. The strongest arguments for a common

origin have been derived from comparisons of clan-specific cultural features. Many of these, and not only those which are consciously used as
group-identifying symbols (name, ostentatious food avoidances, etc.), are
shared between 'brother' clans in different ethnic groups. Common origins
and subsequent splits are also reported by oral history, so the two types of
evidence used confirm each other.

The clan fissions and clan migrations can be seen in a framework of major
ethnogenetic developments. They stem from the time before the Oromo
expansion (sixteenth century) when the present ethnic divisions in this
area did not yet exist. The ancestors of the Gabbra, the Rendille, the
Sakuye and the Garre (and possibly some others) then shared a culture
which I reconstruct from what is left of it. I call this the PRS culture
(proto Rendille–Somali) after the westernmost and easternmost of its
heirs. The question of how many other Somali groups, apart from the
ancestral Garre, once shared this culture will be discussed but cannot be
answered in a definite way. The PRS culture is most conspicuously
marked by a unique calendrical system and a related set of rules for the
proper treatment of camels. Whatever internal divisions existed between
the bearers of the original PRS culture, they did not coincide with the
present-day ethnic boundaries. These latter are due to two factors which
have affected northern Kenya and southern Ethiopia since the sixteenth
century.

The Oromo expansion, which has to be seen in conjunction with a
reorganisation of the *gada* system (see below), changed the power balance
in the area. Some bearers of the PRS culture (e.g. the Gabbra Miigo) soon
accepted Boran Oromo hegemony, others (the Gabbra Malbe and the
Garre) only after a number of migrations which were aimed at removing
them from the Boran sphere but which in the end led some of them back
into it. The Rendille always remained enemies of the Boran. A population
that split from the Rendille in the seventeenth century, however, in
association with other (Garre-like) elements, became the Sakuye and
under this name joined the Boran-centred alliance. Because of these
developments some heirs of the PRS culture speak the Oromo dialect of
the Boran (the Sakuye, the Gabbra, and some Garre) while others speak
their original Somaloid and Somali languages (the Rendille and the Garre
Kofar).

These ethnic divisions were deepened by another factor, Islam, which
affected some groups (the Garre, other Somali) more, others (the Sakuye
until recently, the Gabbra) less, and yet others (the Rendille) practically
not at all. Many of the inter-ethnic clan relationships discussed in this
book thus stem from the fact that the original population split and became
ethnically differentiated across clan boundaries; others stem from later
inter-ethnic migrations.

The historical circumstances of how these clan relationships came to be are also of some sociological interest. In the past historical anthropology has been regarded as a continental tradition[11] and the sociological variant as typical of Britain. Anthropology thus divided into two disciplines which were pursued in different places by different people. What I want to demonstrate is that it is not the diachronic nor the synchronic perspectives on their own from which new insights are to be expected but from a combination of the two: we should not be exclusively interested in systems nor in processes but in both, and we should try to observe how systems change through time. The fact that many of the clans in different ethnic groups of northern Kenya are related by origin and the fact that the relationship is supported by historical memory also make them different on the sociological level from clan brotherhoods which are purely contractual. A relationship which is based on nothing but an agreement needs to be constantly renewed and activated or it soon becomes obsolete, as is the case with the clan relationships between the Boran and their former political allies. On the other hand, a relationship by origin defined by socially recognised descent can remain latent for generations and then be activated when the need arises. Examples will be given of inter-ethnic clan relationships which, intermittently throughout the centuries, have been used for economic relief in times of stress, for intermigration, conflict solving, hospitality and other purposes. These inter-ethnic clan relationships have thus been integrated into the wide-spun systems of alliance and mutual help typical of pastoral nomads who subsist in harsh and threatening environments.

CHAPTER 2

CLAN, PHRATRY, TRIBE, ETHNIC GROUP AS DEFINED BY EMPIRICAL FINDINGS

The possibilities of social organisation are so numerous, the rules by which people choose marriage partners or address relatives so different, that even for closely related groups we cannot assume beforehand that social units of the same scale have, even approximately, the same tasks and functions. It is impossible to apply any of the terms we want to define here to any two societies studied in exactly the same sense, that is, to find an interculturally valid definition. For example, what in Rendille we call a 'clan' has – with two exceptions – exogamy as a main feature and this can be used as a definition by both the Rendille and an anthropological researcher. Any member of the same clan will be addressed in kinship terms which correspond to patrilinial relatives – i.e. first ascending generation: Fa, FaBr, FaSi; Ego's generation: elder Br, elder Si (for younger siblings: name); women who have married into the clan are addressed and treated as Mo, MoSi = FaBrWi, or in one's own generation Wi and BrWi. Among the Somali there are social units of the same scale and with very similar kinship terminology, but they are, however, not exogamous. Should we therefore exclude exogamy as a feature of definition also for the Rendille because it cannot be generalised inter-ethnically? Or should we in all cases call the largest exogamous and corporative unit a clan? That would lead to the absurd consequence that in some southern Somali groups we had to call the nuclear family a clan, because for them as close a relative as a FaBrDa is a potential and even preferred choice as bride for Ego. A third possibility would be to use different terms for the respective Rendille and Somali units. If, however, we made that our principle, the diversity and incommensurability of social phenomena in different societies would soon exhaust our stock of words and we would have to invent new combinations of sounds. I therefore chose the lesser evil and use the same terms in different societies in different senses. To reduce misunderstandings I start with a short description of the social structure of each society.

RENDILLE CLAN STRUCTURE

'Rendille' in its widest sense denotes all those who speak Rendille. These include the nine clans of 'Rendille proper', or 'white' Rendille as they occasionally call themselves and are called by their neighbours. A tenth clan is the Odoola (of Rendille) whose special position is described below. 'Rendille' as a speech community further comprises about 9500 Ariaal:[1] five clans with Samburu names, four of which correspond to Samburu sections. The fifth clan is Ilturia – 'mixture' in Samburu, a telling name. Ariaal mostly speak Samburu as well as or better than Rendille. Despite their strong Samburu orientation most of them are of comparatively recent Rendille origin and follow the exogamy rules of their Rendille clan of origin. They thus have a double affiliation. The economic advantage of being an Ariaal lies in better access to the resources of the cattle economy, which is dominated by the Samburu with whom the Ariaal share water the grazing, and with whom they practise stock exchange, intermarriage and joint defence. In addition, they participate in the camel economy and the rituals associated with it, like *almodo* and *sorio*.[2] The criterion used to distinguish Rendille and Ariaal is the initiation rituals: there are differences in the circumcision ceremonies but, more importantly, the Samburu and Ariaal hold various *ilmugit* sacrifices while the Non-Ariaal Rendille, in the year after circumcision, hold the *gaalgulamme* ceremony.

The 'white' Rendille thus define themselves by the *gaalgulamme* ceremony, for which they gather once in fourteen years in a gigantic circle of houses (Schlee 1979: 224). Attached to this fourteen-year cycle is a long series of rituals, which involve a complicated division of ritual labour and require co-operation of the nine clans. The tribe becomes visible here as a corporate whole.[3] But even here there are exceptions: the Gooborre, a subclan of the Saale, speak Rendille, live among Rendille, breed camels and are generally counted among the 'white' Rendille. However, they 'kill *ilmugit*' and do not participate in *gaalgulamme*. The case of the Rengumo subclan, the Ongom, may well be similar. Another clan, the Odoola, participates in *gaalgulamme* but settles outside the great ring.

The 'white' Rendille, whom I shall simply call henceforth Rendille (the Ariaal are not part of our study), divide into three parts: two moieties (*belel*), i.e. Belesi Bahai and Belesi Berri, the 'western' and 'eastern' moieties respectively. The cardinal points become evident in the settlement order at *gaalgulamme*. The distribution of clans into the two *belel* is given in the clan list below. The third part of the Rendille is the small clan

Odoola, which once more proves its special position by not belonging to a moiety.

To arrive at a definition of 'clan' it is convenient to invert the hierarchical order of organisational levels and to define the largest self-contained subunit of a clan, the subclan, first.

The subclan is based on common socially acknowledged patrilineal descent. Biological descent is 'not counted'. The genitor, even if known to be different from the pater, is irrelevant, so irrelevant, in fact, that nobody bothers if mothers of potential marriage partners have had the same lover. Marriage of such biological half-siblings would not be considered incestuous.

It is through the subclan that a given combination of traits is inherited and passed on, rather than through the clan, although it is in the clan and even the larger brotherhood of clans that sexual rights are shared: men of the age set of the husband (Hu), if genealogically junior to Hu, are counted as younger HuBrs and are thus interchangeable in their role as potential lovers. In other words, it is irrelevant to the subclan, as bearer and bequeather of qualities, that the group of accepted potential begetters of children is larger than the subclan. The subclan is the largest socially relevant patrilineal descent group, while clans are composed by adoption after the model of common patrilineal descent. The features believed to be inherited through and typical of a subclan are partly central personality traits, partly anecdotal marginalities. Here are some of the most current ascriptions: Saale – strength and stupidity; Rengumo – 'heat', irritable temper, strong attraction to water from the necessity to cool down; D'ubsaħai – cunning, etc.

Closely related to this are features which are not only inherited but also transmitted ritually. These concepts do not exclude each other: the cultural (i.e. ritual, sympathetic-imitative, magical-analogous) and biological forms of transmission of personality traits are not seen as alternatives but as complementary, as an interwoven, mutually reinforcing whole. Examples of subclan-specific traits which are transmitted in a combined way are the gift of a special power over enemies (Gaalorra), rhinoceros (Saale), snakes (Rengumo), elephant (Tubcha-Gaaldeidayan), and the ability to heal headaches (Uyám, Bulyárre [D'ubsaħai]), skin disease (fungus) (D'ubsaħai-Kulalioorat [Wambíle]), anorexia (Sanchir [D'ubsaħai]), itching eyes (Gaalorra [Gaaldeilan]), burns (Elegella, Nebei [both Saale]). The possessors of the strongest and most numerous curses and the most efficient prayers are collectively referred to as *iibire*. All those who are not *iibir* are *wakhkamur* ('God is rich/mighty'), who can only trust in God, but do not have intrinsic powers of prayer or curse. *Iibir*-ity and the ritual objects associated with it – a bundle of sticks, pieces of ivory, etc. – are – with many variations in character and elaboration – features of a subclan. Although *iibire* power, like other clan-specific features, is believed to be inherited, it is reinforced or actualised by special rituals performed on male babies and on individuals who are adopted into a subclan. All the members of a subclan must be either *iibire* or *wakhkamur*. A clan, however, can be composed of *iibire* and *wakhkamur* subclans. In the tribe-wide division of ritual labour it is generally the *iibire* who do something and the *wakhkamur* to whom something is done. Two *wakhkamur*, for example, are transformed into fools by public magical rituals as a sacrifice for their age set; on other occasions *wakhkamur* have to provide sacrificial animals.[4] *Wakhkamur* are suitable for this because of their harmlessness and freedom from guilt, which make them propitious approximately in the biblical sense of a 'pure' sacrificial animal. The distinction between *iibire* and *wakhkamur* thus runs as a binary principle throughout Rendille society.

A further subclan-specific feature is propitiousness, *munya*, or in its negative form, as a stigma, unpropitiousness, *bidir*. That a subclan is *bidir* can mean that it is believed that children begotten by men of such a subclan on wives of other subclans bring misfortune to their half-siblings begotten by the pater, i.e. their mother's husband, so that in the end they remain as sole heirs. It can also mean that daughters of such a subclan inadvertently bring misfortune to their husbands so that these die early (Schlee 1979: 197ff.).

Apart from personality features, ritual abilities and immanent luck or misfortune, subclans differ in their material culture, in details of the age-set system and in food avoidances. Subclans fill different age-set offices and public roles. The different subclans of the Gaaldeilan, as an example, have different house forms (Schlee 1979: 251f.). Four of them postpone the marriage of the girls of one age set out of three by one fourteen-year cycle, one does not (Schlee 1979: 147). One of the subclans avoids eating game, the others do not. This list of variations could be expanded.

A clan is composed of between two and seven subclans and is the largest group which is exogamous for all its members. Exogamy can extend beyond clan boundaries, but this only concerns adoptive brotherhoods between single subclans. A clan typically consists of several subclans, which can either be the products of fission of a common group of origin or can be of totally different origins but joined together in an adoptive association, using patrilineal descent as a mere model. Terminologically, all members of a clan are patrilineal relatives. At least ideally, a clan should settle together for the boys' circumcision once in fourteen years, and all boys should be circumcised in order of their segmental seniority in one morning at the same place.

The only clan which is not exogamous, is Rengumo. The subclans Ongóm and Bátarr (See, Aicha) marry each other. *Ongóm* means 'side of the neck', *batarr* 'thigh', i.e. the places where their camels are branded. According to one tale, the ancestor of the Ongóm once eloped with a girl of his own clan, Rengumo. Later this marriage was sanctioned by the introduction of new exogamy rules. According to another tradition an old man, Eisimkoro, was left behind by his migrating settlement. A warrior of Rengumo saved him and helped him to the new location of the settlement. Eisimkoro then called his co-elders of Rengumo to the *naabo*, the assembly place, and declared that he had given his daughter in marriage to his rescuer and asked them to give the couple their blessing. Since the patrilineal terminology is kept for the whole of Rengumo, the paradoxical situation arises that somebody can be Hu and Br or FaBr and MoBr at the same time. It is remarkable that DaChi (*eisim*) of Ongóm and DaChi of

Table 1   Rendille clans (capital letters), subclans (italics) and lineages in their order of seniority[4]

I   Moiety: Belesi Bañai

1 D'UBSAHAI =	Guta	Durolo
D'ISBAHAI	Höso	Leba
Wambíle (Farre)	Orguile	Timo
Gaalimogle	*Asurua*	Eisimlesebe
Wambíle	Asurua	*Gaalgorowle =*
Timado		*Gaaldaayan*
Orguba	2 RENGUMO	Arboi
Dabalén	*Bátarr: See*	Gaaldaayan
	Ruuso	Bartigo
Bulyárre	See	Gaalmagalle
Bulyar		Nabañgán
Baayo	*Bátarr: Aicha*	
Deere	Aicha	*Bañaiyeito*
Garab	Intore	Nyargua
		Enkusa
Gudére	*Ongóm*	Munyete
Gudére	Chana	Mirgalkona
Eisimdeele	Suber	Eidimole
Eisimchudugle	Sas	Mindaye
Sanchír	Barnat	
Nolaso	Harabore	5 UIYÁM, UYÁM
Chaule	Garguile	
		Baséle
Mirgichán	3 MATARBÁ	Jalle
Mirgichán	*Gaalgidele*	Baséle
Eisingaalgidele	Gaalgidele	Eisimsanchír
Korante	Kaato	Farrogán
Bokor	Gaasot	Leede
		Adille
Dókhle	*Feecha*	Kombe
Dókhle	Feecha	
Hajúfle	Baltor	*Gaalñaile*
Harrau	Meite	Gaalñaile
		Alyaro
Teilán (= Fur	4 NAHAGÁN	Khalaukhalle
ti balladan)	*Durólo*	Gaalmagár
Gaalmagál	Machán	Gaalwórsi
Arandiide	Gaalnañagalle	Rabhaio
Kiráb		

II Moiety: Belesi Berri

1 SAALE, SAALE

Nebei = Fofén
Neibichán
  Reiko
  Jilbogalle
  Ilkede
  Dammal
Ilwas = Herleñ
  Berrika
  Garawañle
Bagaajo
  Burroya
  Eisimmirdana
  Eisimbasele
  Torruga
  Gelebán
Elegella
Obeile
Orkhobesle
Khobes
Sarrehe
Gaaloroyó
Gudurro
Eisimékalo
Beilewa
Kakuche
Deigarr
Eisimgaalája
Baaro
Gooborre
Inde
Orre
Ngoléi
Eisimgaalalle
Orañle
Ilkibayang'i
Nobosu
Indilaalo
Goobanai = Kimogól
Burra
Chichia
Dañaleyo
Gaallagán
Kimogol
Bargeri
Segelán
Ilmoodi

Haile
Ildani
Malén
–
Chorrodo
Ruufo
Eisimgaalgorow
Sambakañ
Gaabanayó
Elimo
Ribayo
Eisimbaltór
Orsorio
Sañmal
–
Bullo
Nahiro
Lafte
Orkholám
Liito
Eisimbulyár
Daharo
Nkuchi
Eisimbaltór

2 URWÉN, URAWÉN

Jaale
Ubane
Jaale
Ikimerre
Eisandáb
Arigele
Mirkoro
Eisimrea
Silamo
Silamo
Adisómole
Ogom
Gaalsaracho
Letiviai
Kisambu
Eisimfofén
Tirtiri
Dokhe

3 GAALDEILAN

Keele
Búrcha

Elémo
Gaalorra
Narugo
Chormárro
Mórsa
Súda
Eisimtokón
Eisimmónte
Ukúrro
Baaro
Tombóya
Tanyági
–
Eisarboi
–
Gambárre
Adichárreñ
  Eisimfeecha
Eisobeile
–
Eisimlukhumulhau
Tarwén
Eisimgaalbooran
Madácho
Medero
Inkurlé
Eisimgadi
Kolong'o
Buleiya

4 TUBCHA

Gaalálle
Gaalálle
Orbora
  Eisimñarrau
  Gaalfure
–
Bolo
Deele
Lüñmorrogo
Ortoya
Gaalwab
Dirgell
Haanu
Neiyaba
Fañanto
Eisimgaabana

Outside the moieties

ODOOLA
Makhalán
Mañabolle
Timbór
–

Dafardai
Mooga
(Adibille)
–
Nurre

Keinán
–
Bursúnna
Gaerre

Bátarr, like the DaChi of an exogamous clan, do not marry each other but 'respect' each other as MoSiSo and MoSiDa.

In the strict sense, Odoola is not a clan, but, like its Gabbra equivalent, a phratry or confederation of clans. As Odoola, however, is smaller than the smallest subclan of many other clans, it is, in any enumeration, either listed as a clan or forgotten altogether. Odoola consists of four exogamous units and has a special position, remarkable both culturally and organisationally, which I shall discuss below.

A very large clan with symptoms of an advanced stage of fission into independent units is Saale. Saale has six subclans: Nebei, Gooborre, Elegella, Goobanai (Kimogól), Gaabanayó and Gaaloroyó, of which Nebei and Gooborre on one hand and Kimogól and Gaabanayó on the other hand are believed to be of common origin. Gaaloroyó and Elegella each stand alone. For a few age-set cycles the four parts thus defined have now been marrying the DaChi of each other. Further, these DaChi are allowed to intermarry, although it is normally forbidden to marry someone whose mother stems from the same clan as one's own mother. Both rules are recent introductions, on the grounds that Saale is such a large clan that marriage partners would become scarce if rules valid for the typical clan were applied. In 1976, the year of marriage of the age set Ilkichili, when a boycott against the girls of the opposite moiety led to a shortage of brides, it was even allowed that DaChi of all subclans of Saale marry each other and – even further – that Chi, i.e. members of Saale, marry DaChi of all subclans of Saale but their own. This means that classificatory MoBrSos marry FaSiDas and MoBrDas their FaSiSos.

GABBRA CLAN STRUCTURE

The Gabbra[5] consist of five phratries – Gār, Galbo, Sharbana, Odoola and Alganna – which are the political and ritual foci of Gabbra social organisation. Such is the relative self-sufficiency of the phratries that one is tempted to ask what constitutes Gabbra as one tribe or one ethnic group. The coherence is weak indeed. The only traits which constitute 'Gabbra' as a corporate whole are, first, the linguistic usage which combines 'Gabbra' conceptually and allegorically as the 'Five Drums'; and, secondly, the common ritual calendar which requires the Gabbra phratries to pass certain age-set rituals at given times in a given order. This needs coordination, i.e. co-operation.

The five phratries or 'tribes', gos, clearly appear as corporate units. To define them is easy because they define themselves. Each of them – and for Odoola this is valid with modifications – has its own moiety structure expressed by paraphernalia like a drum and a horn of ivory as central objects of ritual and identification, and a nomadic settlement, the yaa or capital, in which rituals important for the wellbeing of the whole phratry and processes of political and jural decision take place. Furthermore, there is a system of offices shaped after the lineage and age-set structures with *hayyu*, *jallaba* and *qallu*.

The *hayyu*, of whom there are two per phratry (i.e. one per moiety) and initiated elders' age set, hold a good share of the jural and political authority in this society. They do not speak first in a meeting; on the contrary, they have the last word. Although a decision may be reached by a communal discussion, it is only the *hayyu* who by his verdict finalises it. The symbols of power which the *hayyu* holds, the whip (*licho*) and the sceptre or club (*boku*), underline this aspect which may appear surprising in a society which shares so many acephalous and segmentary features with the neighbouring Rendille. A number of features of the *hayyu*ship (*hayyoma*), such as its close association with luck or propitiousness, the *hayyu*'s function as a war leader and his inevitable downfall if the divine grace seems to have been withdrawn from him, are reminiscent of kingship. But Gabbra phratries are not kingdoms and so I prefer to keep the Boran terms *hayyu* and *hayyoma*.

Jallaba are more numerous and may be called the bearers of middle-range political authority. 'Age-set speakers' would be an acceptable translation.

The *qallu*, third in order of conspicuousness and first in order of importance, possess an innate power which is independent of the age-set structure and which is not conferred on them by human action. The *qallu* is the one who holds the most powerful prayer and curse of all, and whatever power the *hayyu* holds is bestowed on him by a member of the senior *qallu* lineage of his moiety.

Each of the five phratries has holy sites where age-set rituals take place. The rituals are very similar to one another, and each phratry performs its own rituals for itself without the participation of members of other phratries. This is in vivid contrast to the Rendille, among whom, on similar occasions, there is a high measure of ritual differentiation, division of labour and resulting co-operation: for certain age-set rituals, ideally, the whole Rendille society has to assemble (for others only the age sets concerned) and each clan has to perform a specific part of the ceremony. Between the Gabbra phratries, on the other hand, we find parallelism and division. As internally differentiated communities of co-operation it is the single phratries, and not the whole of Gabbra, which in their age-set rituals resemble the Rendille tribe.

Each Gabbra phratry has two moieties: Yiblo and Lossa. Yiblo is translated if a Gabbra chooses to speak Rendille, as Belesi Berri, while Lossa is equated to Belesi Bahai. This may sound strange because the Rendille regard Belesi Bahai as senior while the senior moiety of each

Gabbra phratry is Yiblo, i.e. Belesi Berri. But seniority has to do with power, and power with politics, and politics consists of ups and downs. The Gabbra and the Rendille disregard such unstable features. The equation between the Rendille and the Gabbra moieties is established instead by the dates on which they hold their *sorio* sacrificial ceremonies.[6] These dates correspond for Belesi Bahai and Lossa on the one hand and for Belesi Berri and Yiblo on the other. It is due to this common structure of their societies and the recognisability of its constituent elements that Rendille migrants who wish to join the Gabbra can be ascribed their 'correct' moiety and soon find their way around their new social environment.

Below this level it is difficult to define units. It is best to ignore a number of vague intermediate forms of aggregation and start again from the bottom with the base of social organisation, the lineage. The lineage is similar in many aspects to the Rendille subclan. It would sound odd, however, to call it a subclan because of its small scale and because I have not yet found a clan of which it could be a subunit. Analogous to the Rendille subclan, the lineage for the most part is not an adoptive-associative but an actual patrilineal descent group. A further shared feature is the fact that the lineage is the bearer of traits and abilities which qualify its members for certain ritual roles.

Similar to the *iibire* of the Rendille, there are *qallu* lineages whose curse and blessing are powerful in special measure. There are younger and older acting *qallu* at the same time performing ritual tasks for their own and other age sets. *Qallu*ship is based on a power inherited in a lineage; it is not an age-set office. The ceremony performed on newborn children to transmit the curse power to them is formally and functionally equivalent to the corresponding Rendille ceremony. Further, it is the non-*qallu* lineages which, like the *wakhkamur* of the Rendille, not only distinguish themselves by lack of power but also by propitiousness. There is something threatening, mysterious and suspicious about the curse power of the *qallu* or *iibire* in spite of their social acceptability and utilisation. Fortune is not part of their outfit. For this reason members of *qallu* or *eebiftu* ('praying') lineages are not eligible for the propitious *hayyu* office.

Also, in Gabbra as in Rendille, prayer and action largely exclude each other: somebody who prays for a lost flock of camels will not join the search himself. Typically, it is the elder men who are believed to have the strongest prayer and the younger men who are credited with the most effective action. But behind the visible power of the *hayyu* there is the power of the *qallu*, who have bestowed it on the former. '*Abartu qurt, eebiftu galc!*' is the formula by which in *qallu* lineages the power is transmitted to children and by which the *qallu* allow the *hayyu* to share in it: 'Kill what you curse, and lead home what you pray for!'[7]

As in Rendille, so in Gabbra there are lineages which are believed to be unpropitious and whose daughters are to be avoided in marriage. These are despised groups, to whom various past sins or antisocial behaviour is ascribed. The curse, however, sticks to them and is inherited, a part of their nature, quite independent of individual good deeds and misdeeds which figure in our notion of guilt.

Despite their socially integrated role and in spite, or because, of their power, a little of this unpropitiousness attaches itself also to the *qallu*. One avoids marrying their daughters if the latter are very young, because it is believed that otherwise one will meet an early death. All this is not compatible with the positive, propitious role of the *hayyu* as a figure of social identification. Thus the *qallu* remain in the background of the power play.

The two binary divisions which cut across any Gabbra phratry – *Yiblo* versus *Lossa* and *eebiftu* versus non-*eebiftu* – are also reflected in the composition of the *yaa*, the mobile capital. The holy drum (*dibbe*) and the horn (*magalada*) are kept in the *yaa* and sounded on Fridays, the evening of the new moon and on other ceremonially important dates. While the custodian of the drum (*abba dibbe*, 'father of the drum'), who has to keep the instrument in his house, belongs to one moiety, the *abba magalada* belongs to the other. The two gates of the ritual enclosure (*naabo*) and a number of other spatial arrangements for ceremonial purposes, some of which are discussed in the course of this book, also reflect the moiety structure. For sacrificial ceremonies *eebiftu* lineages give sheep while non-*eebiftu* give goats.

As well as being the bearer of powers such as cursing and blessing or the holder of heritable offices, the lineage also tends to be the largest exogamous group, although in many cases exogamy is extended to a group of lineages.

In some cases there is a taxonomical level between the phratry and the lineage. Thus five lineages in Galbo combine under the name Baráwa and seven under the name Yohóma. By their scale and taxonomic position we are tempted to call these units clans. But these clans are neither exogamous nor in any other conspicuous way relevant for behaviour, nor do their myths of origin point in the direction of common descent; they are associative clusters. So we can be fairly confident that there are no clans in Gabbra but only phratries and lineages. If we use the word 'clan', we do so in reference to this intermediate level of loose lineage associations.

It is usually at the level of lineage, though in some cases at the intermediate 'clan' level, that kinship terms are generalised and members of the same sex and same generation are addressed by the same terms. For instance, the children of a daughter of the lineage Qoshobe of Galbo address all men of Qoshobe of the corresponding generation as *abuya* (MoBr). In the case of the five lineages of Baráwa, however, the use of such terms is extended to all of Baráwa.

Some informants succeed in tracing the names of their patrilineal forefathers back to the eponymous lineage ancestor. Not all lineages, however, derive their names from such ancestors, and models such as the segmentary lineage system derived from the Nuer (Evans-Pritchard 1940), the Tiv (Bohannan 1953), etc., do not apply to the Gabbra. Lineage differentiation and fission can be observed at the lowest, small-scale level (we may call it the sublineage level), where seniority and settlement order are determined by order of birth and the order of birth of the common ancestors.[8] On higher levels of social organisation it is, however, difficult to apply such models – which better fit with the northern Somali[9] – because of the high emphasis on lineage or clan identity supported by the belief in heritable qualities, and the relatively low demographic growth of the Gabbra. Gabbra lineages and clans, like those of the Rendille, are seen as fixed categories, not as transient constellations that change their names and identities as they split, grow and split again. So when we speak about 'clan relationships' between the Gabbra and the Rendille, we generally mean a relationship of a lineage or a subclan on the Rendille side and a lineage on the Gabbra side. These relationships may exist between units of different size, function and taxonomic level.

Table 2   Gabbra clan list

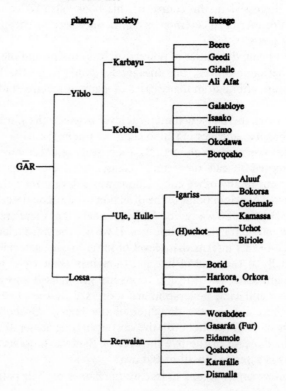

SAKUYE CLAN STRUCTURE

In describing Sakuye clan structure we have to distinguish between two periods of time. During and before the colonial period the Sakuye were highly mobile camel pastoralists and clanship played a role similar to that described for the Gabbra or the Rendille. During the secession war that followed Kenya's independence, however, practically the entire livestock population of the Sakuye and a large part of the human population perished, either in the keeps, the camps in which they were concentrated, or after the emergency, when they were trekked back to North-Eastern Province. On this trek they were guarded by Boran militia (homeguards, police reserve) who took this opportunity to torture and kill people with impunity. This greatly affected the demographic structure, the residence pattern, the authority structure and the mode of livelihood of many

Table 2   (cont.)

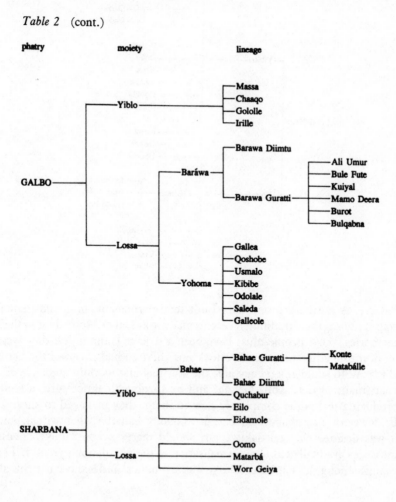

phatry	moiety	lineage

Table 2 (cont.)

page 30

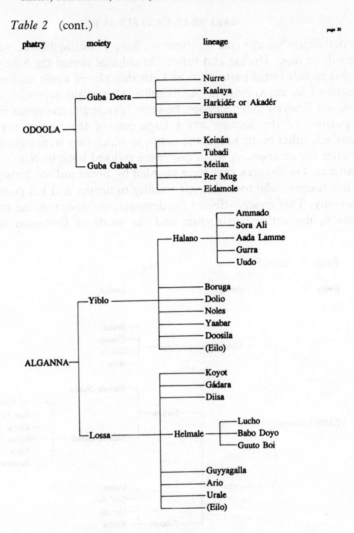

| phatry | moiety | lineage |

Sakuye. A northern group later built semi-permanent, mud-and-thatch, round huts at their traditional ceremonial site at Dabel. According to their memories, these people must have been a strange community: they were all destitute adults; neither livestock nor children had survived the hardships. With some emergency aid, the spiritual and worldly guidance of a charismatic leader, Abba Ganna, and by turning to agriculture, a food-producing technique completely new to them, they managed to survive. Bridewealth was abandoned because nobody had the wherewithal, and it was decided that no Sakuye girl should marry a non-Sakuye. These measures gradually led to a normalisation of the population pyramid. The change among the southern Sakuye was less radical and less permanent: all

Sakuye were impoverished after the emergency, many became sedentary as peri-urban paupers or farmers on irrigation schemes, but some managed to build up herds and to take up nomadism again. In the following description I focus on the role of clanship among the pastoral Sakuye, as it is still alive in the memory of the elders, because this earlier form has greater relevance to the subsequent reconstruction of ethnogenetic processes and clan history. I hope to be able to discuss the agricultural Sakuye and their cults more fully elsewhere.

The Sakuye are a union of two originally different ethnic elements. We shall discuss their ethnogenesis below (pp. 115–22). For this reason they distinguish among themselves between Sakuye (in the narrow sense) and Miigo. This binary distinction is overlaid by another one, the moiety division. Like the Gabbra, they call these moieties Yiblo (in their pronunciation sometimes Jiblo) and Lossa. A Sakuye thus can be Sakuye and Yiblo, Miigo and Yiblo, Sakuye and Lossa or Miigo and Lossa (Diagram 2).

The clans are exogamous and are believed to have heritable characteristics. Two clans, one per moiety, namely Saale and Arsuruwa, are *qallu* or *eebiftu* and have sticks as their ritual insignia. All other clans qualify for *hayyu* offices which, as among the Gabbra, are not compatible with *eebiftu* status.

Sakuye

	Sakuye	Miigo
Yiblo	Saale Worr Suya ⎨ Fofle / Buleta Deele Kurno Ilani Gaalorra	Tuulo Diima Jiriwa Mailan
Lossa	Matarbá ⎨ Muja / Nyabare Fur ⎨ Fur Gudda / Fur Diqa Arsuruwa	Shirshiro = Tubadi ⎨ Madera / Jaaro / Charri

Diagram 2 Sakuye clan list

Other clan-specific customs and characteristics are that the Deele have a special power over iron and spit on cuts or spear wounds to heal them, that the Kurno spit on burns, the Matarbá on wounds inflicted by thorns or the sharp sanseverias (*algi*) from which fibres for mats are made. The Miigo have a special power over *ibid Waaqa*, 'the fire of God' or watery boils on the skin. The Matarbá, being the first-born of their moiety, march ahead of the others on war expeditions, are the first to pray when communal prayers are held, and are the first to make their camels kneel down in a new settlement site.

Traditionally, the social structure of the Sakuye becomes focused and visualised in the *jila* ceremonies when a new set of *hayyu* and *jaldab* office holders are proclaimed. There were three ritual sites to which the clan had to go in the course of these ceremonies. The Sakuye in the narrow sense had to send a group of men to Mount Deemo, north-east of Marsabit, a place which plays a significant role in Sakuye history.[10] From there they collect red earth which is later smeared on people's foreheads and on the udders of camels. The Miigo do the same at Lensayu, an outcrop north-west of Buna, from where they are believed to originate. The big communal ceremonies are held at Dabel.

This ideal pattern has not been followed on the last three occasions. As early as 1947 the sourthern Sakuye could not co-ordinate their organisational efforts with the Sakuye around Dabel and held their own ceremonies. This indicates that the split of the Sakuye in two regional clusters, one in the northern part of Marsabit District and one in Isiolo District on the Ewaso Ngiro (Waso River) does not date from the emergency of the sixties but started much earlier. About this ceremony we read in the colonial Isiolo District Annual Reports:

> The chief event of their [the Sakuye] year was the holding of the first Jilla [= ceremony] since 1910. The traditional site was at Dabel but after much discussion the Uaso Ngiro Sakuye decided to split from those at Moyale and hold their ceremonies at Damballa Dika. They were concluded on the 12th July. 17 "Haiyu" or kings were elected and 18 "Jaldabba" or princes. In all 18 head of cattle and 40 goats were slaughtered.[11]

In 1965 the southern Sakuye held renewed installation ceremonies at Yamicha in Isiolo District. Apparently only eight *hayyu*, four for Yiblo, four for Lossa, were proclaimed on that occasion. The attempts to hold joint promotions with the Dabel Sakuye failed again in 1982. By then Islam had taken such firm root that only a minimal version of the traditional rituals was carried out. Instead of every *hayyu* candidate slaughtering a bull, one bull was slaughtered on behalf of all. No red earth was collected and accordingly no foreheads were smeared with it. Traditional Sakuye rituals were replaced by prayers led by Muslim sheikhs. Also the economic circumstances of the impoverished Sakuye altered the character of the meeting. Instead of entire settlements migrating to the ritual site

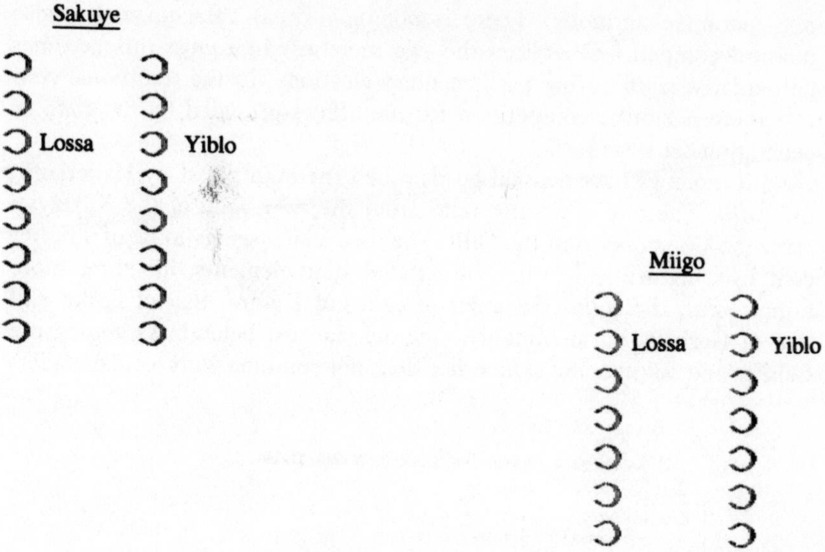

Sakuye

Diagram 3 The settlement order of the Sakuye at the site of the *hayyu* and *jaldab* inaugurations

with their loading camels, only the participating males went there by foot. The social structure of the Sakuye, which was made visible by the traditional spatial order of the ceremonial settlement, thus no longer became manifest. Traditionally, the Sakuye on such occasions settle from north to south in long rows of houses in order of seniority, the Lossa moiety of the Sakuye to the west of the row of the Yiblo moiety, and the Miigo segment, also in separate rows according to moiety affiliation, at some distance from them (Diagram 3).

The fact that the Dabel Sakuye did not participate cannot be attributed to a self-sufficient or separatist attitude on the part of their southern brethren but, I believe, rather to a certain lack of interest on their own part. A new community structure had developed among them, in which clanship and traditional authority played a rather subordinate role. This sedentary and largely agricultural community had found new ways of expressing their communal feelings.

BORAN CLAN STRUCTURE

The Boran clans[12] are grouped into two moieties, Sabbo and Gona. Gona in turn is divided in two submoieties, Haroresa and Fullele, while the composition of Sabbo does not reflect the binary principle. Among other Oromo the moiety exogamy has been relaxed, but the Boran moieties are still exogamous: Sabbo marries Gona and Gona Sabbo. Intermarriage does not guarantee harmony. There is not only ritual antagonism but also political competition between the two moieties. In Kenya this becomes particularly acute during parliamentary elections. In the traditional context there is similar competition for the offices provided by the *gada* or generation-set system.[13]

Both moieties have a ritual head, called the high priest by Haberland, the *qallu*. The one of Sabbo stems from the *worr qallu* of the Karrayyu clan, the Gona one from the Odítu. Sabbo, which seems to be of a rather composite nature and to have integrated alien elements, has three more minor *qallu*, the *qallica* (singular of *qallu*) of Karara, that of Ķuku and that of Garjeda, all in Matt'arri (see the clan list below). As among the Gabbra and Sakuye, the *qallu* office does not combine with secular leader-

Table 3   Boran clan list

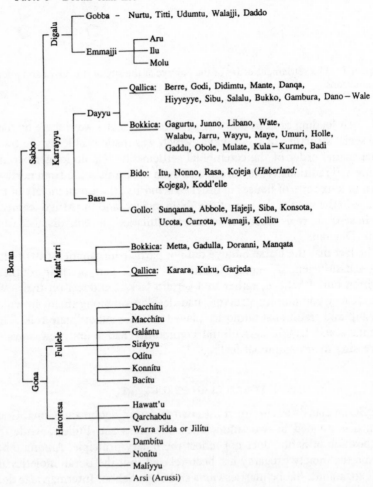

ship. The *worr boku* (people of the sceptre or club; singular: *bokica*) always stem from non-*qallu* lineages.

Boran clans and lineages are also differentiated by special ritual gifts (the presence or absence of *woyu* status), by their relative seniority and by different food avoidances. We do not need to go into details here.

For the orientation of the reader in the following chapters we here give a list of the Boran clans (Table 3). This list is based on Haberland (1963: 123ff.) and Legesse (1973: 40). The clan names have been transliterated using the newer orthography, but this has proved no problem because both Haberland's and Legesse's phonemic transcriptions are largely correct, although Haberland seems to economise on geminated consonants. For comparison we add the clan list of the sixteenth-century 'Galla' according to the contemporary Amharic monk, Bahrey (Table 4) (Schleicher 1893; Guidi 1907; Huntingford 1955).

Table 4   'Galla' clan list (sixteenth century)

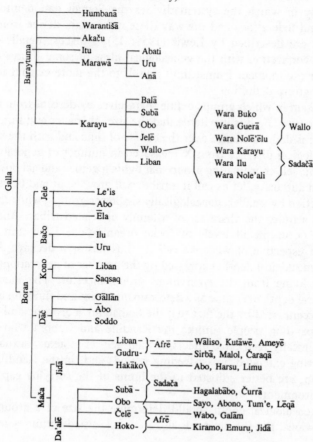

SOMALI CLAN STRUCTURE

The juxtaposition of Somali on the one hand and Gabbra and Rendille on the other may appear incongruous because the Somali are an internally strongly differentiated nation of several million people while the Rendille are a traditional tribal society of some 12,000. However, the Somali have to be discussed as a whole since they form one big segmentary system. This putative genealogical system ultimately traces the patrilineal descent of every single Somali alive today back to the Quraish, the tribe of the prophet Muhammad. African ancestry, which is obvious from the physical features of the Somali, is attributed exclusively to female links.[14] It is obvious that this is not an image of reality but a massive ideological construct. Nevertheless, the system deserves to be studied, not for being true, but because it defines for every Somali his identity and the expectations of loyalty demanded of him. Thus this genealogy does not perhaps describe history so much as make it.

The way in which the system divides the Somali nation into tribal families and federations and the way these units again derive from Arab ancestors, are described by Lewis (1955: 15). I discuss details of this system in connection with the genealogical ideas of some Kenya Somali below; for the moment I must limit myself to the more general features of Somali group definition.

In a system in which groups define themselves by descent from a given named ancestor (X) it is inevitable that the size, character and function of a group thus defined change over the course of time and with the increasing genealogical distance from X measured in number of generations. A co-resident, self-coordinating group that fights together and acknowledges a common authority, let us call it a tribe, will grow, split and be replaced in its function by smaller, genealogically shallower groups, while the tribe itself will acquire the character of a family of related tribes. Analogous processes occur on all levels of social organisation. Each unit of the Somali, irrespective of what we call it, thus has as a decisive defining feature genealogical depth, expressed by the number of generations separating the living from the eponymous group ancestor. The increase of genealogical depth over time as a determinant of size and function of social units is accentuated by the fact that the Somali are a growing and aggressively expanding people, unlike the Rendille and Gabbra who by the demographically restrictive effects of their age-set systems, sexual abstinence during extended breast-feeding periods and, in the Rendille case, emigration, are better adjusted to the limits of the carrying capacity of their environment.

That genealogical depth should determine the size of a group seems rather obvious. But the inverse is also true. Size also determines genealogical depth, meaning, of course, the depth of the mental representation of genealogies. I. M. Lewis (1961a: 99ff.) has observed that among the Dulbahante, a section of the Darood Somali of northern Somalia, small units count fewer generations to a given ancester than living members of larger lateral branches who derive from the same ancestor. A fast-growing branch of agnates splits often and therefore has to remember more ancestors to record the genealogical position of the resultant units in relation to each other than a demographically more stable branch that basically only reproduces itself. Some Dulbahante lineages therefore only count six generations to the man Dulbahante, while others, the more prestigious, faster-growing 'long' branches, count up to twenty generations to the same ancestor. This variation is higher than any similar variation which I found in northern Kenya. The Garre and the Ajuran of Kenya do not have a history of growth and expansion which is as dramatic as the recent Darood expansion[15] since the nineteenth century. According to Lewis's 'size factor' (I. M. Lewis 1961a: 105) (the influence of telescoping genealogies or 'genealogical amnesia', i.e. forgetting those ancestors whose descendants did not form a different unit) we should therefore expect Ajuran and Garre genealogies to be rather short (a factor we have to take into account when we are trying to construct a chronology of historical events using genealogical information).

Growth and expansion are not natural factors blindly obeyed by the social system, but the declared collective aim which is forced beyond the limits of biological increase. For every Muslim it is easy to become a member or vassal (*sheegad*) of a Somali tribe. *Sheegad* is a derivative of the verbal form *ku-sheegada* ('I name you', i.e. 'I name your ancestor when asked for my ancestor'). The difference between *sheegad* and consanguine members of a Somali group may be blurred by time, and presumably more quickly among the southern groups than in the north (I. M. Lewis 1959: 274–93). This form of alliance or adoption, which was highly desired because it augmented the numerical and fighting strength of a group, was not always irreversible. This is exemplified by the penetration of the Darood tribal family to the south and the south-west in the nineteenth and twentieth centuries. The Darood often succeeded in renouncing their *sheegad* hosts and even in occupying a dominant position (Turnbull 1955). In the same manner Ajuran and Garre Somali joined the non-Muslim (!) Boran, and later, when the power of the Boran declined, renounced them again. During the colonial period it was also very popular to declare oneself Boran by *sheegad*[16] in order to be able to cross the Somali line which the British had drawn to stop the westward expansion of the Somali (a goal which this measure did not achieve; we shall see in chapter 3 that this line might even have had the opposite effect of furthering this westward advance).

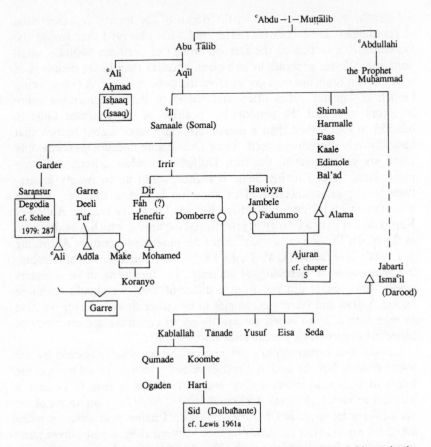

Diagram 4 The position of Isaaq, Degodia, Garre, Dulbaḣante and Ajuran in the genealogy of the Somali nation.

Apart from the agnatic links which all Somali claim to have to the Quraish, i.e. the tribe of the Prophet and more specifically to his FaBr Abu Ṭālib, the importance attributed to female links to Irrir, the son of Samaale, should be noted. The Ajuran, who are often referred to as Hawiyya, claim to descend from Fadumo d/o Jambelle s/o Hawiyya. The whole Darood clan family is also Somali (in the narrow sense of descendants of Samaale) through Darood's wife Domberre d/o Dir s/o Irrir. Also Isaaq and Saransur are ascribed Irrir wives, Isaaq one of Dir, Saransur, the father of Degodia, one of Hawiyya descent.

Cerulli (1957: II,251ff.) reports a story about the origin of the Ajuran in which the sons of Hawiyya found Ajuran's father in a tree and had to persuade him to come down, promising him, among other things, their sister. Similar stories exist about Darood and Domberre, the daughter of Dir. These stories seem to follow the same pattern.

Sources: Kenya National Archive, Wajir Political Record Book; I. M. Lewis (1961a, 1982); Schlee (1979: 286ff.); and the Ajuran informants quoted in chapter 5, pp. 209–30.

The northern Somali regard the *sheegad* relationship as rather shameful. Their means of acquiring strength is growth by agnation (*tol*) and by contracts (*heer*) which oblige smaller units to joint defence or joint payment of blood compensation (*diya, mag*) if they do not wish to fight. Only a group whose very existence is threatened would give up its separate identity and become *sheegad*, who, as 'pretenders', '... claim the lineage affiliation of those to whom they are currently attached and are generally scorned for their lack of lineage pride. [This] status ... betrays weakness and insufficiency' (I. M. Lewis 1961a: 100–101) In northern Kenya, by contrast, the term *sheegad* does not seem to have such negative connotations. I have already said that *sheegad* affiliations were very common and I illustrate this by many examples below.[18] Even Isaaq and Darood traders, northern Somali whose fathers and grandfathers came to Kenya mostly as soldiers in the British forces, make liberal use of *sheegad* mechanisms although as non-pastoral minorities with a professional specialisation in which they do not compete with the pastoralists they are not subject to any military pressures. I once asked a Marsabit businesswoman from the 'Idagalle section of Isaaq, who claimed that 'Idagalle was just another name for the Rendille clan Elegella, how she came to believe this. She pointed to the similarity of the two names, an argument which did not convince me. She then gave her argument a pragmatic turn: 'It is much better to have people than to be alone.' That is why she and her family *sheegdeen* 'Elegella since their arrival in Kenya, had become known as 'the Somali of Elegella' to the Rendille. (Many Somali traders relied heavily on the help of such Rendille 'brothers' in the beginning and only later, when they had accumulated wealth, developed cultural arrogance towards these 'pagans'.) I have not met a Somali who regarded this ubiquitous type of relationship as shameful.

In northern Kenya the frequent and unstable *sheegad* relationships have not superseded the agnatic relationship but have only formed temporary additional links. In Diagram 4 I show how the major Somali groups of northern Kenya fit into the total genealogy[19] of the Somali nation. A more detailed internal genealogy of the Ajuran can be found in chapter 5.[20] Here I concentrate on the Garre and the Degodia and their relationship to the other major Somali clan families without going into detail on the subgroups of the latter. Diagram 4 provides a rough orientation. It does not point out variants, contradictions, inconsistencies and adjustments to ideological or social needs. Some of these problems in relation to the Ajuran are discussed and illustrated in chapter 5.

CHAPTER 3

THE HISTORICAL FRAME

I here give a historical sketch of the area of study, partly derived from written sources, partly from my own investigations described in later chapters. Conclusions normally belong at the end of an argument. Also the order of presentation should ideally follow the order of epistemological steps, so as to enable the reader to follow the argument critically as it proceeds. Here I invert this order. I present part of my conclusions first, with little reference to their empirical base (apart from the few written sources), because the multiplicity of facts demands that the reader be given some orientation in the form of an overview of the main historical tendencies and the more conspicuous population movements in this historiographically neglected part of the world. The critical reader is thus called upon to test the generalisations offered here against the data on single clan histories given in later chapters.

In the absence of a written history the explorer of the past has to draw his/her conclusions about the historical process from its results, i.e. from what is observable today.[1] The most economical historical explanation is the one which requires the smallest number of speculative and unlikely events and which can explain the present-day linguistic and cultural complexity by the mechanisms of differentiation and exchange in a satisfactory manner.

This type of reconstruction with the present as a starting point has been developed farthest methodologically in the field of historical linguistics. Features which cannot be explained by independent development serve to group languages according to the number and closeness of the correspondences between them and postulate proto-languages for groups of similar languages. For these proto-languages one can postulate populations of speakers. From the distribution of these languages and from the nucleus of strongest differentiation one can draw conclusions about the geographical origin of the proto-language speakers.

Language, however, is only one sphere of observable culture and other subsystems of culture are equally suitable for the reconstruction of common origins. Where, for example, a complex of ritual prescriptions and a calendar of festivities and other types of culturally conditioned behaviour mark a group as belonging to cluster X, while the language and traits of the political organisation correspond to cluster Y, it seems probable that the origin of the group is to be sought in the domain of proto-X, and that the politically dominant Y have imposed their own form of political organisation and their language. Adopting a language seems to occur frequently; some groups are even bilingual in Boran and Somali, the two dominant languages of the region, although there is evidence that neither of these was their original language.

The reconstruction from observable cultural and linguistic facts is supplemented methodologically by the collection and interpretation of oral traditions. There are no good and no bad oral traditions. Everything that is handed down is handed down because it corresponds to a social or psychological interest and is thus, sociologically, of equal importance. But for both the historian and the sociologist the question of historical content arises: the former wants to know whether a tradition corresponds to historical truth, the latter, why, possibly, it does not. The method is critical-comparative: do the versions of independent informants of different social standing and different ethnic affiliation agree? The approach is similar to that of criticising ideology. Where the improbabilities of the tale support a positive social self-definition, they are to be tested more rigorously for their historical truth than where they contradict such a positive self-definition of the informant.

Where categories like right and wrong are difficult to apply for lack of hard evidence, different versions of history have to be discussed on their relative merits. What follows may be a very rough history with only approximate dates but I do not know a better one.

NORTHERN KENYA AND SURROUNDINGS C. 1500 AD

Five hundred years ago the hot, dry lowland from Lake Turkana in the west to the Juba River in the east and beyond it was, as it is now, populated by pastoral nomads and hunter-gatherers.[2] The climate may have been more favourable; the specialists are not agreed on long-term climatic changes and posit different theories of desert encroachment. A larger area of the country might have been suitable for agriculture, but we

can, however, safely assume that nomadic pastoralism was the dominant
and most prestigious way of life.

Elements of this culture of herdsmen – a complex of rituals for the
wellbeing of the herds – can be found today among Somali and Boran-
speaking groups, among Muslims and pagans alike, as the remains of a
common cultural substratum. These consist of a cycle of sacrificial festivals, four *sorio* in accordance with the lunar calendar and a festival geared
to the solar year, in which fire and milk play a special role, and which in
Rendille is called *almodo*, in Boran *almado*.[3] Today these festivals are
performed by the Rendille, who speak a language of their own, related to
Somali, and who are pagans; by the Gabbra, Boran-speaking pagans with
isolated Islamic borrowings; Gabbra Miigo, Boran-speaking Muslims; and
by the Garre, an Islamic Somali group. They were performed until recently
by the Sakuye, who are Boran-speaking Muslims. In recent centuries
pagan groups have often copied elements of Islamic culture but rarely have
Muslims borrowed pagan rituals – their self-awareness is too strong for
this. We may therefore conclude that this complex of rituals is part of the
pre-Islamic proto-culture. (It is, by the way, not a law of nature valid at all
times and places that pagan groups do not proselytise. Rather, we here
extrapolate recently observed forms of cultural flow into the past). Apart
from the fact that they celebrated these festivals, we thus know two things
about the bearers of this proto-culture: first, they had a lunar calendar by
which they timed their *sorio*, and second, they were able to determine the
solar year either by counting 365 days from one *almodo* to the next or by
adding a number of days to the span of twelve months. There were no
efforts to combine both cosmic cycles in a single calendrical system (see
Schlee 1979: 82ff.). We call this culture PRS (proto-Rendille-Somali) after
the westernmost and easternmost of its modern heirs. Whether it was ever
shared by all Somali cannot easily be determined, but it was and partly is
shared by some. The language of the bearers of the PRS culture was
Somaloid. The Somaloid languages are closely related to the Baiso language of southern Ethiopia (Fleming 1964: 35–96). Together they belong to
the Eastern Cushitic subfamily, most of whose branches are spoken in
south Ethiopia: Oromo (Galla), Konso, Gidole, Gato, Arbore, Warazi,
Gawata, Tsamai, Geleb, Sidamo, Kambata, T'ambaro, Hadiya, Alaba,
K'abena, Marak'o, Darasa and Burji. Some languages which belong to
'this family have apparently moved away from this cluster to the north-east
(Afar, Saho) or to the south (Magodogo) (H. S. Lewis 1966: 39). Eastern
Cushitic belongs to the Cushitic language family which, in turn, belongs to
the Afro-Asiatic macro-family which also includes, among other branches,
Semitic. This macro-family is so differentiated that it must be much older
than Indo-European, yet even beyond this time span there is room for
speculation: Indo-European and Afro-Asiatic must either have undergone

early intensive mutual influences or stem from the same root; if we assumed separate origins, these language families would have to be even more different from each other than they actually are. This Noahitic language, as it might (if it ever existed) be called by analogy to Cush-itic and Sem-itic, defies, however, all attempts to locate it in space and time, not to speak of reconstructing it.

So much for the narrower and wider linguistic contexts of the Somaloid language of the PRS people. Since this language covered such a wide area, we probably have to assume even for this early time a considerable degree of dialect differentiation. The numerous different dialects of southern Somali may have begun to branch off from each other centuries earlier. Rendille might have started on its course of development into a separate language. Many dialects that were placed geographically and linguistically between these – i.e. the dialects of the ancestors of the present-day Gabbra and the Miigo Sakuye, and of groups that now count themselves among the Garre and possibly the Ajuran – were probably only much later replaced by Boran and modern Northern Somali or, in other cases, assimilated to dialects of Raħanwein affiliation. The northern Somali, who in comparison to their southern cousins show a remarkable degree of linguistic uniformity, can be seen as a comparatively recent migration to the north out of this proto-Rendille-Somali cluster. (Their recent expansion to the south thus appears as the counter-movement of the pendulum.) Also by that time the eastern Horn down to the coast had already long been populated by proto-Rendille-Somali.

This process of dialect differentiation, however, is counteracted by the process of homogenisation (Möhlig 1976: 699ff.; 1979; 115–16). The pastoral nomads often migrate hundreds of kilometres in a single year. It does not make much sense to try to localise any particular group precisely, for example, to ask whether the ancestors of the Sakuye originated in what is now northern Kenya or southern Ethiopia or Somalia. They may have ranged through wide stretches of all three countries in the course of a few years. Their oral traditions describe migrations from the slopes of the Ethiopian highlands to the country east of the lower Juba and back. Thus new contacts in fresh neighbourhoods occur continuously and with them new alliances and antagonisms, new links by fraternisation, marriage, adoption, capture, vassaldom, trade, and so on. These lead to linguistic approximation and cultural exchange. As the linguistic boundaries, so the borders of organised tribal units have to be regarded as fluid. It is perhaps due to the high degree of reciprocity of linguistic influences that it is difficult to pin down regular phonetic equivalences between the single languages for the entire Eastern Cushitic group (Andrzejewski 1964b).

As well as the ritual calendar and what we know about the language we can assume, as a further descriptive feature of the proto-Rendille – Somali, that they had an age-set system. We do not know whether this system primarily followed the principle of generation, so that men and boys of very different ages are combined in one set, as among the majority of present-day Gabbra, or whether it utilised a compromise of the principles of generation and age, as with the Rendille and the Galbo phratry of the Gabbra. It is, however, common to all descendants of this proto-group and even to the Afar, the Saho and the northern Somali who had emigrated northwards to the Red Sea and the Gulf of Aden prior to the time discussed here that they have an age-set system, or, as can be concluded from rudiments, that they formerly had one. The Rendille and the Gabbra Miigo, who, it would seem, have not had any contact with each other for centuries, have a number of age-set names in common. The Gabbra Malbe, however, who live between then, seem to have been influenced by the Boran more strongly with regard to their age-set system. We can probably conclude that the Rendille and the Miigo nomenclature is the earlier one.

The ethnogenetic process that transforms a part of these proto-Rendille–Somali into the Somali proper, has Islamisation as its mainspring. Arabic influence on the coast is older than Islam and presumably there has been a mixed population for a long time. Since the seventh century, Arabic influence has taken an Islamic form. Islamised groups suppress their pagan origin and place stress on mostly fictitious Arab ancestors. They even construct complicated genealogies back to the tribe of the Prophet, the Quraish. The aspects of Islamisation and Arabisation – by redefining ethnic identity and claiming a new origin – are not separated. Today, as the mythical equation of Somali origin with the family of the Prophet is accepted as a fact by all Somali, newly converted groups still try, after the old pattern, to fit somewhere into this genealogical frame. It is a standard myth that at one time on a long migration a group got lost from its Somali relatives and now has found its way back into the tribal family. The ethnogenesis of the Somali, a process that continues, thus has two closely related features: Islamisation and the claim of a position in the Somali genealogy. Islamisation proceeds inland from the coast. Among the more recently converted groups, at any given time we find a richness of pagan cultural heritage under the mantle of Islam and often rather tense efforts to reinterpret this heritage in Islamic categories or to suppress and hide it.

At the western margin of their area of distribution these proto-Rendille–Somali met Nilotic groups and influenced them linguistically and cultur-ally, so that the resulting mixed form became known as Nilo-Hamitic. (This expression has taken root, although the term 'Hamitic' in this context has long been replaced by 'Cushitic'.) This process, which at different times may have affected the Teso, the Maasai, the Nandi, the Suk and others, is difficult to delineate in time and space. The evidence we have for these contacts is based on lexical comparisons (Fleming 1964: 90–91). We know little about the nature of these contacts with the exception of the recent example of the Rendille, especially the Ariaal Rendille, who maintain a virtually symbiotic relationship with the Maasai-speaking Samburu. To elaborate here about the interaction with Maa speakers in the nineteenth and twentieth centuries, however, would mean jumping to the last chapter of a long history of interaction. Like Islamisation, proceeding from the coast, so Nilo-'Hamitic' interaction is one of the historical constants of the last millennium.

NORTHERN KENYA 1550–1850 AD

The lack of written historical sources, which for the earlier periods has forced us to rely on speculative reconstructions, gives way in the sixteenth century to events that have been recorded in Ethiopian and Portuguese sources. We thus know that the expansion of the Oromo in the Ethiopian highlands began about 1540. It is believed that this expansion occurred simultaneously on all sides – perhaps within a few decades. The southward expansion of Oromo from their southern Ethiopian nucleus into Kenya presumably did not take place much later. In any case a strong concentration of Oromo on the lower Juba is documented for 1624 (Turton 1974: 533).

The wave of Galla or Oromo that moved farthest into Kenya were the Wardeh, Warday or Warr(a) D(a)ay(a) whose descendants are the Tana Orma. 'Orma' is a common southern dialect form of 'Oromo'.

I have dealt with the problem of the affiliation of the Tana Orma in the wider genealogy of Oromo peoples elsewhere (Schlee forthcoming). Here I therefore limit myself to a summary of the main points.

The Warra Daaya are believed to have inhabited at one time or another almost all of northern and eastern Kenya and the Jubaland. Graves marked by large stone circles and many wells are attributed to them. (There is a certain confusion in the oral traditions between Warra Daaya and Madanleh[4] as welldiggers.) They originate from the Dirre and Liban areas of southern Ethiopia, from where they are said to have been expelled by the Boran. After the Daarod Somali expansion of the late nineteenth and early twentieth centuries those Warra Daaya who had escaped death or captivity by the Somali were, for safety, restricted by the British to the right bank of the Tana River.

A comparison of the clan lists of the present-day Tana Orma and the Boran with that of the sixteenth-century 'Galla' by the Ethiopian monk Bahrey reveals a clear pattern of fission which has not been obscured by numerous later cross-migrations of clan groups. Bahrey's 'Galla' had two moieties: Boran and Baraytuma. These moieties must have been localised to some degree, since a subsequent split occurred at the line separating them. The Boran moiety of the early 'Galla' has formed the core of the Gona moiety of the modern Boran, while Baraytuma has become a moiety of the Tana Orma. The products of this split must have each rebuilt the moiety system by incorporating groups of different origin as the second moiety, thus enabling them to continue moiety exogamy and a moiety balance of ritual functions. Some of the clans of the Boran moiety Sabbo seem to be of Baraytuma origin, others have been co-opted from elsewhere. The Irdida (Arsi) moiety of the Tana Orma likewise show some elements of the early Boran moiety of the 'Galla' (Diagram 5). This pattern of fission along the moiety line with subsequent reconstitution of the moiety system has already been observed by Haberland (1963: 120) as typical for Oromo ethnogenesis.

I want to end my speculations about the role of moieties in Tana Orma origins with one observation about spatial arrangement. All the nomad peoples I know of the northern Kenyan lowlands have the doors of their houses to the west, including the Boran, the Gabbra, the Sakuye of Oromo speech, as well as the Rendille and the Somali. Although there are many ritual elaborations involving spatial orientation, the main reason seems to be a practical one: the constant wind blowing from the east. In accordance with this, north is called the 'right' and south the 'left' side. Among the Tana Orma, all this is inverted: their houses face east, north is 'left' and

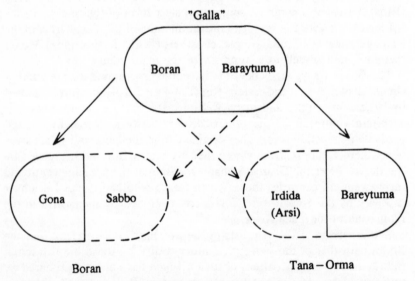

Diagram 5   Fission along the moiety division and reconstitution of moiety systems in Boran and Tana Orma ethnogenesis

south is 'right' (Werner 1914: 129 and 132; Jaenen 1956: 176). As this orientation of the huts does not seem very functional because of the dust, the most likely explanation may be that it once marked a ritual opposition to the Boran, the other moiety, a phenomenon not unfamiliar to anthropologists. The custom may stem from the time of their common residence in the Ethiopian highlands, where the mountain ranges produce irregular wind patterns.

It was the Warra Daaya who drove the first wedge into the settlement area of the proto-Rendille–Somali, which had until then been continuous, and separated the Rendille in the west from the Somali in the east. 'Somali', however, may at that time not yet have been the flag under which these tribes sailed. It is more likely that this identifier became attractive to many groups in the southern interior only through the expansion and dominance of the (northern) Darood Somali in the nineteenth century. At that time one was either Garre or Madanleh and, although one was not opposed to Islam, greater importance was attributed to the wellbeing of the camels as guaranteed by *almodo* and *sorio* rituals. In the period of their widest extension the Warra Daaya inhabited – although presumably not alone and not permanently – the whole country from the Ethiopian highlands down to the ocean and from Marsabit to beyond the Juba.

A more lasting and deeper influence on their neighbours emanated, however, from another Oromo group, the Boran. They succeeded not in building up an empire – that was reserved to their Amhara rivals in the north[5] – but in keeping a large federation of tribes of different origins in a loose, internally peaceful association, in which they themselves, especially their two *qallu*, were the undisputed centre of ritual power. Also the Warra Daaya kept their eyes on Dirre and Liban, the heartland of the Boran.

The centre of this network were the two *qallu*, priest-kings of the Boran, each of whom stood for one of the moieties, Sabbo and Gona. The dependent peoples paid livestock tribute to these *qallu*.[6] This was not, however, a unilateral tax, but a fee for the ritual services by which the *qallu* guaranteed the wellbeing of people and stock and provided a blessing, an umbrella extended over all those who paid these tributes. Certainly the activities of the *qallu* were awe-inspiring; even today fireside stories about how the *qallu* kept snakes in baskets – the one of Odítu (Gona) cobras, the one of Karrayyu (Sabbo) pythons – and handled them with familiarity[7] have a wide currency. Also in less likely variants these stories circulate among the inhabitants of northern Kenya far outside the sphere of Boran hegemony: the snakes roam freely in the compound of the *qallu* like dogs, *Katebo*, the sacred cattle of the *qallu* Karrayyu, are not castrated but only touched with a stick on the back and ordered, 'Be an ox', 'Be a bull', and as it grows the calf obeys this order.

Although submission to Boran hegemony may have been a rather light burden, there was considerable pressure to take this burden on oneself. The *gada-* or generation-set system of the Boran, which may have been established in its present form in the sixteenth century (i.e. at the same time as the dramatic Oromo expansion), and which in the first decades of its existence was an effective means of recruiting a warrior set (and then gradually 'underaged' by the fact that more and more Boran were born too late to fit into this system), produced once in eight years a new set who moved into the warrior grade and who went on a ritually prescribed raid in order to secure trophies: the severed genitals of slain enemies. Prospective victims avoided this treatment by submitting to the Boran hegemony and putting themselves under the umbrella of the *pax borana*.

Boran pressure, however, was not in all cases answered by submission. Among the Sakuye, the Garre and the Ajuran we find traditions about a vast exodus out of the triangle Moyale–Wajir–Mandera to the south-east. There are very similar traditions among the Gabbra and the Rendille – with, however, a westward flight. These migrations are of great importance for the genesis and the scattered distribution of the present-day ethnic groups, in the Garre's case from Moyale to – as splinter groups among the Rañanwein – Mogadishu. I examine the historical and sociological aspects of these tales in several variants in the following chapter.

The outcome of these population movements seems to have been that, after an eventful migration and re-migration, numerous groups of refugees nevertheless found themselves under Boran hegemony and – at least in romantic retrospection – experienced something like a *belle époque*, or, at least, peace for many generations.

Before the Boran were toppled from their position in the nineteenth and twentieth centuries by two groups of invaders – northern Somali, mainly Darood, and the British – groups bearing the following names lived in the area of Moyale, Wajir and Mandera under Boran tutelage: Gabbra (Malbe and Miigo), Sakuye, Ajuran, Warra Daaya and Garre. We have no evidence that around 1700 or 1800 these people were also grouped in these constellations and under these names. On the contrary, it is, for example, unlikely that it was the Islamic Hawiyya Somali of the tribe of Ajuran s/o Alama and his wife Fadummo d/o Jambele s/o Hawiyya, the conquerors of Mogadishu in the fifteenth century, who established this relationship with the Boran. With regard to those Ajuran who paid tribute to the Boran in northern Kenya, the Degodia (who on the threshold of the twentieth century came into hostile contact with them) report that they were pagans, indistinguishable from the Boran and unable to speak Somali. With which justification do both groups now claim the name Ajuran? The oral traditions are contradictory: on the one hand the present-day Kenyan Ajuran stress their Somali genealogy and their descent from Aqīl bin Abu

Ṭālib, the uncle of the Prophet; on the other hand they claim to descend from the legendary well-digging giants,[8] Madanleh, the autochthons of the country. Both claims may have an element of truth and certainly contain one of ideology: the first proves Islamic legitimacy, the second justifies a territorial claim. It seems most likely that an older, non-Islamic or only marginally Islamised group, which was originally called Madanleh and temporarily also Bal'ad, assimilated more and more Hawiyya Somali elements. Under Boran dominance the soil was not suitable for the flowering of Islam, so its practice became lax or forgotten. When, however, the Boran were replaced by Muslim Somali as the dominant ethnic group, people remembered their share of Hawiyya and then, in the main, sailed under the flag 'Ajuran', although this might have corresponded to genealogical truth only for a minority. The clan relationships between the Rendille and the Ajuran, in any case, which are believed by both sides to be genuine and genetic, become improbable if we assume that these 'Ajuran' were recent Islamic Somali.

Collectively these peoples who lived under Boran hegemony were known as the Worr Libin or Liban, after a region in southern Ethiopia, the Boran cradleland, which in this context had given its name to a much wider area (see Avanchers 1859).

The Oromo expansion in the sixteenth century and their subsequent hegemonial position in northern Kenya should not lead us to conclude that all the cultural influences the Oromo exerted on their neighbours happened after 1540. Before this time proto-Rendille–Somali and the Oromo of the regions Dirre and Liban were close neighbours, and there may have been centuries of relatively peaceful interaction, since the Boran and their ancestors kept cattle in the highlands. These highlands were too cold and wet for the camels of the proto-Rendille–Somali, and they would start to cough and lose weight. We can thus assume that, as today between the Gabbra and the Boran, there was little grazing competition between the proto-Rendille–Somali and the Boran, because at least the majority of the former specialised in camels and the latter in cattle. There may instead have been trade: cowhides for sleeping mats in exchange for smallstock. In any case there are many oral traditions in which the Boran do not figure as lords of the land, but as equal partners or as enemies with whom, again and again, one tries to find a *modus vivendi*.

When the Boran then established their overlordship, this was not an invasion from outside but a shift in the balance of power between ethnic groups which had known each other and interacted for a long time. This familiarity, however, was a familiarity of mutual intercourse, not a feeling of kinship: even today it is most unpropitious, even sinful, if Sakuye/ Somali/Rendille or Sakuye/Gabbra/Rendille kill each other. (An alienation has only occurred between non-Odoola Gabbra and Somali.) The killer 'has blood', brothers' blood, loses his mind and perishes. None of these groups, however, cares much about killing a Boran. Peace with the Boran is due to political expediency and not to higher imperatives. Also a Boran is not affected by any feeling of sin if he rips the belly of a pregnant Somali, Gabbra or Rendille woman, castrates the embryo and dances with the trophy. Among the Gabbra and the Rendille there are quite a number of unfortunates who were castrated as babies by Boran eager to acquire killer status: cut and run. 'The blood of Boran is different' is the current explanation for this state of affairs. Inside the Boran community, on the other hand, violence is considered deviant; one would even think twice about punishing one's child (Baxter, 1965: 65).

In the Mandera area during this period the Islamisation of the proto-Somali and their gradual incorporation into the Somali identity, which had long been formed in the east, continued. Presumably this mainly happened via the immigration of Muslim Somali and their association with local lineages which thus became doubly affiliated: an older affiliation to one of the tribes into which the local branch of proto-Rendille–Somali culture was organised – we here think of names like Madanleh, Jiddu, Bal'ad and Gassar Gudda without knowing much more than the names – and a newer affiliation of the modern Somali type with a pedigree extending right back to the uncle of the Prophet. Among the Garre this process often takes the form of a re-migration from Kofar, the southern part of the East Juba country, of those who had formerly escaped from the Boran. Apart from these, members of all possible tribes might have thought it convenient to claim a position in the local society. A strengthening of modern Islamic Somali culture in this period may have been limited to such immigrations, because the power constellation was not favourable for mass conversions. The Boran may not have been against Islam, but certainly they did not favour it either.

In the west of the area of the former proto-Rendille–Somali continuum, which was now divided by the Oromo expansion, the Rendille remained largely untouched by the two processes which were dominating this period: Boranisation and Islamisation. Instead they were culturally influenced by Maa speakers. They pierced their earlobes and their circumcision rituals, in many details, became assimilated to those of the Maa speakers. (In the case of the Nilo-'Hamites' the age-set system itself and circumcision as such, seem, however, also to have older roots which are ultimately Cushitic.) Some few Maa loan words were introduced into their language. In the area between the Ewaso-Ngiro in the south, the Chalbi salt pan in the north and Lake Turkana in the west, a mixed culture developed among the ancestors of the Samburu and the Rendille: the Ariaal, bilingual and interested in both camels and cattle. The 'white' Rendille, i.e. those who were not Ariaal, migrated far beyond these boundaries to the north and east, since their camels are much less dependent on water than the Samburu and Ariaal cattle. With the Dasanech, relatives from earliest times, when, as the tale goes, 'Lake Turkana had not yet split mankind into different parts', pasture and water were shared peacefully. Occasional mutual raids occurred with the Gabbra and Boran. The latter were mounted and thus tactically superior, since they could stampede a camel herd by beating against their shields and drive them away at a gallop in broad daylight, without any fear that the Rendille would catch them. The panicking camels would simply follow the horses. (Keeping horses was forbidden by the British who regarded horses as weapons of warfare and giraffe poaching. Until recently in northern Kenya a licence was required to keep a horse.) The Rendille, who could not reach the raiders, took vengeance on the nearest Gabbra settlement. There is, however, a mechanism for restoring peace. Nebei, the Rendille subclan whose name means 'peace', provide a female sheep, *neibichán*, which is sacrificed by Saale-Goobanai at peace negotiations. Neither Gabbra nor Rendille have a similar mechanism with the Nilotic Turkana. Thus there are two categories of enemies: the ones one can talk to and the ones one cannot.

Even if it is wrong to believe that the present area of Rendille is the same as their area at that time, we can nevertheless assume that their former area included their present one. There are a number of indicators that the Rendille have lived in their present area for a long time: Korolle, the permanent water on the margin of the Chalbi salt pan, without which one can never be really healthy, Farre and Algas, the sites around which clan origin myths have been wound; Lake Turkana, which has to be visited once every fourteen years for the *gaalgulamme* ceremony; the *ulukh* sites, groups of trees and rock formations which form ritual gates for migrating herds and settlement groups – the density of this ritual topography leads to the conclusion that the present-day Rendille area has been their heartland and centre for a long time. Gámura, on the northern fringe of the Chalbi, where today there are only Gabbra, was, with its sweet waters, as much a part of the Rendille heartland as Korolle. Containers woven from Gámura palm fibres brought luck to the camels that were milked into them, and for many ritual uses the palm fibres from Gámura were considered to be the best. The strongest concentration of Gabbra then may have been farther north around their sacred sites of Farole, Magado, Turbi, Hobok and Gorei on both sides of the Ethiopian border. The area around Maikona was only Gabbra-ised by refugees from Ethiopia in about 1915.

In perhaps about 1830 a settlement cluster of Rendille which contained a whole series of different clans – call it a cross-section of Rendille – ventured far in search of pasture and water and for four or five age-sets (some sixty years) lost contact with the other Rendille. They settled to the west of the Mountain with the White Neck (Mount Kenya) in the lowlands and, like the Ariaal and the Samburu, lived in close association with an alien people (the Laikipia or other Maasai?). This offshoot of the Rendille came to be called Kirima. The Kirima were later decimated by the Rendille and their remainders reincorporated.

1850–1910

The second half of the nineteenth century saw the first wave of invasions by the Darood, who expanded partly at the expense of other Somali, the Hawiyya, who had preserved a higher share of pagan (proto-Rendille–Somali) culture and were allied to the Boran. At times the invasions brought advantages for the Boran, who, profiting from the defeats of the Warra Daaya, acquired land and watering rights. Whatever the temporary advantages, however, gained by the Worr Libin, and whatever the set-backs suffered by certain Somali groups, the final results of this period are unambiguous:

1 All Oromo groups, from whose internal dissent the Somali finally profited, suffered large territorial losses.
2 Autochthonous Somali groups were culturally assimilated by the ˙northern Somali, with the consequent unification of Somali culture.
3 All Somali made territorial gains.

After a slow penetration into east Jubaland, into which the Ogaden Darood and splinter groups of other northern Somali associated with them by *sheegad* had expanded at the expense of the Tunni, the Raħanwein, the Dirr and the Warra Daaya in 1865 the Warra Daaya suffered a smallpox epidemic which led to a dramatic shift in the balance of power (Turnbull 1955). The Ogaden took the opportunity to attack from the east, and the Boran–Ajuran–Garre alliance, which included a federation of smaller tribes from the Dawa River which flows by Mandera, made life difficult for the Warra Daaya in the north. If, as according to oral traditions, we assume that the Warra Daaya themselves once belonged to this alliance, what then broke it up? We have to content ourselves with conjectures. First, the Boran might have seen the Warra Daaya, a group very similar to them-selves and the strongest single group of their entourage, more as rivals in their claim for hegemony than as allies. A practical reason, and one confirmed by the further course of events, was that the Boran and the Ajuran were envious of the Warra Daaya's possession of the wells of Wajir. In the same way, by the expulsion of the Warra Daaya the Garre gained access to the wells of El Wak. Those of the Warra Daaya who were left after the pincers had been closed were mostly sold by the Ogaden into slavery. They ended up in the markets of Lamu and Zanzibar. Others withdrew to the south-west, to the Tana River. The numerous women captured from the Warra Daaya enriched the Ogaden with a mixed population.

These events changed the ethnic composition of northern Kenya roughly as follows: the Darood Somali, mainly Ogaden (Telemuggeh, Mohamed Zubeir, Maghabul, Habr Suleman) entered what is now Garissa District and later expanded into Wajir District, and the Ajuran and Boran expanded in Wajir District.

Darood expansion, the dominant tendency of this epoch, continued without leading to any dramatic changes. The first attempts of the British to administer Jubaland (after 1895) and the NFD (Northern Frontier District) of Kenya had no effect on the course of history.

In the north another group expanded mainly under the umbrella of the Ajuran, as their *sheegad*, i.e. as second-degree *sheegad* of the Boran. They counted themselves as Hawiyya, but claimed, like the Ajuran, to descend only by a female link from Hawiyya. These were the Degodia. This form of genealogical reckoning may very well be a posthoc justification of a political alliance and does not necessarily have anything to do with actual descent relations.

The one group of the Degodia which went farthest in integrating itself into the Ajuran tribal community, and which, for decades, was not generally regarded as Degodia at all but as Ajuran, was the Gelible. Because of a slightly discriminatory attitude on the part of the other Degodia against them – when in anger, they call them *kufaar* or 'unbelievers' – and because of some cultural attributes the Gelible share with the Rendille and the Gabbra (elements of the proto-Rendille–Somali culture), I suggest that the Gelible are a relatively recent addition to the Degodia and that their ultimate affiliation to one of the major tribes at that time was still open.

Also the other Degodia did not come from a different world, however, but from the region around the rivers Dawa Parma and Ganale Doria in south-east Ethiopia and from El 'Ali in Somalia, where fellow tribesmen of theirs are still present today. This means that even before their southward expansion they lived in the vicinity of other groups and there may have been a wide range of contacts. Further, they are rooted in the same proto-Rendille–Somali culture, which, in the southern interior later than elsewhere, ceded to modern 'Somality'. Thus we do not need to wonder too much about similarities between them and their pagan cousins.

It is this recent migration of northern and central Somali to the south and south-west, in combination with their pious traditions to have originated at Mecca and Medina, that misled a whole generation of scholars into believing that the Somali as such originated in the north and have moved from there into the rest of the Horn, replacing an earlier population for which the Oromo (Galla) are the most likely candidates. Not only the more general historians (e.g. Low 1963: 321) but also the best specialists (e.g. Huntingford 1955: 19; 1963: 65–6; I. M. Lewis 1955: 45; 1980: 22–3) have succumbed to this error. There is no way to reconcile this erroneous view with the evidence of historical linguistics or cultural history and one wonders why it took so long to die.

1910 TO PRESENT:
NOMADS IN THE COLONIAL AND POSTCOLONIAL STATE

British colonialism, although it had been present officially for some time, only began to make its influence felt in the area in the second decade of this century.

During the early half of the colonial period the relative strength of the Boran-centred alliance and the Somali newcomers became inverted: today the Boran hegemony has been broken while the Somali continue to be vigorous and expansive, although often at the expense of their own subgroupings.

The entry of the British into this power struggle seems to provide at least part of the explanation for this reversal. Paradoxically, however, the British did not join forces with the Somali against the Boran but, on the contrary, with the Boran against the Somali. It seems to have been to the advantage of the Somali not to have been allied to the British.

In order to trace how it came about that the involvement of the British in this region benefited their declared adversaries and harmed their declared allies (the British themselves could only win, whatever the outcome of these rivalries) we have to consider the question of what, after all, the British were looking for in northern Kenya. The answer is nothing, but they did not want to leave this nothing to anybody else.

The northern boundary of the Kenya Protectorate was the result of a race against Ethiopian expansionism under Menelik. They met at the halfway point and formed a boundary commission. Northern Kenya thus came under state control because two empires tried to prevent each other from expanding into the power vacuum between them. From the very beginning northern Kenya was just a buffer zone against Ethiopia and later, in the war against Italy, it had exactly this function. The government wanted to keep hostile powers at a distance of a few hundred miles of semi-desert away from the White Highlands, the Brooke Bond tea plantations and the Uganda railway.

The north-eastern boundary with what today is Somalia is the result of a retreat. Up to 1916 the British presence extended into Jubaland where the military post Serenli was maintained. This post was sacked by Aulihan Somali, the garrison was massacred and the British Maxim guns were taken by the enemy. Thereupon the British also thought it wise to evacuate Wajir, hundreds of kilometres farther west, and left the whole region for several months to the free play of local forces. in 1924 Jubaland was ceded to the Italians, perhaps with relief. Why? Was the British empire unable to win a war against a few thousand herdsmen most of whom were only armed with spears? The answer is simple: no one wanted to invest in the wrong place.[9] Northern Kenya was of no economic interest and as long as it was shown in British red on the maps and a formal claim was maintained, the British were content. True to this stand, hardly any roads or schools or hospitals were built in northern Kenya. Even the Christian missions were not allowed in, because the administration feared they might instil new desires in the local population which could not be satisfied later. Thus the aim of the British can be defined as visible presence at the lowest possible cost and not as effective control.

The most mobile, most pugnacious and least controllable part of the local population were the Darood, of whom the Auliħan, whose unpleasant acquaintance the British had already made at Serenli, are a part. To save military expenditure it was an obvious option for the British to join forces with the Boran and their allies who were trying to check the Darood expansion. In a way the British became the sixth tribe in this alliance. Some months after the flight, the district commissioner was in fact escorted back to Wajir by the Ajuran *hayyu* (or 'sultan') Ido Robleh[10] and his men to restore order there.[11] It is difficult to decide who protected whom on the journey.

The answer of the administration to the incessant conflicts over pasture and water was to map tribal areas. This created economic and ecological problems:

1 Did the extent of the areas take into account the uneven and unpredictable spatial distribution of the rains? Only large areas had a reasonably high chance of sufficient rainfall in a particular locality even in a bad year.
2 Why else were border violations so frequent? In the dry season some groups obviously regarded their rights of access to wells as inadequate.

As the term 'desertification' had not yet been invented, the British, according to the established patterns of explanation of that period, attributed all ecological and economic difficulties to soil erosion due to overgrazing, i.e. to the nomads themselves. After reading through the archives and becoming familiar with constant laments of this nature it is surprising to find that in photographs from now and from fifty years ago no difference in the type and density of the vegetation can be found.[12] But then, just as during the Sahel drought of the seventies, nomads with their purportedly negative environmental impact were convenient scapegoats where planners and politicians had failed.

In their attitudes, and thus also in the degree of rigidity with which they

enforced territorial boundaries, the British administrators differed. While
some were generous in granting exceptions by opening such boundaries to
livestock movements in years of drought, others took positions like 'this is
a hard country and if God does not send rain to particular tribes it must be
accepted as God's will that they perish.'[13] For someone for whom God has
assured a government officer's pension, such things may be easy to say.

These ecological and economic problems were closely linked to the
ethnic and political ones:

1   What is a 'tribe'? What were the criteria the British used for dividing
    and subdividing the population into such units with territorial rights?
    And what effect did this have on the self-definition of the people
    concerned?
2   What were the long-term consequences of declaring such boundaries
    and making single herd owners pay fines for trespassing without being
    able to guarantee these boundaries militarily?

As to tribal divisions, the British distinguished two gross major categories: 'Somali' and 'Galla'. (This book aims to show how much more
complex things are in reality.) Thus, in accordance with this view, a first
rough cut was made: the Galla–Somali line.

Internally, the 'Galla' country was subdivided into Boran, Gabbra,
Ajuran, etc., grazing grounds, and the 'Somali' part into the territories of
the Degodia, Muḥammad Zubeir, Marreḥan, etc. Later, with the growth
of motorised traffic, the resultant tracks, which led radially from all sides
to Wajir, were declared territorial boundaries and the sectors between
them were allotted to different 'tribes'.

According to their ritual and political affiliation to the Boran, the
Ajuran were allotted an area on the western or 'Galla' side of the Galla–
Somali line. But there was also one section of the Ajuran which had never
belonged to the Boran-centred alliance and which neither linguistically nor
politically nor ritually had been 'Galla'-ised: the Waqle. The Waqle had
lived farther east and thus, as Somali among Somali, had undergone quite
a different history: they had become representatives of the mordern Islamic
Somality. In the course of the general south-western trend of Somali
migration since the late nineteenth century, more and more Waqle joined
the Kenya Ajuran and exercised an Islamising, 'civilizing' influence on
their 'lost brothers' which in the long run resulted in an ethnic redefinition:
all Ajuran perceived themselves more and more as Somali.

The matter was further complicated by small groups which, according
to the famous Somali motto 'Be a mountain or attach yourself to one',
joined longer-established groups as *sheegad*. These latter tried to attach
themselves as closely as possible to the sultan Ido Robleh, in order to
benefit in terms of pasture and water from his good relationships to the

Boran. The longer this process lasted, however, the more often we hear of frictions and armed conflicts because the Boran were being driven away from their own wells by this proliferation of 'guests'. Also Ido Robleh perceived the advantage of joining the stronger side and repeatedly broke his loyalty to the Boran. Finally, in 1934, the British legalised the new state of affairs and incorporated the Ajuran territory into the Somali area – an act which amounted to shifting the Galla–Somali line westwards.[14] The Boran were thus badly paid for accepting and supporting the British as arbiters.

In the same period, 1932, the Boran also had to give up the wells of Wajir because the British wanted to avoid conflicts with the Somali, who were there in greater numbers. In compensation the Boran were given (at the expense of the Samburu) what is now Isiolo District much farther west.

Boran informants believe that it was a mistake to trust the territorial guarantees given by the British and to go along with their continuous attempts at appeasement. If, in the second decade of this century, free rein had been given to the Boran cavalry, the Somali, they claim, could have been contained.

In fact the British have weakened those under their protection not only indirectly by their ill-defined stand but also directly and materially by prohibiting the possession of guns and horses, both of which were classed as arms. (It is perhaps easier for an administration to control empty-handed pedestrians.) They succeeded in enforcing such prohibitions, however, only in the case of their friends, not among their adversaries, so that this step also resulted in an indirect furthering of Somali interests. Another factor was that the armed force of the British, the Red Turbans (the Duub As, or Administration Police as they are known today) were largely recruited in British Somaliland. Naturally, these soldiers were not keen to fight against their Muslim brothers. In a similar context Dalleo (1975: 226) quotes the remark of one district commissioner: 'A straight Somali force is not only a useless unit but a positive danger.'[15] The one or two whites per district were no counterweight to this. Further, the British did not have transport facilities of their own but depended in Somali areas on hired Somali camels and thus had to rely on the goodwill of those whom they pretended to control. One can also doubt that all British administrators really meant to stop the Somali expansion. In a report by District Commissioner Sharpe we read: 'We try to stop him [the Somali]. Are we right? He is obviously of better material than many of our own tribes.'[16] By 'our own tribes' he did not mean the various nations that make up the British (Scottish, Welsh, etc.), but the populations, like the Boran or the negroid central Kenyan Bantu speakers, who had been resident in the Kenya colony for a long time. Some British seem to have discovered related spirits in the Somali, who conducted themselves as a warrior aristocracy. Apart from this, the British, whose principle was indirect rule, allied themselves wherever they went to those in power, not to the losers. Why then, once the tide had turned, oppose the Somali, if they were obviously the more successful?

The expectation that – at least from one boundary correction to the next one – the British policy of territorial allocations provided well-defined territories inhabited by well-defined populations has to be disappointed, too. The nomads understood, of course, the principles of land allocation and also knew and welcomed the gaps in administrative information. Thus all types of masquerade, not only by *sheegad* but also by simple change of label, were practised to ensure that the herds could graze wherever the pasture was greenest: one more advantage for those whom the British did not know so well and a disadvantage for those close to them.

To prevent such circumvention of the law, British administrators collected more and more elaborate Somali genealogies, and some of them became specialists in the inter-relationships between the diverse groups. In their annual reports we find again and again little sketches of pedigrees by which the officers tried to explain the intricacies of the matter to their superiors. Occasionally an officer would boast of having traced a 'false' Ajuran group who had pretended to be 'real'. Such usurpers then were repatriated somewhere and had to pay a fine in livestock for trespassing. The officers acted as if biological and not the more changeable social descent was the principle behind tribal affiliation. More problematical than this is the fact that acceptance into the community, which since time immemorial had been in the competence of local elders, was now regulated by a colonial power from overseas.

The readiness with which Somali became *sheegad* of other Somali was matched by the willingness with which they were accepted by their hosts. This openness of Somali society and its readiness to accept strangers as long as they were Muslims or prepared to convert, is part of an ecological-economic-military strategy which can be called maximisation. Marriage at a relatively early age and shorter periods of sexual abstinence after the birth of a child are other aspects of maximisation. The differences in camel management between the Rendille and the Gabbra on the one hand and the Somali on the other provide a vivid contrast (Schlee 1987b): while the camels of the former are allowed relatively short spans of grazing or browsing, go without water for long periods and only receive rather rudimentary traditional veterinary care, Somali camels are herded with a much milder hand, even being allowed to browse at night, watered more frequently and taken much care of. As a result the Benaadir strain of camels kept by the Kenyan Ajuran and Degodia Somali was able to develop into one of the largest and fleshiest type of camel in the world, with abundant milk, whereas Rendille and Gabbra camels are smaller, more mobile, hardier and have a higher resistance to drought. While Somali management maximises inputs and outputs, the Rendille management minimises both; the neat gain achieved by the two forms of management might not differ that widely since both systems are successful adaptations to very similar environments.

Baxter (personal communication) told me that in the fifties this maximising strategy of the Somali, both in terms of demographic growth and pressure on the environment, was exactly what the Boran complained about. The Somali had to expand – and with their numbers have the power to do so – 'after eating up all behind them. . . . It was to what they saw as Somali fecklessness that the Boran attributed the continuous erosion of the Somali line.'

I shall dwell on ecology a little longer, because ecological strategies underlie the ethnic dynamics which are the motive force of the history we are discussing. In ecological terms the comparatively conservative form of Rendille camel management finds its parallel in the management of people.

As we shall see below (chapter 5), there is a flow of migrants from the Rendille to the Gabbra, the Sakuye and the Boran, to whom they are assimilated. The reverse does not hold. The history of the Ariaal (Spencer 1973) confirms that there is a constant flow of migrants from the Rendille to the Ariaal and the Samburu, but hardly any migration in the reverse direction. The Rendille themselves use the following words: *Rendille inenyet asaħta* ('The Rendille sort people out'), that is, they discriminate, segregate and differentiate.

The Ariaal have a mixed economy with camels and cattle as their large stock, while the Rendille neglect cattle in favour of camels. Someone who favours cattle should therefore join the Ariaal because they adjust their management and movements to the needs of their cattle; also it is possible to acquire Ariaal and Samburu stockfriends.[17] So far, so good. But Ariaal settlements in the immediate vicinity of the Rendille and which consist mostly of Rendille speakers seem to find no impediments to cattle keeping. On the other hand, increasing numbers of Rendille try cattle breeding in spite of the ecological hazards involved. So is it really necessary formally to break with Rendille society by non-participation in the age-set rituals and to declare oneself Ariaal in order to became a cattle herder? There may be other reasons. A number of Rendille who have become Ariaal told me that they left Rendille society because good neighbourliness (*oluħ ti ħaagane*) can be found more easily among the Ariaal and because there is constant gossip (*mededél*) among the Rendille. It is difficult to measure the intensity of gossip. But once friction ceases to be verbal and seeks its outlet in violence, there are some quantitative indicators: the number of dead and wounded. In my book on the Rendille (Schlee 1979) I devote a chapter to the chronology of the conflict about the marriage rituals of the Ilkichili age-set, in which I point out that the roots of the conflict can be traced back for many decades. Cases of suicide and murder are recorded. The main line of conflict was the moiety division between Belesi Baħai and Belesi Berri whose protagonists were the warriors of the clans D'ubsaħai and Tubcha respectively. Between writing that book (1977) until the present (1984) nearly all of Ilkichili have married and settled down to the peaceful life of elders, but the inter-clan conflict became more heated. The succeeding warrior age set, Ilkororo, has already paid a death toll of four and the wounded have ceased to be counted. Tribe-wide rituals, which I describe as an integrative force because of the degree of co-operation they impose, have become increasingly difficult to organise. In 1984 Tubcha was excluded from a sacrificial ceremony (órlagorraħo) and the whole clan may well cease to be regarded as Rendille at some time in the future. This book is the wrong place to delve deeply into the internal mechanisms of any one society. Suffice it to say that Rendille internal affairs are characterised by constant politicking and occasional violent outbreaks. Though it is small, Rendille society shows clear tendencies towards fission.

Violence is the domain of warriors: elders are believed to inflict damage through their curse. Many instances of misfortune – and misfortune is recurrent in the harsh environment of the Rendille – are attributed to curses, envy, the evil eye and occasionally even sorcery. For example, the large, heavy Somali camels do not thrive in the arid, stony Rendille country because their nutritional demands are too high (see Schlee 1987b). If you ask the Rendille why their imported Somali camels die, they tend to give a different answer: 'They are larger than our camels and everyone stares at them. These eyes finish them off on the spot. Rendille eyes are bad.'

On the micro level, the poverty of junior sons, who are disadvantaged by the inheritance rules, which radically favour the first-borns, has already been described by Spencer (1973) as a factor causing emigration.

All these elements combine to make Rendille a society which is very easy to leave and very difficult to join.

We shall see below[18] that certain clan groups which have been among the Rendille for many generations are still sometimes referred to as 'Boranto'. Two hundred and eighty years, it seems, is not long enough to become fully accepted by the Rendille.

One immediately attractive explanation as to why the Rendille are so exclusive, is the nature of their environment: their arid country does not support many people and so they have to get rid of some. But the Gabbra live in just as harsh an environment, yet they are largely composed of immigrant groups and are hospitable to new arrivals. The environment alone does not seem to be a sufficient explanation. We might need to take livestock management strategies and herd mix into account as well. The Rendille are specialised camel herders, while the Alganna phratry of the Gabbra, which has absorbed most of the recent Rendille migrants, also keep cattle.[19] Perhaps the mixed economy of Alganna is more flexible and better suited to accommodate newcomers than the Rendille camel mono-culture. Be this as it may. On the other hand there are, as we have seen, certain Somali groups which are as specialised in camels as the Rendille are and which nevertheless readily accept strangers, who strengthen their numbers. In fact, there seem to be two opposite cultural responses (and possibly some mixed intermediate strategies) to ecological limitations. One can react to scarce resources either by self-restriction or by expansion which breaks the limits of a given environment by penetrating into another environment.

There is not only an ecological aspect to Somali expansion and Rendille exclusiveness, but ecology also helps to explain why Boran hegemony and the *pax borana* lasted so long. The Boran seem to have respected the principle of the ecological niche: that peace can be most easily maintained among peoples who do not compete for the same resources. The Boran hegemony incorporated many camel-keeping peoples under a loose ritual umbrella and relied on their military assistance. Boran people and herds, however, do not seem to have expanded into the grazing grounds of these allies to a significant degree. The Boran remained mainly cattle herders and restricted themselves to the higher parts of the country. Very few Gabbra lineages[20] and no Sakuye claim Boran origin. The Ajuran have only absorbed individual Boran and the latter have left no traces in the clan structure because they reaffiliated themselves to their host clans.

Shortly before independence, in 1962, the British held a referendum in the NFD[21] to find out whether the population wished territorial integra-tion with the young Somalia or with the future Republic of Kenya. There was a majority for Somalia. It would have been better if the referendum had never been held. To hold a referendum and then to act contrary to its results is asking for trouble: trouble not for the British who withdrew but for the Kenyans who took over. Because of the referendum central Kenyans knew exactly what to think about the northern Kenyans and war was the immediate result. Guerrilla actions of varying intensity flared throughout the decade. This was the so-called *shifta* emergency, derived from the Amharic word for 'bandit'. Although anti-Somali feelings among the Boran and the Sakuye were so strong that they might have been won over to the Kenyan side, the central Kenyans, who had the greatest say in the new government, mistrusted everybody who lived as a nomad. The Sakuye in particular were suspected of feeding and sheltering guerrilla fighters, although these very Sakuye were regarded as enemies by the

Somali and had to defend themselves against their raids. But instead of joining forces with the Sakuye the government forces preferred to destroy the purported Somali food supply and machine-gunned the Sakuye camel herds. Since camels have a very low reproduction rate, very few Sakuye even now have succeeded in building up their herds again. Thousands of them still live as peri-urban paupers around Isiolo and other townships.

In so far as the *shifta* activities were based on support from Somalia, this guerrilla war was part of an international conflict which shifted in the seventies from northern Kenya into the Ogaden. In the triangular con-stellation Ethiopia–Kenya–Somalia good relationships were maintained between Ethiopia and Kenya as if there had never been an Ethiopian revolution. Shared aversions have proved stronger links than shared pre-ferences. Somalia tends to woo Kenya harder the worse her own relations with Ethiopia become. Peace at the international level did not mean that northern Kenya was entirely free from collective violence in the seventies. Apart from the traditional forms of warfare, with spears and some old-fashioned guns, to acquire booty and the honoured status of killer,[22] Somali gangs equipped with automatic weapons continued to raid, although no longer backed by Somalia. A recurrent pattern seems to be that men got arms in Somalia by pretending that they wanted to join the guerrilla fighters in the contested Ethiopian Ogaden and then diverted to Kenya where life as a marauder and parasite appeared sweeter than death on the Ethiopian battlefield. By appeals to ethnic loyalty, accompanied by some intimidation, these bandits managed, for a certain period, to enjoy the support of the local Somali population; but they overreached themselves. In 1980 Isiolo District was flooded by pastoral Somali from Wajir and Mandera districts who were fleeing from constant harassment by their fellow Somali, who roamed about robbing and raping at gunpoint.

That these Somali could infiltrate so heavily into Isiolo District, which in colonial times was reserved for the Boran and the Sakuye, seems to suggest that the colonial boundaries have become obsolete. This, however, is only partly true. Although in theory all Kenyans are supposed to be citizens of the whole country without any section having special rights to any part of it, nomads are still forcefully repatriated to their districts of origin. A quarrel between one faction of the Marsabit County Council, which wanted to reserve the Moyale area to the Boran, and another faction, which pointed to the constitutional rights of Kenyans of Somali origin to move where they please on the open range, was resolved as late as 1978 by the detention of the 'constitutionalists'. But normally, especially if no Somali are involved, movements by one ethnic group into the custom-ary grazing grounds of another are agreed, after prior announcement to the government-appointed chiefs, consultations among the elders and admonishment of the youngsters to keep peace. Some ethnic boundaries such as that between the Rendille and the Samburu are permeable any-how. Thus in very bad years Rendille herds have been able to graze hundreds of kilometres away from their usual grounds, even though in normal years herdsmen prefer to stay close to their home areas.

In spite of the principle of freedom of movement and in spite of the fact that restrictions along ethnic lines smack of tribalism, it is understandable that the authorities should want to have a say in who is allowed to graze where; if they did not, it might be difficult to keep the peace and impossible to introduce ecologically acceptable forms of grazing management which, in the long-term, are in the interest of all.[23]

Whether it is regrettable or not, ethnicity, clanship and inter-ethnic clan relationships continue to be of great social and political importance. Newer forms of relationships, such as those arising from the monetarised economy, have made the picture more complex but in part they run parallel to the older set of relationships. Without studying clanship it is, for example, often impossible to understand the results of local and national elections.

The systematic neglect and the wilful retardation of the development of northern Kenya by the British, who only perceived it as a buffer zone, has meant that, until today, the northern nomads are under-represented among Kenya's elites. In most areas it is only now that the first generation of school-children is growing up, whereas in central Kenya some of the grandparents and great-grandparents of today's children underwent formal education, with the result that their families are today firmly established in the state and the economy.

The circumstances of colonisation, decolonisation and the final integration of the north into the Republic of Kenya have caused the relationships between the central powers and the northern nomads to be characterised by estrangement and aversion. Because of their isolation and belated access to education and power the nomads lack spokesmen and middle-men who think in their terms and who could work with them, for example, in organising mobile schools, improved systems of production and marketing and in balancing the interests of mutually hostile groups.

CHAPTER 4

ELEMENTS OF A PROTO-CULTURE:
A COMPARATIVE APPROACH TO HISTORY

This chapter is divided into two parts: the first deals with non-verbal aspects of culture, the second with oral traditions. Subdomains of culture can be defined in many other ways, and this bipartite organisation stems from pragmatic considerations only. One feature which distinguishes oral traditions from other cultural phemonena is that the former have history as their subject matter, while the comparison of artefacts, institutions, rules, rituals, etc., only allows indirect conclusions about how they came to have their present shapes and distributions – that is, about history.

THE CAMEL COMPLEX

Huggung' ki gaal dakhamba a ko kaldach[1] – 'The custom of camels is only one,' say the Rendille. By this they mean that there are uniform rules about the ritual treatment of camels which are observed by all camel-keeping peoples. Within the Rendille horizon this is true. Their neighbours, no matter whether they speak Boran or Somali, share with the Rendille many cultural traits relating to camels. The Nilotic Turkana, by not following any of these rules and treating camels like cattle, in the Rendille's opinion demonstrate that they are not legitimate camel owners. (The Turkana acquired camels only relatively recently in raids on the Rendille.) Had the Rendille had contact with the pastoral Darood Somali, however, they would have known that not all camel people keep these rules; the dividing line between those who do and those who do not runs through those groups which today we call Somali.

Many of the rules which form the complicated codex about how to treat camels relate to what to do with a camel on a particular day of the week. The names of the days of the week in the languages of all the peoples discussed here[2] are ultimately of Arabic derivation. There are, however, remnants of an older set of names, all relating to domestic animals.[3] Thus, for the Gabbra, Sunday is the *ayaana gaala*, the Day of the Camel. Neither Rendille nor Gabbra nor Sakuye may move their settlements on Sundays or take camels on a journey which would oblige them to spend the Sunday night[4] outside the settlement, except in an emergency and with special ritual precautions. Camels should not be bled on Sundays, nor can the promised gift of a camel be collected or even camel milk be taken out of the settlement on this day. The Garre of Mandera District, who are Somali and Muslim, share this fear about Sunday, although, as Muslims, one would expect them to be more concerned about Friday. Mu'allim Mukhtar 'Usmān, a Garre (Tuf) and Qur'ān-teacher, describes the Garre restrictions about Sunday thus (in Boran):

> *Ayaani godanan ínjir. Ammo ayaan seerat jir. Ka seera ka ingódanin ínjir. [. . .] Worri gaala Ahad ingódan. Eegi at alkan kud'an on kan kébult, ingódan. Ammarki Waaqa aki chufa ammo wan kud'ani irre diqoo, ka ammo fulá sun faan marre fa inqábne ka atini jete, ka ammo galgali bori Ahada ingódana fa jed'ani, wo lamma duub wo lamm taat: inúmolti, godanti injírtu; yo d'ad'abani, moona gaali kébule chufa, kossi gaala kan fudan. Akas íngodanan.*

> There are days on which one migrates. But there are [also] forbidden days. There are forbidden days on which one does not migrate. Camel people do not migrate on a Sunday. Before you spent ten nights in that settlement place, one does not migrate. But if, by God, by all means, it is, however, less than ten, and that place does not have pasture and so, you said, and they say, tomorrow night, Sunday, one does not migrate, then there are two things [to do], two things happen: you stay, there is no migration; if they cannot [stay], from all enclosures in which camels spend the night, they take that dung of camels with them. Like this, they do migrate.

To circumvent the rule about not migrating on Sundays, the Garre take the camel enclosures in symbolic form with them. (The Gabbra do the same.) This device makes it evident that the camels are the reason why one may not migrate on a Sunday. If people could take their houses on their own backs and leave their camels where they are, they might well migrate without this precaution. It is the camels which may not spend the 'Sunday night' in a new or alien enclosure. A young baggage camel must not be introduced to training on a Sunday; training should always start on a Monday. To circumvent this rule one can symbolically touch the tongue of the camel with the mouth part of the leading rope on a Monday and then start the real training on any convenient day (Rendille, Gabbra, Sakuye).

Of course, apart from the propitiousness of the day of the week, it also matters who spits on the rope and then ties it around the camel's lower jaw. One man may have good 'spit' (*ħanjúf*) that contains a blessing; another may have a 'hot hand' (*daħanti kulel*) that hurts, brings misfortune; another a 'cool hand' (*daħanti khobo*) that leads, heals, protects, makes things succeed, prosper and multiply (*daakh*) (Rendille).

As well as being the day for training unbroken loading camels (R: *leilei*; B: *lenjis*),[5] Monday is the preferred day for various transactions involving camels.[6] The two most usual forms of loaning a female camel are as R: *maal*, B: *dabarre* or as R: *kalaksimé*, B: *kalassime*. The customs concerning these two forms of loan and the legal principles involved are so similar to all groups discussed here,[7] that they can be described as a single system.

Both forms of shared rights over a camel have important functions in balancing economic risk, in establishing social bonds, in redistributing wealth and reallotting labour. We find similar institutions in many pastoral societies, since nomadic pastoralism is a high-risk enterprise amidst war-like competitors in an insecure, ecologically marginal environment. Here the need arises for insurance against loss from drought, epidemics and human and animal predators or simply against the ever-present possibility that an entire herd may stampede for no apparent reason and be irretrievably scattered. The need also arises for widespun networks of mutual help and solidarity for shared defence, shared labour and political and jural assistance. Sharing beasts helps to meet both these needs.

Maal and *kalaksimé* camels differ in regard to the rights in their offspring and the period of the loan. The more attractive form for the recipient is *maal*. While I know of no etymology for the term B: *dabarre*, the Rendille word *maal* is derived from *a-maala*, 'I milk'; *a-maald'a* (autobenefactive), 'I milk for myself' – e.g. *aitó maald'a*, 'I milk a she-camel for myself', 'I have a she-camel milked for me' (i.e. 'milked for my household, by whoever does the actual milking'[8]). Usually a *maal* camel needs to be asked for, formally applied for or begged for (*a-daaħa* – e.g. *aitó daaħa*, 'I ask for a she-camel', *inantó daaħa*, 'I make suit for a girl'; *chiling'kó daaħa*, 'I beg for a shilling'.) The applicant, after a long introduction which stresses the good relationships between himself and the owner, as well as between their respective kin groups and ancestors, will carefully and respectfully approach the subject, since he is the interested party and in the weaker position. Once the transaction of a camel has been agreed, it is necessary to wait for an occasion, for example, a *sorio* festival, when the camels are in the settlement and not in the satellite camp, so that the loan camel can actually be collected. This is only possible, however, on the appropriate day of the week (see above). On the morning when the recipient comes to collect the promised camel, he has a twig of R: *gaer*, B: *mad'er* (*Cordia sinensis lam.*)[9] in his hand. As he leads away his camel, usually a recently weaned calf or young heifer, he deposits the twig on the house of the donor as a ritual payment.[10]

This camel, although a loan, would normally never be recovered by the original owner. Indeed, it would even be slightly shameful for him to be too inquisitive about the animal's condition and that of its progeny, and the prestige gained by loaning out the animal would definitely be diminshed if he were so (see Spencer 1973: 37–40). The male offspring of a *maal* camel is the full property of the holder, i.e. the borrower; in other words, it becomes *alál* (R, B).

The word *alál* is easily recognisable as derived from the Arabic حلال (*halāl*), an Islamic concept that means (a) ritually clean, slaughtered in the prescribed way (the Islamic equivalent of *kosher*), and (b) rightful, legal (as in 'rightful' wife as opposed to 'mistress'). In Rendille and Boran the use of the word is restricted to camels and, with a slight undertone of irony, to women.[11] In this context a close English translation would be 'own'.

Any female offspring of a *maal* camel, however, belongs to the original owner, at least in theory; it is branded with the brand of the clan of origin and ear-clipped or otherwise marked correspondingly by the holder. Thus every herdsman must know how to apply many different brands to his camels. This nominal ownership of the original *maal* giver does not entitle him to actual possession. A giver who asks for repayment of a female calf is likely to be stalled and told that the camels are still few, the holder is in need, and to try again a few years later. Forcibly to repossess a camel would be considered unworthy behaviour. One Rendille elder who sought a girl for a second marriage was reminded of how he took back by force a *maal* camel from a clansman of the girl years ago. He had to pay a fine in excess of the bridewealth to assuage the anger of his future affines and was only then promised the girl. It was never contested that the camel which caused this turmoil bore his brand, was known to be his property and offspring of his property; but possession and 'ownership' are two different things.

On the other hand, a *maal* holder can very well give a female calf or heifer of the *maal* herd to a third person, thereby making the animal second-degree *maal*. Then the following rule applies: *Gaal et lama malakakhabo* (R), 'A camel is not owed to two people' – i.e. the second-degree *maal* holder owes gratitude to the first-degree holder and nothing to the original owner, although the property marks of the latter will be retained throughout the generations. The offspring of a camel given by clan A to clan B, and in the next generation by B to C may thus end up in clan D, while all camels connected by uterine descent to the camel originally given retain the property marks of A. It is difficult to see the advantage of giving a *maal* camel, since the gain so clearly seems to be on the side of the taker. Spencer (1973: 38) is right in stressing the prestige acquired; giving a camel is considered generous and makes the giver appear *mejel*, a worthy man.

Apart from the prestige, the giver retains latent rights in animals of the *maal* herd. He can use these rights if he has a plausible need, such as the imminent circumcision or marriage of a son or his own second marriage, where *alál* camels are required for bridewealth. Such a need can be made more plausible by pointing to losses by drought, epidemics or raids. A *maal* giver who has lost the herd in his possession can use his widespread latent rights to the offspring of camels he or his ancestors originally loaned out. On the other hand, no compensation can be claimed for *maal* camels received from others which may have belonged to the lost herd. (*Maal* givers often are at the receiving end of other *maal* transactions.) An *alál* ('own') camel that was given away as *maal* may thus entitle the victim of a major loss to a heifer. The one he kept, on the other hand, may have died or been taken by enemies, i.e. it has gone without being replaced, and so may the *maal* camels he received from others. In the latter case, however, the loss is alleviated by being shared. Thus the insurance factor favours giving and taking shared beasts. The only camel really lost is the dead or stolen *alál*.

Another incentive to lend out a camel may lie in the human:animal ratio of a given household. A wealthy man with few sons and few other junior patrilineal relatives may be forced to hire herdsmen to handle his vast herd. These herdsmen would customarily be provided with tyre sandals, cloths, smallstock for slaughter and paid a female calf every other year. An animal given to a hired herdsman is one that has changed from the side of benefits to the side of costs and remains there for generations, although, in the case of a camel it nominally is *maal*, while camels given as *maal* to an independent herdsman may diminish the need for hired labour, establish claims on camels if at a later time the human:animal ratio has changed, and may at the moment not be necessary for subsistence anyhow, since at present the human:animal ratio is low. A man whose sons are too young to herd may prefer to loan out camels, so that he can claim back some of their offspring when his sons are grown up and, especially, when they marry, instead of spending them on hired labour.

The rules for the other type of loan (R: *kalaksimé*, B: *kalassimé*) are completely different. The *kalaksimé* animal is always an adult female camel which has just given birth and is given to a household that is short of milk. After the lactation period the camel is given back to the owner. The latter can now say *niyrakh kagoi* (R) 'Cut the calf away (from the mother)' – i.e. 'Keep the calf!' – or he can take back both animals and thus limit his gift to the milk. *Kalaksimé* thus is the preferred form of helping a poor person without necessarily establishing a long-term relationship.

Yet another form of transfer of stock is *darnán* (R) or adding (*ka-dara* [R], *iti-dara* [B]) animals to someone else's herd. The giver rather than the recipient is regarded as the beneficiary of such a transaction. One gives stock to somebody to herd, because one is short of labour. No rights exist on the herder's side, except usufruct of the milk and the usual gifts which reflect the number of animals herded and the generosity of the owner. *Darnán* thus is a service to the owner, not to the herder.

With the inheritance of original brands through the generations of *maal* camels, camels can be thought of, in a sense, as forming matriclans. This mode of categorisation is illustrated further in the category of camels called *dorr* (R) or *doro* (B) (see Torry 1973: 93ff.). There are different camelid 'matriclans' of *dorr* which are owned by different human patriclans and lineages. The latter, however, can very well own other strains of camels besides the *dorr*. Being a *dorr* camel thus does not depend on being owned by a certain clan but exclusively upon being the daughter of a *dorr* camel.

Dorr have to be treated differently from other camels. As a general rule, their milk cannot be mixed with the milk of other camels. They even have to have their own milking containers (R: *murúb*, B: *gorfa*), which are marked by a cowry shell or shells (R: *eléll*, B: *eleelani*) sewn onto them. There are different rules as to the categories of people who are allowed to consume the milk and other observances which differ according to the different strains of *dorr*. For example, the *dorr* camels of Hajufle (D'ubsaħai, Rendille) are known by the family name Ilal. This is the story of how Hajufle got Ilal and how Ilal imposed special conditions on Hajufle:

Hajufle once, going his way, passed by a vast hyena hole in which a female camel was sitting. That was at a time when the animals still used to speak. Hajufle demanded that the camel come out, but she refused. So he started to make promises. 'I will make you sacred [*lagan*], come up, I will surely make you sacred.' She remained in the hole. So Hajufle continued: 'Come out, you will not be milked into the container in which water is given to the goats, come out!' She still just refused. 'Come out, while you are in the settlement[13] your milk will not be brought near the cooking pot!' She is still sitting. 'Come out, your milk will be kept away from women. Women will not drink you,' he said. So she came out. This is why women do not touch her.

The camels of the Ilal strain are thus specially protected against pollution by goats and women. The avoidance of contact with goats is shared by the Atire strain of Gaalgidele (Matarbá, Rendille) and by the camels of Gaalorra (= Riyodiido, i.e. the 'goat-hater'), a subclan of Gaaldeilan.

A certain ritual opposition between reproductive female camels and women is general to Rendille and Gabbra societies. Women should not milk camels; nor should men who have sexual intercourse with women. 'So and so milks camels' means that the person referred to is in his boyhood and early warriorhood and has not yet taken up sexual relations, or that he has given them up in old age.[14] Other observances connected with the *dorr* of Hajufle, which are more numerous and more rigid than for other *dorr*, are: women may not carry their calves; the meat of their male offspring may not be eaten by Ḥajufle; a sterile cow may not be used as a beast of burden, as they usually are, because then she would come into contact with women. All rules concerning *dorr* have to be observed by those who might take a *dorr* camel as *maal*. The specially marked milking containers, set apart for *dorr*, can thus be found in the most diverse clans.

An important element of the explanation of the special status of *dorr*, as given in the story quoted above, is that they are *lagan* (R), *lagu* (B), i.e. sacred, special or set apart. There are parallels of this cognitive category with the status ascribed to human ritual leaders (Schlee 1979: 354–7).

Mu'allim Mukhtar 'Usmān[15] remembers from his childhood that Garre had *doro* camels which had separate milking containers (*gorfa*) and storage containers (*cico*), woven from plant fibres, and these were at that time common among the Garre. They are still common among the Sakuye, the Gabbra, the Boran and the Rendille. Mu'allim Mukhtar says that the Garre only learned from the 'Somali', i.e. Degodia, Ajuran, etc., how to carve the large wooden containers which are now in general use. The milk of Garre *doro* camels could not be served to guests. The *doro* quality of camels was heritable in the female line, as among the groups discussed above.[16] A feature peculiar to the Garre *doro* seems to be that they are preferentially given by a MoBr to a SiSo, and that the former must never reclaim any of the offspring, because it is feared that then the whole strain of camels will die out.

Another category of camels is those given as a reward for killing an enemy. These are called *sarma* by Boran speakers and *aiti magaň* – 'she-camel of the name' – by the Rendille. The special status of these animals is only conferred by the transfer, that is, contrary to *dorr*, they are not camels with any inherited peculiarities. This institution is shared by the Rendille,[17] the Gabbra (see Torry 1973: 95), the Sakuye and the Garre in more or less identical form. The *sarma* should be given by the MoBr of the killer being celebrated. Among the Rendille it is the MoBr who gives a camel if the killer is a first son, while a younger son receives a camel from his elder brother. To justify their claim to be a killer, Rendille, Gabbra and Sakuye have to present the penis and scrotum of their victim. (This, of course, implies that women are not counted, although they are killed as well.[18])

For the Garre, Mu'allim Mukhtar denies that castration of victims was practised. (Mutilation of bodies was forbidden by the Prophet after the battle of Uhud.) In other aspects, however, the institution he describes is very similar to its Rendille or Gabbra equivalent. Also in this case it is the MoBr who gives the *sarma*. This camel cannot be shared out as *kalassimé* or given away, nor can it be used for *maher* (Muslim allocation to a bride which remains hers if there is a divorce).

Among the Rendille and Gabbra, if a *sarma* gives birth to a female calf, women have to sing praise songs for the *sarma*.[19] Also the Garre know praise songs about *sarma*. In a former, more warlike, period, when the 'Ejji' (northern Somali: Darood, etc.) and the Boran and their allies, which included the Garre, constantly raided each other, war dances called *jemo* were performed which comprised such praise songs and which often led to possession-like fits among the warriors.[20] Yet another category of camels that requires special treatment is *fugo* (R), *fugu* (B), that is, the products of a breech birth. The rules concerning them are practically identical to those of *dorr*, the important difference being, of course, that the quality is not heritable. As the milk cannot be drunk by women and children and as male offspring cannot be castrated and become loading camels, their use is limited and they are consequently not highly desired. To avoid misfortune it is, however, very important to treat a *fugu* camel in the appropriate way if the circumstances of its birth are known. While among the Rendille and the Gabbra all males can drink the milk of *fugo* and *dorr* camels, among the Sakuye its consumption is limited to boys and old men.[21]

There is also a special aura surrounding humans who are breech births, as there is with twins. When the Rendille remove the two central lower incisors of such children[22] and pierce their earlobes, they perform certain precautionary rituals (see Schlee 1979: 209, 216). The Gabbra, who do not observe such practices, show the specialness of *fugu* in a different way. They believe in their healing powers:

> FUGGU – colui che alla nascita è uscito dal grembo materno prima coi piedi che con la testa. Poichè si ritiene che una tale persona abbia proprietà curative con i suoi massaggi, vanno da lui coloro che hanno avuto fratture di ossa. Inoltre gli è proibito di mangiare la carne della gamba degli animali. [Tablino 1974: 25]

I have already mentioned the importance of the day of the week in connection with camels in general and with *maal* camels in particular. There are many other such rules concerning camels, other kinds of stock and also humans. These rules sometimes refer to the day of the week, sometimes to the day of the lunar cycle, or to a combination of the two.

In the same way that camels cannot be given away on a Sunday or spend 'Sunday night' in a new enclosure, so cattle have their special day on Saturday and smallstock on Monday (Rendille, Gabbra). The rules for camels are more numerous. The following days of the lunar month have the same rules as Sunday: new moon (R: *maanti hai d'elati*, B: *ilbaati*); the fourteenth, full moon (R: *haugdéer*, B: *hoideera*); the fifteenth (R: *gobaan*, B: *gobana*). The importance of this category of days for the wellbeing of camels and camel people is further illustrated by the fact that Gaalorra, a subclan of Gaaldeilan (Rendille) who, unlike other Rendille and Gabbra, do not pour libations of milk every evening, do so on Sundays, *haugdéer* and *gobaan*. On the same days all Rendille and Gabbra households tie a female sheep to the doorpost of their house and 'wash' it ritually with milk, in the same way as they do for *almodo* (see below).

As Spencer noted, Wednesday is an unpropitious day; 'No camel settlement should move at all on a Wednesday' (1973: 66). What makes Wednesdays even less propitious, however, is when they fall in the second half of the month, from the sixteenth day onwards, the time of the waning moon, and especially the moonless period. This second half is called *mugdi* in Rendille and *dukana* in Boran (i.e. 'the darkness', the idea being that after sunset the moon has not yet risen, so there is an increasingly longer stretch of night between sunset and moon-rise towards the end of the month, accompanied by a decrease in the width of the visible moon. The opposite, i.e. the first half of the lunar month is R: *d'akhnán*, B: *addesa* – 'the whiteness'.) Within *mugdi/dukana* there are two Wednesdays: the first one will 'come around' in the weekly cycle in the shape of the second one, which will not 'come around' – *arba dukana immarín* (B).[23] The nearer the end of a month such a Wednesday is, the worse. The son of a Gabbra elder, Mamo Wario (Sharbana), was born on a Wednesday which was the thirteenth day of *dukana*. Such a child is dangerously strong, *jabba*. A week later the young mother died. Mamo said that her death was lucky, since otherwise he, the father, would have died. Now, as fate had missed him, Mamo saw the 'strength' of his son, who is now (1980) a circumcised youth, cheerful, and a good hunter, as a positive trait. The Rendille have similar fears about boys born on such Wednesdays; they are dangerous to their seniors. First, their elder brothers may die under strange circumstances, apparently unconnected with the existence of their younger sibling; then the father, so that the child remains as the sole heir. Similar beliefs exist about the children begotten by lovers from unpropitious lineages.[24] Rendille fathers may therefore order such sons to be suffocated by putting the intestinal fat of the birth sacrifice over their faces. They may also try to cheat destiny by treating such a boy ritually as a girl, i.e. by sacrificing a female instead of a male kid.

Of Garre practices concerning boys born on a 'Wednesday of the darkness that does not come around' Mu'allim Mukhtar says:

> Sila abban isá d'állate inféed'u. Wo ma tokko immíd'asan. Ingúbesan. Wo maan intólcani. Hamasso le inqábu. Duub índ'allate iní. Sirbi inqábne malle, Wakhlal le ínqaba, fula iti-wakhlallan injira. Yokhaan baati sadi amma d'allate, lammán sun aki takká jib.

That one, the father does not want that he was born. They do not do anything [of the customs required]. They do not hold the dance for newborns. But he has been born. Although there is no dance, there is [however] *wakhlal* [the Muslim ceremony of naming on some other day], there is a date for making *wakhlal*. [Whether a child is born on the last Wednesday of *dukana* or] whether he is born on the third day of the new moon, those two are disliked in the same way.

Wani irra sódatani: hark isat hamma jed'ani, burcigi isa hamma jed'ani. Nam rig jed'ani. Yo durri jarole fa qallu gugurdo fa laf jirtu, wo fa mid'asani. Hark isá kan akan wolthidd'ani, duub wo iti-tolcan.

What they fear about him: his hand is bad, they say, his birthday is bad, they say. They call him an unpropitious man. Before, when elders and big people of prayers and so were in the country, they do something about it. They tie his hands together like this, then they make something with them.

Wo iti-mid'asan. Woni sun wan durriti beek, ka durri an arge. Hojja sun woni irrá-miirfat. Wo mid'asani, hark isa ka kekayan talishi fa tufani.

They make something with them. That is something of long ago, you know, what I saw long ago. Then that [the unpropitiousness] cools down. They make something, put it into his hands, they spit with *talishi* water[25] on it.

Wan d'ibbi ammá-lle armát hidd'an: ergams jed'ani. Hojjum sun wo iti mid'asaní, irra-hiikhani, deem. Wa sun duub yo baate, bas.

Now, they also tie something else here [to the hands]: they call it *ergams*.[26] Then they definitely repair it, un-tie it [the unpropitiousness together with the hands], they go. When that thing has left, it is enough [i.e. the trouble is over].

The lunar cycle also determines the dates of sacrificial ceremonies (*sorio*, R, B) held for each house.[27] Of the four *sorio* of the Rendille, three are common also to the Gabbra, the Sakuye and the Garre, while the fourth (in the month of Harrafa) may be linked to the Muslim ritual calendar. The other three *sorio*, in the months Sondeer I, Sondeer II and Daga (in Gabbra usage, Somdeera I and II and Yaga), are part of the proto-Rendille–Somali culture. The division of all three societies into moieties[28] plays an important role in the timing of these sacrifices. Although this binary distinction in the different societies is made on different (though in all cases high) organisational levels, the principle of division into moieties seems another established feature of proto-Rendille–Somali culture. *Sorio* would normally be held on the ninth day of the lunar month by Belesi Baħai or Lossa and on the tenth by Belesi Berri or Yiblo. This has nothing to do with seniority, since in Rendille Belesi Baħai is regarded as senior and in Gabbra Yiblo, which would correspond to Belesi Berri. Groups that emigrate from Rendille to Gabbra would be asked on which day they hold their *sorio* and would be ascribed their moiety accordingly.

The list of months in Table 5 shows how the domestic *sorio* are spaced over the twelve-month cycle. (The solar year is treated as a unit of time independent of the course of months.)

Cultural comparison shows which parts of the *sorio* festival are accidental and which are essential and invariable for all groups performing *sorio*. A marginal feature seems to be where the meat is eaten: the Rendille

Table 5 A comparative list of the names of months

Rendille	Gabbra	Garre*	Wajir Somali †		Arabic
Sondéer I	Somdeera I	Rajab Somdeera I	Rajab	7	Rajab رجب
Sondéer II	Somdeer II	Sha'abaan Somdeera II	Sha'baan	8	Sha'bān شعبان
Scom	Soom	Soom	Soon	9	Ramadan رمضان [fasting: صوم]
Furám	Furám	Furam	Soon-Fur	10	Shawwāl شوال
Dibiál	Didial	Didial	Sidataal	11	Dhu-l-Qi'da(ti) د والقعدة
Haráfa	Arrafa	Arrafa	'Arrafo	12	Dhu-l Hijja(ti) ذ والحجة
Dága	Yaga	Zaka§	Dago	1	Muharram محرم
Ragarr I	Ragarra	Safar	Safar	2	Safar صفر
Ragarr II	Regarra	Moulid	Rabii'al Awal	3	Rabi'ul Awwal ربيع الاول
Haitikelée	Faite	Jibor I	Rabii'al Aakhir	4	Rabī'uth-thānī (Rabi'ul Aakhir) ربيع الثاني ربيع الاخر
Haibórboran I	Jibor I	Jibor II	Jumaadal Awal	5	Jumādā-l Awlā جمادى الا ولى
Haibórboran II	Jibor II	Jibor III	Jumaadal Aakhir	6	Jumādā-l Aakira(ti) جمادى الاخرة

* According to Mu'allim Mukhtar.
† After Grum (1978b).
§ *Zakat* is the Muslim tax on one's possessions for redistribution to the poor, which is collected in this month.

do this in the house, the Gabbra have a communal feast in the open. Instead of giving lengthy descriptions of such details, we limit ourselves to the essential, invariable elements as they are common to Rendille, Gabbra, Sakuye[29] and Garre.[30]

An animal (usually a head of smallstock) that is going to be sacrificed is first 'washed' (R: *a-la-dikha*; B: *ín-diqani*) by touching mouth, back, tail and belly with hands wet with milk or by splashing some milk on it.[31]

The next common practice for all groups is *harir* (R, B) in which a stick is passed gently over the back of the animal with the word(s) *sorio* or *nagaa nu ken* (B), 'Give us peace'.[32] Rendille and Gabbra use a *gumo* (R), *ejjers* (B), a well-oiled black stick with a phallic head which is handed on from father to eldest son; later sons have new sticks cut for them.[33] The Sakuye do not have *gumo* but *meti*, literally 'palm fibres', here meaning a bundle of fibres, which they use in the same way. The *meti* of the Sakuye corresponds to the *sed* of the Rendille, which is the same object used in the same way. All Rendille, with the exception of the Gaalorra subclan of Gaaldeilan, have *sed* and use it along with the *gumo*. The distribution of *sed/meti* and *gumo/ejjers* in Gabbra, Rendille and Sakuye is shown in Table 6.

Next the animal is thrown to the ground and its throat is cut.[34] The blood or part of it is allowed to flow into a small pit in the ground hastily dug by one of the bystanders with the tip of his stick. In one way or another all the groups discussed here use this blood for the blessing of animals and sometimes of people. Among the Rendille and the Gabbra everyone present is smeared on his forehead with a spot of blood, taken on the fingertip from the dripping knife. Small boys run with a handful of *eima* (R), *algi* (B) fibres (wild sisal, *Sansevieria robusta*, *Agavaceae*), which are used for plaiting mats for roofing, dip them into the bloody sand and smear the camels on the right side below the hump with blood, marking them with a simple line. The pattern drawn on the hump of a herd sire may be more elaborate (Schlee 1979: 103).

Sakuye mark the camels in the same way, and the Garre may do so if the camels are ill or need special protection for other reasons. One less explicit way of marking the camels is to splash some blood in their direction, as the Sakuye sometimes do after becoming Muslim, feeling ambivalent about their pagan heritage.[35]

Khalli (R), *medica* (B), i.e. strips of the skin of *sorio* animals, are worn around the wrists and ankles, tied around the *gumo* below its phallic head, and may be tied to the neck of favourite camels or, among the Gabbra, to a stool, as a visible sign of having participated in the sacrifice and as a symbol of the blessing emanating from it.

If a *sorio* falls on a Sunday and because blood must not be smeared on

Table 6 Distribution of the tools of consecration

	Gaalorra (Rendille)	All other Rendille	Gabbra	Sakuye
meti	−	+	−	+
ejjers	+	+	+	−

camels on Sundays (see above), the smearing is restricted (Rendille) or, as the Gabbra prefer, the *sorio* is postponed to *haugdéer*, or full moon, four or five days later.[36] In all cases, whether the camels are smeared with blood or not, they should be present and in their enclosures whenever a *sorio* or any other important ritual takes place, even if this means that they cannot go to pasture for several hours.[37] There can be no *sorio* without camels and no gainful camel management without *sorio*.

The branding of camels takes place on the day of a *sorio*. Most of the many transactions involving camels which I have discussed above should be carried out in a *sorio* month. Another way of referring to these months is therefore *ji gaala* (B), 'camel months', an expression used even by the Muslim Garre.

The performance of *sorio* thus is limited to settlements which own camels. An impoverished Sakuye who, like the bulk of his people, lost all his camels during the *shifta* war, explains the relationship between camels, ritual and self-awareness as follows:

Question: *Sakuye ammálle sorio qaba?*

Do Sakuye still have *sorio*?

Answer: *Gaal inqábtu; sorioon ta gaalati, looniini. Gaal inqában; hag gaal d'abani duub mataiyu yád'abaní, mataiyu inqábu.*

They do not have camels; *sorio* is for camels, not cattle. They do not have camels; since they lost their camels they also lost their heads, they also do not have heads.

Among the Ariaal, irrespective of their ethnic origin (Samburu or Rendille) and their language, those groups that keep camels perform *sorio*, and those who have only cattle and smallstock see no necessity to do so. A man may have one wife in a camel settlement and slaughter *sorio* in front of her house, and another wife in a cattle settlement where he does not perform this custom.

If *sorio* months are camel months, then the two consecutive months of Ragarr are the opposite. One should never give away a camel or any other stock in Ragarr; nor should one give a girl in marriage. Most restrictions again concern camels. No camels should be introduced to training in these two months. Nor should the ears of camels be clipped or those of human children pierced in these months. In fact, all such operations, including removing the two central lower incisors and circumcision, should happen in a *sorio* month. Marriages in Gabbra are limited to *sorio* months; in Rendille there is a preference for *sorio* months, although any month will do, with the exception of the two Ragarr.[38] *Rendille Ragarre diida*, the Rendille 'hate' Ragarr, and so do the other groups discussed here. Mu'allim Mukhtar says, however, about the Garre that only Safar, i.e. the first Ragarr, is connected with such avoidances, while the following month (which is regarded by Rendille and Gabbra as only slightly less unpropitious) is completely free from negative characteristics. This is understandable in a Muslim society, since the second Ragarr is the month of Maulid, the birthday of the Prophet – an Islamic '*sorio*'.

One faction of Rendille and Gabbra, however, does not follow any of the avoidances of Ragarr and 'hates' Soom instead. *Soomdiid*, 'those who hate Ramadan', is the praisename of the camels of the Rendille clan Odoola, and the camels of Gabbra Odoola 'hate' Soom/Ramadan in the same way. In addition to the rules that other Rendille and Gabbra observe in connection with Ragarr, the avoidances of Odoola in regard to Soom are said to have in former times included the collection of firewood. Thus large piles of firewood had to be gathered before the new moon of Soom. Odoola say that this is their way of 'fasting' and some of them take this as a sign of ultimate Muslim origin. *Soom* in fact means 'fasting' (in Rendille and Somali[39]) and the following month – Soomfur – means 'untying', i.e. lifting or breaking the fast. The first day of Soomfur, in fact, corresponds to the Muslim 'Id-al-Fitr. The correspondence with the Muslim practice, however, can only be found in these names. The observances themselves differ in form and content. We may take this as support for our assumption that the proto-Rendille–Somali, before they split into the present ethnic groups, had absorbed some features of Islamic culture but did not have Islam as a central part of their ritual or self-definition.

Quite independently of the cycle of twelve empirical lunar months the groups under study calculate and mark the solar year. There are no leap months or other mechanisms of the type Spencer (1973: 123) postulates to make the two cycles match.

Odoola not only differs from the other parts of Rendille and Gabbra in 'hating' a different month, but also in their customs concerning the solar year. They kindle the *dab Odoola* (R), *ibid Odoola* (B) – i.e. the fire of Odoola – to mark the beginning of the autumn rains.

Customs involving fire to mark some point on the solar cycle are widespread. Cerulli describes the *dab-shid* as a general Somali feature:

> The day of the Somali new year is celebrated with the festival of *dab-šid* – 'light-a-fire'. It is characteristic that this festival, although very popular and generally observed, may in many regions not receive the approval of the men of learning, who indeed call it 'the festival of Pharao', thus acknowledging by this very appellation its pagan character. The festival is of a domestic kind and consists in lighting a huge fire of branches near every hut, over which the head of the family then jumps, passing from one side to the other. Sometimes throwing a spear right through the fire is substituted for the jump. This ceremony then is accompanied by public dances which last throughout the following night; in the villages by processions of armed youngster who sing special songs; by solemn sacrifices, etc.

The Tuesday year of the current cycle started on 12 August 1919 (or better, on the sunset of 11 August); the Wednesday year on 11 August 1920 (on the sunset of the 10th); the Thursday year 11 August 1921 (on the sunset of the 10th); the Friday year 11 August 1922 (on the sunset of the 10th). [Cerulli 1957: Vol. I, 186, my translation]

In a report about British Somaliland,[40] 4 August is given as the date of *dab-shid* for nine consecutive years from 1944 to 1952. The difference of one week to the dates given by Cerulli for the early 1920s is easily explained if we assume that in the Gregorian calendar the *dab-shid* moves forward one day in four years by not taking into account the intercalary day. This, however, would not allow *dab-shid* to be on the same day of the Gregorian calendar for nine consecutive years. Shifts by one day should have occurred in 1948 and 1952. We have to leave open whether, in the time between our two authorities, an adjustment has been made to the Gregorian calendar, or whether the dates of the later source have been 'corrected', or whether different Somali indeed celebrate *dab-shid* on different days.

In the case of Odoola, the fire ceremony mentioned above is only an addition to a similar ceremony they share with the other Rendille, Gabbra, Sakuye and Garre: *almodo* (R), *almado* (B). The Rendille rules for the timing of *almodo* enable it in the long term to be closely related to the solar year, if the rules were strictly followed and *almodo* held on the earliest permitted date; but in practice the Rendille tend to postpone *almodo* for all sorts of reasons and different clans even have *almodo* at different times and in fuller or abbreviated versions.[41] We may thus conclude that the Rendille *almodo* was at one time meant to be timed according to the solar year and is now out of step. The Gabbra are more rigid. Father Tablino (1975) gives 4 November as the date of the central part of the *almodo* celebrations for four consecutive years from 1972 to 1975. For the four-year period before that he assumes 5 November and so on, *almodo* moving backwards twenty-five days per century in the Gregorian calendar, because the Gabbra simply count 365 days from *almodo* to *almodo* without having leap years.

The fire of Odoola precedes *almodo* in the following way: after three seasons of 100, 100 and 66 days have been counted, the three fires of Odoola are burned over a period of two weeks. After the last of these fires exactly ten weeks are counted to the beginning of *almodo*, which ends fifteen days later (Tablino 1980: 82). As the whole cycle lasts 365 days, i.e. 52 weeks and 1 day, each year *almodo* is concluded a day later in the weekly cycle than the previous year's *almodo*. A link is thus established between the seven-year cycle and the days of the week: a Monday year would start with a Monday, a Tuesday year with a Tuesday, etc. This, of course, makes it possible to determine the recurrence of any solar date in the following year without counting days. One simply waits for the recurrence of the lunar date in the following year, knowing that the solar date one wishes to determine will be in the second week after that on the day of the week following its day of the week in the last year.

Descriptions of the chronological course of events at an *almodo* festival and the manifold social and religious dimensions accentuated by its rich symbolism are given for the Gabbra by Venturino (in Tablino 1974: 60–62) and for the Rendille by Schlee (1979: 108–27). Here I simply enumerate the main elements common to Gabbra and Rendille which enable us to recognise a ceremony as *almodo*, or related to it, if we find it elsewhere.

Milk At *almodo*, on three occasions, one a week, female sheep and lambs are 'washed' with milk at the doorpost of the house and at the ritual gate (see below). The washing is done in the same way as with the sacrificial animal in *sorio*. At *almodo*, however, no animals are slaughtered. These milk-washings are not restricted to *almodo* and *sorio*, but are performed at new moon, on Sundays and on similar occasions. Milk is also taken to the *naabo* (Rendille) or an improvised assembly place (Gabbra) and drunk, or sipped ritually and exchanged by the assembled elders, who also hold collective prayers.

The Gate The animals, and in Rendille also the women, have to pass through a ritual gate (R: *ulukh*; B: *uluqo, gool*. Again *almodo* is not the only occasion for passing an *ulukh*.[42] It is thus this combination of elements, not the elements themselves, which is typical of *almodo*. To pass this gate is a blessing and blessings may be shouted at herds or women as they pass it. The two other elements of *almodo* are also found at this gate: milk and fire. Two lambs may be tied to the gate, one to each of the piles of thorn branches marking it, and 'washed' there with milk. Fire is also lit on both sides.

While *almodo* is a distinctive feature of the PRS culture and the *ulukh* is an integral part of *almodo*, *ulukh* ceremonies as such are not limited to the cultures deriving from the PRS but can also be found in other contexts outside this ethnic cluster. According to Haberland (1963: 94) all Galla (Oromo) have similar ceremonies which they call by the same name (*hūlúko* or *ūlúko*[43]) in order to avert misfortune which might befall the herds. (The Rendille perform an *ulukh* ceremony to the same end after a lunar eclipse, an event which is considered unpropitious.) Among the Boran such a ceremony should be performed at least once a year, preferably at a certain date. Lambs and milk ablutions apparently are not used in these Oromo ceremonies, nor is fire, but ashes are. Prescriptions instead concern the species of plants used to build, mark or be attached to the ritual gate.

Fire Apart from the *ulukh*, fires are burned at all gates in the outer fence of a Rendille settlement. (The Gabbra do not have these fences.) The repeated use of fire shows that *almodo* and the fire of Odoola might be two variants of the same thing. Among Rendille and Gabbra Odoola the two may have been recombined after developing separately for a time.

Also among some Garre, although no longer universally, the 'washing' of a female sheep, communal prayers and drinking of milk by the elders are found in connection with *almodo*.[44] Mu'allim Mukhtar also mentions *saddet ibida*, 'eight fires', one a week, at the end of the dry season, leading up to *almodo*, which marks the beginning of the autumn rains (*hagaya*).

According to a large number of independent informants, both Gabbra and Sakuye, the customs surrounding *sorio* and *almodo* are identical for both peoples. One special feature for Sakuye is a sacrifice in connection with the pre-*almodo* fire. This fire itself is shared by Odoola of Gabbra and Sakuye, but the sacrifice is unique to Sakuye. This is the *sorio ibida*, the '*sorio* of the fire'.

What then is the meaning of *almodo* except that it marks the solar cycle? One clue is given by the ritual symbols and the verbal expressions, prayers, connected with it. Obviously a blessing is bestowed on herds and women, giving health and fertility. The prayers are for peace, rain and all the other things for which nomads usually pray. There is, however, one aspect of *almodo* which is nowhere alluded to in the course of the ritual itself: its origin. There are tales about the origin of *almodo* which may or may not be mythic post hoc explanations of a ceremony whose meaning has been forgotten. Irrespective of this, I quote the following story because in itself it is an interesting cultural feature:[45]

> *Nam durri foor gaala tae. Nadd'een algi mid'aasu yaate, foor tae. Bulti buufate. [. . .] Niitin taan duub intal d'alte. Nam kaan duub gaaf kaan tae, imbéekhu, intal taan qad'ate, fuud'e, intal ta isii.*

Long ago a man stayed in the camel camp. A woman went to prepare wild sisial, stayed in the camp. The herder of the camp raped her. [. . .] This woman then gave birth to a girl. The man then stayed, he does not know [anything], asked for the girl, married her, her daughter.

> *Duuba intal taan maqa Fooro baafte. [. . .] 'Maqá kanke maanif Fooro baasaní?' Intal jennaan: 'Ayo foor gae. Bulti foori ayo gabe.' 'Nami si d'alle sun eenu?' jed'e. 'Almado jed'ani.' Duub challise.*

Now this girl was called Camp by name [. . .] 'Why are you named Camp?' The girl then [said]: 'Mother got to a camp. The herdsman of the camp got hold of mother.' 'Who is that man who begot you?' he said. 'They call[ed] him Almado.' Then he remaind quiet.[46]

> *Qoraan cabsum cabse, waan kaan mid'aafate, qoraan cabsum cabse. Yo sun waan arra kalétini. Ilmán-lle chuf yad'ad'alte. Qoraan kaan, gaal qalle, d'ad'a itinanaggé, qoraan kaan mani chufaan marse, biyyá dámate.*

He broke and broke firewood, he prepared something, broke and broke firewood. Even then it [the marriage] was not something of today or yesterday. She had already given birth to all children. He slaughtered a camel, poured fat on this firewood, put the firewood around the whole house, called the people.

'*Guyyá kan deebitani, ind'edina', yo guyya sun gae duuba akum* Kenyatta day *jed'an, kan* 'siku kuu *[sw.] tolca' jed'e. Dámate, ibidan dae, man kan due duub.*

'When you come back to this day [i.e. next year, this day], do not forget it', when that day comes, then like what they call 'Kenyatta day' he said, 'make a holiday'. After he had called them, he lit the fire, then that house died.

Worri kaan, dubr jed', d'iir jed', haad jed', abba jed', tokkó-lleen incéén, artumat lufe. Duub guyya kaan yo ini gae, waan kaan siku kuu *tolcani, éebifata. Almado tanum gul baate, aada tolfataní, duub itum-deebiani, inlákifne.*

Those people, say girls, say boys, say mother, say father, not one of them escaped, they died on the spot. Now, when that day comes, they make it a holiday, they pray. *Almado* has developed from that, they make it a custom, they go back to it again and again, they did not leave it.

Garrí-lle durri inúmqabt. Gabbri Miigólle inúmqabt. Rendillé inúmqabt. Gabbri túlle inúmqabt. Yo sun mal kiyya nami sun gargar imbááne. Eege sun gargar bae.

Even the Garre used to have it. Also the Gabbra Miigo have it. Also the Rendille have it. These Gabbra also have it. At that time, I think, these people had not yet separated from each other. Only after it they separated.[47]

A slightly different version of the myth about the origin of these fire rituals is given in chapter 5.

The majority of the groups who perform *almodo* or *almado* (if we discount those who perform similar but not identical rituals like *dab-shid*) today speak Boran. This might lead us to the conclusion that *almodo* is of Boran rather than of proto-Rendille–Somali origin. However, such a hypothesis cannot be maintained for two reasons. First, the Boran themselves do not perform *almodo*, and second, in the *almodo* chants even of the Boran-speaking Gabbra and Sakuye we find remnants of their earlier Somaloid (proto-Rendille–Somali) language which have been preserved in this conservative ritual context.

These chants are called *dikir* (from the Arabic ذكر – 'remembrance', 'praise', 'invocation'). The language of these chants, which for the uninformed listener is rather cryptic, contains, besides Boran words, Arabic and elements derived from proto-Rendille–Somali. (The Gabbra call it Af Daiyo.)

1 *Nuuru nuuru nuur Allahe*
2 *nuuru Makka Medina*
3 *nuurassiye malimme gante*
4 *waale salaamu*

Translation and comment:

1 'Light, light, light of God' (all in Arabic)
2 'light [of] Mekka [and] Medina' (all in Arabic)

3   lights [Arabic with PRS plural suffix + emphasis marker] of daytime [PRS]'
    (*gante* is cryptic, perhaps connected to R: *gan*, 'to shoot')
4   Interpreted by the informant[48] as *hanán woltisalaaman* = *hanán woltinanagan*,
    'they pour milk for each other', 'into each other's milk containers' (≙R
    haanu iska-maalata); 'they milk [autobenefactive] milk from each other',
    an act performed during the communal milk drinking of the elders at *almodo*
    or at festivals connected with the age-set cycle (the *nanesa* of the Gabbra).
    Salaamu, of course, is Arabic for 'peace', and shows, in accordance with the
    visual symbolism, that the whole action is meant as a prayer for peace.

Apart from *almado*, *dikir* are chanted on all possible ritual occasions.
There are also *dikir* about the days of the week. Here is the one about the
Day of the Camel.

1   *Ahadooo sher gaala waane*
2   *sher gaaliye gaal luf d'eere*

1   'Sunday, the day [*sher* is PRS, the corresponding B word would by *ayaana*]
    of the camel [which is]'
2   'the day of the camels, the camels with the tall humps' (*luf* [R, B] literally
    means the longer hair on top of the hump).

1   *Ahadooo sher gaala waane*
2   *sher gaaliye gaali arbaiye*

1   As above
2   'the day of the camels, the camels with abundant milk' (R, B: *arbad* (adj.),
    'with much milk')

1   *Ahadooo sher gaala waane*
2   *sher gaaliye gaali t'alabye*

1   As above
2   'the day of the camels, the camels that climb [R: *dalabsad'a*, 'I step over']
    [difficult places]'

1   *Ahadooo sher gaala waane*
2   *sher gaaliye, gaali mululye*

1   As above
2   'the day of the camels, the camels which are *mulul*' (R, B: 'big with young
    while still suckling the previous calf'[49])

The vocabulary of these verses, some of it archaic, is mostly common to
Rendille and Boran, so that it is difficult to determine where these words
stem from. Some morphological elements (*gaal-iye d'eer-e*) remind one of
Rendille (in other words, they would have to be interpreted as being
derived from PRS). Some of the words do not exist in Boran at all, but
only in Rendille (*sher* ≙ R: *ser*, *t'alab* ≙ *dalab*).

The point that the whole camel complex, i.e. the cluster of cultural
features associated with camels which we have just described, not only has
no equivalents in Boran culture but is also in marked opposition to
Boran-ness is further illustrated by marriage behaviour. A Boran girl

married by a Gabbra or a Sakuye would not be allowed to 'tie the ewe' for the ritual washing for *almado* or to participate in these camel-oriented rituals in many other ways. For this reason Gabbra and Sakuye should not marry Boran girls. They are 'bad for the camels'. Impoverished Sakuye who have no camels drop this restriction. Gabbra and Sakuye girls, on the other hand, because of the relative scarcity of camels for brideprice and for the maintenance of families and the accordingly low polygyny rate, are never in short supply. They are eligible for Boran suitors. As the Boran played an hegemonial role in the area for several centuries, we have here a peculiar situation in which the dominated groups reject potential brides who belong to the dominant groups because they are unpropitious. Marrying a Boran girl would not be regarded as 'marrying upwards' but as marrying a girl the camels do not like.

These marriage restrictions, as well as many other customs directly or indirectly relating to camels, once more show that the Darood Somali, although they are camel keepers, do not share the particular form of camel complex discussed here. The Darood see no connection between the well-being of their herds and the ethnic origin of their brides. This was demonstrated on a large scale by the mass capture of Warra Daaya (Orma) women during and after the 1860s by Muhammad Zubeir and Telemuggeh. The descendants of these women are known as Weil (i.e. child) Tullo, while the Muhammad Zubeir of uterine Somali descent were called Weil Tagok (Turnbull 1955: 7).

Another aspect of the societies discussed here that deserves attention is the different forms of age-set organisation and the customs associated with promotion in such systems.

Not only the principle of having formal age sets as one of the basic structural features of society, but also many of the details of ritual elaboration, are shared by many Cushitic groups from the shores of the Red Sea all over the Horn to Kenya as well as by Nilo-'Hamitic' groups in the Kenyan and Tanzanian Rift Valley. The distribution of many features that are unlikely to have developed independently points to a very old common origin of all these age-set systems, or to intense mutual influences between them, or both. The groups sharing the PRS-camel complex only form a small fraction of this wider spectrum of related societies.

To put it more precisely, the age-set systems of the Rendille, the Gabbra, etc., as well as those of the Boran and other Oromo, are not age-set systems but generation-set systems.[50]

To illustrate the principle of organisation along generation lines, I shall examine one such system, that of the Rendille, in some detail, before I proceed with my comparison.

The word for generation is *óyo*. In its basic meaning it stands for 'father' or 'owner'. An *óyo* can be calculated from a fixed point in any age-set cycle of a set of fathers to the corresponding point in the age-set cycle of their sons and always comes to 42 years because sons, if old enough, are initiated into the third age set after their fathers, i.e. 3×14 years after them. Two *óyo* are one *achi* 'grandfather, double generation': the span between a fixed event in the life of a man and the corresponding event (circumcision, marriage, etc.) in the life of his grandson is $2 \times 42 = 84$ years.

These cycles start in a *sorio* month of a Friday year[51] with the circumcision of an age set. The newly initiated warriors, after whom the following 14 years (two seven-year cycles) are named, now enter into a phase of their lives which is virtually free from day-to-day labour and correspondingly richer in martial and amorous exploits. After its termination they will spend a great deal of their time telling stories about this period of their lives. Subperiods of warriorhood are marked by *gaalgulamme*[52] and other rituals and festivals (Schlee 1979: chs. 3 and 4). In the second Tuesday of this period, i.e. 12 years after their circumcision, an age set is allowed to marry. The eldest sons of this age set will be born during the subsequent Wednesday year and will be initiated after two intervening age sets at the age of 29, 42 years after their fathers.

All this is valid for all age sets and their sons. The starting point of an *óyo* can be shifted back and forth in time. In the case of a *fañán*, however, the starting point is fixed. The *fañán* is a ritual generation which is opened by a given age set and closed by the second after it, i.e. by the third in the row, when they have become elders. So, any age set is either the first, second or third in a *fañán*. All first age sets of a *fañán* are called *teeria* and descend from each other: the sons of *teeria* are *teeria*. We can therefore speak of all *teeria* sets as an age-set line. Likewise all number twos and all number threes of all *fañáns* correspond to the same numbers of all other *fañáns* and form the age-set lines 2 and 3 respectively. This can be depicted in a diagram in which time is shown on the vertical and different descent on the horizontal axes (Diagram 6).

A *fañán* is ritually completed and established as a corporate unit by a man of Tubcha (see Schlee 1979, chapter 2.8.8.1.1). Also the lineage Harrau[53] plays a part in these rituals. When a *fañán* is complete with the age sets 1, 2, and 3, a new *fañán* is 'opened' with the circumcision of a fourth age set who ideally are the sons of 1. But this new *fañán* will not be proclaimed before it is complete, i.e. before the age sets 5, the sons of 2, and 6, the sons of 3, have married.

Elders who belong to a 'closed', i.e. a complete and formally established *fañán*, have a special ritual status. If a stick belonging to such an elder should lie on the ground, one may not step over it. Should this happen to somebody inadvertently, he has to retract his steps and repeat the action correctly: he steps backwards over the stick, lifts it up and puts it against a wall or tree and then moves on. The destruction of the headrest or the stool of a *fañán* elder require drastic compensation.

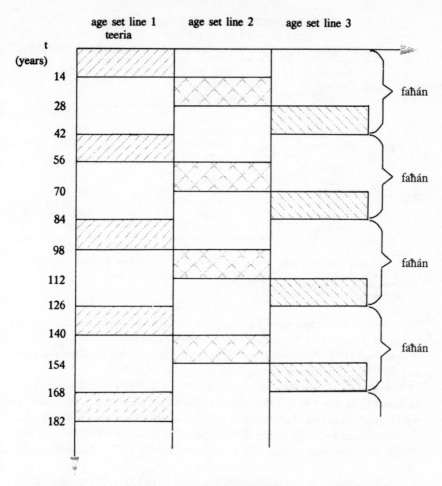

Diagram 6 Age-set lines and the *faħán* cycles in the Rendille system

The timing of the *faħán* proclamation leads to the following spans: in our example, the age sets 1 and 4 have to wait 2 × 14-year cycles, the age sets 2 and 5 have to wait 1 × 14-year cycle, while the age sets 3 and 6 do not have to wait, until they reach *faħán* status.

In agreement with the breaking down into generations, the names of age sets often recur after two, five or eight intermittent age sets in the same or a similar form (Table 7).

Ideally, in an age-set line (fathers, Ego, sons, grandsons, etc.) the same names recur. No. 10 should have been called D'ismaala after their grandfathers, but as the period between 1881 and 1892, when D'ismaala were warriors, was a hard time for the Rendille, the unpropitious name was avoided and the name D'ifgudó, although it stems from a different age-set

Table 7 Rendille and Samburu age-set names

No.	Rendille age-set name	Samburu equivalent[1]	Initiation year (Rendille)[2]
1	Kipeko	Il-kipeko	1839
2	Libaale	Il-kiteku	1853
3	D'ibgudó	Il-tarigirik	1867
4	D'ismaala	Il-marikon	1881
5	Irbangudó	Il-terito	1895
6	D'ifgudó	Il-merisho	1910[3]
7	Irbaalis	Il-kiliako[4]	1923
8	Libaale	Il-mekuri	1937
9	Irbánd'if	Il-kimaniki	1951
10	D'ifgudó	Il-kichili	1965
11	Irbangudó	Il-kororo	1979

1. See Spencer (1973: 33).
2. The horizontal lines mark *fañán* boundaries. The initiation years are extrapolated, except for the last four for which there is historical evidence.
3. Postponed by one year because of drought.
4. Rendille pronounce this Ilkilegú.

line, was given to the new warriors. To avoid confusion, the age set is normally referred to by its Samburu name Il-kichili.

Spencer (1973: 33) thinks that there is a similar reason for the exclusive use of a Samburu name for age set 1.

The double generation, *achi*, marks the cycle after which history is believed to repeat itself. This idea of cyclicity is called *daji* in Rendille, a word which may have been borrowed from the Boran although it refers to a different span of time in the Boran prognostic calendar. Rendille beliefs about *daji* have been illustrated elsewhere (Schlee 1979: chapters 0.6.5. and 4).

It is impossible to check whether droughts, epidemics, wars and so on recur every 84 years, but certain constellations in the Rendille age-set system do. Part of this cyclicity is thus man-made.

Apart from the above-mentioned categories of age sets, there is another which sequentially links age sets in pairs.[54] By this rights and duties which one has in relation to members of one's own age set are extended to the members of the linked age set. Thus there is a two-beat rhythm which overlies the triple rhythm already described.

We have already seen that the three age sets of a *fañán* differ in a number of features: all first age sets of a *fañán* have an eminent position as *teeria*, all second age sets have to wait the same number of years as all other second age sets to become *fañan*, etc., in other words all age sets repeat the constellation of their fathers and more so of their grandfathers, whose name and fate they ideally share.

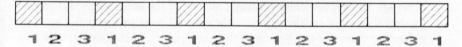

1 2 3 1 2 3 1 2 3 1 2 3 1 2 3 1

Diagram 7   The *teeria* age-set line in the time sequence

Teeria men have to delay the marriage of their daughters by a full age-set cycle. This means that the girls cannot marry for two age-set cycles after their fathers and one before their brothers, as other Rendille girls do, but have to wait until their brothers are about to marry. They are clitoridectomised in the Monday year before the Tuesday year of the marriage of their brothers and may marry any time after clitoridectomy. This category of girls is called *sabade*.[55] A consequence of the *sabade* institution is that the brothers of these girls, i.e. the *teeria* warriors, have a large choice of potential brides: the ones of their own age set and of the subsequent age set. On the other hand the choice of brides for first, and more so for second, marriages is somewhat limited in the case of an age set which precedes a *teeria* set because many of the girls of the right age are *sabade* and still have to wait.

In Diagram 7 the *teeria* line because of its special status is shown by a dark square. If we imagine that this sequence of three is overlaid by a sequence of two, the paired age sets just mentioned, we arrive at the configuration shown in Diagram 8.

In Diagram 8 the *teeria* age set on the left is combined with the following age set (No. 2) in a pair. The members of No. 2 address members of the

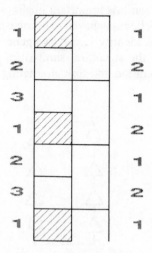

Diagram 8   The *teeria* age-set line in relation to adjacent linking

teeria age set as *mbó* ('elder brother') instead of the more respectful *abáya* ('father's younger brother') which they would have to use if the age set preceding them did not belong to the same pair.[56] These two age sets are expected to behave like brothers. The senior set do not resent it if members of the junior set have temporary affairs with their wives. Thus the lives of an age set are also determined by whether it is in senior or junior position in such a pair.

If we combine the two sequences, there are six different combinations: a senior *teeria*; a junior second; a senior third; a junior *teeria*; a senior second; a junior third. After this the first combination, a senior *teeria*, recurs and the cycle starts again. Thus a given combination of marriage options, sexual rights, potential conflicts, etc., recurs after a double generation, just like the prognostic calendar predicts. This part of the prophecy thus is self-fulfilling.

The equation between someone and his grandfather which is evident from this system is also reflected by kinship terminology and a number of joking relationships. A little boy can call his grandmother 'sister-in-law' or 'mistress' (*dumaassi*), because she is the wife of somebody of 'his' age set. Accordingly the two can make sexually tinged jokes about each other.

This idea also underlies the preferential marriage rule that somebody should marry a girl of his father's father's mother's clan and lineage (Diagram 9). This is called 'marrying one's grandfather's bones' (*lafo achi*). If everybody kept this rule, a patrilineage would always marry girls of the same three clans in the same order, say A would always marry B C D B C D ... (Diagram 10). By this rule Ego takes care that his son becomes a 'daughter's son' (*eisim* = 'leftover') of the clan of which Ego's grandfather was also a 'daughter's son'. As important qualities are believed to be transmitted by this link, the boy is believed to become like his great-grandfather in some respects. This identity jumps two generations and is established with the third, while the structural similarities provided by the age-set system jump one generation and link alternating generations. But never-

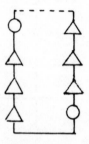

Diagram 9   The Rendille ideal marriage with a bride of one's FaFaMo's clan

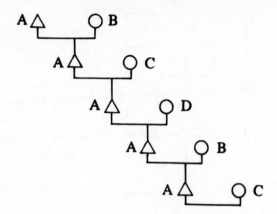

Diagram 10 The cyclical recurrence of marriage constellations in a Rendille descent line

theless the *lafo achi* rule is an important aspect of Ego's relationship to his paternal grandfather: it is Ego who marries a woman of his grandfather's mother's clan and with her begets a son in his grandfather's likeness (Schlee 1979: 97).

The Boran have a similar system of generation sets, but in their case a son is not initiated into the third but into the fifth set after his father's. Among the Gabbra there are different variants: Gār, Galbo and Odoola have a system which only combines two sets into one generation cycle, so that every other age set consists of the same descent lines: After A follows B, followed by A's sons, followed by B's sons, followed by A's grandsons, etc. Alganna, Sharbana and the Gabbra Miigo, however, have a threefold basic structure like the Rendille (Diagram 11).

As in the Boran case there are eight years between the initiations of successive age sets, while in the Rendille case this span consists of fourteen years (two seven-year cycles), Boran sons enter the cycle $5 \times 8 = 40$ years after their fathers, while Rendille sons do so $3 \times 14 = 42$ years after their fathers. Here we encounter the problem which is discussed at some length by Haberland (1963: 179, 181ff., 184ff.) that these spans do not always correspond to the length of natural generations. Even if the average length of a generation among Rendille and Gabbra fathers and sons is about 40 years,[57] the age difference between brothers can be great because old men continue to have children with young second and third wives while their elder sons may already be grown up and heads of families themselves. The Boran have created the category of 'children of the elderly' (*ilma jarsa*) for these late-born (Haberland 1963: 184ff.). The Rendille deal with this problem by initiating such boys one or even two full 14-year cycles later, thus breaking the generation-set principle in favour of the age-set principle, but

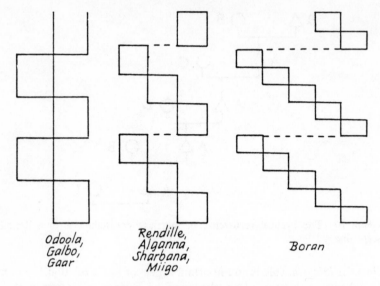

Odoola,
Galbo,
Gaar

Rendille,
Alganna,
Sharbana,
Miigo

Boran

Diagram 11 Age-sets per generation in the various systems

on such a wide grid that individual hardship cannot be avoided. An age difference of a few years, for example, may lead to putting a junior brother one step down, especially if it is foreseeable that not enough stock will be available for all sons to marry at the same time. As an uncircumcised boy he will then be treated disparagingly for an entire 14-year period by initiated warriors who may be about his own age, and he will have to wait 14 years longer until he can marry.

In more favourable economic circumstances the son or grandson of such a man can move up again to join the age-set line which his father or grandfather has left. This can be done simply by enrolling him into the second age set after his father's instead of in the third by circumcising him with the former.[58] In certain cases Rendille youngsters can also be moved up into an age set which has been established already by circumcision, but only if they can claim the right to join that age set by pointing to the age-set affiliation of an ancestor who belonged to the respective age-set line. Stewart (1977: 112) describes a number of such cases.

Among the Gabbra Malbe there is a tendency for initiations to be delayed by a seven-year cycle and yet another seven-year cycle, so that some age sets never reach certain grades and other grades are over-aged. The ritual journeys, *jila*, on which age-set promotions are carried out, seem to have a religious appeal of their own and the age-set system linked to them is not so emphasised. Although age sets are sometimes not promoted formally, every Gabbra knows his position in the system by referring to the age sets of his father and grandfather.

The Boran and other Oromo speakers call one of the grades through which their generation sets pass *gada*. Haberland takes this term up and defines *gada* systems as different from other age-set systems in being marked by a rigid order of numbers. This is an important difference, for example, from some Nilotic systems, like those of the western Nilotes and the Karamojong' cluster among the eastern Nilotes. In general the Nilotes do not seem to place the same cultural emphasis on calendars and the structuring of long spans of time as do Lowland Eastern Cushites. The Rendille and the Boran, at least, seem to derive pleasure from intricate numerical constructions.

In this sense also the generation-set system of the Rendille is a *gada* system, because it is based on exact numbers. This, however, does not mean that the Rendille have adopted their generation-set system form the Oromo. The PRS must have had a *gada* system because, apart form the Rendille, the distant Gabbra Miigo have a functioning system of this type and the systems of the interjacent Gabbra Malbe, although they are somewhat out of step, show enough reflexes of such a numerical order to allow the conclusion that they once had a proper *gada* system too.

There have been a number of theories on the origin of *gada* systems. These have been summarised by Haberland (1963: 167ff.) Instead of repeating Haberland, I want to limit myself to two remarks.

First, pursuing an argument put forward by Jensen (1942), Haberland (1963: 168) comes to the conclusion that Cerulli's interpretation of the origins of the *gada* system can be dismissed. Cerulli's theory is that the Oromo must have adopted this system from the Bantu on the lower Juba or Tana, because it is '*analogo a quello dei Negri Bantu*' (Cerulli 1938: 38). Cerulli assumes that the southern lowlands of the Horn must have been the starting point of Oromo expansion, and that the Oromo have penetrated into Ethiopia from the south. We have already explained above (chapter 3) that this theory is linked to Somali traditions that they, the Somali, penetrated into the lowlands of the Horn from the north and there met the Oromo, whom they pushed into the interior. These traditions are explained by the desire of the Somali to depict themselves as original Muslims and do not fit in with the linguistic and cultural evidence.[59] By these traditions, and by the various 'Hamitic' theories which were rife at the time, and which were very receptive to any news about purportedly culturally superior groups moving in from the north, entire generations of scholars have come to rather awkward views of the history of the Horn. According to more recent studies (Haberland 1963; H. S. Lewis 1966; Braukämper 1980b) the Oromo cradleland has to be looked for in the southeastern highlands of Ethiopia. The Somaloids, who are linguistically related to them and who expanded into the lowlands before they did, may have originated in the same region (Fleming 1964; Schlee 1987a). The argument of Jensen and Haberland, which is based on cultural comparisons of Bantu (Pokomo ...) and Oromo, is thus supported by the general picture of migrations in the Horn which has emerged since: the *gada* system cannot have been borrowed from the Bantu.

Second, in 1933, Biasutti published a critical review of the second volume of Cerulli's *Etiopia Occidentale* (1933). Haberland (1963: 168) depicts Biasutti's view as being that the Oromo had adopted the *gada* system from archaic peoples (*Altvölker*) living in the southern and central Ethiopian highlands. Biasutti, claims Haberland, thereby has anticipated later findings by Jensen, who regards the Konso and the Darassa as the original possessors of the *gada* system (Jensen 1936: 591–2; 1942: 93–4). This seems to me to be a rather narrow interpretation of what Biasutti actually said. In fact, Biasutti claims, based on Frobenius's classification, that the age-set systems are part of the 'old-erythraic' or 'equatorial' cultures, which have been preserved inside and outside Africa by different peoples, but in Africa by 'some Hamitic groups' among others ('*di preferenza fra i Negri ma anche in qualche gruppo camitico*'). The Oromo themselves or their immediate ancestors are nowhere excluded as potential original bearers of the *gada* system. Biasutti does not so much anticipate Jensen's views as Haberland's own views, although in a very cautious and general way.

Haberland himself regards the *gada* system as being a common possession of all peoples with Eastern Cushitic languages. Among these it is old and not a recent loan from anywhere else (Haberland 1963: 169–70). Ulrich Braukämper (personal communication) would rather limit this statement to speakers of Lowland Eastern Cushitic languages. Either way the Oromo, the Somali, the Gabbra, the Rendille, etc., that is, all the peoples who interest us here, are included. What I have discovered about the Rendille and Gabbra age-set systems confirms this view. They are obviously old, as can be concluded from their advanced degree of different-iation from each other, and so different from the *gada* system of the Boran that they cannot have been borrowed recently.

To substantiate this hypothesis I now want to describe the Gabbra systems in more detail. Looking at the comparison between them and comparing them with the Rendille system will also allow us some insights into what the original PRS system may have looked like.

In Diagram 12 reading from left to right gives the sequence of initiations of Gabbra Miigo age sets: (1) Dismalla, (2) Desgudo, (3) Margudo, (4) Melgus, etc. From top to bottom we find the time dimension with the sequence of generations of fathers and sons: Dismalla are the fathers of Melgus, Melgus of Dibgudo, who in their turn sire another Dismalla age

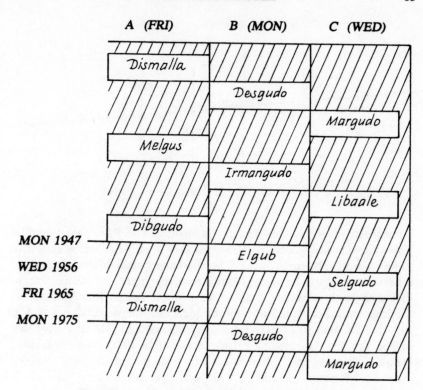

A (FRI)   B (MON)   C (WED)

Dismalla

Desgudo

Margudo

Melgus

Irmangudo

Libaale

Dibgudo

MON 1947

Elgub

WED 1956

FRI 1965

Selgudo

Dismalla

MON 1975

Desgudo

Margudo

Diagram 12   The Gabbra Miigo generation-set system

set. All these form the age-set line (*goges*) A, while Desgudo, Irmangudo, etc., form the *goges* B, and Margudo and their descendants the *goges* C. All member classes of A are initiated in a Friday year, all B classes in a Monday year ten years after the last A initiations, and all C classes in a Wednesday year nine years after the last B initiations.[60] The next initiations of A follow in a Friday year nine years after that. The number of years elapsing between the initiations of a father and his sons thus is $10 + 9 + 9 = 28$.

As a ritual generation of 28 years is usually shorter than the biological generations of polygynous pastoralists,[61] we should expect under-aging to occur, i.e. that a proportion of the male population of the Gabbra Miigo are too young to join their proper age set or were not yet born at the time of their installation, unless the Gabbra Miigo have ways of counteracting or accommodating this phenomenon. The data, however, tell us nothing in this respect. Stewart, in his brilliant analysis (1977), discusses many such demographic problems connected with age-group systems.

The Gabbra Miigo system, except for the shorter age-set cycle (nine or

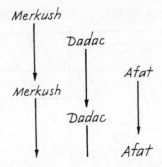

Diagram 13   The Sharbana age-set system

ten respectively instead of 14 years), is identical with that of the Rendille.
This system is also shared by the Sharbana of the Gabbra Malbe and, with
some variations, by the Alganna. The Sharbana system differs from that of
the Gabbra Miigo in having only three recurrent names for the age sets, so
that each of these comes to stand for a whole age-set line: the sons of
Merkush and their grandsons will be Merkush, the descendants of Afat
will be Afat, and so on (Diagram 13). Alganna and Gār only have two
named age sets, so their sequence is a simple alternation: Waakhor,
Dambal, Waakhor, etc. These two names form part of the more complex
set of age-set names of Galbo and Odoola, as does the name Afat, which
also occurs in the Sharbana system: their cycle goes Gurjab, Afat,
Mangub, Dambal, Waguur, Waakhor and then starts again with Gurjab.
The details of these systems and the somewhat irregular unrolling of them
can best be seen from Table 9 which shows all known years of initiation,
the *goges* links between age sets and gives the names of the *hayyu*s at the
head of each age set.

One might hypothesise that the original PRS system (there may have
been different systems) had nine named age sets and three age-set lines
like that of the Gabbra Miigo. The Rendille system only diverges slightly
from this model because, as we have seen, certain age-set names have been
avoided as unpropitious. The Gabbra Malbe systems may then be seen as
various stages of erosion of such a system: the number of age-set names
and in some cases also the number of age sets per *goges* are reduced.
Although the ritual journeys to the holy sites where the initiation takes
place form the central events of Gabbra Malbe life and are key religious
experiences, the age-set systems themselves do not seem to be so
important to the Gabbra: the schedules are not kept strictly and the
systems themselves seem simplified.

I do not want, however, to overstress this point. The strongest argument
that the PRS had such an age-set system and that the present varieties
derive from such an ancestral form does not stem from a comparison of the

various systems. Age-set systems, like other aspects of social organisation, adjust and have to adjust to social needs, demographic changes, etc., and are therefore not suitable as *Leitfossile* of historical reconstruction. The strongest argument, in accordance with Graebner's *Formkriterium*, arises from a rather accidental feature: the age-set names. The highest number of shared names can be found between the two systems which are geographically farthest apart from each other, the systems of the Gabbra Miigo and the Rendille (Table 8).

This high overlap cannot be explained by recent contact which involved mutual borrowing because no such contact is known from written or oral history; also the geographical distance and the hostile groups which lie between the two systems make such contacts unlikely. We can therefore regard these names as surviving elements of a system already in existence at the time of the PRS. (This system can therefore not have had fewer than five named age sets. From a different angle we have already dimly seen that it probably had nine.)

The terminologies of the interjacent Gabbra Malbe contain some names which are of Boran rather than PRS origin: Waakhor and Dambal (*wáhor* and *dámbal*) are mentioned by Haberland (1963: 182) and Baxter (1979: 85) as the alternating names of the *hariya*, i.e. the real age sets which the Boran have in addition to the *gada* classes because the latter no longer accommodate many men of the appropriate age.

The differences between these systems is striking: the Gār have a system in which the age sets of fathers and their sons are separated by one age set of unrelated people. This is reflected by the alternation of two names: Waakhor and Dambal, all Waakhor are sons of Waakhor, all Dambal of Dambal.

Table 8 A comparison of Gabbra Miigo and Rendille age-set names

Shared names	
Gabbra Miigo	Rendille
Dismalla	Dismaala
D'esgudo	D'ifgudo
D'ibgudo	D'ibgudo
Irmangudo	Irbangudo
Libaale	Libaale

Names which are not shared	
Gabbra Miigo	Rendille
Margudo	Irband'if
Melgus	Irbaalis
Elgub	
Selgudo	

The Galbo and Odoola have a similar system. Ego's sons enrol in the second set after his,[62] but they are not called by the same name. As there is a total of six names, there are three names which recur in a descent line: Gurjab beget Mangub, Mangub beget Waguur, who in their turn beget another Gurjab. The other age-set line (*goges*) is Afat–Dambal–Waakhor.

All these system differ not just terminologically but substantially from that of the Alganna (apart from the Sharbana, whose system is meant to

Table 9 Gabbra Malbe age-set chronology

Gär phratry

year of promotion	age – set name	hayyu – names of those age sets who became dabela	brackets linking age – sets of fathers and sons
1908 ?	Dambal	Yiblo moiety: Elle T'elo (Kobola, Galabloye) Lossa moiety: ?	
1922	Waakhor	Yiblo moiety: Guyyo Halake ? Lossa moiety: Sarro Agerte (Borid)	
1957	Dambal	Yiblo: Issako Maderte (Kobola) Lossa: Mamo Isaako (Borid)	
1971	Waakhor	Yiblo: Guyyo Sarro (Kobola) Lossa: Elema Hurri (Biriole)	
1985	Dambal	Yiblo: Hurri Isaako (son of Isaako Maderte, above) Lossa: ?	
?	Waakhor	Afó Jillo T'elo (moiety ? lineage ?)	
?	Dambal	son of Hurri Isaako	

Alganna phratry   Sharbana phratry

year of promotion	names of hayyu of those age−sets who became dabela	brackets linking age−sets of fathers and sons	hayyu of those age−sets who became dabela	age−set names
1923	Yiblo moiety: Harro Duche (Hallano, Ammado) Lossa moiety: Godaana Abudo (Koyot)		Ø	Dadac
1958 (1951?)	Yiblo: D'ad'u Korricha (Hallano) Lossa: Godaana Burale (Gádara)		Ø	Afat
1972	Yiblo ?: Galgallo Harre D'aacha Lossa: ?		Yiblo: Adano Galgallo (Bahae Diimtu) Lossa: Raako Saako (Matarbá)	Merkush
1986	Yiblo: Isaako Harro, son of Harro Duche (above) Lossa: Doti Galgallo (Koyot)		Lossa: Isaako Mamo (Matarbá) ?	Dadac
?	sons of those promoted in 1958			Afat
?	sons of those promoted in 1972			Merkush

Galbo and Odoola phratries

brackets linking fathers and sons	age−set name of those initiated into the dabela grade	year of promotion (Galbo)	year of promotion (Odoola)
	Gurjab		
	Afat		
	Mangub		
	Dambal	1909	1909
	Waguur	1923	1923
	Waakhor	1951	1958
	Gurjab	1972	1972
	Afat	1986	1986
	Mangub		

work like the Alganna's but who, impoverished and decimated by enemy attacks, too often have not found the means to carry out their ceremonies). In the Alganna system fathers and sons are separated by two age sets. While the Gār, the Galbo and the Odoola go on the ritual journeys together with their sons, who become *luba* and install their *hayyu* and *jallab* office holders, while their fathers become *dabela*, in Alganna the age set following the *dabela* will install their *hayyu*, while the sons of the *dabela* will become *hayyu* only two age-set cycles later (Table 10).[63]

The religious significance of the ritual journeys, which consist of long pilgrimages to holy sites (mainly in Ethiopia) and elaborate cycles of sacrificial ceremonies, cannot be subsumed under the heading 'age-set systems'. I describe them elsewhere (Schlee, in preparation).

In summarising those aspects of our comparative description which allow us to throw a glance at earlier age-set systems from which the present ones are derived, we have to avoid the evolutionist assumption that the older systems must be simpler. We have seen that the Gabbra Malbe, although they live in proximity to each other and have synchronised promotion ceremonies, differ in the number of sets per generation, the names of those sets and the offices and roles attached to them. There is no reason to assume that earlier clusters of PRS peoples presented less variety. One of possibly several PRS age-set systems may have had three age-set lines, sons being enrolled into the third set after their fathers. There may have been nine cyclically returning age-set names, so that Ego's set had the same name as that of his FaFaFa. Five of these names may have sounded like Dismalla, D'esgudo, D'ibgudo, Irmangudo, Libaale (taking the Miigo forms, which appear phonologically older than the Rendille ones).

In spite of the marked differences in the length of age-set cycles and in their number per major unit, and thus in their way of functioning the fact that the *gada* systems of the Oromo and the PRS are of a common origin can be seen from a number of features. These are so marked that their similarity can hardly be explained as parallel development. The peoples who are now called Somali, among whom we find rudiments of a *gada* system in various places, originally belong in this context. Haberland (1963: 170) has already explained that these *gada* systems are not recent

Table 10 Installation into offices in the Alganna age-set system

No. of cycle	Dabela	Hayyu
1	Age set 1	Age set 2
2	Age set 2	Age set 3
3	Age set 3	Sons of 1
4	Sons of 1	Sons of 2
5	Sons of 2	Sons of 3

loans from the Oromo, as Cerulli (1957: 73) and I. M. Lewis (1955: 21, 105) believe, but old elements of the pre-Islamic Somali culture. Parts of this cultural complex have been adopted by Nilotes (Nandi, Maasai, Samburu) and have been handed on by these to some Bantu peoples (Kikuyu, Chagga, etc., who are sometimes called Masai-Affen in the early literature because of their eagerness to follow Maasai fashions).

In later times mutual borrowing has occurred between the various branches of these *gada* systems: Oromoised PRS, the Gār phratry of the Gabbra Malbe, adopted *hariya* names of the Boran as their age-set names. The Gabbra possibly have also adopted their particular form of circumcision from the Boran (there are two types of circumcision in North-east Africa and these solve the problem of closing the wound in different ways). The Rendille have adopted some ritual elaborations, but not, as Spencer (1973: 33) seems to believe, their age-set system and its timing from the Samburu. (This is a case of Cushites borrowing back elements of Cushitic culture in a Nilotic remould). Generally, the correspondence of these customs seems to me to be high between the PRS-derived peoples and their Nilotic and Bantu neighbours and possibly also originally comprised other Somali than those now exhibiting a strong PRS complex, while the similarities with the Oromo are more general and remote.

As an example I would like to take the ritual killings which among the Oromo are a central part of their achievement complex (*Verdienstkomplex*), and which by the institutional war expeditions are closely linked to the *gada* cycle. Ritual killings and the killer status exist among the PRS peoples in a very similar way, even with some agreement in details like the severing of male genitals as a trophy, the boasting song, the decoration of the killer with the necklaces of girls or women, ostrich feathers as killers' insignia (Haberland 1963: 208ff., Schlee 1979: 343ff.). But among the Gabbra, the Rendille and their Eastern Nilotic neighbours (Nandi, Maa-speaking peoples) killing human beings is not (or no longer) connected to the unrolling of the age-set systems. In this context we find instead the shooting of birds and small mammals, and this in a remarkably uniform way over large distances. The hunt is carried out with bow and blunt arrows, the bodies of the birds are worn dangling from the headgear, the period during which this is done is the seclusion phase which immediately follows circumcision, this phase is further marked by an interdiction against washing oneself, a prohibition on touching food with the hands, etc.[64] At the end of this seclusion period the young Rendille, Samburu and Gabbra have to slaughter a head of smallstock and to break its thighbone with a single stroke of the club, otherwise they would expose themselves to derision from the women and girls who look on at a distance. Cerulli says that the warrior age set among certain Darood Somali are called the *laf-jebis* ('bone breakers'). This poses the question – which possibly can no longer be answered – as to how much else of their culture the northern Somali shared with the Rendille and Gabbra before Islam replaced or reshaped it.

Haberland attributes considerable importance to the number 40 which marks the ritual generation among the Boran and other Oromo. He also points to the repeated occurrence of this number in Jewish and Islamic traditions. But Haberland himself also utters doubts about the special significance of this number because the Konso and the Darassa replace the 40 with other numbers (1963: 172). I want to underline these doubts. The Rendille have a ritual generation of 42 and the Gabbra Miigo one of 28 years. The number 40 of the Boran to me seems to be product of 5×8 and not to be of any deeper significance.

Nevertheless, Haberland postulates a connection between the elaborate numerical systems, which among the Oromo are not only characteristic of the *gada* systems[65] but also pervade the calendar, and old oriental cultures. If there is such a connection, however, we can at the most regard it as established by stimulus diffusion (rather than the diffusion of the traits themselves) since concrete parallels in details, such as would satisfy Graebner's *Formkriterium*, cannot be found. The cycle of 27 *ayaana*, for example, which the Boran have as the largest unit of time below the month, does not share anything with the oriental seven-day week except the general function of structuring time. Oriental influence is more apparent in the PRS calendar in which the seven-day week – and, as a local derivate from it, the seven-year cycle, which is unknown in the Orient – play a significant role.

The general attitude behind all these phenomena namely the pleasure taken in naming serial events, in counting and calculating, seems to me to be so deeply rooted in Lowland Eastern Cushites that personally I do not feel the need to look to South-west Asian high cultures or elsewhere for its origin.

I cannot present a complete or even well-balanced picture of all the different cultures studied. Other aspects of these cultures have to be discussed elsewhere. One entire dimension of cultural history has had to be left out almost completely: the early and recent Islamic influences (Schlee 1988). I also have to reserve for the future a fuller treatment of the influences of the African cultures of the interior on the PRS-derived cultures. Some political institutions of the groups in question (*hayyu*, *jallab*, etc.) seem to have been fashioned after Boran models, and linguistic and cultural borrowings from the Boran can even be shown in the case of the Rendille, the group most remote from Boran control. Much would need to be said also about Samburu and possibly other Maa influences on elaborations of Rendille age-set rituals, on Rendille youth culture and on Rendille kinship terminology. All these cultural strata deserve the same attention as the complex of that one early stratum, the PRS culture, which I have outlined in this chapter.

My only justification for neglecting them – apart from limitations of space – is that for the present topic the PRS complex is of diagnostic value. The presence or absence of this complex allows us to say that the Rendille, Gabbra, Sakuye and Garre cultures derive from the PRS and that the Boran do not. In the case of Somali groups we can distinguish between those which show stronger or weaker PRS affiliation.[66] The fact that the Rendille, the Garre, the Sakuye and the Gabbra derive from an earlier common culture ties in with their clan histories[67] which date from that early period, and helps to distinguish the inter-ethnic occurrence of PRS clans from other inter-ethnic clan relationships like the later, adoptive *tiriso* relationships with Boran clans.[68]

For this purpose it was necessary to demonstrate that the present-day derivatives of the PRS culture exhibit complexes of traits which share so many formal and apparently accidental details that parallel developments cannot account for them. (Parallel functional adaptations would lead to features with similar functions, not with similar formal elaborations, such as the same rule regarding a certain way to deal with a camel on a certain day of the week. Functional arguments, of course, can be adduced to explain why these features have been maintained.)

The complexes which I have examined in this perspective are: (a) the calendrical system and the rules applied to camel management, society and ritual linked to it; (b) forms of shared rights in camels; (c) the killer complex and its elaborations (*sarma*); and (d) the generation-set systems which show, apart from great variation, some elements common to different PRS-derived cultures and no evidence of direct borrowing from the Boran, thus establishing the generation-set system as an institution which the PRS had already and which probably goes back to the Lowland Eastern Cushitic-speaking ancestors whom the PRS shared with the Oromo.

Fully to establish the complex of features which I have called PRS as a separate phenomenon which calls for the postulation of a historical origin which is different from that of neighbouring cultures, I would have to show the extent to which the PRS complex differs from comparable parts of non-PRS cultures. Ideally I would have to describe the other cultures in the area – Oromo and Islamic Modern Somali – in the same level of detail as the preceding description of the PRS complex. As I do not have enough space to do so, I have to do without it. Suffice it to say, therefore, that the cultures in question also have ritual and prognostic calendars but with different holidays and different days marked as propitious or unpropitious. They also have forms of mutual help and shared rights in animals but different rules governing these exchanges. In other words, these neighbouring cultures respond to similar needs by means which exhibit different formal characteristics and thereby betray a different historical origin.

THE LONG TREK

Like the Jews' exodus from Egypt, the Great Trek of the Boers, the Long March in China, the memory of a long, harsh migration also has a central position in the collective consciousness of the Cushitic peoples of northern Kenya.

There are basically two versions of this tale: one about an eastward migration into southern Somalia and back, and another about a migration to a land Iris, west of Lake Turkana (Rudolph), and back. Some informants try to reconcile both versions as involving different peoples at different times. On the other hand, it can be shown that some elements of the tales are narrative *topoi* which the two versions not only share with each other but also with the Book of Exodus, which, via Islamic traditions, may have been the model on which such episodes were shaped. Other parts of the tradition, however, refer very specifically to the local context, and one of the questions these tales undoubtedly want to answer is how have the present ethnic groups of northern Kenyan camel nomads separated and developed out of a common ancestral group. That they have done so is beyond doubt to the narrators, so the question remains: how?

I first discuss different versions of the account of the eastward migration which stem from the following sources (the short references, to be used in the text, are added in brackets):

1 Interview Godaana Guyyo 'Korinya', aged 57, Galbo, Gabbra, in Turbi, January 1979, and interview Godaana Guyyo and Jirima Mollu, aged 40, both of the Galbo phratry, Turbi, February 1980. Language: Boran (Gabbra 1).

2 Interview Boku Sora, Dabel, February and March 1980. Boku Sora stems from a *hayyu* lineage of Sakuye and is a former colonial chief. He was appointed in February 1945 after his younger brother and predecessor, Ali Sora, had died in a lorry accident in 1944. Some Sakuye[69] attribute this untimely death to magic motivated by envy. Ali is still remembered as a clever advocate of Sakuye grazing rights, and enemies of Boku depict the latter as the person who spoiled Ali's successful policies.[70] In spite of being the eldest son of the *hayyica* and thus most elegible to be government chief according to the usual practice of indirect rule, Boku had originally been bypassed because the British disliked him. In the district commissioner's reports he is characterised as suspected of sugar smuggling and misrule, 'a strong man and good in debate but ... untrustworthy and unscrupulous' (1947). '... he cannot be relied upon to report illegal

activities or to help the police' (1948). 'A violent tempered and ruthless chief very given to indulging in private fetinas [quarrels] with his subjects' (1950). He was finally deposed in 1951. An adversary of his remembers that the British administrator held a public meeting at which he asked everybody who supported Boku Sora to rise. The Sakuye remained seated. When he asked everybody who wanted Boku to be deposed to stand up, the Sakuye rose like one man. Boku in his anger then exiled himself to Ethiopia for a couple of months (Guyyo Cito). It appears that Boku was indeed demanding and high-handed in the way he procured livestock for slaughter for his guests. But now the Sakuye who venerate his memory outnumber his critics. Like all strong men – and he was strong not only in his personality but also in the charisma he inherited from his family – Boku attracted much admiration and much hatred at the same time. 'Once Boku Sora had gone the Sakuye made some progress both in pan digging and tax collection . . .' (Kenya National Archives, Moyale District Annual Reports, PS/NFD/1/6/3). Seen from a post-colonial perspective, all these derogatory statements, of course, can be interpreted as reactions to Boku Sora's strength of character and independence. Although the district reports claim that he had alienated most of his 'subjects', this alienation cannot have been of a lasting sort. When I knew him, as an old man, I found him very much liked and respected by his people.

Boku Sora died in 1983, survived by his widow, a leading woman member of Abba Ganna's possession cult,[71] his grown-up children (whom I never came to know) and his brother Ali's son. The last, continuing the family tradition of being chief, was also criticised for being high-handed and has since been deposed. *L'histoire se repète.* Language: Boran. (Sakuye 1)

3 Interview Rooba Kurawa, Sakuye, in Gafars, June 1980. Rooba Kurawa was the only surviving Sakuye *hayyica* who, six months before I met him, had received word from his age-mate Boku Sora, who lived 300 kilometres away, to give me information. In the meantime, a new set of *hayyu* and *jallab* has been initiated with Rooba Kurawa playing an important role as the only available ritual specialist and the only dignitary who was left to pass his office on.[72] Rooba Kurawa has also been in demand by other anthropologists. Gudrun Dahl and Anders Hjort invited him to a symposium on camel management in Marsabit in 1984 under the auspices of the Institute of Development Studies, University of Nairobi. Rooba Kurawa was deeply impressed by Gudrun Dahl and the number of men who 'obeyed' her. (Sakuye women do not normally join meetings.)

I had another opportunity of long interview sessions with Rooba Kurawa in October 1984. (Sakuye 2)

4 Interview 'Okolla' Ado 'Abdi Bakur, June 1980. An impoverished elderly Sakuye, Matarbá; a shoemaker in Malka Daka, who had formerly lived in Marsabit. Together with Jilo Sora Jilo, Sakuye, Miigo, same age. Language: Boran. (Sakuye 3)

5 Interview Ḥaji Ḥassan, Garre, Tuf, in Gurar on the Ethiopian border, August 1979. A wealthy and respected herd owner of middle age who could afford the pilgrimage. Language: Boran. (Tuf)

6 Interview Boru Sora Suura, Gabbra Miigo, Gurar, August 1979. Middle aged. Language: Boran. (Miigo)

7 Interview Osman Golija and Sheikh Aḥmad Kanoo Maḥad in Gurar, August 1979. Both are Ajuran and beyond middle age. The late Osman Golija, who died in a road accident, was a shopowner. Language: Somali. (Ajuran)

8 A compilation from Garre informants in J. W. K. Pease, *An Ethnological Treatise of the Gurreh Tribe*, KNA: Gurreh District Political Record Book, 1928. Although this source has the disadvantage of being in English, with the result that much of the original savour has been lost, and the informants are not identifiable, its age and great detail speak in favour of including it here. (Pease)

Other minor sources apart from these eight will be cited in the notes.

THE SITUATION BEFORE THE LONG TREK

Both the Garre and Ajuran claim to have lived in their present locations in Mandera District and the northern part of Wajir District before the sixteenth-century expansion of the Oromo. Rendille, Gabbra and Sakuye are said to have split from this original people in the process of the long trek or *kedi guur* ('migration-migration'). That Ajuran are reported to have fought around Mogadishu in the fifteenth century (I. M. Lewis 1955: 47) does not necessarily contradict the claim of the Kenya Ajuran to have lived in their present area for a long time. The Ajuran of Mogadishu may have come from Kenya, or a people living in Kenya may later have absorbed small but prestigious groups of Ajuran coming from the east and adopted their name, or Ajuran may have arrived simultaneously or at different times both on the Benadir coast and in northern Kenya from a third location. We can exclude none of these possibilities and only silently admire the courage of those authors who speak with assured matter-of-factness about Somali migrational history.

Interestingly, Lewis mentions a tribe by the name of Madinle as allies of these early Ajuran (I. M. Lewis 1955: 47). My Kenya Ajuran informants claim that their ancestors (or some of them) were identical with the Madanleh.[73] These Madanleh, however, are enveloped in thick layers of mythical mist. They are said to have been similar to the Jite, the Dabarre and the Tunni with whom they formed an early population of the area. Tunni and Jite in their turn are sometimes grouped, together with Boran and Warra Daaya, as the sons of one Ali. The historical conclusions from such genealogies, of course, should not be pushed beyond the statement of a possible similarity of the units thus grouped together. Madanleh and Bal'ad are said to be earlier names of the Ajuran.[74]

> *Berrigi hora, zamanki hora, dul-ka Ajuran iyou Garrex islafadiyey. Marki dambe Boorana islafadiyey. [. . .] Kedi Guure alayirada, marki dal-ka lagatagga Booran soo-geshey.*

In the early days, in the past, in this country Ajuran and Garre stayed together. Later they stayed together with the Boran. [. . .] The time when this country was [temporarily] left and the Boran entered it is called Kedi Guure.

> *Soo-noqod kan dambe Boorana ayyá lo-yimid. Booran iyou Garrexa iyou Ajuran iyou Gabbra iyou Sakuye waxaan oodan dal-kan ayyey iskudaqdeen'.*

After [their] return [the Ajuran and Garre] met the Boran. It was in this country that the Garre and the Ajuran and the Gabbra prospered together (Ajuran).

Pease writes:

> According to tradition Gurreh district was originally inhabited by a Semitic tribe – the ben Izraeli – or Madanli; these people were very tall and had long prominent noses which enabled them to smell water a considerable distance underground: they extended beyond Wajir, and dug the wells there and also those at Wergudud, Eil Illi, Hogerali, Goochi [Adabli plain] and other places in this district: The numerous graves along the Daua [Dawa] river are also theirs, and their last stronghold was Hambali, near Gerba Harre, where the stone walls of their town can still be seen.
>
> In course of time they were weakened by pestilence and drought and were then attacked by 5 tribes – the Hirap, Jido, Eroli, Dubarre and Mada Ade, some add Ajuran as the 6th; in their weakened state the 'ben Izraeli' were soon finished off.

Pease then describes traditions about the Hirap, the rule of a certain Sheriff Nur and a Muslim view of the origin of the Boran *qallu*. He then turns to the Garre.

> At this time the Gurreh dwelt around Serar in what is now Arusia [Arussi] country having originally come down from near the Red Sea coast through Harrar or Adarre, as the Gurreh call it.[75] Serar [?Surar south-east of Shek Husen] lies about 4 days south [?of Harar] and some 16 days journey north of Dolo. Under pressure from enemies in the north they migrated gradually to the south west till they reached Filtu [between Negele and Dolo] and Wujili [?Wachille on the road from Nairobi to Addis Ababa between Moyale and Negele] which lie only some 40 or 50 miles [100 km ≙ 61 miles and 124 km ≙ 71 miles as the crow flies] from the present boundary between this district and Abyssinia, north of Malka Murri [Malka Mari of the maps] and Jarra [?] respectively: at these places they stayed long enough to build houses and mosques, and it was there that they came into contact with the Boran Kingdom to the west which was then strong and flourishing. They lived thus with the Boran for some

time and spread southwards into the northern and western parts of this district, until the Boran tried to make them subjects and exact tribute whereupon the Gurreh decided they must move again.

Waan an durri d'agei: Garri fulum sun kees d'alate. Laf tán nami iti-galin, kejiru: Garri, Boran, Ajuran, Gabbra. Worri kun laf tan wolumántaa.

What I heard long ago: the Garre have been born [have originated] just here. In this country the people who have not entered [from outside] but were here are the Garre, the Boran, the Ajuran and the Gabbra. These people stayed together in this land.

Kun abraanu jars ínqaba. Wolíntaa. Yo namin wólijjes gafuudan.

These four had elders. They stayed together. When people killed each other they were brought [for judgement].

Akasi laf aki dansani nagean taan. Boraani ka dibbi name iti-ga-gále. Nam kan chuf, nam eege d'ufe: Degodí, Muralle. Muralle eege galle. Aki nu d'agene akán.

In this way they stayed in the land in a good way in peace. Other Boran joined the people repeatedly. Of all these people, those who came last are the Degodia and the Muralle [Murille]. The Muralle came last [much later than the others. Most Degodia groups and the Muralle came only in this century and do not figure in the traditions about the long migration]. This is what we heard. (Tuf)

We can thus summarise that the peoples who were affected in their development by the long trek, either by participating in it or by remaining behind, were those who today are called Garre, Ajuran and Gabbra. We shall see below that Sakuye and Rendille are also described as having derived from these peoples in various ways.

The accounts of the reason for migrating vary only slightly.

QUESTION: *Laf suni marr d'abe moo bisan d'abe moo nyaabe sodaate moo maan laf sun gale?*

Did the country run out of pasture or water or was there fear of enemies or what has entered [happened to] the land?

Marre ind'ábne, bisá-lle ind'abne; walhadan. Sabab-ti wald'agau d'ad'abaní, duub sabab-ti baddi kedi guuran sabab-ti isii sabab-ti sun.

One did not miss pasture nor water; they fought each other. Because they did not understand each other, now, the reason for the flight, the long trek is this. (Tuf)

QUESTION: *Worre suni aki dansá durri wolintae, maan tíyak?*

These people before stayed together in a good way, what heated them?

Wan ini hámmate: Nam tokko ijjesani duub dubbi nami suni hámmate. Garren yo nam Boraana ijjeft, nam sun ga-fuudan. Boraani ammó gadinin-d'úfu.

What made them bad: one man was killed and the talk [case, affair] about that man became bad. The Garre, when somebody killed a Boran, brought that man [to be tried]. The Boran, however, [when one of them killed a Garre] did not come with [that man].

Guyyan kan dubbi dubbat chuf íntolcit. Boraani waan tolca jed'an kan intólcu. Oddu ini eege dubbi sun intolcín guyyan kan kees ejj.

That day [the Garre] fulfilled all the talk that was talked. [But] the Boran did not do what they were told to do. While the end of that case was not concluded, it came to a stand at that day.

Waan taat: nu Islán. Ini diin in-khábu. Nami diina khabu, ka diin in-khábne woldibt.

The matter is that we are Muslims. They have no religion [*diin* دِ ىن]. Somebody with religion and somebody who has got no religion harass each other.

Aki sheriyaa kena kolki d'abi dubbi sun tolcan. Ini sheria in-khábu. Nam sheriaa khabut walin-daqacu danda. Akasi wal-d'ad'ab.

In a quarrel, they make it good according to our *sheria* [the Muslim law]. They do not have *sheria*. People who have got *sheria* can prosper together. This is how they missed each other.

Nam kun Boraana sheria inkhábu. Nam kan waldibsatan. Worri guyya chuf fard fuudate d'uufe. Duuba 'ken' nu jed' 'nam'.

These Boran people do not have *sheria*. People harassed each other. They took their horses every day and came. Then they said to us 'give [us that] person' [i.e. a suspected murderer].

Gaaf kan Islanin mallate̲. Ín- dawat. Duub dawti waan itibaate: godaan.

That time the Muslims conferred. They discussed. What came out of the discussion was [the decision] to move. (Tuf)

The informant being a *haji*, this version may overstress the importance of dogmatic and legal questions. It remains open how far Islam had actually penetrated into Garre, or proto-Garre, society in this early phase of the establishment of Boran hegemony (sixteenth century). Even today, as we have seen in this chapter, there are strong elements of non-Islamic ritual life in Garre and Gabbra Miigo societies. However, in retrospect both these groups, who today are Muslims, stress the importance of religious differences in this conflict. The pagan past of the Gabbra Miigo is explained as an intermediate phase. The motive of Boran occupation is described as the establishment of overlordship: they wanted to reduce people to *garbi*, vassals.

Boraani walahadde. Islaani garán déebie. Ka gari aci bae, ka gari aci bae, ka gari garán hafe. K'haf kun Gabbr. Obolesi jalla hafé Gabbra tae. Islaani yádeete. Nu Boran birát gad-hafne.

There was fighting with the Boran. The Muslims withdrew. One part went to that side [east], one part went to that side [west], one part stayed here. The ones who stayed are the Gabbra. The brother who stayed behind became Gabbra. The Muslims fled. We stayed in vicinity of the Boran.

Otto nu ingódaanin nu qabte. 'Fulá sila garbici jetu, Gabbri jed'.' Irree nu-rr-qaba,

*nu-rre [= nu irre] gudda. Qara durri biyyen tena; diin-ti nu qabnu, oboles kenu jalla
qabe, kara isa na déebise.*

Before we could migrate, they got hold of us. 'Rather than calling us vassals
[*garbi*], call us Gabbra.' They caught us by force, they were more than us.
Before, the land was ours; they took us away from the religion we have, from
behind our brothers and made us turn to their way.

*Harki kennané, harki isii senne. Marki deebie, nam kena deebine, Islan kena
deebine.*

We took each other's hand [hand, gave, reciprocal] and ended up in their hands.
When [after the long trek, centuries later, the Garre] came back, we joined again
our people, our Islam. (Miigo)

THE TRICKS OF SHEIKH BULE HUSSEIN

Once life in the vicinity of the Boran was found to be unbearable, the
problem arose where to move and how to gain time to prepare for the
migration.

One of their [the Garre] leaders, Sheik Bule Hussein, set out with one slave to
prospect for a new country: he travelled down the Juba and through Rahanwein
to Confor [Konfur, Kofar] and decided it was a good country. On his return he
told the Gurreh to spread the rumour among the Boran that he acquired a
dreadful disease on his travel: he and his slaves [slave] then went to a big baraza
[gathering] of the Boran but first prepared a blood red drink by boiling the bark
of a thorn tree: just before the baraza they drank bowls of it, and they had
hardly sat down when the slave was violently sick, apparently vomiting
quantities of blood: a moment later the Sheikh himself was sick and the Boran
got up in consternation and fled. (Pease)

In our Miigo version the Boran had formally announced to Bule Hussein
that his people should be allotted to different Boran clans.

*'Isan qodani, khora bai.' Waan khora sun baef, waan itiyaamanif: ínqodan.
Balbalan qodan.*

'You will be divided, come out for a meeting.' The reason for that meeting,
what they were called for: they would be distributed. Distributed to different
clans.

*Bule Hussein Kofar daqe. Millan deeme, gagal. Yo ini d'ufe yádarisatani, lafti
lakka. Borani 'kora ba' jed'ani 'Waan tee, an fayáánit.' Fussá d'uge, duuba iti-
d'ufe. 'Na yaamín! Illalan. Fayyáánit, índidig. Fussa indidig. Yasobbé birrágalan.*

Bule Hussein went to Kofar. He walked by foot and came back. When he came,
they [the Boran] suspected them to leave the country. The Boran said: 'Come
for a meeting.' 'The matter is that I am not healthy.' He drank *fussa*, then they
came to him. 'Do not call me!' They look at him. He is not healthy, he vomits.
He vomits *fussa*. So he cheated them and they left him. (Miigo)

Unlike Pease's version, in this account the Boran do not fear contagion
but simply leave to wait for Bule Hussein's recovery. The following episode
also differs in the two versions. In the first version Bule Hussein exploits
the fear of the Boran, in the second their piety.

The Sheikh and his slaves then dug two graves and set up tombstones: the Boran returning concluded that the new disease was indeed fatal and retired well away from the Gurreh villages, while the Sheik seized the opportunity to lead his tribe away to the east through the desert country of northern Jubaland. (Pease)

Bor lalu d'ufan. Gombo wayá iti-yisan. 'Yadue' jed'an. 'Injír' jed'an. 'Guyya torba ind'uf'ina huji isá mid'ãsanna. Inhawwalla. Nu gad in-beina. Nu eega' jed'an. Torba kan baqat.

The following day they [the Boran] came back to see. [The Garre] had spread a sheet over a trough. 'He has died,' they said. 'He is not alive,' they said. 'Do not come for seven days, we are busy with his work [the funeral celebrations]. We bury him. Do not come to us. Wait for us,' they said. During this week they fled. (Miigo)

THE ORIGIN OF GABBRA AND RENDILLE

All our versions agree that the Gabbra have evolved from those Garre who were left behind at the time of *kedi guur*, the long trek. The Boran made them their dependants and allotted them to different Boran clans; they divided them up (*qodu*), the institution of vassaldom being called *tiriso*. We will see in chapter 5 that some Gabbra Malbe lineages claim that they *tiriso inqábtu* ('do not have *tiriso*', i.e. have not been Boran vassals), while the majority of Gabbra still have their double clan affiliation – their own and that of the Boran clan to which they are attached.

Disagreement exists about the part the ancestors of the Rendille played in these perturbations. Garre and Gabbra Miigo believe that the Rendille were cut off from the Garre and stayed behind. The Sakuye claim that they, the Sakuye, have derived from the Rendille, who in their turn are Garre or Biimal who became separated from their fellow tribesmen trying to cross the lower Juba. This version thus sees the Rendille as participants of the long trek. We will see below that the Rendille are also believed to have participated in the westward migration to Iris, together with the Gabbra Malbe, from whom they only later separated. We get the impression that everybody seems to claim the Rendille for themselves, linking the history of their own ethnic group to that of the Rendille. This attitude is complemented by the Rendille, who tend to regard the rest of the world as impoverished or renegade Rendille.

The splitting up of proto-Garre – Gabbra – Rendille into the nuclei of the ethnic groups arising from them is ascribed to their local dispersion and the urgency of the flight.

The Miigo version of the hurried departure has been given above in connection with the reasons for migrating. Pease agrees with it.

Two sections [of Proto-Garre] however stayed behind – the Gabbra and Rendille – the Gabbra had many camels and could not take them all in their flight across the desert; they saw it was a choice between their camels and the Gurreh and said 'We can live without the Gurreh but not without camles' so they stayed behind with the Boran. The Rendille were also a section of camel owners who had pushed into the bush further south and did not get the news of the exodus in time; the name, by tradition, is derived from 'Rer Did' 'the people who would not', they were bush dwellers and always refused to live in or near the Gurreh villages and so lost their chance; it is said up here that their elders still recognize their Gurreh origin and say 'We were lost on [in?] Sheik Bule Hussein's day.'

I could not find this tradition in such detail among the Rendille, and I never heard them mention Bule Hussein. The derivation of 'Rendille' from 'Rer Did' is known to the Rendille, but seems to go back to the Somali, as does the story about the Rendille being camel herders in a *for* ('satellite camp') who became separated from an ancestral Somali group which they could not then rejoin. The Rendille themselves for the most part do not think that they became separated from anybody, but that many peoples on earth became separated from them. The nucleus of Rendille – the senior clans of both moieties – have mythical places of origin within the present tribal area, a fact which points to a long-standing presence there (see Schlee 1979: pp. 12 and 228). The only clan which derives itself explicitly from the Garre is the latecomer Odoola, which only joined Rendille when it was an established society with its present moiety structure, into which Odoola, apart from many other peculiarities, does not fit.[76].

The version given by Pease, however, as well as the Gabbra Miigo, is largely shared by the Gabbra Malbe.

Gabbri chufi gaafas Islán. Ulum takká bae. Borani kan Gabbra kan 'kufára' jed'an, Borana Gabbran jed'. Índid. 'Ín-ann' jed'. Gabbra gaafas kórrat. Meeting-i baase.

All Gabbra at that time were Muslims [a claim not shared by many other Gabbra]. They stem from one origin. These Boran said to these Gabbra 'Become pagans!' [*kufār*, plural of *kāfir*] [you],' [the Boran] said. The Gabbra then took counsel. They had a meeting.

'Ulaa kufaar, ín-baqana,' akan dubat. 'Laf-ti tun dansa, fula gaal laf tan keesa baafnu,' hagi tokko 'ín-kufar' jed'.

'May we not become pagans, let us escape,' like this they argued. 'This land is good, instead of taking the camels out of this land, let us become pagans,' one part said.

Nami tokko 'an laf gaala barbád' d'aga, na egadd'a,' jed'e. Deeme duub, t'urre, t'urre, gale.

One man said, 'I will go and look for a camel country, wait for me.' He went, then tarried, tarried and came back.

'An laf gaala ya-arge. Laf-ti fago, nam iti-imbáu, ammo gandi qabti.' 'Bedele laf gandi gaalan iti-gal, laf-ten dansa keesa nbáan! Nu ínkufara.'

'I have seen a camel country. The land is far, people hardly reach there, and then it has got tse-tse.' 'Instead of the camels going to a land with tse-tse, let us not leave our good country. We become pagans.'

Gabbri akana guyya sun gargar-baat. Hagi tokko 'nu in-kúfar' jete, ol bade. Miigo fi Garri 'nu in-kúfar' jete, ol baat. Hagi kaan asum haft.

This is how the Gabbra then split. One part said, 'We will not become pagans' and got lost to the east. Miigo and Garre said 'We will not become pagans' and left for the east. This part stayed here.

Ta haft tan duub gubbe qodatan. Gargar qodatan gos gosan. Guyyan Gabbri-ti Borana kufart, guyya sun. Guyyan Gabbri-ti íntal Boraana fuut guyya sun. Ammá-lle aki Boráána fuudu dide, akum Islaan fuut.

These ones who stayed were then distributed like bows [?like arrows]. They were divided up tribe by tribe. The day that the Gabbra of the Boran became pagans was that day. The day that the Gabbra married Boran girls was that day. Even now they refused to marry them the Boran way and married them in the Muslim way.

Dubbr Gabbri fuut ammá-lle aki haad hid'an, hid'aa-lle. Ammá-lle mata hag isiin orosá in-cíbran.

The girls the Gabbra marry are even now tied by a rope [not to be understood literally. This is the common way of referring to the Muslim marriage contract, which, however, can only be recognised in Gabbra customs with a lot of good will]. Even now the head is not plaited as long as she is a bride. [Tresses in this region are said to be pagan and of Boran origin. In other areas, for example, among the Swahili, tresses have no such connotations. In northern Kenya, however, devout Muslim women wear their hair loose or in a knot, covered by a thin black veil, *hagogo* or *ogogo*, which is tied around it like a headscarf.]

Guyyaan Borani Gabbr qodat guyya sun hag aaf qodat. Guyya Rendillé-llen aci baat-lle guyya sun. Guyya Rendille-llen dubbri Boraana fuut, dubbr Dambítu, guyya sun. Ka Rendille garan galt.

The day the Boran divided the Gabbra up, they divided up as many as had stayed. That was also the day when the Rendille left to that side [south]. That was the day when also the Rendille married Boran girls, girls of Dambítu. The ones of Rendille went that way [south]. (Gabbra 1)

In other versions the allocation of Gabbra dependants to different Boran clans is, as we shall see below, ascribed to a time after the Gabbra had come back from Iris. Also the split of Gabbra and Rendille, as well as the separation of those Dambítu who are said to have become part of the Ariaal clan Lorogushu from Boran, is supposed to have taken place after the return from Iris.

Let me here only stress that the Gabbra 1 version agrees with Pease, Tuf and Miigo in that the division of Gabbra and Garre has to do with submission to and rejection of Boran supremacy. The history of the scattering of proto-Garre can be summarised in the words of the Tuf version:

Wani kudamma fula sadí gargar kaan. Worri tokkoarma-t haf, tokkó-llen aci godaan, tokko-llen worr isan reefu bantan.

At that time people moved apart to three places. Some people stayed here, some people migrated there [east], and others are those you mentioned earlier [Rendille and Gabbra Malbe].

K'arma-t haf kuni, allén afan Somali im-béeku, afán Boraana beeka. K'aci afan Boraana im-béeku kha Somali mele. Ka aci afan isa qofuma, afan ka lacú im-béeku. Worri sun wolîn-d'alate.

And these who stayed here do not know the Somali language, they know Boran. Those from there [east] do not know Boran, only Somali. Those who stayed there [south-east, i.e. Rendille], their language stands alone, they know neither of the two. [All] these people are siblings [have been born together]. (Tuf)

FOUR HOLY MEN PERFORM MIRACLES ON THE JOURNEY

Warri, abó, ímbaqat. Kara Wajera kan. Wajeran senne karan Af Madou. Arma kae, tullu biyyé tana kae. Laf Sidama amm qubat kan. Ji sadí bul qallu qallawidi kaan.

The people, man, fled. [They took] this road of Wajir [the interview took place north-west of Wajir, in Dabel, in the foothills of the Ethiopian highlands]. After reaching Wajir, [they took] the road to Af Madou [west of the lower Juba]. They left from here, from the hills of this country they left. This country where now the Ethiopians settle. Holy men were consulted about [lit: 'were went to'] the moon which had passed three nights.

Qallawidi qallu afur kaan. Ji sadí bul. 'Hag nu galaana [in]-gén ji kan buu dow!'

They consulted four holy men [*qallu* is the word for the Boran high priests and in a Muslim context also means 'teacher' or 'sheikh']. The moon was three nights old [i.e. would set about 9 p.m.]. 'Until we get to the river, forbid the moon to set!'

Kan laméso. Laf ti bele qabti, karaa kan in-céan, ola, 'maan tanu?' jed'anin qallican. Waan jed'e: 'biyye arradijena, rabbi qadana, musinga hatau.'

The second one. In a land of hunger, the road could not be travelled quickly [could not be run], [it was in the] dry season, 'What will happen with us?' they said to this holy man. What he said: 'Collect earth, we will pray to the Lord [ﺭﺏ], may it become flour.'

'Gaaf laf-ti barite, yokha at fūd'at, gudd isii fūd'ad', musinga taa, fūd'ad',' jed', 'ya rabbi qadad', musinga taa.'

'When the day breaks [literally: 'the land has become morning'], when you take it, take much of it, it will become flour, take it,' he said. 'Pray to the Lord, it will become flour.'

Nami yó sun índiba to gari guddo fūd'ata, tokk diqo fūd'ata, oro faatee-ti, godaan.

People then took trouble, some took much, some took little, loaded it on the [camel-] oxen, then they moved on. (Sakuye 1)

It is worth interrupting the account of the four holy men at this point in order to see how the other versions describe these incidents. The Miigo version has the first holy man making a second moon, to give light all night, instead of preventing the moon from setting. The episode with the flour is described in very similar words.

Qallu 'biyye tan guura' jed'. Nami gari guddisé guurate, nami gari 'nu biyye maa guur' jete waan didigo tokko ínlati, jetét guurate. Baqataní, baqataní. Gaaf Af Madou ga-báán, ín-qubate. Yo hiikan, biyyen tan chuf sagale.

The holy man said, 'Gather this earth.' A part of the people gathered much earth. A part of the people said, 'What for shall we gather sand? Let us collect just a little bit to see,' and they collected it. They fled and fled. When they got to Af Madou, they camped. When they untied [their loads], all the earth was food. (Miigo)

Pease gives the name of the 'sheikh' who 'made the moon which was then 5 days old stand still all night' as Abdi Omar Musa (Bule Gabu of the Ajuran version), and lets the sand which was turned into white *mtama* (Swahili for 'millet') be the sand of the Juba. The sheikh who performed this miracle is here called Abubaker Masherre, the Abokar Mashir of the Ajuran and Miigo versions.

Only Pease includes an 'Aunabe Durr [who] made the 3 year old camel heifers which had never calved give milk' in his list of magical helpers. In the Tuf version poles for house building give milk. In the other versions the number is brought to four by the wonderous crossing of a big river and the emergence of water out of the dry ground at Af Madou. The order of the episodes differs significantly and will be discussed below. Let us first compare the episodes themselves.

The crossing of the river:

For kan irr-imbáán. Im-baqani. Torba ya-obate, eegani, d'aban. 'Beena lala,' jed'an. Yo d'ufan laf-ti onn.

They did not go to [inform the] satellite camps, [i.e. left the satellite camps behind]. They fled. A week was over, [the Boran who had been told to wait a week after Bule Hussein's faked death] waited, missed [them]. 'Let us go and see,' they said. When they came, [all] the land was an abandoned settlement site.

Fardi faan kayan. [. . .] Daw-tu yabaate [. . .]. Qallu tokko-llen bahari na kajelca. Wan deema, wan qabatan, wan qabatan. Fardi kan d'ufe. Eege galaan qabat, fard ya-d'ufe.

The cavalry [literally: 'the horse'] came and followed the footprints. [. . .] They [the refugees] reached the Dawa [Daua, Dawwa] river. One holy man made us pass the water [*bahari* (Swahili) literally: 'sea', i.e. big water]. People went, passed through, passed through. That cavalry came. When the end [of the caravan] passed the water, the cavalry came.

Yo fardi d'ufe galaan kan walti-ga-disan. Bisan gargar in-cítan. Ejjan jete duub womu-llá d'abe, 'beena' jet, fard ufi-tin.

When the cavalry came the river was allowed to close. The water did not separate. They stood there, they missed what to do, they said to each other, 'Let us go [back].' (Miigo)

This episode, of course, reminds us of Moses leading Israel across the Red Sea.[77] The Gabbra 1 version consequently gives the name of the

sheikh who performed this miracle as Musa. Pease writes: 'Sheik Omar
Bahar struck the river [the Juba] with his staff and it divided and they
crossed over the dry bed.' Instead of 'Omar Bahar', the Miigo version has
'Amur Bahar', which, if we allow our linguistic imagination to venture
into Arabic, may be read as 'Lord of the Sea'.

The Sakuye 1 version elaborates this episode in beautiful detail:

*Amm galaan qabacu fed'. Galaan ka gar Kisimayu gudda sun. Isan laf ingárne, an
yá-arge, il-tiyya tan. Galaani mume in-qábu, ballen-isa aki̱ Korondille boru isan
milan d'uftani, hag arma̱.*

Now they wanted to cross the river. That big river near Kisimayu [the Juba].
You have not seen the area, I have seen it, seen it, with my eye[s]. The river is
not small [literally: 'has no smallness'], its width is like from Korondille, from
where you have come walking this morning, to here [approximately 15 km].

*Wani d'alate as kees baan injíran. Markabí-lle chuf kees ín-deem. [. . .] Ganaale
Gudda jed'ani. Kisimayo fi Nyoto lammanin jiddú qabat. [. . .]*

There is no born thing that can go through there. All ships go in there. [. . .]
They call it Big River. It passes between Kisimayo and Nyoto. [. . .]

*Guyya sun duub 'kaani' jennan qallici 'Dawíd tai' jed'an, 'galaan kan gargar kut'
jed'an. Qallawidi sen. Galaan, yo 'bismillahi r-rahmani r-rahimi' jed'é, gargar cita.*

That day it was said, 'Let's move on,' the holy man was told 'Sit and read the
Qur'ān, cut this river apart.' He started with the Qalawidi [a sura]. When he
said, 'In the name of God the merciful and compassionate' the river was torn in
[two] parts.

*Kan-lle aci deeta, kan-lle aci deeta, diríra. Hala hamtu halaan yaqaqabt, hala
hamtu kejirt. 'Halaa sun jjesa' jed'. 'Galaan qabacu dowa' jed'.*

This one retreats over there, this one over there, it is passable. A bad she-camel
passed among the camels, a bad she-camel was in there. 'Kill that camel,' he
said. 'Do not allow it to cross the river,' he said.

*'Yo halaan sun galaan sent, gargar isan kuti, halaa tan gogooraa, keesa baasa!' jed'.
Hojja sun duuba hala sun gorani, duub dawá daqani, dawá daqani, d'ad'abani,
warrána jjesani, halaan kan gaal qabat gul qabat.*

'If that camel gets into the river, [the river] will cut you apart. Kill that camel,
cut its throat, do away with it!' he said. Then they went to cut the throat of that
camel, tried to hold it back, tried to hold it back, failed, tried to kill it with
spears, [but] the camel ran among the [other] camels, crossed [the river] with
them.

*Worre guddan qabaté, worre guddan hafé. Worre guddan haf kan-at, galaani
waltideebie. [. . .] Worri gari gar kana hafe̱ gari yau d'abe̱, guci chufumá ya-ra-
kaate̱, gar d'ufefu warran deeta, im-baqat.*

Many people had crossed, many people had remained. While many people had
remained, the river joined itself again. [. . .] The people who had stayed on this
side had nowhere to go, all their tribe had left them, [and] where they came
from they were afraid of spears, they were escaping. (Sakuye 1)

In the Pease version, the interruption of the train, with some crossing the river and others not, is not caused by mystical events but by faintness of heart.

> ... all got safely across the Juba and reached the Confer country where they settled and prospered. A small party, however, from the Kalia, Banna and Birkaya sections were faint hearted and turned aside at the Juba to make for the coast between Kismayu and Lamu where they settled with the Bajun [-Swahili]. (Pease)

This agrees with Turton (1974: 529) who uses different sources from those used by Pease:

> One group [of the Garre] moved to Giumbo, near the mouth of the river Juba, but after being repeatedly attacked were forced to cross the river and eventually moved north to Merca. A second group of Garre moved to the coast and then crossed to the Dundas islands, where they sought the protection of the Bajun and were eventually absorbed by them.

The last miraculous episode to the discussed here is the emergence of water at the present-day wells of Afmadu which saved the migrants from dying of thirst. In some versions this episode precedes the crossing of the river; in other versions it follows it. The sequence of the episodes is summarised in Table 11.

Table 11   The order of narrative episodes in seven versions of the Long Trek Tradition

	Make moon stand still	Convert sand into food	Cross river	Make sticks or camel heifers give milk	Water at Afmadu
Gabbra 1	1	2	3	–	–
Sakuye 1	1	2	4	–	3
Sakuye 2	–*	–*	1	–*	–*
Sakuye 3	–*	–*	1	–*	–*
Tuf	1	2	–	3	4
Miigo	1	2	3	–	4
Pease	2	4	3	5	–*

* No specific questioning about these episodes.

If we compare the Miigo and Sakuye 1 versions we find an inversion in the order of crossing of the river and the Afmadu water. This is because in the Miigo version the river is the Dawa, while Sakuye 1 speaks of the Juba. The Miigo version thus makes the journey start from north of the Dawa and then proceed south to southern West Jubaland. The Sakuye 1 version, however, gives the Moyale area as the starting point and has south-east as the general direction of migration, so that Afmadu is reached before the river, in this case the Juba.

Before we find out exactly what happened at Afmadu, let us examine two more Sakuye versions at the crossing of the river – these are rather different from the preceding accounts. One does not mention the Boran as the foe from whom people fled, but a mysterious Sanga Baale, a gelded steed called Baale.[78] In the second version there is not even an enemy, the people being driven by pure wanderlust. This version is also remarkable in that the Juba is crossed from the east to the west, contrary to all other versions.

The place where the river was crossed is given as Malka Gaala ('camel ford') east of Kisimayo (Sakuye 3).

Gaafi sun, gaaf sun Sanga Baale jed'ani. Sangaan Baale worr sun ín-hadde duub. Worri suni gad-hadde Korondille gennáni laf duute. Eeee worrumaanum namumaanum laf duute.

That time is called the time of Sanga Baale. The steed Baale fought those people. Those people [= the steed Baale] come for war, they reached Korondille and intruded into the country. Yes, these very people, these very men intruded into the country.

Nami dullate. Nami ciise dullate. Nam dullate sun akanumat -lafti cité- laf seene. Laf Garri fulá amm Sakuyeen jil tolfata, halkan yo gaali marat kokken gaala dibbesi hobobsu korbeyi índ'agean. [Aki Gorei][79]

People prayed. People lay down and prayed. Those people who prayed – the earth opened – entered the earth like this. In the Garre country where now the Sakuye make [their] pilgrimage, at night when the camels turn [to sleep on their other side] one hears camel bells ringing and billy goats bleating.

Gaafas gaaf ini arti qaqabate, ga-baqat. Sangá Baale ammá-lle faan-tisa ammá-lle ín-jirt. Dakhá gubbá cift. Faan gaala ta gaafasi.

That was the time when they passed that way, they came fleeing. Even now the footprints of the steed Baale exist. They are on top of the rock, [together with] footprints of camels of that time.

Sanga Baale: fard ka koora lamá. [Namá iti-irre taa?] Nama namaan hadda. Eee, nyaabi. Nam hojja gaala gagayu. Worr sun ínhamate.

The steed Baale: a horse with two saddles. [Do people sit on there?] People fight people. Yes, enemies. Human beings, now, big like camels. Those people became evil.

[Waan sun deetani galaan gataakani?] Ee, galaan gataakan. Galaan duub gargar- kute. Worrini gargar-kute sun gaafas Hawiyya, guyya sun. Anin ya-arge, worr handaar isa dedeera ka Rendill fakat, ka ammá-lle wo hodd'ate waan aki macallá goga hori wan didiqo tokko duub mormat hidd'ata.

[Was it that that people fled from and crossed the river?] Yes, they crossed the river. They cut the river apart. Those people who cut it at that time were Hawiyya, [that day]. I have seen them, people with long fringes [who twist the weft threads of the end of their mantle sheets into fringes instead of sewing seams] like the Rendille, and who tie something small like a leather amulet to their necks.

[Laf Safara kejira?] Safara kúúúno, Háwiyya, kan kúúno galaan sun gam jir, ammátan isumá galaan gaqabaté. [. . .] Gaal isá-llen akum gaal Rendilla wan didiqa.

[Do they live in Somalia?] [They are] those Somali [far away], Hawiyya, those over there, beyond that river, now, [then] they have crossed to this side. Even their camels are like the Rendille camels, [something] small.

'Abó, d'iro tiyya, gaal durri, isan aciit nu irragalle, gaal durri malkaan isan aqbataní baddaní tan, hala tokko nu hafe halan takka sun it hore laf irr-dabre. D'iro, ammátan gaal nu kenna' nu n-jete. Worri sun worr akana. Worri Rendille irragalte Rendillí.

'Man, gentlemen, [of] the camels which, when you left us there, the camels with which you crossed the ford, which were lost, only one camel cow remained with us, that only she-camel we bred until [these camels] became too many for the country. Gentlemen, now give us camels,' they said to us. These people are such people. The people from whom the Rendille came.

A link seems to exist between the ghost camels under the ground, the fabulous beings who leave footprints in the surface of a rock and the cult of *ayaana*, a concept derived from the Boran 27-day week, in which each day is associated with an animal species. *Ayaana* thus also means animal spirit or spirit animal and the states of possession they cause. These widespread beliefs in spirit animals are linked syncretically to the veneration of the Islamic Sheikh Hussein (Shek Husen) whose tomb at the eponymous place in Bali, southern Ethiopia, attracts pilgrims from afar. This, however, is not the place to elaborate on this complex of ideas.

The Sakuye 2 version makes a similar connection between the ancestors of the Rendille, who in their turn are the ancestors of most Sakuye clans, and Hawiyya Somali. It specifies these Hawiyya as Biimal (Bi'mal), over-looking that Bi'mal are not Hawiyya but Dir. Hawiyya and Dir, however, are genealogically close to each other, because their eponymous ancestors are brothers and the sons of Irrir, who, according to Somali genealogical tradition, is one of the sons of Somal. (These genealogies, of course, are not to be taken as being beyond historical criticism. However, they provide a clue as to which groups the Somali themselves believe to be similar or more closely related than others.)

Gos tokko Biimal jed'aniu, Biimal kan gargarbahan, Biimal kan keesa ga-baate [. . .] 'Sakuye' jecun, eege sun malle, guyyá sun 'Rendille'. Rendillen sun-lle eege worrî garán ga-bae maqá sun iti-bae malle, worrî guyyá sun Biimal.

One tribe called Biimal, this Biimal split, they [the Sakuye] came from inside these Biimal. If one says 'Sakuye', [that came up] only afterwards, at that time they were 'Rendille'. Even those Rendille only got that name after they came to this side, at that time they were Biimal.

Rendille jecun – afan Safara fi Rendille woltiduudan – 'Rendille' jecun, 'rer' hojja jed'ani, 'worr' yo jed'an 'rer'. Worr 'rer did' jecun, 'Rendille'.

The so-called Rendille – the languages of the Somali and the Rendille are inter-woven – to say 'Rendille', when they say 'rer', a 'settlement' is called 'rer'. The people who are said to 'hate the settlement' are the 'Rendille'.

Gaal forá godaane, intal dubra kejirt, gurba luba kejira, ín-godaane. Malka Go'-win jed' ani fula worri sun godaane, gaafas qabate, Gowin lafa beek, arman qabate.

The camel satellite camp moved, a girl is in there, a warrior boy is in there, they shifted. The Ford of Gowin [Gobuin, upriver from Kismayu] it is called, the place from where those people moved, that day they crossed, Gowin is a place, you have to know, they crossed to this side.

Lafá ya-ga-baate, 'olum deema, fulum durrat deema,' nam iti-ergani d'ad'aban. 'Worri kun ya rer diide, yaala baha,' jed'ani.

They left [literally: 'came out of'] the country, 'Go upward, go forward,' they sent somebody to them and could not reach them. 'Those people have rejected the settlement, leave them alone,' they said.

Intal tan akanumá fuude. In-qubate. Lafti sun Korren amma achi jirtu sun gaafas aci in-jírtu, chuf galaan kan qubat. Korre tana woltiduude.

They married the girl just like this. They made camp. That country where the Samburu are now, at that time they were not there, they all settled at this river. [The interview took place near Merti on the middle reaches of the Waso (= Ewaso Ngiro) river, well to the east of Samburu District.] They mixed up with these Samburu.

Wol-haadde, wol-haadde, wol-ga-deebie, wol-in-qubate. Nam takkaa tae. Afan wol-in-d'agae. Gaafi worri kun gurr kan qoorat gurre qoora aki Rendille qabtu kan, gaafas.

They raided each other, raided each other, came back to each other, settled together. They became one people. They understood [= learned] each other's language. That was the time when those people made holes in their earlobes like those pierced ears the Rendille have now. [i.e. the Rendille adopted the custom of piercing the earlobes from the Samburu].

Rendill jecun guyya kana Sakuyé-llen gaafas Rendillum-tan. Gargar im-báán. Hawiyya balbal-ti isiin keesa ga-galte Biimal jed'ani.

If today one says Rendille, then also the Sakuye then were just these Rendille. They had not separated. In Hawiyya the gate [clan] they came out of is called Biimal. (Sakuye 2)

In the fuller versions of the tale the next episode introduces a remark-able female who, however, only appears for a regrettably short span.

Af Madou-in dubr, intal mid'aadu, takká infúún, afan issin kun chuf doti jed'an, garrac, cile. Intal akas mid'aadu takk in-d'ágein. Af Madou fula isii-genane lafti bariit.

Af Madou [Black Mouth][80] was a virgin, a beautiful girl, she had never been married, a girl with a black mouth, like soot [or charcoal]. A girl beautiful like this had never been heard of. Wherever one got near her it was [like] daybreak. (Sakuye 1)

[Qallic] tokkó-lle 'deebu, laf tan ola, Waaqi roobu, akanan bisan in-jírani, Waaq nu qadad'!' jed'ani.

They said to one holy man, 'There is thirst, drought, may God rain, there is no water. Implore God for us!'

[. . .] Deebu ya-d'uft. Ji-lle, ya lafti ya-bariite, yafagaatan. Qallici wan jed'e: 'Af Madou, atin dawi baate, yodooté-lle rer Janna taat. Abbaan, haada, goci, hori namá-lle ín-d'abani.' Dawi isiin baate.

The thirst came. The moon [?had set], the day broke, they had gone far. The holy man said: 'Af Madou, the oracle has appointed you (literally: 'you have come out of reading [the Qur'ān]'), even if you die, you will belong to the people of Paradise. Father, mother, the tribe, animals and people are about to be missed.' She had come out of the oracle.

'Ha arm doft, dooti. Duub în-dooti, ya Sin iti-deebifna'. Abba d'uf, duub, haada-llé yaaman. 'Intal tante dawi itim-baate, duub în-dooti,' jed'an. 'Goci tun deebun rawate duub gocin in-jiraati, intalti duub rer Jannat', jed', qallici.

'May she hit here and die. As she will die, let us read the Ya Sin [Sura 36, the Sura for dying people] to her.' The father then came, also the mother was called: 'The oracle has appointed your daughter, so she will die,' it was said. 'The thirst is finishing the tribe, [but] then the tribe will continue to exist, and the girl will belong to the people of Paradise,' he said, the holy man.

'Af Madou,' jed'ani, yaaman, maqaan-isiitu. 'Af Madou, Af Madou!' 'Au!' 'Amm daw-di si iti-baate, goci tante horinf isá deebun in-jíratan, yo atin arm in-dóf. Si in-dósani, atí-llen ín-doot. Atin ammo er Jannat, yo doot Ya Sin si-iti-deebisan.'

'Af Madou,' they called her name. 'Af Madou, Af Madou!' 'Au! [= here I am]' 'Now the oracle has appointed you, your tribe and their livestock are dying of thirst, if you do not hit here. It is not hidden from you, you will die. But you will belong to the people of Paradise, when you die the Ya Sin will be read to you.'

'Fula goci tiyy baddu, ka goci tiyy hobatu, anin aná kubale, ín-dai' jed'. Woni kan 'mindisa' wan akana qar gab, 'mindisa' jed'ani, akan dane, 'tau', duub bisan 'but' jed'ani, cean.

'Where my tribe perishes, my tribe is finished, I agree, I will hit,' she said. That thing, a chisel, that thing with a tip called 'housebuilder' [a PRS word, meaning the instrument for making the holes in the ground into which the poles of the house are stuck], she hit [the ground] like this, 'tau', then the water said 'but', sprang up.

Amm barbá, in-yáátu, in-dúúmani, ado gar feed'ani, ín-d'ugani, in-dúúmani, duuwan-lle eegi isiin doft ya-jirátani, duub 'Af Madou' tan maqa iti-baasan, harre jed'ani.

Now the pasture is lush, they do not move, it does not get exhausted, they drink from pools wherever they want, [the pools] do not get finished, [the pools] have always been there, since she has hit there, then this 'Af Madou' [today a town] was named [after her], a pond, (they call it). (Sakuye 1)

Shorter versions of this episode are also contained in Miigo, Pease and Tuf. The Tuf version claims that the girl Af Madou stemmed from the

Tuf section of Garre, while Pease gives Oordek as her section which is a part of Kuranjo.

THE PENDULUM SWINGS BACK

Most versions of this tale mention Af Madou, i.e. Af Madu in Somalia, as one point on the journey and even claim that the trek miraculously crossed the Juba to its eastern bank. All these traditions, however, stem from groups that today live in northern Kenya, and all of them have some account of a subsequent migration back to the west. In the case of the Garre this return was gradual and incomplete. In fact, many Garre, the so-called Garre Kofar, still live in Somalia.

> The Confer country lies beyond Rahanwein in the coastal area, the principal Gurreh towns or villages being Shan and Musser on the Owdegli i.e. the lower reaches of the Shebelle river where it runs parallel with and close to the sea coast between Mogadiscio and Merca.
>
> When well established and prosperous the Gurreh penetrated into Rahanwein and sent trading safaris and settlers further inland until they reached Lugh and Dolo and re-entered the Gurreh district [today Mandera District] and worked up the Daua district [sic: actually 'river'] again, trading mostly but also making settlements and shambas.[81] Finally they got back to Wujili where Sheik Abdi Hiloli started a settlement and traded with the Boran: his grave is there, and when these settlers reached the upper Daua and Wujili they met the Gabbra section of camel owners who had refused to follow Sheik Bule and recognized them by their camel brands and by their Gurreh section names Banna, Birkaya etc. which they still retained, also by the fact that they still preserved some Gurreh customs and that their women, unlike the Boran, wore 'hagogo', i.e. covered the head in the mohamedan fashion.
>
> The Gurreh count 4 or 5 generations to the time when these traders and early settlers re-entered Gurreh district, say 120 years [i.e. 1800]. (Pease)

Apart from farmers and traders, Garre livestock nomads also move back and forth between Somalia and Kenya. I met Garre herd owners from Kofar ('Confer') at Gurar near Moyale. Let us leave the Garre at these various occupations and examine the link between this migrational history and the ethnogenesis of the Sakuye. We left the ancestors of the Sakuye at the bank of the Juba, where they had gone from Af Madou, cut off from those migrants who had reached the eastern shore by the waters that had suddenly closed in front of them again, and with the enemy at their backs.

> *Waso ful deefate, kara Waso baqat. Inúm-godaane laf nami in-jíru̯. Gaal qaba, loon qaba, ree qaba, chuf ín-godaan fulum chuf godaan. Laf atin d'aget tan; karaa ini gale kara Garba Tullaa kan, ka Garbaa.*
>
> They turned their faces to Waso, they fled [along] the road of Waso. They moved about [freely], there were no people in the land. They had camels, cattle, smallstock, they moved everything, moved everywhere. It is that country you have heard about; the road they took was the road to Garba Tulla, to Garba.

[Worri sun worr Gaal Ilmiti?] Qaal Ilmi jed'ani, abbaan isá Ilm. Qalluni ka deemuni kan. Kalle Galwein Hussein jed'ani. Hayyun galen jar laman, kan qallu, kan hayyu.

[Were those people the people of Gaal Ilmi?] They say Qaal Ilmi, his father was Ilmi. The *qallu* who led them was this one. Somebody else was called Gaalwen Hussein. The kings [*hayyu*] with whom they went were two: this one a *qallu*, that one a *hayyu*.

Worri kara kan deeme. Kara Siolo imbáánee, armumaan d'anqar lafti kara inqábtu. Galaani Waso kuni mirga d'ufe, jal godaane. Addu díatu godaanan. Godaani yennan laf Rendilla d'ufe.

The people moved along that road. They did not take the road to Isiolo, [they stayed] on this side, [it was] bush, the country was pathless. That river Waso came from the right side and they moved west [along it]. They moved when the sun was going to set. They moved, then they came to Rendille country.

Laf feed'ata. Faan Rendilla ka lubá ka salfa deeme arge. Worri-lle Rendilli-lle Korrélle agart. Yawaldúbbis. Ati nyaaba, sí-hadda, jed', Korreen.

They were looking for a country. They saw footprints of Rendille warrior scouts. The people also saw Rendille and Samburu. [The informant henceforth speaks of Samburu only, because he apparently noticed that the existence of Rendille at this stage of the tale does not fit in with his own account of their later ethogenesis.] 'You are enemies, I will raid you,' said the Samburu.

'Na nhaddín' jed' wayaa adi mataa irr-qabat. Wayaa adi hid'at. Warrán mataa irr keiyat. 'At manre?' 'An kedi, gos in-qábu, gos barbaddá.' Woltid'ufe duub. 'Ati maan?' 'An Islaan.'

'Do not raid me!' he said, [and] held a white sheet above his head. He tied the white sheet [as a turban]. He put his spear on his head. 'What are you?' 'I am [a participant of] the long trek, I have no tribe, I am looking for a tribe.' So they came closer together. 'What are you?' 'I am a Muslim.'

'Islaanin kanke maan?' 'Kitāb kan qaba, qallu an.' 'Ati gosi maan?' 'An qallicini Qaal Ilmi, kitaabi tiyá-llen kan.' Kanlle ya-dubbat. 'Gaalwen' jed'. Abba gaal gugurda jecu, beek. 'Gaalwen ka eenu?' jed'. 'Ka Hussein' jed', 'Hawiyya' jed'.

'What does your Islam consist of?' 'I have got this book, I am a sheikh.' 'What tribe are you?' 'I am Sheikh Qaal Ilmi, and this is my book.' Also the other one speaks up. 'Gaalwen,' he said. That is: the owner of 'big camels', you know. 'Gaalwen [son] of whom?' he said. 'Of Hussein,' he said, 'Hawiyya,' he said.

'Hawiyya im-béenu. Yo an si in-hánne waa lam tai' jed'e, 'atin Islan ya-si-arge, hori an gorrae nyaad'! Yo atin in-yááne si-hadda' jed'ani.

'We do not know [about] Hawiyya. If I shall not raid you, do two things,' he said, 'you are a Muslim, I have seen [you], eat the animals I have slaughtered! If you do not eat them I shall raid you,' it was said.

It is forbidden for Muslims to eat any animal slaughtered by a non-Muslim, even in the proper way. The act of eating meat which in this sense is unclean حرام, *haraam*, 'forbidden' here is seen as symbolic of renouncing Islam.

'Gurr qorad'! gurr kiyy illal, lacu huri kees naqad'!' jed', 'mukh! Yo at kan lamán tolcite gos kiyya si n-háddu' jed! Hori gorraee, nyaacise. Yasodate, worri gudda, mume in-qábu.

'Pierce your ear [lobes], look at my ears, pierce both and put wood into [the holes]!' he said. 'If you do these two things, [you are] my tribe, I shall not raid you,' he said. He slaughtered an animal and made them eat it. They were afraid, the people [Samburu] were many, there was nothing small about them.

'Ya-ogolad'e' jed', 'qubad" jed, 'at gosa.' Dubr aci aci wal-fuud'. Taum tae guddate worrí. Kitaab kaan-lle inúm-qabt. Guddate, 'olki uf-irra-dowu dandeta?' Worrá-lle ini-lle labarrate large [= ya-barrate ya-arge].

'I consent' [in Somali], he said. 'Settle!' he said, 'you are [from now on] of the tribe.' On that very spot they married each other's girls. The people stayed and stayed and became many. All the time they had that book. They had become many. 'Can you now defend yourself ? [literally: 'keep war away from yourself ?']' He [the Samburu] had learned about the people, had seen them.

'Na rra-godaana!' jed'. Korren guratti laf ufí-teeti. Saaku datte. Saaku ta amma Marsabit jed'ani. Gul d'ufte 'kitaabu kana indeeminin sí-hadda', jed'. Sodaate gaar tokko jal kae, gaar kana Rendilli muuda iti-eebifata, guyya chuf sorio iti-qallan.

'Move away from me!' he said. The black Samburu [as opposed to Ariaal and Rendille] stayed themselves in the country. They [the future Rendille] moved to Saaku, the Saaku which is now called Marsabit. [The Samburu] followed them. 'Do not go with this book [the Qur'an], [otherwise] I will raid you.' They were afraid and deposited it at the foot of a mountain. To that mountain the Rendille go on pilgrimage, they always sacrifice there.

Gaarini gar ammo yoyu Isiolo deemani, Logologo deemani kulla tokko gaari ejja, gar sun jir. Arti sun gam. Sorio iti-qallt. Iti-eebifat, fula kitaabi durri kayan.

The mountain is where now, if one goes to Isiolo, to Logologo, on a plain there stands a mountain, there it is. Here, on this side. They sacrifice there. They pray there, where before they deposited the book. (Sakuye 1)

In Rendille tradition there are similar tales of Muslim origin and of the Samburu forcing the ancestral Rendille to abandon their Islamic customs. Most emphatically such traditions are volunteered by recent converts to Islam. Also the heterogeneity of these traditions raises doubts about their historical value. The Qur'an is said to have been deposited on Mount Kenya or on Mount Moile, south-west of Laisamis,[82] or to have been eaten by a calf so that henceforth the guts of slaughtered animals had to be used for divination instead of the Qur'an,[83] or to have been burned by the Samburu, a tradition we shall examine in greater detail.

The story goes that a set of nine Somali brothers came with their camel satellite herds. They had lost contact with their settlement[84] and decided to marry Samburu girls. Eight beautiful girls were selected for them, the youngest brother being considered not yet ready for marriage. The marriages were concluded under the same condition as in the account Sakuye 1, namely that the bridegrooms had to renounce Islam.

While the older brothers were in their houses on their wedding night, the Samburu came and burned the book, which was kept in the arbour used for prayer.[85] In another version it is only the eldest brother who wishes to marry while the youngest objects in vain because he regards such a marriage as unpropitious and disadvantageous.[86]

Maantiye Rendille Dafara ka-soo-kharad'e, eti tēn̄e magard'i, Ḥala Ḥaldayan yimi, a gaali foor, lafidie, obori ma-la-khabin, inti li-nokhti ma-la-khabo. Goorat maanti lasoo-fird'e is-la-dīn̄e. Dafara to sagga i-goote, gaalo leimaten. San̄ka goobiye Nyabárrach, a Koorro, Ḥali Ḥaldayan ki-jiro, inám ladaan̄e.

When the Rendille split from the Somali, I do not know who [which clan] that was, they came to Mount Marsabit, they were a camel satellite camp, they stayed, did not have women, did not have where to go back to. They came as refugees; there was mutual raiding. Some Somali had separated [from their main body] and come with a camel herd. On a later day they asked the lineage Nyabárrach, who are Samburu settling on the Marsabit Highland, for a girl.

Iname la Muslim me, a Koorro. Ki nuchul iyeye (inanki nuchul; ki teiyane inám daan̄e): 'Koorro walān̄ iche inno siisso mele, id'a ka ma-dakhamnó, ili baatenyo ki-jirto la ma-garranni, kaale inánta adisán!'

And the girl is not a Muslim, she is Samburu. The small one said (the youngest brother; it was the first-born who asked for the girl): 'The Samburu will not give us anything, we shall not prosper this way, further we do not know where our people are, come, do not marry this girl!'[87]

The prospective bridegroom, however, is not held back by this argument and even the view of the future in-laws that the Qur'an is sorcery and to be abandoned is seemingly accepted. (From Nyabarrach's point of view such an equation is plausible: the Qur'an is a material item, obviously used in ritual contexts, handled with circumspection, believed – not only by mistrustful outsiders but also within popular Islam itself – to have inherent powers, not integrated into his own Samburu legitimate ritual and consequently sorcery and potentially harmful for him).

Inám ladaan̄e inám chi la-daan̄e-ka, Nerugusho man̄ yidan̄ya, Nyabarrach man̄ yidan̄ya: 'Tibaato khabtan' yidan̄. Tibaato la ti iche khabto a kitaab. 'A-rogna' li-dan̄. Derka inam lasiiche.

They asked for the girl, [and] when they asked for the girl, Nerugusho [= Rendille pronunciation of Lorogusho, the Samburu phratry to which the lineage Nyabarrách belongs] said, Nyabarrách said: 'You have got sorcery.' And that sorcery, if they [are said to] have it, is the book. 'We will throw it away,' they said. So they were given the girl.[88]

In this version[89] by former Councillor Arbele, the Qur'an is then kept in the house, the only house in the settlement, because there was only one married woman, and only women have houses, in spite of the agreement to discard it. One evening, when the herds are returning and everybody is busy at the enclosures, the Samburu fill the house with firewood, pour oil over the house and set it alight, along with the Qur'an. But instead of burning down properly the house emits quantities of smoke so that soon the settlement is filled by complete darkness and despair. The youngest brother, who from the beginning has been sceptical about the match, comes running with something like a spotlight that enables him to see only in front of him ('torch' is the Kenyan English word for spotlight: *id'i tooch ort-is kaldach on arga*). This limited source of light enables him to get hold of a young female sheep and cut its throat. However, this does not improve the light, so for another victim he runs to the calves' enclosure and takes a bull calf. When he kills the bull calf and burns the two sacrifices, the smoke lifts and the daylight reappears. On inspection, the shining object the boy had in his hand proves to be a glowing piece of the Qur'an which had jumped out of the fire.

Being a leading elder and a far travelled man, Arbele knows that this account of Rendille origin is most common among their Muslim neighbours and contradicts the different clan origin myths of the Rendille themselves.[90] He discusses the authenticity of this account himself and gives one point in favour of it: the sacrifices mentioned in this myth neatly link to present-day Rendille ritual practice.

> *Suben-tas a suben-ti worran Rendille naabo ka-khallo, suben-ta uu gorreñe. Heer la-gorreñe, ñeerron la: u la a Nyabarrach, a Kooro, goob Lebokholle ileñ, goob Orboya [?. . .] Heer la id'i goorat ínam yidañya: a-la-guba.   Khallinye on la-ka bañchá, de la-guba.*

That young female sheep is the one the Rendille usually slaughter at the *naabo* [the elders' assembly place in the centre of the settlement], it is that sheep whose throat he cut. An ox is killed by the young people [by the candidates for circumcision, *midir*, in the Thursday year before the year of circumcision, which is one Friday year in two], and he [the ox] is [from] Nyabarrach, he is Samburu, the lineage of Lebokholle and so, of Orboya. [. . .] This ox is done like before the boy did: it is burned. Only hide strips [*khalli*, to be worn as bracelets or around ankles or knees by the participants in a sacrifice] are taken from it, then it is burned. (Dadio Arbele)

That this sacrificial animal for an important Rendille age-set ceremony must come from the Samburu lineage Nyabarrach, even if it has to be brought from afar and costs dear, and that this lineage is identical with the owners of the sacrifice in the tale rendered are taken as corroborative evidence for this tradition.

The piece of the Qur'an is said to have been kept by the subclan Durolo of Nañagan until that clan was nearly annihilated by the warriors of the Ethiopian Boran many generations ago at Kirinyal, south-west of Laisamis.

There is no Rendille tradition about a Qur'an formerly in their possession and disposed of in this way, however, which points to the locality described above by Boku Sora (Sakuye 1).[91] This Sakuye account goes on to state that after this incident the Rendille, newly emerged out of this connubium, prospered and multiplied.

'An Rendill' yetét, duub maqá baafat. Balbal of chuf gosisit ta durri taan dahatét. 'Ya durri wolin-fuudne wolin-háánu, nu sodda,' wal-kees qubat. Amm duub Korrén gam sun qubata, nam gan kan qubatu Réndill.

He said [meaning: they said] 'I am Rendille', so he had got a name. They called themselves by all the [earlier mentioned] lineage names. 'We have formerly married each other, we do not raid each other, we are affines,' they settled together. But the Samburu settled to that side [South-west] and those who settled to this side [North-east] are Rendille.

Yo Boran haddan walín-haddan male, walin-háddu. Akas 'Saaku, Saaku' jed'-anin, Saaku baaten, akan. Sakuye-llen armá galte, Sakuyén tan.

When they raid the Boran they raid together, but they do not raid each other. So they said, 'Saaku, Saaku [= Marsabit],' they appeared at Marsabit, like this. And the Sakuye came to here, the Sakuye are these [same people].

[. . .] Nam tokko ka gaal qofum nyaatu ijjesani, jenan laf sun inténnu jetét garán ga-galt.

One man who used to eat a camel alone was killed and then [his followers] said, 'We do not stay in that country' and came to this side. (Sakuye 1)

THE SPLIT BETWEEN RENDILLE AND SAKUYE

With the appearance of the legendary glutton who ate whole camels by himself, we close the chapter of Rendille ethnogenesis and enter that of the fission between the Rendille and the present-day Sakuye, or more precisely those Sakuye who are not Miigo, because the Miigo only joined them later.[92]

The story of Haara or Aara, the camel eater, exists in nearly identical versions among the Rendille, the Gabbra and the Sakuye. I start with one of the fuller accounts, that by Rooba Kurawa.[93]

The Sakuye separated from the people because one man had died. That man was Aara of the Reer Rug of Worr Furá.[94] These Worr Furá also exist among the Gabbra; all these Gaar are Worr Furá.[95]

One man became strong. Also his size was not human, it was bigger. And he became very bad. Now, you have seen the warriors of the Rendille who walk alone [do not join the settlements], haven't you? He went with those warriors. One day they slaughtered a camel, not a head of smallstock, a camel, a young bull of five, six years. One side of the camel was eaten by the warriors, the other side by him alone.

I did not see that, you know, I just heard it from my father and also from the Rendille. I just tell you what I heard; it is not something I have seen.

That man eats camels. One side of each camel is his: the others do not even try to get a share of it, they just roast it for him. That is his habit.

The camels came to the Korolle waterholes [in Rendille country] and rested there. Among these camels there was a she-camel, a *sarma*. A *sarma* is a camel heifer which the mother's brother gives to a man who has killed an enemy and comes to his gate. The Gabbra, we ourselves [the Sakuye] and the Rendille, we camel people have got such *sarma*.[96] He said, 'Come, get hold of that she-camel, slaughter it for us!'

And the heifer was red, so red. She had never given birth. Beautiful. 'Ai, how can one slaughter and eat the *sarma* of your maternal uncle?'[97] [Aara replied,] 'The [ceremonial] rope has been tied to its neck by a human being and its mother is just a camel. My uncle can tie the rope tomorrow to some other camel. What is the thing you call "custom" because of which you refuse to slaughter the camel for us? Come and get hold of the camel!'

The warriors became angry. One cannot refuse Aara's orders and so the camel was slaughtered. The camel herd to which it had belonged went back to the settlement after the stay at the waterholes. All elders joined in the lamentation. 'Now that Aara has eaten a *sarma*, the next thing he will eat will be a human being. Do away with Aara!' 'We cannot kill Aara with spears, so how can we kill him?'

After he had eaten this she-camel, he went to sleep at sunset. 'Tomorrow he will not get up before noon.[98] Put ten spears into the fire, the ones with the long metal tips, pierce him with five from this side, five from that side, then run away!' [So they did.] When Aara cried out he knocked down and killed with one movement of the hand three men who were standing on one side and then two on the other side. And he kicked with his feet and killed more. Anyone kicked or hit by him did not rise again. And Aara himself died too.

The clan the Rendille call D'ubsahai, Worr Fura, Aara's clan, said, 'We shall not stay in the country where Aara died. Even if we get lost, even if we find hardship, we shall turn our faces towards the place where long ago we came from and go back there. We shall not stay where Aara died.'

This informant is not alone among the Sakuye in believing that the 'Rendille', and thus the ancestors of the Sakuye, originally came from an area farther east which they shared with the future Garre (Mandera District). Among the Rendille this tradition is only shared by the Odoola, for whom such a connection can also be shown in terms of clan history. In contrast, the most senior elements of Rendille society, the nuclei of the two moieties, point to mythical sites of origin (emergence from the ground) within present Rendille territory. It is this tradition of eastern origins which prompts Rooba Kurawa to say that the emigrants wanted to go 'where long ago we came from'. By this he means that they were heading east.

One clan the Sakuye call Worr Suya, with whom Fur frequently intermarry, said, 'We cannot stay in the place left by the clan of our maternal uncles.' Of the Fur clan itself many stayed and people who were dependent on them stayed with them. That is how the clans split. The name 'Sakuye' means people from Marsabit [Saaku, Saakhu] and was brought up by the Boran. At that time they were just called Rendille. Then the people who migrated from Marsabit were called Sakuye. That is how the Sakuye came from the midst of the Rendille.

The element of this tale which is relevant to our historical reconstruction is the claim that the bulk of the Sakuye have split from the early Rendille. The reasons for and circumstances of this split appear to be somewhat fantastic or at least embellished. We might well doubt that Aara here stands for a historical figure, and if he does, we might ask ourselves whether attributes like his physique and the size of his appetite or even the fact that he is thought of as a single person reflects a historical reality or rather a pattern of folk tales. As the tradition of this split and of the reasons for it can be found in an identical form among the Rendille and the Gabbra (also with reference to the Fur element among the Gabbra), we can at least conclude that this story is non-controversial, presumably old, and that its basic content must be historical.

Rendille informants add more details to this story. The camel, a reward for killing an enemy, aiti magañ, by the consumption of which Haara (Aara) provoked his death, is said to have belonged to the Mirgichán lineage of D'ubsañai.[99] The killing is described in very colourful terms:

'Take out the swords, bring the spears, let us put them into the fire!' They heated and heated the fire until the iron became hot, burning, red.
[Comment of a listener:] 'The gentleman is going to be killed.'
One sword was introduced through the clavicle pit, one through the anus. He roared, and when he roared the camels at the Lake [Turkana] stampeded.[100] He hit the people who had pierced him with spears with his feet and broke them. He roared like God when He thunders. 'Ai, what has killed Haara?' it was said.[101]

The reason for the dispersal of Fur, Haara's clan,[102] is attributed, logically but not quite compellingly, to Haara's usefulness as a herdsman and protector and to the sudden panic at his loss:

'Ai, gáaai Haara wae málawaina?' Fúre tad'éñ. 'Chi nah Haara wáine, chie gélla.' Haara, góorat ínenyeti hóölaka inenyet riba. Hóöla u góya tólolo ínenyet mañéllo. Oot us sóojito gédiye gárñiñañ dirñisa jita, ñóölañi D'ubsañáie us ón oota. "Gaali Háara wae málawaina?" tidáñ dérka seleibáabate.

'Ai, the camels which lost Haara, aren't they lost?' Fur said. 'If we lost Haara, we will go to the enemies [join other tribes].' Haara as a herdsman had protected the people. Livestock among which he stands, people [raiders] cannot get. He pulls more thornbushes for fencing than your car,[103] he alone fences the stock of D'ubsañai. They said, 'The camels which lost Haara, aren't they lost?' and scattered at random.[104]

D'ubsañai succeeded in preventing only two people of Fur from leaving. All the others went to the 'Boranto' [Gabbra] and Sakuye. Fur is said occasionally to produce people of extraordinary wildness and strength to this very day.[105]

The Rendille thus split into two factions, one of which was later to become the majority of the Sakuye. Sakuye ethnogenesis, however, apart from out-migration from Rendille, consisted of two more steps: the fusion of the ex-Rendille, i.e. the Sakuye proper, with the Miigo Sakuye and the alliance with and ritual subordination to the Boran, which was accompanied by a shift of language.

As the founder of the Miigo Sakuye the traditions mention one Hassan Buro who was forced to flee from his people, the Garre, because of an offence.

> So he came to this side; in his own country the Garreñ had said that he had made a girl heavy. So they had tormented him; he sorted out his camels by the name of Harrau[106] and got lost.[107]

Other versions deny that Hassan Buro had a whole herd of camels:

> A single man was chased away from the Garre, just one. He was expelled and got a limping she-camel which was left at an abandoned camp site. I have only heard it [. . .]. Even if it is a lie, I just tell you this talk of the people of old, be aware of that! At a place from which people had moved away he found a limping she-camel.
>
> That man had made a girl pregnant. Among us, the people of the mat,[108] formerly a man who had made a girl pregnant could not walk abouit in the country. He would be chased away, get lost, die. He knew that the limping she-camel was at that place from where people had moved. When he got there, it was standing there. He drove it with him. So he had a she-camel.
>
> The place was called Lensayu, that hill south of Korondille. He came there with his she-camel. It had no milk. He collected *tunale* [R: *surr*, the honey of a small fly] and bee honey. There was plenty of it. The wild fruit easily filled a large milk container. He had arrows, a quiver, an axe, all that. (Sakuye 3)
>
> The country has rock caverns where rain water gathers. He put the honey down there and left it. The country had fresh vegetation and the she-camel could graze anywhere nearby. When he came back one day, the honey had disappeared. There were no people in the area. He had left the honey in the cave and how he could not find it. He wondered and looked around and found wax which had been spat out on the ground. (Sakuye 2)
>
> There were footprints of small children, small children like these here of mine. One adult was with them. They used to drink water in the cave and did not move far from there. He looked to this side and to that side and did not find anything. He climbed the glittering rock [granite] and saw the reflection of eyes, a human being. 'I have got a woman!' 'I have got a man!' 'Come out!' She came out. She was a daughter of Boran. (Sakuye 3)

According to the Sakuye 2 version the woman was not Boran but Waat, i.e. from a hunting and gathering population of low status, with whom pastoralists do not like to intermarry. She was an outcast like Hassan Buro himself:

> That woman was Waat. She had got pregnant and born a boy. She had gone to join the Boran and they had chased her away. She had this baby boy. Also she used to come back to these caverns with water. As long as she fetched water from these caverns and saw that food she was afraid of the man. He waited near that [the food he had deposited there]. When he waited and the woman came for it, collected it, he caught her.
>
> He asked her for information. 'Become my wife!' he said. 'Where have you came from?' 'I have come from there, like this and like that.' And he married that woman and drove that camel [and] came to the Boran.

They asked him for information. They also asked her for her tribe. There was somebody who could tell when she had got lost. They asked the man how he had come. They took him and said, 'Go and settle here, [you shall belong to the] tribe!' He just had that one camel, they did not give him more stock. He used to tie a rope [as a trap], he tied it for giraffe, oryx and such things. Still he just had got no companions apart from that woman, allowing for those Boran he had seen. (Sakuye 2)

The version of Sakuye 3 lets Hassan Buro meet the Boran much later and first describes at some length how the small family goes on to acquire some modest wealth in terms of their basic hunting and gathering economy:

The she-camel gave birth. 'Drink milk!' They drank milk. They ate honey. There was a giraffe, heavy with calf, with fat running out of its nostrils, *Dak!* – he shot it with an arrow. They cut the meat in strips and dried it, they extended the skin, tied its edges together, collected the fat in it like in a bucket and kept it down there among the rocks.

The she-camel multiplied and became five heads. The bull Maddo used to serve her.[109] [All these camels were] black with white faces. The entire legs white like this.[110] Then the woman asked one day, "We have got wealth now, but do you know what is going on in the country?' 'I do not.' 'Look for the tail hairs of a giraffe bull, bleached with age, white, white!' She sewed a garment like that of the Hofte[111] or a Rendille woman's skirt of the skin of a gerenuk antelope. They filled a milking container with honey, took the giraffe tail hair and took all this to the *qallu*.

'High Priest, how do you do? Wife of the High Priest, how do you do?' They gave them all this, this giraffe tail hair, this milking vessel, this honey. 'Children of Sakuye,[113] flow through the gate of Katebo!'[114] That was it about Miigo, about Hassan Buro. (Sakuye 3)

The account stresses the episode of handing over the gifts to the *qallu* because it establishes and symbolises *tiriso* between the Boran and their associate peoples.[115] For some centuries, most people of northern Kenya had such a relationship with the Boran and took gifts to the *qallu* at regular intervals which were determined by the *gada* cycle.

Since the Boran and their associate people also formed a military alliance, the institution of *tiriso* was a means of expanding Boran power. We shall see presently that the Boran also sought to bring the other, major, part of the future Sakuye, the out-migrants from Rendille, under this *tiriso* umbrella. According to our sources it was due to Boran initiative that the two groups were joined together and both integrated into the Boran system of inter-ethnic alliance.

The Sakuye [proper, as distinct from the Miigo] came from the Rendille. They met scouts [people who were examining the pasture conditions], caught them and took them to their settlement. 'What is in this country?' they asked them. 'Boran are to that side.' They let them go and the scouts returned to the Boran. 'Such and such people are in this country and have settled here,' they told them.

The Boran visited the Rendille settlement. Then they discussed among them-

selves. 'These Rendille cannot raid us anyhow. We make them part of our tribe.
Let us incorporate them into our tribe.' Then they sent the *hayyu* and *jallab*
[higher and lower generation-set officers] to the Rendille. Animals were slaughtered for them. The delegation just stayed in the shade, where the Rendille had
asked them to sit down, and animals were slaughtered for them. The elders of
the Rendille did not come. Only animals were slaughtered for them.

'Come, let us meet!' 'There is no way to have a meeting. One boy has killed
an enemy out there in the land where the sun rises and has come here to this
settlement to receive a *sarma* camel from his maternal uncle. According to our
custom we cannot have a meeting before the end of this month.'

So the delegation went home. 'Never mind, that is how these people are. We
shall divide them among our clans nevertheless.' It was heard that the Boran
were going to divide us up lineage by lineage. Therefore, when they came back,
the Boran were told that it was impossible to have a meeting.

These people cannot be groped at with hands [i.e. should not be provoked],
do not try to fight them.' They have come from Saaku [= Marsabit], and also
their name is Sakuye, the tribe that found them first, the people who found
them first were Karrayyu [a clan of] Boran. On the surface they are all Boran.
And again, they and Karrayyu take [gifts of] animals from each other, they
are tribesmen to each other. That is how Sakuye and Miigo first found each
other. (Sakuye 2)

In this text only the final phrase reveals that the Miigo were included
under the broad label Boran. Other versions make the special relationship of the Miigo to and their role as mediators between the out-migrants
from Rendille and the Boran much more explicit. The Sakuye 3 version
describes those fragments of the Rendille that were to become Sakuye as
youngsters who lived in satellite camps, not as whole settlement groups of
refugees. The rich detail of this account and its divergence from Sakuye 2
demonstrate how much this story is a living part of folklore and how time
can add to diversity:

There [near Marsabit] the satellite camp of camels and the one of smallstock
moved away from the settlements. They came to Deemo [a mountain 38°38′
E, 2°47′ N, i.e. 80 km North-east of Marsabit]. They came to the country
[around] Deemo. A bull got lost from them. A camel bull got lost. Miigo was
at Lensayu [39°17′ E, 2°52′ N, i.e. 70 km east, of Deemo.] That bull came
there and joined the camels of the Miigo.[116]

Two [Rendille] came following the footprints in order to look for the bull.
Finally they saw the bull but did not demand it back because they were afraid
of those Miigo. They spent the day nearby. When the camels were driven to the
settlement at nightfall, they came closer and stayed just outside the settlement.

The Miigo were bleeding a camel by piercing the nasal vein. One of them
said, 'Boy, it does not come out. Why doesn't the blood come out!' One of the
Rendille who sat just outside the fence responded, 'Damn, man, it will come
out if you put something under the head!' 'What was that?' [The Miigo rushed
to where the voice came from and] got hold of the Rendille. 'Somebody else
will look after your bull,' they told them and took them by force to their huts
where they interrogated them. 'What tribe are you?' 'We are Sakuye.' 'What
does that mean?' 'We come from Saaku [Marsabit], we are Sakuye.' These
Miigo took them away and brought them to the Boran. At that time there were

only Boran in the area and no other people. The Boran interrogated them too. 'What tribe are you?' 'Sakuye.' 'Not Sakuye.' 'How that?' 'Boran.' I am not Boran.' 'How that?' 'I am Sakuye.' 'How Sakuye?' 'I have come from Saaku.' 'You are Miigo.' 'I am not Miigo either, I am Sakuye.' The Boran gave up.

This scene does not reflect a conflict of mere ethnic terminology but of political ambitions. The Boran try to persuade the captives to declare themselves Boran and thus to acknowledge the political supremacy of the Boran. As this does not work, Miigo is offered as another choice, since by declaring themselves Miigo, who in their turn are Boran dependants, the captives would indirectly acknowledge Boran supremacy. This, however, fails because of the obstinacy of the newcomers, which is also apparent in the subsequent episode, along with choosy eating habits, which connote a special ritual status.

They showed them oxen to choose one to be slaughtered for them. They brought them a hornless one. 'I never ate one like this.' 'Have the black one!' 'I do not want that one either!' ' I do not want it.' [The Boran nearly became exasperated.] 'Ah, what is wrong with these people?' Finally a meagre grey ox with long horns and a tail which was dangling down to the earth was brought and they accepted it. [Finally the question of their future affiliation was decided thus:] 'If you cannot be Boran, become brothers of the Miigo. You and Miigo are one.'
That is how the Sakuye and the Miigo found each other and became one. [The Sakuye belonged to a] satellite camp of camels to which also girls belonged. All the warriors [bachelors] married those girls, and Matarbá became Matarbá, Fur became Fur, Yalle became Yalle, Deele became Deele, Arsuwa became Arsuwa. They all call themselves by the names of the gates [descent units] they had come from.

That Matarbá became Matarbá and Fur became Fur, etc., means that all Rendille clans and subclans represented in the emigrant group became their Sakuye equivalents, that is, they remained the same and became something new: subunits of a new and different political structure.

Also in the Sakuye 1 version it is Hassan Buro who introduces the newcomers to the Boran *qallu* and mediates in establishing the ritual patron–client relationship. Sakuye 1 puts it in slightly different terms and compares the Boran to a 'government' to whom 'taxes' (*ancurti*) are paid. This version, however, differs from Sakuye 3 in stressing a common origin for Hassan Buro and the emigrants from Rendille. They are not strangers who establish a new relationship but relatives who rediscover and re-establish an old relationship. They only lost sight of each other during the long trek. This is consistent with the participation of the proto-Rendille–Sakuye in the journey to Jubaland, which Sakuye 1 and 2 postulate.

The Sakuye came. They turned to Korondille, they stayed in the plain of Lensayu, there is a plain and there is a lava field, they climbed onto the lava field and saw camels, smallstock, settlements, large settlements.

These people spoke Rendille. And this one knew Somali, so they and Hassan Buro talked to each other.[117] 'What are you?' he said. 'We are people who got lost on the Long Trek,' they said. 'Talk to us as Muslims.' 'I have also got lost from those people,' he said.

The account continues with Hassan Buro showing the country's path-ways to the new arrivals and introducing them to his ritual head, the *qallu* of Karrayyu, i.e. the high priest of the Sabbo moiety of the Boran. '*An galtu ballet arge, warr gos kiyya ka durri ballet arge*' ('I have found migrants who had got lost, I have found people of my tribe who had got lost'). We shall come back to the nature of the link thus established with the Boran after examining a body of other traditions about a long trek, this time to the west.

THE MIGRATION TO IRIS

In the Gabbra Miigo version of the account of the long trek the Miigo are those who were left behind and submitted to Boran supremacy. The Gab-bra Malbe of Marsabit District confirm this tradition as far as the Miigo are concerned, but have an entirely different account of their own his-tory which only after a formidable attempt at evasion ultimately led to the same result: submission to the Boran. Another point independently confirmed by Gabbra Malbe traditions is that Gabbra (both Malbe and Miigo) and Garre are of the same original stock. Like the oral histories rendered above, these tales also include the Rendille, but not as parti-cipants of the migration to Jubaland, as the Sakuye recall, nor as lonesome bush dwellers who could not be informed in time, as the Garre describe them, but as participants in the same western migration as that under-taken by the Gabbra Malbe, and as a faction of the latter who split from them only later. The Rendille thus are claimed by peoples of eastern and of western migrational histories alike as specially close relatives and travel companions, while paradoxically their own clan origin myths point to a long residence in their present area. Maybe this apparent contradiction can be solved by the composite nature of Rendille society.

Our reconstruction of the tale is mainly a collage of the accounts of numerous Gabbra Malbe and one Boran informant. At first I wish to introduce some of the informants who are given more space on the fol-lowing pages, so as to put each narrative into a personal context with its own background, as well as to give credit to those who share in the merits – but not in the responsibilities – of the authorship of this book.

Godaana Guyyo and Jirima Mollu have already been quoted in the first part of this chapter. The short reference to the interview with them – Gabbra – will be retained here, although most other informants are also Gabbra.

A full account of the migration to Iris was given in an earlier interview by Jirima Mollu alone (Bubisa, February 1980). In fullness Jirima's account matches those of older men. Working with him was made more rewarding by the fact that he not only recounts but discusses history. He patiently went back again and again to explain details of his own account and asked for help from others where his own explanations failed. He is one of those who would better be called a fellow historian than an informant. This source will be referred to as Galbo 1, the name of Jirima's phratry.

The second full account (Odoola) of the migration stems from Boru Galgallo, the ritual, juridical and historical specialist of the Odoola phratry of Gabbra, an old man himself and the son of the late Galgallo Gurracca who performed the same prestigious informal role before him. Their settlement is the Yaa Odōla, the mobile capital of that phratry where the holy drum is kept. Boru Galgallo is a more convinced citizen of the wider Boran federation than other Gabbra and displays signs of ethnocentrism and cultural arrogance towards the Rendille, whom he describes as violent barbarians. He is noble with all the positive and negative connotations of that word. The interview took place in Bubisa, September 1979.

Halake Guyyo of Burot lineage in Galbo phratry is an influential elderly man who owns a permanent house in Kalacha, a trading post on the fringe of the Chalbi. The interview took place there in August 1980 (Galbo 2).

Waako D'iriba, to whom I was introduced by his son, an administration police corporal, is a Boran and thus adds a non-Gabbra perspective to these traditions. His age (he was born about 1883), his direct involvement in important historical events like the fighting over the wells of Wajir in the second decade of this century, his personal knowledge of most of northern Kenya and his humorous narrative make him an interesting informant. In 1923 he came to Marsabit where he practises cattle transhumance up and down the mountain. (Marsabit, April 1980, short reference: Boran)[118]

THE SEPARATION OF GABBRA MIIGO AND GABBRA MALBE

Gaaf worri gargar-bae gaaf Kedi Guure jed'ani. Wolin Borani hadde, Gabbri chuf ta wolin-jirtu, nyaabi dibbin hadde. Worri wan jed'u: gaaf sun jarsi Miigo tokko wan jed'e: 'Saabu umná Soráán yamnan dide, sororo teeso worri did.' Jarsi Miigo tokko guyyán Malbe-f Miigon gargar-baate kan jed'e, ka amm worri sirbi sadéka dawwatu.

The time when people separated is called the time of Kedi Guure.[119] Boran raided them all, all Gabbra as they were staying together were raided by an outside enemy. People say that at that time one elder of [Gabbra] Miigo said, 'In Saab [a regional name] where one is afraid, Sora did not want to be called [out], the red ones [camels] rejected the place where the settlement group stayed too long.' One Miigo elder said like this when Malbe and Miigo separated, and now people sing it when they play the *mbao* [Sw.] game.[120]

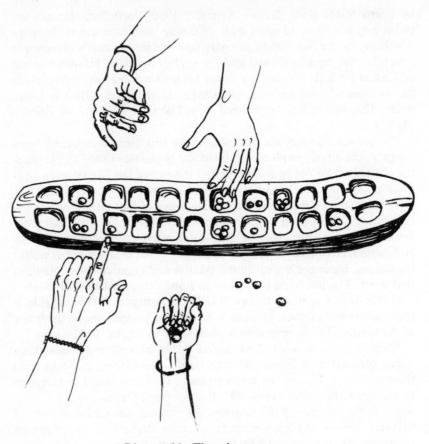

Diagram 14   The *mbao* game

Gaade, ijjesu feed'a Borán. Ya-ga-bae, yokana yaga-mulate, 'Soraa, Sora,' diide. Yennaan ya godaanu feed'e, sadeka bir gaqubanné. Saaba jed'ani, aci, laf Konsó, lafti tuni horí in-qábtu, baqumá d'ufén.

They plot, they, the Boran, try to kill. They had come out, when they appeared [they called], 'Sora, Sora,' he refused. But he wanted to move away, so he squatted down lightly [ready to run] at the *mbao* game [to announce his decision and give no pretext to accuse him of treason (?)]. They call [the land] Saab, there in the Konso country [Jemjem District (Awraja) in Sidamo Province of southern Ethiopia], that country has no livestock, so he escaped and came.

'Saaba umná yaamnán Soráán diide. Sororo teeso worrí diide.'

[So he sang while playing,] 'In Saab where one is scared, Sora did not respond to the call, the red ones rejected to stay at the overstayed place of the settlement group.'

Guyyáán ini gargar-bae, Malbéén gad-báqate, isiin miilum suni Irisi galt. Guyyan gaaf kan duub, guyyan kun guyya Kedi Guure kan.

The day [the Gabbra] separated, [when] the Malbe escaped to this side, he [= the latter] went directly [literally: 'on the same foot'] to Iris. That time, now, is called the time of Kedi Guure.

Boranat hadde gaafas. Borani hadde, Miigoon ol baddé, kan garán bae. Aki Gabbri heddu, héén Gabbraati bari gaaf suni, bari gaaf Kedi Guure barbarána ka shiftaan d'ufe. Shifta onana harréti ta Rooboe-itiini.

The Boran raided [them] at that time. The Boran raided [them], the Miigo got lost to the east, these came to this side. As the Gabbra recount, in the account of the Gabbra, the anniversary of that time, the anniversary of Kedi Guure was recently when the *shifta* [Somali bandits] came. The new *shifta* of the recent days, not the ones of the Year with Much Vegetation [1962].[121]

Booranumat arrá-lle hadde laf Heesiti kan Gabbra hadde. Ganni sun kud'ani mar, adál. Ganna sagal nageumaan wolin-tae jennán gann kud'ani Boranumaan Gabbrat hadde. Gaaf arrá-lle Boranumaan Gabbra Miigo hadde.

Even in those days the Boran raided the Gabbra [Miigo] around Hees.[122] That year comes around in the tenth year, it is *adál*.[123] Nine years they stay together in peace, but in the tenth year the Boran fight the Gabbra. Even now the Boran have raided the Gabbra Miigo. (Gabbra)

Other versions ascribe the same cause to the separation of Gabbra and Garre. Therefore, if we take the above quoted traditions of Garre and Gabbra Miigo into account, all versions agree that the distinction between the three peoples does not date farther back than the Boran expansion.

Gaaf worri wolhadda kan, Boraní guddo nam dibbe. Gabbra chuf qara ín-qodan. Qodum kan kees wol-hamate. Duub Gabbraaf Garri gargar kaate. Garrin ol hafte. Gabbri garán deemte.

At the time when people raided each other, the Boran tormented people a lot. At first all Gabbra were divided up. In this process of dividing up they became bad to each other. So Gabbra and Garre moved apart. The Garre stayed in the east. The Gabbra went to this side. (Galbo 2)

Our Boran source agrees in attributing the flight of the Gabbra Malbe to Iris to the Boran, although it does not claim that the Boran at this stage tried to divide the Gabbra up among themselves. In this it agrees with the Odoola version, which, as we shall see below, assigns the allocation of the Gabbra to Boran lineages to the time after the return from Iris. Rather than an attempt to establish political dominance, ritual raiding is given here as the reason for the Gabbra's flight.

Ínhaddan, raab ini ín-duul, duule raabá, farde qaba, nam gudda, godaane qubacu qubata, ka sangán jale yau, ufumá horí nyaatu.

They were raided, the *raab* went to war, the war of *raab*, they have horses, have a leader [literally: 'big man'], they move and make camp here and there, they follow an ox, they only eat livestock. (Boran)

Raab are the new warrior generation set that go on a ritual military expedition once in eight years, that is, once in every promotion cycle of the *gada* system. According to Legesse (1973: 75), the animal which the *raab* follow is not an ox but an entire bull, to whom, apart from the whole expedition looking after him, a special guardian is assigned so that he is always in optimal condition. The bull is secretly let into a herd of an enemy camp to fight with the sire. If he wins, this is taken as a good omen and the camp is raided.

> *Guyyá Gabbra had ín-qaba, in-fítan, nam nama jallate nam hada d'ad'aba malle, hori írra bannatan.*

When they raid the Gabbra, they do not kill [people], except for somebody who hinders people and with whom the expedition cannot deal otherwise, they take their livestock out [of the enclosures].

> *Guyya qallún kenne; yo qallún in-kennín iti-in-dúúlan. Gabbr sun ín-d'ad'aban, gaaf isiin aci badde. Itum-déebian, haddan. Sum ím-badde, Irisi galte.*

The *qallu* fixes the day; if the *qallu* did not fix it, they do not go to war there. They missed how to deal [peacefully] with those Gabbra at the time these got lost to that side [Iris]. They came back and raided them again and again. Those [Gabbra] got lost and migrated to Iris. (Boran)

IMPOTENCE AND THE SEARCH FOR RITUAL STRENGTH

Strangely, both our two major Gabbra sources stress the impotence and defencelessness of the early Gabbra, who appear like hunted animals. This early period of supposed disorder and fear is depicted as forming a contrast with the subsequent introduction of ritual order and social organisation which brings spiritual and political security.

> *Gabbri oluma baat, gara Garri iti-baat. Ga-baate lafti isiin iti-ga-baat, Boraani qabti. Waan nu abooti teen irrá-d'agene: nami yo sun worraná-lle in-qábu, wan chuf ín-deet. 'Nami ga-bae' jennán Bórani akum nyaaba háddata.*

The Gabbra came from the east, they came out of the Garre. They came, and the country they came to had Boran. What we heard from our fathers: people at that time did not even have spears, they were afraid of everything. It was said, 'People have come' and the Boran raided them the way enemies do. (Galbo 1)

> *Nami ín-deem. Kuun aci deem bahrini tan gam deeme. Biyo tan Booraana fa tan Rendilla fa ya-d'ufte, Boraana gaafi Irisi jed'. Gaal Gababo, Galbo challa, amm galaan sun gam jirti. Aci Gaal Gabab, arma Galbo. Rendill at keesa d'ufte kan, waan Rendill jed'ani, Boraana tokko, Iris wolumán-d'aqan.*

People move. Far away there, beyond that sea [Lake Turkana or Rudolph] they went. These people of Boran [meaning the Gabbra Malbe[124]] and the Rendille came, the Gabbra call that the time of Iris. Gaal Gababo [People of the Short Camels], all of them Galbo [one of the Gabbra phratries], are now behind that lake. There they are called Gaal Gababo, here Galbo. These Rendille you came from, what they call Rendille, and the Gabbra were one, they went to Iris together.

Boi kuuni, Boi gadi, fulanu tenu kana aci, gati. Bahrini duub. Nami busawa huma, inum-badaa, hindiin deeta, sotowa ín-deeta, binesa allá kan chuf ín-deeta, laf-ti yó sun worrán in-jíru, duub, deeme duub laf sun daqa.

There, beyond the lake, from our place to that side [west], yonder, behind the sea. People are game, they get lost, gazelles stampede, giraffes stampede, all the animals of outside [= wild animals] stampede, in the land at that time one did not have spears, so they went [escaped] to that country. (Odoola)

This migration included the Rendille but did not involve one of the present-day Gabbra phratries, Alganna, which only later evolved around a nucleus of Boran immigrants.

Gabbri Alganna challa kees in-jír; dibben tan abrán wolumán-jirti.

Only Alganna was not among the Gabbra; the other four drums [phratries] were together. (Galbo)

Nam durri dawe, dawen tan ín-baqati. Isiinu kúún Iris galte. Iris um-teet. Worri kun raag qaba. Worri waan jed': Waan ijolle jarolen dooft:

The people of old were fools, these fools panicked. They went far out there to Iris. In Iris they stayed. These people had diviners. These said what now the children and old people sing:

(The following are counting verses for children which are not generally known to refer to Iris. I include these verses here together with the exegesis later given by the informant.)

1 *Tokko ka tokkoci Bonu saaka*
'One is that one [son] of Bonu is of the earthen pot', i.e. is thrown or to be thrown into a cooking pot. This is interpreted as a reference to the sacrifice of a young man who finds death by jumping into the lake in order magically to open a ford for his people to pass. (A new variation of the Moses motif which we shall meet in the course of the narrative.)

2 *Lamma ka miil Kate Doiyu*
'Two is of the foot of Kate Doiyu' or 'Second, the foot of Kate Doriyu' No exegesis obtained.

3 *Sadíí ka sadeen ared ree jabba Mammo*
'Three of the three is the goat's beard of the strong Mammo [the Gabbra variant of the name Muhammad]', i.e. third, the goat's beard of the strong Mammo, who is said to be Mammo Bere, one of the diviners who were active during the time in Iris.

4 *Afuri ka abrán dubr gooro*
'Four [of four] are the girls of *gooro*.' *Gooro* is the way of pilgrimage or the road of the ritual journey (*jila*) undertaken by the Galbo phratry to Farole, a mountain on the Kenyan – Ethiopian border and on to Melbana where the age-set promotions are performed. Four girls and four female sheep are taken along on the journey. Camp is made at the foot

of Farole and the sheep are sacrificed at the camel enclosures. Other rituals are performed by selected elders on top of the mountain.

5   *Shani ka shanan Abai saatu koti daqe d'abe boboya galle*
'Five [of five], Abai went to dig for *saatu*, missed them and went home crying.' *Saatu* are edible grass roots (R: *chaanto*), considered inferior food and sometimes eaten by children.

6   *Jahán Abai qulumme nyaat daqe dabe boboya galle*
'Six, Abai went to eat *qulumme*, missed them and went home crying.' *Qulumme* is a kind of wild fruit.

7   *Torban gusuméti darte wayya d'irá bubute*
Seven, the divorced woman was unclad [unprovided for] and pulled at the sheet of a [sleeping] man.

8   *Saddet muc sará*
'Eight are the tits of a bitch'.

9   *Sállan ka laakos: ékerá*
'The ninth [thing] of the account is the spirit of the dead.'

While the first four verses are difficult to categorise, we can group the remainder of the verses in two categories: 5–7 on the one hand and 8–9 on the other hand. The former are descriptions of various kinds of dearth. Emergency foods to which pastoralists revert in a drought cannot be found and a single woman can find no lover to maintain her. Galbo 1 takes this as a description of the sad state of the Gabbra/Rendille in Iris, which forced them to leave that land. The last two verses both refer to unclean, dangerous and unpropitious things and are explained as pointing out the necessity of sorcery – itself potentially anti-social and not permissible in everyday life – to get out of a dire situation.

> *Unú-kun ak raaguma dubbi jajabdu [. . .] Amma hasa gubbá iti-deebina. Yo nam chuf it-deemté-lle, Gabbra guddon at agartu nam tokkot wo beek.*
>
> That is the way of diviners, difficult talk. [. . .] Now we come back to the surface of the story. Even if you go to everybody, if you see many Gabbra, only one [or the other] knows something.
>
> *[Namici raaga kun, ini gos tam?]*
>
> [Of which clan was that diviner?]
>
> *Woni kun na durra wol-marte, ammo Usmalo. (Raage kaan lammesan) – ka waan takkan himu: sadíi sadeen waan takkanin waan kan waan takkani himu: laf Iris tana in-taaína. Tokko Mamo Deera, raagi kunin Usmalo, raagi kun Chaaqo. Sadeen kan.*
>
> That has turned around before me [i.e. I failed to mention it], but he was of Usmalo [≙ R: Harrau[125]]. (The second diviner) – they were three who predicted one and the same thing – and the one thing these three predicted was:

do not stay in this land Iris. One was of Mamo Deera, that one [the above mentioned] Usmalo, that one of Chaaqo. These three.[126]

'Gabbra, galaan kan kunne, aada tolciné keesa baan. Laftí isan fidu, gará Waaqa fin ka isan ya ol dae. Ol deebia!' jed'e.

'Gabbra, let us cut this lake, let us perform a ritual and get out. The land where you will prosper, the belly of God [= the starred sky] has pointed out life for you in the east. Go back to the east!' he said. (Galbo)

As in the Garre traditions about the migration to the Juba, we once again are confronted by a big water that is impossible to cross by everyday means. The similarity between the two stories is reinforced by the same word being used: *galaan* can mean a large river or a lake, as in *galaan Boi*. The means employed for separating the waters, however, are different.

'Akam deebinu?' jed'an. 'Gurba Alkóra, qofum d'alate, galaan kees buusa, intala Elfure, Kibibe, harm haada duda hanan baaft, harm isii galaanat elma, galaana duub gargar cit, yo akan tolcan.' 'Beena gurba gaafada!' jed'an.

'How can we get back? it was said. 'Throw a boy of Alkóra [a lineage of Gär phratry], an only son, into the lake, and milk the breast of a daughter of Elfure, Kibibe [a lineage of Galbo], for whom the sealed breast of her mother gave milk [i.e. who is a firstborn child] into the lake,[127] the lake will then be torn apart, if it is done like this.' 'Go and ask the boy!' it was said. (Galbo 1)

Gurba kan yaamaní, gurbán luba, nam gudda. 'Boraani Haw-Adan birrá-d'ufe, amma ka aci in-débin in-jíratu. Bisan kan yo att ké-buut ín-citani, yo at bisan ké-buut worran jireeni iti-deebia. Yo at bisan kan im-buín Boraani jireen iti in-déébiu, bisan kan bui!' jed'an.

They called this boy, the boy is a warrior, a grown-up. 'The Gabbra have come from Haw-Adan [Hawa and Adan, i.e. Eve and Adam, here taken as the name of a locality somewhere in the east], now if they do not go back there they will not live. This water will separate if you jump into it, if you jump into the water, life will come back to the people. If you do not jump into this water, life will not come back to the Gabbra, jump into this water!' they said.

'Yo an galaan kan bui galaani kun ín-cita?' 'Ín-cit.' 'An nám tokk. Badíí Boraana wali-im-bítani gosi-tiyy guddo, an ím-bua, isan mid'áfadd'a!'

'If I jump into this lake, will it separate?' 'It will separate.' 'I am [only] one man. If [my own] doom can be traded in [to avert] the doom of the Gabbra, my tribe is big, I will jump, and you, recover!' (Odoola)

The next episode is known to us from almost identical Garre traditions about the Juba.

Nami raaga waan tokko jed': Yo gurban kun bisan kan bui, gaali abba in-qábne gudda, gaali kun beek gaal badii, ka nam seseenu. Yo gaali sun bisan kan kees in-ejjatín, ji gurban kun bisan kan bú, ji kud'ani lamma itú-martan, olum godaantan. Yo gaali dullatín tokk kees ejjat, guyyani ini wolti-deebiu sunuma.

The diviner said one thing: When the boy jumped into the water, the camels without owners are many, these camels, you know, are stray camels which joined other people. If those camels do not go into the water, after the boy jumped into the water, twelve moons will come around and you will just migrate to the east [all the time]. If even one of those camels gets into the water, the waters will close again on that very day. (Odoola)

As with the Garre traditions, this account claims that enormous numbers of people and animals were involved in the migration. Twelve months were thought to be necessary for them all to pass through the lake. The passage, however, is interrupted by an unclean camel entering the lake with the result that the waters close again and cut the caravan in two. The unpropitiousness of this camel lies in its doubtful ownership. Rendille and Gabbra consider it highly important to distinguish between one's own and borrowed camels[128] for generations – indeed, for ever after.

The supposedly disastrous effects of indeterminate ownership are illustrated by the following case history.

A young man of the age set Dismaala, who were warriors from 1881 to 1895, of the lineage Harrau in the Rendille clan D'ubsahai went as a herdsman to the Gabbra. He was nicknamed Konkomane (the short one) and was a daughter's son of the clan Matarbá. (Lineage, age-set, nickname and clan of the mother are the only available identifiers since the name of a senior, and more so of a dead, person must not be spoken by Rendille and will consequently be forgotten.) Among the Gabbra he joined his own lineage, Usmalo, the Gabbra equivalent of Harrau. (I discuss this as an example of inter-ethnic clan identities in chapter 5.) One day he stole two young she-camels and drove them home to the Rendille. At some time later the original owners or their descendants demanded the return of these camels or their descendants. They were told that both strains had died out. The truth was that they thrived and multiplied. This, however, could not be said about the progeny of the man, Konkomane. In order to rid themselves of sickness and death, which hit them with unusual frequency, the family of Konkomane later admitted their fraud and asked the Gabbra to take their camels back. This could not be done because the ownership was not certain. Of the two camels originally stolen, one was *alál* of Usmalo, the other one was borrowed. Both, however, had the same brand. (The camel brand of Usmalo, the *alif*, is shared by the whole Lossa moiety of Galbo, of which Usmalo is a part – see Diagram 15.)

The Rendille, of course, knew which camels had descended from the one long-dead ancestral cow and which from the other, but there was no way of ascertaining which ancestral cow had belonged to which Galbo lineage. So the Gabbra refused to accept the camels, fearing that a mistake in allotting them might bring death to their own children.

The house of Konkomane died out and another man of Harrau, the next one up in order of seniority, inherited the camels. He was of the

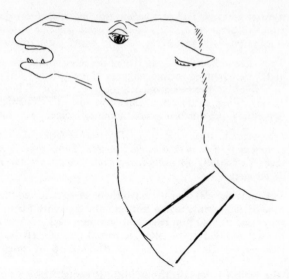

Diagram 15 Alif Lossa of Galbo

sublineage Eisimsee, his age set was Irbālis (= Ilkilegu) who were warriors from 1923 to 1937, and his mother was a daughter of the clan Matarbá. We can be sure that he did not want the camels, but as Rendille do not slaughter or sell fertile female camels, he had no choice but to accept his inheritance. He had two sons who as grown-up warriors died of sickness. His only daughter is married and childless. In the absence of male heirs, Inchuni, the next in order of seniority of Ḥarrau, inherited the camels. There are two sons of Inchuni in the age-set Ilkichili (warriors from 1965 to 1979), one of whom is married and has a child with a daughter of the clan Gaabanayó in whose settlement group near Kargi the family is living. May God protect them.[129]

The belief that such camels are highly unpropitious is shared, as this example shows, by Rendille and Gabbra.

To secure safe transit through the lake, the returning migrants from Iris are reported to have taken great pains to exclude such camels from the journey.

Gabbri laf jaare. Gool jed'an, gool kan jaare. Gam sun ruuf qabani, gam sun ruuf iti-qabani. Gabbrí karibu ji afuru ji shan chuf ín-godaane. Jarolle im-baate guddo arm ciift. Horín kun wan badí gaafatan armumat gorsan.

The Gabbra fenced [the country]. They call it *gool*, they made this gate.[130] They held a *ruuf*[131] at this side and a *ruuf* at that side. The Gabbra migrated nearly four or five whole months [one after the other through the gate]. The elders came out and stood there in large numbers. They asked for stray camels among the stock and sorted them out on the spot. (Galbo 1)

Àyyanit hereganí, ji Arrafa, alkan isiin kud'ani, dirám d'ufanini duub kébusan, bisan ya-gargar-citan, duub ín-deem, duub gódaane ol taak. Gaala lafi jaaraní. Gaal yo ini d'ufe 'gaal kanke maan iti kejir?' Waan akana monum tan naggan.

They determined the proper day of the week, in the month of Arrafa, its tenth night, they came in the morning and threw [the boy] in, the waters divided, so they went, so the trek passed through eastwards. They made a fence for the camels. When a camel herd came [they asked], 'What is among your camels?' Something like this [camels of unknown owners] was put into the corral.

Itum guurani, itum guurani, ji afur, ji afur deeme, ji shanééso, isi sagali, rocón takkan utale, dowum dowan, duub baafate, bisan ke-bue, galaan kan kees ejjet. Ín-taak. Ya-baafate. Ya wolti-deebie duub galaaní. Galaan Boi sun agarté? Wolti-deebie duub.

They [the camels] were collected there, were collected there, four months, four months they went, in the fifth month, the ninth [day], a single gelding ran, they tried to hold him back and hold him back, (so) he escaped, jumped into the water, stood in the lake. He passed through. He had escaped. So the lake closed again. Have you seen Lake Rudolph? So it closed again. (Odoola)

In the Galbo 1 version the gelding is replaced by a barren she-camel, the common element being that in both stories sterility seems to be introduced to illustrate unpropitiousness.

Ol godaante, halaan yaqaa, yaqa qabti – 'hala tan gaal keesa deebisa!' – halaan tun rima in-qábtu, hanan in-qábtu. Ín-cete; 'dowa!' Ud dowan dowanu galaan sente. Galaani kaan ín-fargat. Gabbra kan gargar-kute.

They moved to the east, an unpropitious she-camel, that had unpropitiuousness – 'Drive this she-camel out of the herd and back!' – that camel cow did not get heavy with calf, she had no milk. She ran; 'Hold her back!' For as much as they tried to hold her back and hold her back she got into the lake. The lake closed. It cut these Gabbra apart.

Rendillé-lle tanum. Gabbrí nami niitin garán d'ufte dirsi aci iti-haf. Worr tokko Chaaqo jed'ani intalti ogogo qabti dirsa aci-t haf, intalti amm Eilo jed'ani Alganna galte. Akanumát worr abaa keteet.

Also the Rendille are just these [the same people]. Of some Gabbra, the wife has come to this side and the husband remained there. Of a lineage called Chaaqo, a girl with a black headscarf [= a newly married bride], her husband remained there, the girl is now called Eilo, joined [the phratry] Alganna. That way she stayed in the clan of her father.[132]

Ka Sharbaná-lle worra kute ka fa akasum ke-teet gaaf Iris. Rendillen ín-deebit, afan Galaana irra deebit. (Gabbri gul deebite.) Odōlá-lle gul dēbit, diqa. Worri gul deebite ka Borana: Korrot, Harrau. Diqa tokko-lle Gabbra gul deebie, gargar bae.

Also the Eilo of Sharbana phratry: a family got separated and so on and they stayed there in the same way at the time of Iris. The Rendille turned sidewards, went along the shore of the lake. (They had followed the Gabbra.) Also some few Odoola followed them.[133] The people who followed them [the Rendille] from the Gabbra: Korrot, Harrau. Very few of the latter two also followed the Gabbra, so they separated.[134]

Godaane, gar Jibis aci bae, Boróle Naqaio. Kuuno eela aci ... Gorei-lle, Jal, Hobok jed'ani, aci qubat Sharbana. Borale Naqaio. Balál genán qubate. Gár godaane, Gorei genan, Dakha Qaqalla qubate. Galbó-lle deemte, Farole, gete genán ín-qubat.

They migrated and turned to that side at Jibis, to Borale Naqio. There, a well, far there [north].... Sharbana settled at Gorei, Jal, a place called Hobok, Borale Naqaio. They came to Balal [a species of trees which gave its name to a river bed] and settled there. Gār moved, came to Gorei and settled near Dakha [= Daqa] Qaqalla. Galbo went, got to Farole and settled there. (Galbo 1)

Although these settlements or encampments were, of course, temporary, emphasis is put on them because they are the ritual sites for age-set promotions and all of them have to be passed on the ritual journeys (*jila galani*) of the respective phratries.

Yo Turbi gean Odool ín-qubat. Rendillen deema suni arma deemte; yo isii galgu-lámme jetu galaana ga-débiti bisan isii Korolle tana, armum teete. Odōlí gaafas Rendille gul gorre. Tokko tu Boraana-f Rendille.

When they got to Turbi, Odoola settled.[135] The Rendille on the same journey came to here;[136] when they say [= perform] *gaalgulamme*[137] they go back to the lake and their water is this Korolle,[138] they stayed just here. At that time Odoola followed the Rendille. They were just one, Gabbra and Rendille.

Korren Boraan, Boraan-bor. Booraani Iris in-dánne. [...] Gaaf beni wol-deebi Gabbrí Boraana wolti-d'ufe, gaaf kan Boraani nam argan.

The Samburu are Boran, Boran-bor.[139] The Boran had not gone to Iris [...] When people converged, when Gabbra and Boran came together, at that time the Boran appropriated people.

Gabbri tiríso in-jéd'ani? Nam argán duub nam kan duub gosan qabat. Worr kan dowan duub. Jars tokko Babo Sibu jed'an Dambítu yamt. 'Kota mukh sun teena!' jed'.

Don't the Gabbra say *tiriso* [= allocation of Gabbra lineages to Boran clans]? They appropriated people and incorporated them into the tribe [literally: 'got hold of them with the tribe']. These people [the Boran clan Dambítu] were refused [= the other Boran refused to allot Gabbra to them]. An elder called Babo Sibu [who must have been responsible for the refusal] was called by Dambítu. 'Come, let us sit under that tree!' they said.

Dambítu jars in-ijjeft. Dambítu baqate, ful bita deebite, baqat. Lag Dambítu d'ufte, qubat. Godaante, hedado Rendilla sent, gar jallo baat, Korre taate duub.

The Dambítu killed the elder. The Dambítu fled, turned their faces south, fled. They came to the Dambítu seasonal river [which is called after them, near Maikona], entered the thornbush steppe of the Rendille, left it to the west and so became Samburu.[140] (Odoola)

Both versions stress the connection between the establishment of Gabbra official ritual and the Boran threat which it was meant to avert. That the Boran built up their hegemony nevertheless and that many Gabbra, although proud of their separate customs and traditions, at the same time regard themselves in their wider political affiliation as Boran does not diminish their claims that their rituals originated in opposition to the Boran and were imported from Somali.

Lafti guddo Boraana qabti. Arge yennán baafat. Gubbe qodata iti-bae. 'Nam argad'e!' Aki hori irát. Duub jarole deemte, 'worri sun qallu qaba' gar Garri barbadacu datte. Odooli gaaf aci jiru: Abábur, Galbo-fi Gāri gaaf aci jiru: Makkamadina. 'Nu deemne, laf tana baane, laf tan d'ufne, amm aada laf tana feena, qallu.'

The country had many Boran. When they saw them they fled. [The Boran] divided them up like arrows. 'I have found people!' They divided them up like livestock. So the elders said, 'Those people [the Garre] have got sheikhs'[141] and went to the Garre to look for [sheikhs]. When Odoola were living there, [they lived at] Ababur, when Galbo and Gār were living there, [they lived at] Makkamedina.[142] 'We have gone [out of], have come out of this [Garre] country, have come from this country, now we want the custom of this country, [we want] a sheikh.' (Galbo 1)

In the Odoola version priority in time and importance is attributed to the new rituals acquired by Odoola.

Duub Safari Au Maro jeti Odool Ababur jed'a, ín-daqan duub, worri durri birrádeeman kan. Au Maro nam chuf Odoola durr daq. Ol ol ol. Laf Safara. Bahrini gamma. Gaaf sun duub aci Safarí qallu duub aci iti-ga-baasan.

So they went to a place called Au Maro by the Somali and Ababur by Odoola where people before had gone out from. All people of Odoola originate from Au Maro. East, east, east. In the Somali country [meaning the Somali Republic]. Near the sea. At that time the Somali installed sheikhs there.

'At amm kitaab in-dándetu. Waan at dandetu si tolca. Mashashid [also masajid, *from* مسجد *, pl.* مساجد *= 'mosque'] Turbi qar fite kan jaarán. Fulá sun waan Waaqi tolce fakati namumá tolce̱.*

At present you are not able to deal with the book. I will set up something you can perform. The mosque of Turbi was built [or fenced] for the first time. That place looks like something God made but only people made it.

It is surprising to hear that an Islamic religious leader should advise the delegation of a 'pagan' (or, in their own terms, semi-pagan) people not to bother about the Qur'ān because it is too difficult for them and – as we shall see shortly – to adopt other rituals than those of Islam. This episode, however unrealistic it may be, here serves one purpose: it describes the Gabbra tribal ritual as equivalent to the practice of Islam and as sanctioned by Islamic authorities. The stigma of paganism is rejected. Both the fear of being called pagans by the Muslims and the ambition to have their own rituals respected as being on an equal footing with Islam show a certain degree of acceptance of Islamic ideas or at least of the prestige accorded to Islamic neighbours.

The second surprise is to hear of the Gabbra as mosque builders. In fact, the present-day Gabbra build practically no permanent structures. However, round stone settings of 5 or 7 metres diameter would also be referred to as 'mosques', whether they are temporarily roofed with branches and twigs or not. The meanings of *masajid* and *naabo* thus largely overlap. The use of the word *masajid*, however, makes the same point as the episode of the Somali sheikh instructing the Gabbra: it suggests that they are equal to Muslims.

> *Gabbr chuf as wolti-yaaman. As wolti-yaamani liyat, karsó, karsó kud'ani lamá as qallan.*

All Gabbra were called together there. They were called together and the *liyat*, female sheep, twelve young female sheep were slaughtered there.

The following paragraph makes clear that the *liyat* sacrifice is not linked to the Muslim ritual calendar in any way and that its origin, despite the pious tale that a Muslim sheikh established the custom, has to be sought elsewhere. The closest Muslim ritual in time would be Maulid, the birthday of the Prophet. This, however, is not held on the date of the *liyat*, which, in the version below, is the 6th of Ragarr – if not specified otherwise that means the first month of Ragaar (Arab. Safar) – but on the 12th of the second Ragarr, i.e. Rabī'ul Awwal. No connection to Maulid, however, is even claimed. On the other hand, *liyat* is linked by the informant to other Gabbra public rituals, both annual and heptennial (i.e. belonging to the seven-year 'week'), which are all clearly non-Islamic. The localities which follow are all the sites for age-set promotions of the different Gabbra phratries.

> *Arma deemaní duub Farol d'ufan. Farole-lle aada iti-tolcan. Gāri yabate, gubba Melbaná jir. Sun-lle d'aqaní, artumát aada tolcan. Sharbana-lle d'aqaní, laf tokk deeme Dillo gam sun aada tolcan. Fulá tan chuf naabo iti-jaaran.*

They went from there and came to Farole. Also at Farole they performed customs. Gār climbed, [their site] is up-mountain from Melbana. They went also there and performed customs right there. Also Sharbana went to one land, beyond Dillo, and performed customs. At all those places *naabo* were fenced [or laid out in the case of stone settings].

> *Worri kan chuf naabo jaarani. Laf tokko Ees jed'an, Dirre, arma fuud'aní fulá sun d'aqan. Dabela, nam hiitu iti-hid'an, fulá sun d'aqan. Eesi taan qabsisaní gaal arti qallen, gurbó.*

All these people [phratries] build *naabo*. One country is called Ees, in Dirre, they take [people] from here and go there. The *dabel*, the people who get the ritual headdress. [i.e. the ritual elders, the most senior age grade to which there are formal promotions], go there. They put [the sacrifice] on top of this [mountain] Ees, they slaughter the camel there, a young male one.

> *Gaaf karso kud'ani lamma qallan, ji sun Ragarr, adési jaa. 'Itum-deebité, womá in-sódatu, wom tokk at amm deete in-déetu, wani si-qabata.'*

When the twelve young female sheep were slaughtered [the *liyat*], it was the 6th of the month Ragarr. 'If you do that regularly, you will not be afraid of anything, you will not fear anything of what you fear now, nothing will get hold of you.' (Odoola)

With the establishment of ritual order, the time during which the proto-Gabbra stampeded like antelopes and were afraid of everything came to an end. This reminds us of the functionalist theory which claims that religion serves to reduce anxiety. Other sociological theorists might say that the establishment of public ritual furthers emotional unity, necessitates co-operation, and thus tends to create larger political units, thereby widening and intensifying social cohesion and, indirectly, military strength. Boru Galgallo is simply a believer and for him the effect is direct: having learned the right ritual, the Gabbra had acquired a means of securing God's blessing, which includes protection against their enemies. He therefore elaborates on further rituals which are deemed necessary to guarantee this blessing.

Duubo-um tana saddét gannat heregát, hiitu hid'ád'. Naabo tan jaarád', halkanif guyyá-lle galgalif diramá-lle iti-eebifád'.

For the *duubo* [the ritual headdress of the *dabela*] count eight years.[143] Build this *naabo*, pray there night and day, in the evening and in the morning.

Ji sorio mid'aaga sadíi: Somdeeri lama, Yaka sadí; ji sadéen sun jabád'i irre-in-dabríni, sorio qalád'! Aki dansa. Ragarra addési jaha, karso tan illakisín! Ji kan guyya at wolin-jirtu sorio qallád'!

The good months for *sorio* are three: the Somdeer are two, Yaka is the third; keep these three months holy [literally: 'make them strong', 'take them as something strong'] and do not let them pass, hold *sorio* [literally: 'slaughter (sacrifice) the *sorio*']! In a good way. On the 6th of Ragarr do not leave out these young female sheep! These [above mentioned three] months, if you are together, hold *sorio*! (Odoola)

In this context of assertion of new ritual strength, the holy objects of the Gabbra phratries, which each have a drum belonging to one moiety and a horn belonging to the other, is also believed to have been first established. The proverbial Five Drums figure prominently as the visual symbols of Gabbra identity.

Worr kan chuf ammá-lle dibbe-f magalád wolin-itin-d'ufan. Chuf Gabbran kan. Nam chuf durrát Odoola kennan. Gul Gaará kennan, Galbo kennan. Gaafas Algannan in-séene. Duub eege Sharbana kennan. Ammá-tan ammo Gabbr chuf yaa-i shani, chuf ammá-tana angáfi Shárbana.

All these peoples [phratries] now also each were given a drum and a horn. All these Gabbra. Of all [phratries] Odoola was given [them] first. Then they were given to Gār, then to Galbo. At that time Alganna had not entered [= joined the other Gabbra]. At last they were given to Sharbana. But today of all the Gabbra, of the Five Drums, the first-born is Sharbana.[144] (Odoola)

THE GABBRA–BORAN RELATIONSHIP

A strange contrast arises between this description of the origin of the main collective identity symbols of the Gabbra and the establishment of their public rituals as a means of asserting their independence from the Boran on the one hand, and the present-day close alliance between the two peoples on the other. If we accept the PRS origin of the Gabbra, as suggested by cultural comparison,[145] migrational traditions and clan histories,[146] it is in fact their Boran-ness, that is, their political association with the Boran and their use of the Boran language, that sets them apart from the Rendille (who even call them 'Boranto') and establishes their separate identity. Today their similarity to the Boran is so close that they are treated in the literature as an Oromo group or a camel-keeping branch of the Boran rather than as a Somaloid group. To understand the nature and development of the Gabbra–Boran relationship we must return to Boru Galgallo's (Odoola) account of the events after the establishment of the Gabbra rituals.

The spirits of the Gabbra had been strengthened by the words of their Somali ritual adviser:

'At ammatan woma insódatu, ya gara si-jabbese, woma insódatu, taa!'

'Now you do not need to be afraid of anything, I have strengthened your belly, you are not afraid of anything, stay!'

So the Gabbra stayed and awaited the arrival of the Boran, who would come to divide them up. In the resulting fight the Gabbra put the Boran to flight, but were nevertheless pursuaded by their foe's numerical strength to seek peace. They agreed on a *modus vivendi* and stayed for a while in the neighbourhood of the Boran in the Ethiopian highlands, until the pasture requirements of their camels, which did not prosper in the cold, damp uplands, made them move away.

Waaqi roobe duub, roobi jabbate, Gabbri waan jete: gaal ín-d'ala, boqeni roobe, ya-guddate. An ammá akán in-d'andau. Laf gammoji, laf diida, sababu gudda in-qabne, an amma laf akasi barbad'a. Ati dubbi chuf hobbas, aada ati maan chuf dubbadd'i hobbas. An si-mirá odu fuud'a.

God/the sky now rained, the rain became strong, and the Gabbra said, 'The camels are about to calve, it has rained, rained much. I now can not [stay] like this. I will look for a hot country, a low country, because it does not have much rain. Finish all the talk [alone], finish all the talk about the custom. I will ask you about it [later]. (Odoola)

Even if this text does not render the exact course of historical events (which is unlikely because of the strong and independent position it ascribes to the Gabbra), it clarifies two important points. First, the main factor which at all times has prevented the Gabbra and the Boran from merging into one political unit (all they ever became is an unequal alliance) has been the different ecological requirements of their economies, namely the high, wet lands preferred by Boran cattle and the low, hot, dry pastures of Gabbra camels. (This, on the other hand, may have made their alliance stable by excluding territorial competition.) Second, the Gabbra were not fully integrated into Boran public ritual and law (both included in the term *aada*). The two ritual and social systems remained different and intact, although links were established between them, as we shall see below.

At this time, the informant claims, the Boran were still under the rule of a woman, and their political system, as we know it today, was only about to be established. To achieve this, however, the woman ruler, named Banoiye, first had to be disposed of. We here quote the fuller account by a Boran informant, Waako D'iriba.

Niitiin nam chuf isiin moot. Murraan isii. Qallu isiin challa. Waan lafa d'alate chuf 'taha' jet. Waan isiin 'taha' jet chuf in/tahan. Waan isiin eege irrá doot [. . .]: 'T'affi ta marrá gami chuf rifesa qabu kéjirt fuuda!' jet.

The woman was king over everybody. Hers was the command. She was the only priest. She said, 'Do [like this]!' to whatever was born in the country. Everything she told [people] to do was done. What she finally died of was this: 'Bring me fleas in a skin bag with hair on both sides [= inside and outside]!' she said.

Nami gar walaale, mucca diqaa yabbi tissu irr d'ufan. 'Maal isan injéte?' 'Badd akan jet. Ya-walaale waan isiin jetu.' 'Badda, gurr harre mura!'

People missed what to do and went to a small boy who looked after the calves. [They reported Banoiye's demand to him and he replied with astonishment,] 'What has she told you?' [The elders said,] 'The one who may get lost said like this. We do not know how to do what she said.' [But the boy advised them,] 'Go and cut the ear of a donkey!'

'Qora udan harret iti-gurra, ibid garát hidd'a, yo sadíi bulte, taffi mijju.' Itind'ufan. 'Taná-lle na garsisan.' Ya waan taatu d'abte, 'beena, loon kun imbobaín, moona in-olín, in-elmín, birri in-olín!'

'Collect donkey dung in it [in the bag made of the ear of the donkey], hang it up above the fire, when it stayed three nights, it will be full of fleas.' They [did so and then] went to [Banoiye again]. 'They have shown me even that,' [she said]. Now she missed what to do [i.e. had difficulties to invent more chicaneries], 'Go, these cattle shall not go to pasture and shall not stay in the enclosures, do not milk them and do not leave them unmilked!'

Gar walaalan. Imbóban, agábu in-ólan. Jennan mucca diqa kan iti-d'ufan; muccá ya-jaalataní.

They missed what to do. The cattle should not go to pasture and not stay with an empty stomach. Then they came to this little boy; they had come to like the boy.

'Ya-walaaltani?' 'Eee.' 'Beena, bol qota, ya finn walaalte, korá kora, kor isii kora,

bol qota, gurbi isiin irr-afa. Isii yo gasa-t baatu, itille jalaan deemani. Itille sun irrá-
t-aaf.'

'You miss what to do?' 'Yes.' 'Go and dig a hole, she has lost her claim to lead
[*finn*: 'her proper conduct', 'her way to manage and make herds and people
prosper'], call a meeting, call a meeting for her, dig a hole, put her cushions on
top of it. When she goes to the tree of assembly, they carry her cow skin along.
Put that cow skin on top of it.'

Kori durrá bae. Isiin laanum faan d'ufte. Ya itille ballesani-fi itille taan irre teeti,
laanum d'ufte. 'Hooobób!' jete, ke-badde.

The meeting started. She came slowly slowly. Already they unfolded the cow
skin and put it down [on top of the pit], she came slowly. '*Hooobób!*' she said
and got lost in it.

'*Arrrarrr baddi nadd'een, baddi nadd'een,*' *in-daamati,* '*dubbi micirám hayét, fin-*
caani boró dubát hayet, hanan abbá worrá diqica hayét.' *Waan isiin daamat chuf,*
bool akanuman ballé buusan. Had Wejja tan, Had Wejja ta baanan tan kuuno.
Akanam ballesan, akan.

'Arrrarrr, the women are lost, the women are lost,' she made her last will and
testament [shouting out of the pit], '[Women,] talk only twisted talk, urinate
right behind the house, save little milk for the head of the household!' All this
is her last will and testament. This is how she was thrown into the depth of the
pit. This Mother of Wejja [married women in Boran are respectfully called
'Mother of So-and-so'], this is the Mother of Wejja people talk about. That is
how they did away with her, that's how. (Boran)

It is clear that the emphasis of this tale is not to recount a historical
event but to make a point about the nature of women, or, as a Boran
might say, to explain why women behave as they actually do, that is, why
they do not speak the truth, why they do not go a decent distance away
from the settlement to urinate and why they do not feed their husbands
properly. All this is Banoiye's legacy. Also, implicitly, this tale praises
the blessings of male dominance by showing the calamities to which earlier female rule had led. Thus it serves the functions matriarchal myths
have always had in male-oriented societies from Homer and Sophocles
until today.

From the accounts of other informants it appears doubtful that, at the
time of the extension of their hegemony over the Gabbra, the Boran should
still have been under Banoiye's rule, if indeed they ever were. On the
contrary, it appears to have been the new order, namely the *gada* system,
of which *hayyu* and *jallaba* are functionaries, which led to this political
expansion.

Eegi isii ijjesan, gadá tolfatan. [. . .] Qallu, raabi, gadán, waan kan chuf Borani
tahe. Duub gadana nam fidu iti tae, qallum fidu iti tae, raabi nam fidu iti tae. Yo
nami amma raaba gada jed', akanan, finn kan argate.

After they had killed her, they made [= established] *gada*. [. . .][147] The Boran
made *qallu* [priests], *raab* [uncircumcised warriors], *gada*, all that. So the *gada*

became the way to manage people, *qallu* became the way to manage people, *raab* became the way to manage. If people now say *raab* and *gada*, this is how this custom was established. (Boran)

Here follows the account of the war expeditions of the *raab* and the bull oracle they consulted before raiding an enemy camp which we have recorded above.[148]

Thus, in agreement with other sources, we arrive at the following relative chronology:

the violent end of Banoiye's rule[149]
the establishment of *gada* with its recurrent ritual wars
the flight of the Gabbra to Iris in the west (and the flight of other PRS peoples towards the east)
the return from Iris
the continued Boran threat leads to the establishment of the Gabbra public ritual
the extension of the *pax borana* over the Gabbra

For the period since the establishment of Boran hegemony over the Gabbra until the time of colonial rule – and in certain ways until today – the Gabbra–Boran relationship was characterised by the following traits: (a) relative peace; (b) *tiriso*, i.e. the equation of each Gabbra lineage present at the time of 'dividing up' with a Boran lineage, thereby establishing a mild form of dependence; (c) regular visits to Boran ritual leaders by Gabbra delegations bearing gifts.

The peace between Gabbra and Boran at times seemed, and seems, uneasy. This may perhaps be explained by the strong emphasis on warriorhood and martial exploits imposed on the Boran *raab* by their role in the *gada* system and the short supply of enemies within reach which certain groups might have experienced after the Boran had pacified a large proportion of East and North-east Africa.[150] The *tiriso* relationship did not prevent the Gabbra from defending themselves, sometimes even successfully.

We give the story of such a Gabbra success in the words of a Boran informant:

Aki tokko duub ka hadis fakatu jir. Boranii 'raab' jed'a, 'gada' jed'a. Guyya raa-bum kana duub 'd'id'a' jed'a, iti-duula.

There is one way which is similar to raiding.[151] The Boran say *raab*, say *gada*. At the time of this *raab*, they say 'war camp', they went there for war.

D'ufe duub iti-qubata. Wa hadan malle, d'id'a tan im-báhani. Yoosi d'ufe iti-cabse duub in-hádu, iti-qubat. 'Hori ga-báása' jed'ani, Gabbri duub in-sodata. Duub hori ga-fuud'ate gallan.

They came and settled there. Unless they raided something, they did not leave the war camp. When they came, when they intruded, they did not raid, they [just] settled there. They said, 'Surrender livestock!' and then the Gabbra were afraid. So they took livestock and went home.

Akanum ole gaaf tokko duuba 'hori ken in-kénnin.' Gabbri duub raab Boraná akan haat. Gabbri duub Boran dabsat. Rra-débie, 'ya na dabsate, aada malle, in-gállu, hori yau ken' jed'.

So it was until one time [the Gabbra said], 'Let us not give them our animals.' The Gabbra then just raided the *raab* of the Boran. The Gabbra defeated the Boran. These came back and said, 'You have defeated us, according to the custom we cannot go home, give us those animals which walk [there]!'[152]

According to Gabbra informants, the Boran were given an old she-camel as their 'spoil'. A camel ox, however, broke away and ran after her, so that two animals were lost.[153]

Such war expeditions occurred until the British and the Abyssinians ('Habash') established their respective overlordships.[154] Boru Galgallo mentions that such expeditions also aimed at killing a man and taking his genitals as a trophy. If a Gabbra was the victim, the Boran withdrew after killing only that one man. This also underlines the ritual nature of these wars. Even today, long after the end of organised *raab* expeditions, Boran occasionally shoot and mutilate single Gabbra herd boys. The use of guns from a safe distance makes these incidents appear especially ugly and explains the bitterness of the Gabbra, who claim that these trophies are used for 'boasting in front of the women'.

We should recall[155] in this context of bloodshed between allied peoples that Gabbra and Boran are bound together by ritual ties and treaties[156] but do not regard each other as brothers. Their 'blood' is 'different'. The relationship between the two peoples being merely political, murder may be regarded as a disruption of this relationship but not as a sin.[157] Consequently the power of the Boran, their leading political role and the prestige of their ritual offices are given as reasons for their ability to incorporate and dominate other peoples, and it is striking how little use is made of the language of kinship which otherwise is so common in ethnic politics. Sometimes the Boran are equated with the later British rulers, by being referred to as *serikali* ('government') or by having other terms from colonial phraseology applied to them.

Worri sun gaafas biyye dabsat. Nam kan chuf mpaka ciratta. Ammálle biyye sobba. 'Isan challááni, nu-lle yo akas gos wolin-taana, nu-lle si gosa. Atí-lle nu gosa. Yo hori wol-dowwane cubbu.

Those poeple [the Boran] at that time were superior to the common populace. They incorporated all these peoples [of northern Kenya] into their boundaries [using the Swahili word *mpaka*, introduced by the British, who enforced territorial boundaries between what they perceived as tribes]. But they also cheated people. 'Not you alone, also us, if we become tribesmen to each other, we shall also be tribesmen to you. And you will be tribesmen to us. It is sin if we refuse each other [gifts of] livestock.

'Isan wan moona itin-d'uftanif in-d'ábtani. Nu-lle in-d'ábnu. Akana gos wol-tolfannu.' 'Eee' jed'ani, duub qoodani.

You will not miss [livestock] if you come to [our] enclosures. Neither shall we miss [livestock if we come to your enclosures]. Let us make ourselves one tribe [literally: "Like this let us make each other tribe"].' 'Yes,' said [the Gabbra] and were divided up. (Galbo 2)

This 'dividing up' was done lineage by lineage. Each lineage was ascribed to a Boran clan without taking their internal relationships into account. Brother lineages thus ended up in different Boran clans. This new order, however, has never replaced the old one; it was only relevant in Gabbra–Boran interaction, while for all other purposes the old clan structure was utilised and the new Boran names were not even mentioned. To illustrate this, I give the set of equivalences for Galbo phratry (Table 12).

This alignment of the Gabbra clans with the Boran clan structure does not mean that they gave up their cultural identity, which, as we have seen, had been formulated as an assertion of their independent existence under Boran pressure. The following may be regarded as a Gabbra charter or as their manifesto against the Boran.

Table 12 **Tiriso** relationships of Galbo

Gabbra lineage		Boran clan
	Massa, Chaaqo	Odítu
	Gololle (Carriye)	Digallu
	Gololle (Chooro)	Konnítu
	Irille	Karrayyu (Wòrr Bokku = Bokkica)
Barawa:	Bule Fute	Odítu
	Kuiyal	Karrayyu (Danqa)
	Mamo Deera	Karrayyu (Berre)
	Burot	Karrayyu (Danqa)
	Bulqabna	Qarcábdu
Yohoma:	Gallea	Dambítu
	Qoshobe (Hidábu)	Digallu
	Qoshobe (Bule Sora)	Karrayyu
	Usmalo (Korrot)	Siráyyu
	Usmalo (Cirratte)	Karrayyu Didimtu
	Kibibe (Elfure)	Worr Jidda
	Kibibe (Eldaiyo)	Digallu
	Odolale	
	Saleda	
	Galleole	⎰ Matt'arri ⎱ Karrayyu ⎰ Hawatt'u

Jarsi Gabbra Borán yaam. 'Wo hagám tofauti qabt: wo sadíi. Woni tofauti qabu chufi kiyy. Ati wo lama qabta: Woni tofauti inqábu kaan kanke.

The elders of the Gabbra called the Boran: 'Three things are different.[158] These are all mine. You have got two things: what is not different is yours [i.e. the Gabbra share the two central elements of Boran culture and have three more central cultural traits which they do not share with the Boran].

'An durri Gabbra. Si-t na Boran-se, mata cibrad'e, maqan Gabbra tofauti. An Borana ammo Gabbr uf-in-jed'.

'I used to be Gabbra. You made me Boran, and I plaited my hair [i.e. my women-folk adopted the Boran hairstyle], the name Gabbra is different. I am Boran but call myself Gabbra.

'Loon nu chuf woliman-qabna. Loon'jenne maqa gaala bir kena. Loon jenne re maqa bir kena. Maqa re-lle tofaut. Maqaan gaalá-lle tofaut. Maqaan tofaut in-qabne loon.

'We both have cattle. If we mention cattle, let us also consider camels. If we mention cattle, let us also consider smallstock. Smallstock constitutes a differ-ence. Camels constitute a difference. What we have in common is cattle.

'Maqaan Boraaná-lle kanke. Maqaan looni kanke. Gutu loon ín-dawat. An gutun tiyy gaalu. Gutun tante loon.

'The name of Boran is yours. The name of cattle is yours. You make your tress with cattle. My tress is camels. ["tress" is here figurative for personality or cultural focus since Gabbra, with the exception of some Alganna lineages, do not wear the tress, *gut*]. Your tress is cattle.

'Duub anáf si looni wol-sodanu, nam wol-sodataanu. Ijjefne, wol-murraccu lakifnu.

'So, both of us respect cattle, let us become people who respect [or fear] each other. Even if we kill each other, let us cease mutilating each other.

'D'ufne, wol-irra-dabiiti dinnu. Fula intalti dubrá d'ufte keesa wo d'abtu, fulan duub tirison d'ufte keesa wo in-d'ábtu.'

'We have come, let us stop to miss something from each other. Where one's own daugther came and missed something, may the *tiriso* partner not miss any-thing.' (Gabbra)

Any interpretation that reads this passage as referring only to the ecol-ogical and economic differences between the two pastoral systems and the greater importance attributed to smallstock and camels by the Gabbra would be too narrow. 'My tress is camels' means that camels are culturally central to Gabbra society and implies the whole camel complex with its ritual elaborations described in the first part of this chapter. To underline camels means to underline the core of Gabbra culture; and it is the cores of their cultures which the two societies do not share, although they arti-culate smoothly on the fringes.

This articulation takes its visible form in the journeys Gabbra under-took to pay tribute to the Boran *qallu*. Such journey (*muda*), however, were by no means peculiar to the Gabbra but were undertaken by delegations of other dependent peoples in the same way. We have already heard of the gifts handed by Hassan Buro, the first Miigo Sakuye, and his wife to the Boran *qallu*, and this description does not stand for a single event but for a permanent relationship.

THE PAX BORANA AND ITS DECLINE

The accounts of the long migration often end with the refugees returning and being incorporated into the hegemonial system of the Boran which originally they had tried to evade. This marked the beginning of a pluriethnic political system which was the major unifying factor in the region before the introduction of modern statehood. In what is now Kenya this system comprised the Gabbra (Malbe and Miigo), the Sakuye, the Garre, the Ajuran and the Warr Daaya, and other peoples belonged to it on the Ethiopian side. These peoples were also collectively known as Worr Liban, or, in Somali, Reer Libin, i.e. the people of Liban, after a region in southern Ethiopia.

For our present purpose the hegemonial role the Boran played during three centuries is important, since it explains the distribution of languages in the area. It explains why, between the Somaloid Rendille in the west and the Somali in the east, there is a wedge of Oromo speakers.[159] These Oromo speakers are PRS who have given up their original language in favour of Boran and have only kept some Somaloid phrases for ritual use (like the Af Daiyo above).

The decisive event for the emergence of the inter-ethnic clan relationships between the societies we are studying was the establishment of Boran hegemony and the ethnic differentiation processes across clan boundaries which it triggered in the form of the 'long migrations' and the ethnic reshuffling resulting from them. These have been described. To go into the details of the subsequent political history, the ascendancy of the Boran and their decline with the advent of the Darood Somali and the British, is not necessary in this context. The subject is far too interesting to be treated as a side issue and deserves fuller treatment under separate cover.

CHAPTER 5

THE INTER-ETHNIC CLAN CLUSTERS

The two preceding chapters have depicted the present ethnic groups as emerging out of a more uniform proto-Rendille–Somali population in more or less their final shape. A PRS population split into Garre, Gabbra and Rendille, who later split into Rendille and Sakuye. Now I must, at the risk of causing the reader annoyance, ask him/her to abandon this picture again. Such a view of the ethnogenetic processes is no more than a rough model of some basic trends. We have to regard it as a temporary structure which is pulled down once it has completed its purpose, just as a scaffold is taken down once the building is finished. As a scaffold approximates the shape of the construction which it helps to erect without depicting it fully or replacing it in any way, so the implicit model of ethnogenesis I have developed so far is neither arbitrary nor completely wrong but neither is it final. I have so far maintained the fiction that once a group has split into two, the products of this split lose all contact with each other. This idea is familiar to us from phylogenesis or the more primitive models of his-torical linguistics, which are often compared to a tree: a trunk splits into branches, branches split into twigs.[1] (The word *phylum* itself means 'trunk'.) In linguistics newer approaches try to overcome the simplifications of this simplistic model.[2] To adjust the tree model to the complex courses ethnogenetic processes can take, we have to invent a new type of tree: one in which twigs can again join the branches they spring from or join other branches or grow together with other twigs from their own or other bran-ches. In other words, we have to take into account the fact that differen-tiation is reversible and that the products of a split continue to exchange parts of themselves, and do so the more easily the more recent the split is. For example, the Kirima at one time split from the Rendille, who later destroyed some of them and reintegrated the remnants. Today there are no Kirima but only Rendille, some of whose ancestors at one time were

Kirima and others not. The history of single clans can vary greatly from the general model, which assumes that PRS became Garre, Gabbra and early Rendille who in turn became modern Rendille and Sakuye. We should not be surprised to find that certain Gabbra lineages derive from the Rendille or an earlier Rendille-like configuration, or that a Sakuye clan stems from the (ancestral) Gabbra, or that certain Rendille clans claim to come from the Garre, etc. The very ethnonyms were use are nothing but a projection into the past, because we do not have any evidence that two hundred years ago all or any of the ancestors of the Gabbra referred to themselves as 'Gabbra'; nor do we know how old names like 'Rendille' or 'Garre' are. So we have to examine each of the clan histories in its own right and can only use the major ethnic processes described above as rough indicators, to which some clan histories correspond and others not, to provide a crude chronological orientation.

The method I apply to the history of clans is the same as the one I have applied in chapter 4 to the reconstruction of the major ethnic currents. In the first part of chapter 4 I have used the comparison of cultural elements to distinguish a cluster of historically related peoples from neighbouring groups whose cultures respond to similar needs but derive from different sources. In the second part of chapter 4 I then examined and compared one special domain of culture more closely, namely the historical traditions. This comparison was of a more complex nature since, in addition to the search for formal similarities in texts (which can be compared like those of rituals, artefacts, words or systems of time reckoning), the study of oral tradition opened up a dimension of content which can be discussed in the light of the historical and philological methods of source research, the analysis of narrators' motivations, folklore patterns versus historical realism, and so on – in short, all the categories of historical criticism which are also applied to written sources.

I now apply the same two procedures at the level of clan history and compare clan histories from the origin myths to recent migrational traditions; and I also compare other clan-specific cultural features such as avoidances, ritual powers or elements of material culture. While in chapter 4 I had a fixed order – non-verbal sources first, verbal sources second – I now relax this order because in some ways clans appeared to me like personalities. When describing a personality one starts with a conspicuous feature, a characteristic event or a telling quotation – whatever one finds particularly distinctive. The following eight sections are independent essays in each of which an inter-ethnic cluster of clans is described in its own right as an individual entity. The reader who is interested in a more systematic form of comparison can, however, easily extract lists of features and synopses of traditions from these essays and represent them in tabular form or any other convenient way. I hope, however, that the way these clan histories are presented here permits a sufficiently clear picture to emerge.

ODOOLA

Groups which refer to themselves as Odoola or Adoola can be found among the Rendille, the Gabbra and the Garre, and two lineages, which among the Rendille and/or the Gabbra are part of Odoola, appear among the Sakuye as independent clans. For easy orientation let us start with the subunits of Odoola and the different forms their names take in the four ethnic groups (Table 13). The order adopted is the relative seniority of these groups among the Rendille. Whether or not these groups actually share a common origin the reader will be able to judge at the end of the discussion.

In chapter 2 I have already mentioned that Odoola of Rendille has very atypical marriage rules. Although as a whole it is smaller than the exogamous clans of Rendille, it is not exogamous itself but comprises not less than four exogamous units – in this way it resembles a whole Gabbra phratry or a supra-clan unit of some other society. As mentioned in the same chapter, Odoola does not belong to either of the Rendille moieties, thus forming an independent – although demographically negligible – third part of Rendille society.

The Rendille remember a time – it may have been around the turn of the century – when Odoola camels were taken by force by other Rendille (*maanti Odoola gaal lasare*). To minimise such risks, Rendille Odoola have

Table 13   Synopsis of Odoola lineage names

Garre	Gabbra	Rendille	Sakuye
Adoola	Odoola	Odoola	
	Meilán	Makhalán	Mailan
Ma'abile		Mañabolle	
	Kaalaya	Timbór	
		Dafardai	
Rer Mug	Rer Mug	Mooga	
	Keinán	Keinán	
	Nurre	Nurre	
Hodomai or Bursunni	Bursúnna	Bursúnna	
		Gaerre	
	Akadér, Harkidér		
Tubádi	Tubádi		Tubádi
	Eidamole		
Kalwein			
Kalmasa			
Meda			

established clan equivalences with other Rendille clans: Makhalán with
Gaaldeilan, Dafardai and Mooga with Tubcha, Nurre with Saale, Busúnna
with Elegella.

Of a different nature is the relationship of Adibille to Nahagán. This
lineage descends from a wife of a Nahagán man who remained childless
until she settled with Odoola. In Rendille terms of legitimacy this lineage
therefore belongs to Nahagan, although it lives with Odoola and shares
their customs.

The special position of Odoola in the social organisation of the Rendille
becomes visible in the spatial arrangement of the *gaalgulamme* settlement.[3]
On this occasion all Rendille ideally join in one large settlement. The two
moieties settle in one large ring, the western Belel (Belesi Bahai) starting with its most senior segment in the west and the eastern Belel (Belesi
Berri) in the east, whereby the most junior clan of one moiety become the
neighbour of the first house of the other. Odoola settle outside the ring.
Apart from the obvious reason that Odoola cannot claim a settlement position in the ring because it has no moiety affiliation and no place in the
seniority order of the Rendille, Odoola informants also give another reason
for this arrangement: *Jibanjib naabotiche a yer. Baa makakhaianto* ('Jibanjib has a separate *naabo* [assembly place]. She does not join the people').
Jibanjib is the only drum in Rendille-land with a function similar to the
holy drums of the Gabbra phratries. Odoola uses the powers of this drum
to exercise influence throughout Rendille society and beyond it.[4] The
drum has significance also for one other institution: the *dabel* or elders of
a special status, which is also bestowed by Odoola on selected elders of
other Rendille clans. We have seen in chapter 4 that *dabela* also play a role
in Gabbra and Gabbra Miigo societies where they are an age grade which
is passed through by all males who live long enough. (Rendille–Gabbra
comparison shows that the importance and prestige of *dabela* decrease
in the same measure as their numbers increase.) The separate *naabo* and
the separate settlement ring around it which houses Jibanjib have one
characteristic which needs to be borne in mind in the course of this chapter: they are always found in the north of the *gaalgulamme* settlement of
the two moieties. The Harrau lineage of D'ubsahai[5] also has a similar
special relationship to the north, perhaps for the same reason.

While talking about spatial arrangements, I should also mention that all
Rendille houses are built with their doors facing west, or, more precisely,
converging on a point outside and to the west of the settlement, approximately where the *ulukh*, the ritual gate, is built at *almodo*.[6] Gabbra houses
likewise face west, the difference of settlement arrangement being that
Gabbra settlements are lineal whereas Rendille settlements are circular.
The first house in order of senority of a Gabbra settlement is in the north,
the most junior house at the southern end of the line. The whole orienta-

tion is modelled on the spatial arrangement of the settlement: if one faces west, north becomes associated with the right hand and south with the left hand[7] (B: *mirga* – north, right, *bittaa* – south, left; R; *miig* – north, right, also: strong (!), *gurro* – south, left). The inside divisions of a house are just as closely associated with the cardinal points as the orientation of the house in the settlement and that of the settlement in the cosmic order. The private sphere is the eastern half of the house (R: *berri*, B: *ol*), where the bed or the sleeping skins are found, while the western half (R: *baħai*, B: *jal*) is open even to people with whom social intercourse is restricted, such as strangers or certain categories of affines. In Gabbra houses the two spheres are divided by a lattice of twigs and a curtain. This division is called *dinqa* by Gabbra and throughout Oromo. The difference between the Rendille division of a house and that of the Gabbra is the relative location of water and fire. In a Rendille house the water containers of woven plant fibres (R: *ħan*, B: *bute*) are in the south of the house (the 'left' side facing the door, i.e. the right side as one comes in) and the hearthstones are in the north. This also determines the place of the woman, who works, sits and sleeps near the hearthstones. In a Gabbra house the fireplace is in the south and the water containers are in the north. Coming back to Odoola we find that the house of the Rendille Odoola is divided like a Gabbra house – in other words, it is the wrong way round, a mirror image of the standard Rendille house.

If in this field of spatial orientation the Rendille Odoola follow the Gabbra pattern, in another field of spatial orientation, namely slaughtering, the Gabbra Odoola follow the Rendille pattern. When they throw a sheep or goat on the ground to cut its throat both Gabbra and Rendille orient its longitudinal axis towards the east. Thus if the slaughter takes place inside the settlement in front of the house the head points towards the house. But a Rendille animal lies on its left side with the legs and the face pointing south, whereas the Gabbra animal lies on its right side with limbs and face pointing north (Diagram 16). (Contrary to some claims by recent converts, neither of these two forms is due to old Muslim influence, since Muslims would turn the animal with the head in the *qibla*, i.e. towards Mecca, which in Kenya means north.) All Odoola slaughter animals in the Rendille fashion, as do also the Sakuye, while the Gabbra use the Boran way. This suggests that the original PRS way would correspond to the Rendille orientation which, in the case of the non-Odoola Gabbra, was later replaced by the Boran way. That Odoola, contrary to the other Gabbra, did not follow the Boran example fits well with their general opposition to Boran-ness and their self-perception as 'Somali', which I discuss below.

As well as the similarities between the Rendille Odoola and the Gabbra and between the Gabbra Odoola and the Rendille, we also find many features which are shared by both groups of Odoola and which distinguish

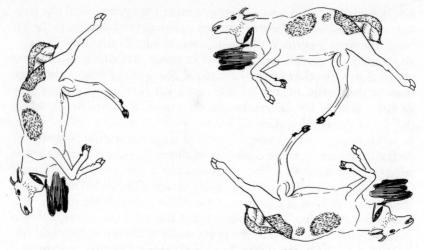

Diagram 16   Orientation of sacrificial animals

them from all the other Rendille and Gabbra. Such specific traits of Odoola are that they 'hate' or avoid the month of Ramadan (Soom), during which many activities are or were forbidden to them.[8] I have already mentioned the fire of Odoola which, just like *almodo*, is said to be celebrated as a reminder of a mythical relation of incest between a genitor and his bio-logical daughter.[9] Boru Galgallo (Gabbra, Odoola)[10] gives a new variant of this myth in which the husband is not only genitor but also pater, adding social to biological incest.

> *[Aadan ibida teesan eesá baate?] Gaar irrá d'uf. Nam Gaara maqá Almado. Niitin isaan baddé. Arsi galte. Gaaf sun ulfo. Niiti sunti aci doote. Dubr d'alte, intal maan jed': 'Abbaan kanke maqáán almado.'*

> [Where does your custom of the fire spring from?] It comes from the Gaar. A man of Gaar was called Almado by name. His wife got lost and joined the Arussi. At that time she was pregnant. That woman died there. She had given birth to a girl, she said to the girl, 'The name of your father is Almado.'

> *Amm intaliti [. . .] guddo. 'At amma laf Boranat deebi!' Laf Borana d'ufte duub. Niitin tun gaaf badde kan nittin eege fuud'e. Jarti qar ini fuud'e haad ijolle gugurdo taani duub iní-lle ya-jare, isiin duub doote.*

> The girl was grown up now. 'Go back to the Gabbra country now!' So she came to Gabbraland. When that wife had got lost [Almado] had married another wife. The woman he had married had big children, he himself had become old and she had died.

> *Intalti lafum Borana kejirti, ijolle isa duub agarté, hawadatte duub, fuuté d'ufté, abba jal keete, Almado kan, in-fuusift duub. Abban amma jarsa, ufuman gosé taa. Fuute jal keete.*

The girl [now] was in the Gabbra country, his sons saw her, abducted her and brought her to the feet of [or 'under the eyes of', literally: 'under' (*jal*)] their father, this Almado, and made him marry her. The father now was an old man and stayed alone near the livestock enclosures.[11] So they put her at his feet.

Intalti yo dubbate 'wa Almado kiyy baddee' jete. Waan chuf Almado maqa dooft. In-gaafatan duub. Haad maqá gaafatan. Haad hiimte. 'At garami d'alate?' jed'ani. Laf iti-d'alate hiimate. 'Haati maant aciin daq?' jed'. 'Ufumaan badde aci datte,' jet. 'Duub isiin amm jirti?' jed'ani.

When the girl was talking [cursing, lamenting, e.g. about spilled milk or other mishaps] she said, 'Oh, my Almado is lost'[12] on all occasions she mentioned the name Almado. So they asked her. They asked her for the name of her mother. She named her mother. 'Where have you been born?' they said. She named the region where she was born. 'Why had your mother gone there?' he [Almado] said. 'She got lost by herself and went there,' she said. 'Is she alive now?' they asked.

'Gaaf durri laf tana badde garaac qabti,' jet. 'Garaaci sun ana. Duub amma dooti yennan, "at biyye Borana deebi, naan jet."' Abbaan ijolle ya-yaamte. 'Intalti tan haati ta isan maqá beetan; intal tan anumá d'alle,' jed'. "Ammo isan na jal keetan", jed'. "Amm isan duuba yo an isan woldaanu malle middi in-táátan", jed'.

She said, 'When she got lost from this country she was pregnant with me. [literally: "she had a belly. That belly was me".] Then, when she was about to die, she told me, "go back to the Gabbra people!"' The father called his children. 'You know the name of the mother of this girl; I begot this girl myself,' he said. 'But you brought her to me [literally: "under me"]. Now you cannot prosper unless we do something.

Ji iti-erregé, ji dukani shane, Somdeer, diram 'beena, roco ga-daa,' jed'. Aadu goos amma tan Gabbri daabt kun, 'goos na jaara' jed'. Yo goos kan jaaraní: 'Shabash chufana gudda iti na ga-murra! Roco kan duub ga-daa, kota, qalla!'

He counted the days of the month, in Somdeer, the 5th of the darkness [the 20th of the lunar cycle], in the morning, he said, 'Go and bring the [fattened] camel ox.' Like these arbours the Gabbra build, he said, 'Build me an arbour!' When they built the arbour, he said, 'Cut a large door branch from the *shabash* tree[13] for it. Then bring the ox, come with it and slaughter it!'

Goos kaan ya qoran cabsani, hagganaan gaani. Foon roco kaan chuf iti-deebisan, 'foon roco kan dallu inkutatín!' jed'. 'Duub ann ibid kan uf-kaa ibidi kan ha na gubu. An irresi kiyyá-lle kanuma. Duub in-tuqína!

At that arbour they broke firewood until it reached up to here [meaning a huge pile of firewood]. They put there all the meat of the camel-ox, he had said, 'Do not cut any of the meat [fat] of the hump of this camel-ox for yourselves! Now I will expose myself to this fire, may this fire burn me. Also my grave will be just this. So, do not touch it!

Bulti tan heeda, duub bulti taan gul deema, aada tolfadd'a!' Almado duub arma baate ini kaan ibid uf-kaae, due. Nami wolin laf jiru Odoolaf Gaar. Odooli duub heedum heete, nu heeni lafa aki jiááni, halkan kaan ka ini ibid uf-kaae, halkan kan jed'ani, bar ganni dabre, ak ibid onana kan. Duub Odooli bobes.

Calculate this date, follow this date, hold a custom!' Like this Almado origi-

nated, that one exposed himself to the fire, died. The people who were together
in the area were Odoola and Gaar. So Odoola calculated and calculated, not like
you calculate the month [a lunar date; because Almado follows the solar year],
that night when he burned himself, they say it was this [meaning: such and such
a] night, the anniversary is when a [solar] year has passed, like that fire of a few
days ago. [The interview took place shortly after the last repetition of the Fire of
Odoola.] Odoola kindled that one.

*Gaari, guyyá durri kaan, yo ini guyya sun gae, ayyaani barri iti gad aanu kaan,
duub ini hanan diram wolti-kae duub ibid kan bobes. Wol-yaame. Hanan d'uge.
Qar duuba chufana jida iti-murr.*

The Gaar on that day, when that day arrived, when that day broke, they came
together bringing milk and kindled that fire. They called each other. They
drank milk. Before that they had cut a fresh ['wet'] door branch [for the camel
enclosure].

*Odooli ibid bobesa kaan iti-ga-dabr. Almado duub Almado jed'an kaan gaafum sun
gad-umant. Almadon nam chuf taate, ibid Odoolumaan challa bobes. Ibid Odoola
jed'an duub.*

Odoola stuck to burning that fire. So Almado, as it is called, was brought into
existence that day. All people performed Almado, only Odoola burned the fire.
So they call it Fire of Odoola. (Odoola)[14]

This account does not mention where all this happened and whether
'Odoola' and 'Gār' then lived as Gabbra in the present Gabbra country
or whether other ethnic constellations and localities were involved. The
informant for the other version of this tale, quoted in chapter 4, concluded
from the distribution of these customs that they must have originated
before Gabbra, Gabbra Miigo, Rendille and Garre separated.

Leaving Almado and the fire, we proceed to a feature that is common to
all Odoola and distinguishes them from all other clans of all ethnics groups
discussed here: they do not cut the navel.

Rendille boys have small incisions made around the navel, with the
result that when they grow up, the scarred skin contracts and only leaves
a small round hole in a shiny circle of scar tissue the size of a shilling. If
irregular growth results, a man will hide his navel in shame and, so people
say, will even die with one hand covering it.[15] This is not done by the
Rendille Odoola. No Gabbra of whatever clan makes such an incision, but
both Rendille and Gabbra Odoola carefully cut around the navel of an
animal when skinning it. They share the rule not to cut navels.

Odoola also have clan-specific practices associated with the life cycle
which are unlike those of other Gabbra. If a father is absent at the birth of
his child they do not wait until his return to offer an animal sacrifice, nor,
mirroring this, do they wait until the return of an absent son before bury-
ing an old man. Further, no Odoola male may marry unless he has performed the sacrifice *mogasan*, which is peculiar to Odoola and is compared
to the Boran *mogati* ceremony.

One more word about spatial arrangements, this time in connection with burial. The Rendille bury their dead, in Spencer's words and confirmed by my own observation, 'on [their] right-hand side with arms together and knees tucked right up (this may or may not be a prenatal position, but it is certainly one of the most effective ways of fitting a body into a small hole)' (1973: 59) What Spencer does not mention is that women are laid on their left side with the head pointing east, as in the sleeping position in which the feet point west, towards the door. (Anyone who sleeps with his head to the west may be reproached for adopting an unpropitious position. This may or may not have to do with the sun setting in the west.) The Gabbra bury their dead in a similar posture, but with the head pointing north, the only exception, as we by now have learned to expect, being Odoola. These are also buried with their heads pointing north but on their back with their limbs straight, thus resembling Muslims, for whom north means Mecca.

Boru Galgallo explained this by saying that people came from the north, from Makkamedina, before venturing to the east and finally arriving at their present location. This leads us to the migrational history of Odoola and their claim to be of Somali origin and therefore their avoidance of killing Somali. Boru Galgallo's grandfather, Gurracca, was killed by Somali at a time when much livestock was stolen and many people were kidnapped. Of these captives, two are said to have returned much later and reported that the Somali section that had undertaken the raiding had died out. Similarly, it is believed that the families of Odoola men who have killed Somali do not multiply, nor do their herds grow.

Rendille invoke the ritual names of their ancestors or of their strain of camels when swearing or expressing astonishment or making protestations. Odoola may exclaim *Ababur*, their supposed place of origin far in the east,[16] or *Somaliħi dakħan* ('white Somali').

I postpone the discussion of the significance this may have for the migrational history of Odoola because I want to begin their story as they would do it, with the mythical first appearance of their lineage ancestors, which is not specified in time or space.

The first man of Odoola was the eponymous ancestor of the lineage Keinán. While his son was out herding camels, he met another boy, who had come from the sky, and invited him home. In the following days, so the story goes on, he met other boys, all of whom made their entry into human society accompanied by signs of their special ritual vocations. These boys became the lineage ancestors of Odoola and the descendants of each of them keep their specific characteristics and powers to this very day.

Tokkoon iti-d'ufe. Worri kun [Nurre] qar fite kanat iti-d'ufe. Kun gurba ka gaal tissu d'ufe. Gurba: 'abbó jabbá?' 'Ee at jabba?' Gurban kan: 'at garamí d'uft?' 'Gar Waaqati d'uf.'

They came to them one by one. Nurre came first. He came to the boy who herded, the camels. The boy said: 'Hi man' [literally: Man, are you strong?] 'Hi' [literally: I am, are you strong?'] This boy said, 'Where are you coming from?' 'I have come from God/the sky.'

'Amm garám deemt?' 'Amm wael laf tolfadd'' Wolín-galan. Galgali yo gaal gal-siftu, yo abban gurba isa yaame 'galcumi nagaa?' fuud'e, kun bir ejj. 'Aabo, gurban kullééni "gar Waaqati d'ufe wael na tolfad'!" jed'.' 'Maqaan isa een? Maqaan gurbá kanke kan een?' 'Nurr.'

'Where are you going now?' 'Now I look for companions among the people.' They went home together. In the evening when they brought the camels in, when the father called his son and greeted him with 'Has the drive home been peaceful?' he was standing near. 'Father,' this boy said, ' "I came from God, make me your companion!" ' 'What is his name? What is the name of this boy of yours?' 'Nurr.'

'Beena, bisan d'uga, gosé gala, halan teesan wolt isan quubsiti?' 'Ín-quubsit.' 'Beena, wolingololfadd'a, wolin-d'uga!' Gurbaan kaan halan isan tana duub ini gam kan ga-marré duub raf.

'Go, drink water, go to the sleeping place, is [the milk of] your camel cow enough for both of you?' 'It is.' 'Go, have your meal together, drink together!' This boy came round to this side, [next to] their camel cow, and slept.

The spatial arrangement in which the boys sleep is important because it gives the mythical basis for the settlement order of the lineages of their descendants and thus their relative seniority. As the gestures of the informant show, young Nurre sleeps to the north of the Keinán boy, thus unknowingly assuming the more senior position.

Yo worrí hagi lamma kan ole, ka Bursúnna ya-d'ufe. Ijolle gaal tissitu ya-iti-d'ufe. 'Gurba!' 'Aaa.' 'Garami d'ufte?' 'Gar Waaqati d'ufe.' 'Amm garám deemt?' 'Waaq, "fula ijolle suni d'aqe, waeli kanke suni!" jed', waeli kiyy isan, wael na tolfadd' a!'

When they had spent about two days, the one of Bursúnna came. He came to the children who were herding the camels. 'Boy!' 'Yes.' 'Where have you come from?' 'I have come from God.' 'Where are you going now?' 'God has said, "Go to those children, they are your companions!" You are my companions, so make me your companion!'

Wolin galgal galte. Yo abban 'galcumi nagaa?' fuud'e kun duub ejja. 'Abbo, gurban tokkó-lle ya nu d'ufe, "an gar Waaqati d'uft", jed'a, "been ijolle sun iti-q'aq, ha ijolle sun wael tolfadd'a," jed', akan jed'.'

In the evening they went home together. When the father greeted them with 'Has the drive home been peaceful?' that one was standing there. 'Father, one more boy has come to us. He says "I have come from God" and says that [God] had said, "Go to those children, may you and those children become companions." '

'Beenaya, halan teesan isan quubsiti, nu-lle irrá-haft, beena wolin-d'uga! Gololfadd'a, wolin-d'uga!' Yo gololfate irribat dacaat duuba ka Nurre uf duuba aci lakisé ka Keinana garam lakisé, duub jiddu worri kan lamman iti-seene duub.

'Go ahead, your she-camel will be enough for you, there is [milk] left over from us, go and drink together!' When they had finished their meal and went to sleep, he [Bursúnna] left the one of Nurre to this side and the one of Keinán to that side and lay down between the two.

The deictic gestures of the informant make the arrangement clearer than the verbal account alone does: the north–south sequence now is Nurre, Bursúnna, Keinán.

Yo dirama abban bulé kae, moona gaala ga-bae, gaali lamma, ijolle tan lacú akan gubba ejjani, tokko bisan kees ejjit, tokko ruuf morma qabti. Jarsi ijolle taan kaase, 'orge ruuf qabti tana, ata qallu, ruuf tan irrá-hiik, at marad'! Orge bisan kees ejjit tana, at tante tan, tan horád'!

When in the morning the father awoke, got up and came to the camel enclosure, two camels were standing like this above these two [newly come] children, one was standing in water [although there had not been any rain] and one had a *ruuf* sheet[17] around the neck. The old men woke the children. 'This camel heifer with the *ruuf* sheet [is yours], you are a *qallu*,[18] untie this *ruuf* from her, put it around yourself!' [he said to Nurre; and to Bursúnna,] 'This camel heifer which is standing in the water is yours, take her for breeding!

Ammo gaaf adun baate, hanan orge tana lafa buusif, Waaq biyya, yaamad'! At boqá roobsita.' Odool worri boqa roobsit kana. Gaali sun ammá-lle inum-jira, gaal Odoola ka durrá sun. Keinán ammá-lle inúm-qaba. [. . .]

When the sun has come out [meaning in a drought], pour the milk of this heifer on the soil, pray to God for the people! You will make rain.' This is the lineage of Odoola that makes rain. These camels still exist, the original camels of Odoola. Also Keinán still has them.

Kun [Akadér] duub yo torban tokko bula ya arti d'ufe. Kun yo iti-d'ufe, hala qaba, halaan orgé qabt, irmaana, ijolle taan iti-d'ufe, dubbatan. 'Garami d'ufte?' 'Gar Waggati d'ufe.' 'Amm garám deemt?' 'Hala tante tana fulum gaal sun in-daqi, waeli kanke suni na injéd'an.'

When they had spent one week, Akadér came here. That one, when he came, had a lactating she-camel with a female calf, he came to these children and they talked. 'Where have you come from?' 'I have come from God.' 'Where are you going now?' [God has said to me,] "take this she-camel of yours to those camels, there are your companions."'

Akadér [. . .] ka gaal Harrau jed'ani. Duub galgalla, hala tan gaal ke-galcan. 'Abbo, gurban tokkó-lle ya nu iti-d'ufe, Waaqi "fula ijolle suni d'aqé, waeli kanke suni!" jed'e, halan isá-lle irmana ín-qaba.'

He was called Akadér with the Harrau camels.[19] In the evening they drove this she-camel home with the other camels. 'Father, one more boy has come to us. God has said, "go to those children, they are your companions!" He also has got his own lactating she-camel.'

'Beena, teesani wolti-daradd'a, isan chuf woluman-d'uga!' Jal kan lamman aci uf durr lakisé, duub ka Keinána kan aci uf durr rahiise, duub ini jari sadéen kan wolt mirg lafa kae, duub akan rafe. Yo abban dirám bulé d'ufe, ka isát duub gam kan jir.

'Go, pour your [milk] together, drink all of you together!' [When they went to sleep] he left those two ahead of him, separated them from Keinán, so these three people [the newcomers] lay on the earth together to the north [of Keinán] and slept like this. When the father woke up and came in the morning, his own one was on this side [south].

The order of seniority up now reads Nurre, Bursúnna, Akadér, Keinán.

Worr kan sadeen dubr ufi jal nag. Odooli worri wolti-d'ufe haganum.

To these three people he gave girls. As many as these are the people of Odoola who [originally] came together.

Thus the three boys from the sky became the sons-in-law of Keinán and the foundation for Odoola was laid. The account directly continues with those lineages that came later and makes the interesting distinction between people who came before the migration to Iris and those who joined Odoola after the return from there, thus linking the history of the single lineages to the major migratory movements related above in chapter 4.

Nami eege d'ufe ka durrá bae lamm, worri tun Tubádi jed'an tan, fiite biyyá bae kun, Iris in-dánne eege Irisi ol deebie d'uft, worri keenaf ka Barowa [Timbor] sun-lle diqo wal-hanqata.

Of those who came later, the first two were these people called Tubádi, they came to the end [the descendants?] of the [above mentioned?] people, they have not gone to Iris, after people returned to the east from Iris, they came. Our lineage [Kaalaya] and that of Barowa [Timbór of Rendille, corresponding to Kaalaya in Gabbra] came shortly after them.

Worri keená-lle Iris in-dánne, Worr Daaya keesa d'ufe. Worri sun worr Iris in-dánne. Armá-lle arm ín-jiran, ammá-lle gargar, armá-lle diqa, worri sun.

Also our lineage did not go to Iris, they came from the Warra Daaya.[20] These are the people that did not go to Iris. Also here they are, even now they are different, here they are few, these people.

Guyyá qara aada iti-kennan suní-lle kees in-jír. Gaaf d'ufe gaalan d'ufe keen. Dubbumaan angaf irrafuud'at. 'An fula aadat hafe, at deemte, Iris datte, ol deebite, ammátan d'ufte, an nam tokko malle nam tokkó-lle na durr in-jírru,' jed'.

When the custom was brought to [the Gabbra] he was not with them. Our [lineage], when they came, they came with camels. They got their senior position only by talking. 'I have stayed where the custom is, you have gone, migrated to Iris, returned to the east, you have come only now, apart from one lineage nobody is ahead of me,' he [Kaalaya] said.

Gaalum qaba, gubban tokko tu. Gaal worr sadíi gubban tokko: Worr Nurrefi Akadér takka, ka isat yo ini gaalan d'ufe gubban tokko tu. 'Ati deemte badde, an fula iti-d'aladd' iti-hafe̲, amm Nurre malle nam tokko na durr in-jíru.' Dubbumaan irra-fúd'ate duub.

He had camels, the brand was just one. The camels of three lineages have one brand: Nurre and Aradér are alike, and his [Kaalaya's] when he came with his camels, was the same. 'You have gone and got lost, I stayed at my place of birth, now only Nurre and nobody else is senior to me.' So he got it just by talking. (Odoola)

The richness of this account shows that Boru Galgallo's own skill in talking rivals that of his ancestor. Having come to know the different lineages of Odoola with their different features we now have to solve the puzzle of how these lineages came to be represented in four different ethnic groups. From the start we can abandon the idea that an originally united PRS clan or phratry Odoola was split in several parts in the course of the major ethnic splits described in chapter 4 (the flight from the Boran, etc.), because that would imply that the Odoola lineages which were to form a part of the future separate ethnic units were simultaneously and originally present in the new ethnic nuclei at the moment of fission. This would contradict what we learned in the preceding paragraphs from Boru Galgallo, namely that the different lineages of Odoola joined the developing Gabbra society at different times. It would also contradict the fact that Odoola is a relatively recent addition to Rendille society, as shown by its structural position and confirmed by oral history. In other words, it was well after the Rendille had established a separate identity within the former PRS cluster that they were joined by Odoola. The migrations of Odoola lineages thus cannot be explained by the major movements of people but have to be examined each in its own right; to do this, in some cases we can treat a cluster of lineages as a unit, in other cases we shall have to proceed lineage by lineage.

If we trust Boru Galgallo's account that Nurre, Bursúnna, Akadér and Keinán were with the other Gabbra in Iris[21] and that, as described in chapter 4, Odoola – as represented by these four – played a leading role in the establishment of Gabbra public ritual, we can assume that these four lineages were originally part of the emerging Gabbra society. Whenever the Gabbra split from the other PRS, this split must have divided each of these four lineages. We have no evidence against this view. On the contrary, this view is indirectly confirmed by the explicit statement that other lineages came later. (There does not seem to be an overall tendency to claim to be 'ancient Gabbra', as there is an overall tendency among Muslim Somali to claim descent from the uncle of the Prophet.)

On the other hand, we have accounts from very different places[22] that Odoola split from the Garre and on their way west split again, some of them to join the Gabbra and others to take a more southerly route to join the Rendille. We should not be surprised to hear of 'Garre', 'Gabbra' and 'Rendille' as if these then were well-established units, because from the twentieth-century perspective of the informants the present-day ethnic groups provide the only available frame of reference. We can hardly expect them to speak about 'PRS', 'Somaloid peoples', 'emergent Gabbra', 'nucleus of Rendille formation', etc. What remains of these traditions, if we allow for these terminological difficulties, is the synchronicity: the Odoola of (today's) Gabbra and of (today's) Rendille are believed to have split from those Odoola who, at the same time, remained in the east among (today's) Garre. If we accept this assertion and combine it with the apparent newcomer status which the Odoola have among the Rendille, we can only conclude that the ancestors of the other Rendille had acquired a separate identity within PRS earlier than the ancestral Gabbra. To summarise this conclusion: Gabbra Odoola and Rendille Odoola split from the eastern Odoola at the same time. While the Gabbra Odoola became founding members of the Gabbra society, the Rendille Odoola became an appendage of an already well-established society. Ergo, the nucleus of a separate Rendille formation is older than the Gabbra nucleus.

This is not compatible with the Gabbra accounts that claim the return from Iris as the time of the Gabbra – Rendille split, which would imply synchronicity of the ethnogenesis (Gabbra being those who did not become Rendille and Rendille being those who did not become Gabbra) and a relatively recent point in time, since the split of the common ancestors of both from those parts of the former PRS who escaped to the east must have been earlier. We have, however, good reason to take these accounts as Gabbra-centric. In Rendille tradition, the story about Iris has a very marginal role and does not relate to the politically important clan histories. The Rendille accounts about people who were separated by the lake only involve two clans (Gaaldeilan and Rengumo) and parts of a third (Bolo in Tubcha) and do not mention the Gabbra at all. These Rendille accounts only describe this migration as causing the split between these Rendille clans and their supposed clan brothers among the Dasanech ('Geleba'). (The Arbore, who seem to comprise some of these lost clan brothers among their numbers are not commonly known to the Rendille, since their knowledge of the Dasanech is shady and the Arbore live even farther away. That a large proportion of the present-day Gabbra belong to lineages which are also represented among the Rendille is not due to an original split between Gabbra and Rendille which cut across these lineages, but to later emigration from Rendille.

There are other arguments which support the view that the Rendille separated from the remaining PRS earlier than the Gabbra. We remember Pease's account, quoted in chapter 4, in which the Rendille are described as 'bush dwellers [who] always refused to live in or near the Gurreh villages'. The Rendille thus seem to have acquired a certain degree of separation from the other PRS before the long trek.

Another such argument is that Arab-Islamic influences among the Rendille are fewer than among the Gabbra. Boran dominance, between 1550 and 1900, did not favour Islamic forms of expression, and because of the apparently old assimilation of these elements into the local culture we have to suppose that they found their way into PRS culture before 1550. (Recent conversion finds quite different forms of ritual expression.) We have shown above, in chapter 4, that the central elements of PRS culture were not Islamic, but there seems to have been a constant influx of fashionable elements of Islamic culture from the east, and possibly from southern Ethiopia where Islam at that time had a much stronger position than it did in later periods when one of its wings was cut by the Amhara and the other by the Oromo. If this influx was continuous, we can assume that the earlier a group separated from the main body of the PRS and went west or south-west, the fewer the Islamic elements in its culture.

If the relative chronology of Rendille and Gabbra articulation is a matter of conjecture, more or less plausible as the reader may decide, all available information agrees that the emergence of the Sakuye out of the Rendille was the last of the ethnogenetic processes discussed here. (All later developments, the Hofte Boran, the Ariaal, the Ilgira-Turkana still refer to themselves as emigrant or composite groups and not as separate ethnic units.) Although two clans of the Sakuye – Tubádi and Meilán – are Odoola,[23], we have evidence that, unlike the bulk of the Sakuye, neither of them come from the Rendille. This raises the question whether Odoola was already present among the Rendille when 'Hāra was killed'. Rendille Odoola informants answer this question in the affirmative. This implies that Odoola at the time of the split between the Rendille and the Sakuye lived among the Rendille and that none of them went with the migrants, the future Sakuye, at least no one whose descendants survived to form one of today's Sakuye lineages. This is perfectly possible since the Sakuye emigration did not comprise the whole clan spectrum of the Rendille: the Rendille clans Rengumo and Naħagan have no equivalents among the Sakuye.

If Tubádi and Meilán did not come from the Rendille, the question remains where they came from. The history of Sakuye Tubádi is largely implied in what we heard about Hassan Buro in chapter 4. The pauper whom the Garre expelled because of his fornication is said to stem from the lineage Tubádi[24] and his strain of camels is called Harrau, like that of other Tubádi elsewhere.[25] Sakuye informants[26] claim that, according to genealogies and identical camel brands (vertical on the right shoulder), the identity of these Tubádi with those of the Garre and certain Ajuran – the Garjele of Ido Robleh in Gelbaris – and Gabbra Miigo is established. I shall return to the Gabbra Miigo shortly. As to the Garjele, this would imply not that Ajuran is a monolithic block of agnatically related people but that it has a composite nature. This would fit perfectly with my general picture of ethnic processes but belie the generally accepted genealogical model of the Somali themselves. Unfortunately I could not examine this claim from the Ajuran side.

According to Boran and Sakuye informants,[27] Hassan Buro lived a lonely life with his wife, also a runaway, and their children. It is perfectly possible that the accounts quoted in chapter 4 are telescoped, and that it was not Hassan Buro himself who later met the emigrants from Rendille but a descendant of his. If the isolation of Hassan Buro lasted no longer than one generation, there is no reason why he should have permitted narrow endogamy among his children. Given the general PRS rule of exogamy between rather large agnatic units, such behaviour would only be plausible if mates from outside were lacking. The accounts differ slightly about these rules. One says that Hassan Buro permitted those of his children to marry who did not directly follow each other in the sequence of births. From other accounts it appears that Tulo, the son of his wife, married a daughter of Hassan Buro, i.e. his half-sister, and that a son of Hassan Buro married a full sister of Tulo. (In chapter 4 we have learned that the stray woman picked up by Hassan had 'children', possibly a boy and a girl.) This second account offers a variation, and probably an improvement, on the first. Those Sakuye Miigo that go back in the male line to Hassan Buro today are called Shirshiro, while Tulo's lineage is called after its eponymous ancestor. Shirshiro and Tulo continue to intermarry.[28]

Mailán, another clan of Sakuye Miigo, is undoubtedly identical with the homonymous groups elsewhere classified as Odoola. Sakuye and Gabbra informants agree that Mailán is a relatively late arrival from Gabbra Odoola.

Mailán of Sakuye stems from a single man who had left the Gabbra. Wario Guyyó, a medical assistant, is a member of this lineage and from his genealogy it is possible to approximate the time of this emigration. Wario was born in 1924 and insists that his father at the time of his birth was a very, very old man. We might thus set the father's year of birth at around 1850. For the following ascending generations we assume an average length of 40 years. This might appear long by European standards but fits in well with observations of the Gabbra and the general tendency of the age-set system to delay the marriage of young men and the fact that old men continue to marry younger and younger wives and to have young children, begotten by themselves or others. The average age difference of fathers and sons thus is considerably higher than in Europe.[29] To the ancestors of Wario we thus ascribe the following dates of birth:

Wario	1924
Guyyó	1850
Boso	1810
Madera	1770
Bakajo	1730
Ali	1690
'Abdi	1650
Orrot	1610

Bakajo is said to have followed a lost camel bull until he came to the Sakuye. As men who follow the footprints of lost animals and undertake arduous journeys are more likely to be young then old, for lack of more precise information we date this event around the year 1750, with a low probability of having hit the right year and a high probability of having hit the right century.

According to Boru Galgallo (Odoola), the man who joined the Sakuye was called Bagajo Bonso, not, as Wario says, Bakajo Ali. He tarried among the Sakuye until he had missed the promotion of his Gabbra age set to *dabela* status. The Sakuye then decided to let him participate in their own customs and even made him a *hayyu*.

There are, however, more stories about him and it must have taken some time for his status to be elevated. He apparently had no camels and we do not even know whether the bull he was looking for was his own and whether he ever found it. What he had was a donkey, and he tied oryx horns to its head and, hiding behind it, he stalked oryx herds. He hunted with bow and arrow and in this occupation he was unfavourably, according to general opinion, compared to the Waat, the endogamous hunter caste (Odoola and Sakuye 1).

We also have the report that he or one of his descendants herded the camels of Kurno, another Sakuye clan. When one day he miraculously discovered a 'mosque' at Deemo, the later ceremonial site of the Sakuye,[30] the elder of Kurno who had employed him claimed this mosque for himself as Mailán was in his service. He had, however, to drop this claim since he could not approach the place to hold a sacrifice there because of aggressive spirit animals. Only Mailán succeeded in pacifying the spirits and he became ritually associated with the place. The disagreement with Kurno, however, made him leave Kurno and join Miigo (Sakuye 1).

Thus Mailán joined Miigo, of which he, that is the lineage he founded, is still a part. We do not know whether he was aware that, after all these hazards, he had joined his own clan again: Odoola. Mailán, who belonged to the Guba Gababa (= Lossa) moiety of Gabbra Odoola, now joined the Yiblo moiety of Sakuye Miigo. As he changed sides, so did his camel brand: Mailán of the Sakuye marks his camels on the right side of the neck and Mailán of the Gabbra on the left side. Apart from this their brand is identical: it is the *alif*, as we know it from the Lossa of Galbo (chapter 4).

In recent generations many Rendille Odoola have joined the Gabbra, become fully integrated into their brother lineages and also acquired positions of influence, like Orto, an elder still recognisable as Rendille by his pierced earlobes, whose son, Sori Orto, is a rich trader, butcher and 'hoteli' owner, who has twice been chairman of the Marsabit county council. Orto enjoys equal respect among both Rendille and Gabbra and is thus a useful contact for Rendille travellers in Gabbraland. In spite of the identity of

clanship he shares with his Gabbra neighbours, and in spite of his volun-
tary switch of ethnic allegiance, he is still proud of his Rendille origin and
volunteers such statements as 'All real men among the Gabbra are Rendille.'
There are many parallel examples among the older men, among whom
Orto is the most prominent. Since the late nineteenth century emigration
from the Rendille to the Gabbra has not only affected Odoola, but Odoola
more than other clans. The small size of Rendille Odoola – apart from a
Turkana raid in the 1890s – may be largely ascribed to this emigration.
Anders Grum[31] counted 92 Odoola houses, which were mainly concentrated in two settlement groups.[32] Children of Rendille emigrants to the
Gabbra find marriage partners there. Migration is a phenomenon which
concerns houses, i.e. husbands with wives, children and herds, not single
young people who contract trans-ethnic marriages. Gabbra Odoola, in
spite of good neighbourly relations, rarely ask for Rendille Odoola brides
and the only two Gabbra wives of the Ilkichili (junior elders) age set of the
Rendille Odoola belong to 'people of the letter, people of the government',
i.e. state-employed school leavers. In spite of their special relationship with
the Gabbra, their privileged security from Gabbra raids, their frequent
contacts with the Gabbra, especially those of Odoola, and their proximity
to them (one Odoola settlement group usually settles north of all other
Rendille), Odoola by its marriage links is closely embedded in Rendille
society. In the one settlement group I investigated, about half of the wives
were of Rendille Odoola origin and the other half stemmed from other
Rendille clans.

   I conclude this part of the chapter with a diagram summarising the migrations of Odoola and its distribution in the present day ethnic groups
(Diagram 17). To tie this to a rough chronological frame, I assume that the
long trek started around 1550 and that the Sakuye split from the Rendille
around 1650. Odoola migrations are symbolised by uninterrupted lines,
the movements of the main ethnic bodies by interrupted lines.

HARRAU/USMALO

We have seen in chapter 4 that, when the Gabbra found themselves in Iris
and short of even the less palatable wild plants for food, one of the diviners
who pointed out the necessity of returning to the east was of Usmalo.
Usmalo thus is an old part of the Gabbra phratry Galbo; under the name
Harrau, it is also an integral part of the Rendille clan D'ubsahai with
special and irreplaceable ritual functions. That the two groups are aware
of their relationship and that they have been interacting throughout the
centuries – although not always in a brotherly way – is apparent in the
story about the stolen camels of Usmalo which, by their unpropitiousness,
have exterminated whole patrilines of Rendille Harrau (chapter 4).

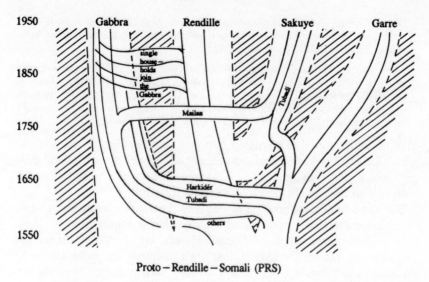

Diagram 17 Migrations and present-day distribution of Odoola

Both Harrau and Usmalo have historical, social and ritual links with Odoola, without ever having belonged to Odoola. They are travel companions but not brothers of Odoola. Before considering its migrational history, however, we must examine the lineage itself in detail because the elements of our inter-ethnic puzzle are not cardboard chips which all look alike at first sight, but collective bodies with recognisable characters, political functions and ritual powers. Each of them has its own relationship with God, nature and people.

The Rendille Harrau should not be examined in isolation but as a part of their subclan Dokhle, which comprises Dokhle proper, Hajufle,[33] Harrau and Ogorjebo. This subclan seems to be an old agnatic unit, as evidenced by the similarity of their ritual functions. (Composite clans, like D'ubsahai as a whole, although 'brothers', are often characterised by quite different inheritable powers of their subunits, some being *iibire*, some *wakhkamur*, etc). Dokhle as a whole, not just Harrau, has a special relationship with Odoola. When a new *jibanjib*, a new drum of Odoola, is made,[34] which happens once in 56 years, Hajufle has to initiate the action by making the first three strokes of the axe against the trunk of the tree to be felled. After the wooden part of the drum is complete, a female sheep is sacrificed, and this sheep belongs to Harrau. The first skin strips which are tied to the drum have to be cut from this sheep. This co-operation shows how closely Dokhle and Odoola are articulated. Asked how this special relationship came to exist, an Odoola informant responded:

Doodas Harrau, Dokhle, Hajufle, dooda tuuman saggane nañ iskalesoobeñe D'ubsa-ñai khaate. Doodenyo goorat nañ ñuggum kañaagsanni, saggaka nal ang'ka lesoo-bañane, chi D'ubsañai khaate lakka, makadíin.

These people, Harrau, Dokhle, Hajufle, all these people have come together with us from there [from the Garre], and D'ubsañai took them. Even if D'ubsañai took them, we have not stopped [to perform the custom together with] our people with whom we performed it before, with whom we settled together there and with whom we have come together.[35]

This triangular ritual relationship between Hajufle, Harrau and Odoola thus is believed to have remained unchanged through a trans-ethnic process: it has existed in an earlier ethnic constellation, the 'Garre',[36] and it continues to exist in the frame of Rendille society.

The same informant goes on to describe these ritual co-operators also as preferred marriage partners and claims a similar relationship for their Gabbra equivalents. Girls of Usmalo/Harrau are preferred brides for Odoola. The reason for this is that their children are believed to be 'stronger' and more resistant to misfortune. Such matches therefore are propitious.

Even in those rituals which are performed by Harrau alone, where they and not Odoola are the ritual proprietors and main actors, certain elements are reminiscent of Odoola: both groups share a special relationship to one cardinal point, the north. The camel bulls of Harrau 'know' what is going on in the north and the west, but they are ignorant about the south and the east. They are used in an oracle to find out whether an area is safe or vulnerable to enemy attack. If the bulls which are led to pasture in a pair browse quietly, the area is considered safe. If they refuse to advance or play up, the area will be immediately evacuated.

As I have described the relationship between Harrau and the Gabbra lineage Usmalo in detail elsewhere (Schlee, 1985b: 25–9), I only summarise it here.

Powers similar to the Harrau bulls are attributed to the male camels of Usmalo, especially those of one particular strain. They are also used against enemies: to find out where they are or magically to deter them.

Much of this book could be rewritten as a history of the strains of camels rather than of human clans. These strains have special characteristics, avoidances, rules and ritual powers ascribed to them and are distinguishable entities. Such a history of camel strains would closely parallel that of human lineages, since the association between the two is a very close one.

Both the Harrau camels and those of Usmalo are used for ritual purposes in connection with age-set promotions into the highest age grade of elders. Both are thus instrumental in transmitting to these elders an especially strong power to curse (*ibid.*: 17).

Other rituals which point to a historical relationship between Harrau and Usmalo involve young girls and female sheep and aim at rainmaking (*ibid.*: 26).

The identity of the two lineages is not questioned by either and frequent use is made of this relationship. Apart from the case history cited above (chapter 4), other case histories of contacts between the lineages for mutual help in times of emergency or by people who were driven to emigrate by personal frustations or by people who just wanted to see their clansmen are given in Schlee (*op. cit.*: 28–9). These contacts have recurred throughout the generations.

The ultimate origin of this clan relationship is clad in mythical mist. Mankulo, or Gaal Gurracca, the One with the Black Camels, fell out of the sky together with a female camel which was miraculously saved from death by falling into a lake. (This Gabbra account does not say whether Mankulo himself survived in the same way.) Mankulo took his sword and cut the umbilical cord with which the camel was still connected to the sky.[37] (This is a mythical allusion to the divine nature of these camels, whose ritual functions have been mentioned above). Mankulo had a son Shefa, Shefa a son Abdalla, Abdalla a son Ali, Ali a son Bulo and Bulo a son Abudo. The sons of Abudo are Cirátte and Korrot (Diagram 18).

The two informants[38] have different opinions about the ethnic context of the early section of this lineage. Inquiries from other informants reveal that the statement that they were Boran is unique while the view that they

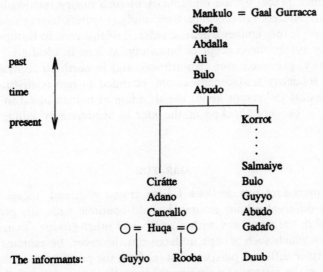

Diagram 18 Some genealogical relationships within Usmalo

were some sort of Somali is widely accepted. There is full agreement, however, that 'Korrot' has some connection with the word 'Korre', i.e. 'Samburu', which, if used by Gabbra, may include the Rendille.[39] There is a
story (Schlee 1985b: 28) how Korrot fled from the Boran to join his clan
brothers among the Rendille from whom he also had to flee to join the
Gabbra branch of his lineage.

It is not clear how Usmalo/Harrau came to be represented in these
different ethnic groups, but we can be sure that this lineage has had a
multi-ethnic character for a long time, that they have been conscious of
these relationships and made use of them for exchanging livestock and as
bridgeheads for inter-ethnic migration. A well-known Usmalo ex-chief
and shopkeeper, Duub Gadafo, gives Abudo as the father and Guyyo as
the grandfather of his father Gadafo. The next two in the line, Bulo and
Salmaiye, he believes to have been Rendille. His lineage among the Gabbra is counted as Korrot, although he does not give Korrot as his ancestor.
A Rendille informant of Harrau[40] claims the same Bulo as an ancestor and
says he was of Libaale age set (warriors from 1853 to 1864 or, one double
generation removed, from 1769 to 1780 – the second possibility would fit
better with the generation spans; then this informant, like Duub, would
be a SoSoSoSo of Bulo). Lineages thus not only split but also merge
again.

Apart from linking a few dozen or hundred people in one ethnic group
to another small group in another, such inter-ethnic identities of clan or
lineage serve another purpose in the arguments of those who appeal for
inter-ethnic peace: by the multiplicity of such binary relationships and
the many indirect relationships they imply (brothers having uncles and
affines, etc.), they convey a general sense of relatedness. In Europe it took
centuries before the concept of humanity, at least in ideal ethics if not
in practice, prevailed over clannishness, and in northern Kenya, where
human solidarity traditionally is not extended to non-relatives, people
who are deaf to laments about the shedding of human blood in general
might yet be very shocked at the idea of inadvertently killing a clan
brother.

GĀR, FUR

In the preceding two sections I have traced clan and lineage groups
through different ethnic groups. I could continue with this procedure
and deal in the same way with a number of other groups. Trans-ethnic
processes which such groups undergo can, however, be examined from
at least three different perspectives: (a) from the perspective of those left
behind, as the history of a fission; (b) from the perspective of the group
itself, answering the question of how a lineage or clan came to be repre-

sented in more than one ethnic unit; and (c) from the perspective of those to whom the group concerned became associated as the result of their trans-ethnic re-identification. Those who are in the centre and focus of perspective (b) would be regarded as newcomers from perspective (c), the view of those who form the earlier segments and the nucleus of the resulting new social formation.

The history of Fur has already been dealt with from the first perspective in chapter 4, with the tale of Haara, the terrible fighter and eater, a man of Fur, who caused the split between Rendille and Sakuye. The same event is believed to have caused the migration of Fur from the Rendille to the Gaar phratry of the Gabbra, and it is from the perspective of this phratry that I now want to resume my account. I start with the older and ritually senior parts of this phratry and then describe how Cushites from many sides gathered around this nucleus to form a large and powerful phratry.

The ritually most senior lineage of the Yiblo moiety of Gār is Kárbayu. As Gār is the phratry that precedes the others in the age-set promotions (chapter 4), in one sense Kárbayu is the 'first born' of the whole Gabbra society. Our informant from this segment, on whose information the following account is based,[40] is very conscious of this position: *aada nu-t harka qaba* ('we have the custom in our hands'). Within Kárbayu the first three lineages are later additions, while the fourth, Ali Afat,[41] is the nucleus. It is customary throughout Gabbra for adopted segments to be given a settlement position north of, i.e. ahead of, the segments which adopt them. Ali Afat are *qallu*, people with the power to bless and to curse, a property which adds to their ritual seniority. *Jallab namá tolc, hayyu namá tolc, qallu Waaqa d'ale* ('*Jallab* are installed by people, *hayyu* are installed by people, [while] the *qallu* is born [or begotten] by God').

Like many clan origin myths, the story of Ali Afat combines different kinds of reality: social reality – it makes claims of seniority; ritual reality – it links sacrificial sites of the *muuda* journey (chapter 4) to the origin tale; and historical reality, which is interwoven with and overlaid by the first two dimensions. The historian who pursues only one type of truth might find it difficult to isolate what he is looking for. He should be warned, however, against discarding too easily everything which is obviously unhistorical, unempirical, supernatural or mythical since these elements of the myth may underlie social behaviour or be instrumentalised in important social relations, and thus make history even if they do not describe it.

'The country we originally came from was a cattle country.'[42] This place of origin is thought of as situated to the north of the present Boran territory, in Liban, i.e. far into the Ethiopian highlands. The two mythical personalities which are in the centre of the tale are a father and son. The son got lost and the father came looking for him, following his footprints.

Dakha Qaqalla, the stones of Qaqalla, are two isolated rocks in the plain north of the Hurri Hills, or the Misty Highlands as they are more descriptively called in Boran. These two rocks have been given a new function by the Anglo-Ethiopian boundary commission: they are one of the landmarks which form the boundary. This is a task they share with the mighty Farole mountain, which is venerated and invoked as a holy place by the Galbo phratry. Different types of people thus put the landscape to different uses. The question remains how these two lonely rocks, which appear to be totally unrelated to their surroundings, came to be in this isolated location. The Gabbra have found an answer: the larger rock miraculously followed the father on his way south and now represents him symbolically, while the smaller one stands in a similar relation to the son.

Before the father, the son and their respective rocks came to what now is Kenya, however, a number of important events took place. The boy came to Mingeda Gorei (north of the boundary) a steep crater or cave where 'even now' one can hear the noises made by invisible camels. The boy recognised the place as holy, a place to hold a ritual, a sacrificial site. He spent the night there. It rained and in the rain his father found him.

Abbán d'ufe, abbaan boka ked'ufe. D'ufé nagaa wolfuud'an. Yo nagaa wolfuud'an: 'abbo at eesa baate, at eesa baate, at eesa baate, amm maal barbanu?'

The father came, the father came in the rain. He came, they greeted each other. When they had greeted each other: 'Father, where do you come from, where do you come from, where do you come from, what shall we look for now?'

'Nu ammatan Gabbra. Amm laf aada Borana laf gaala.' Yokaan gaali beeta arm fula tan ciisan fula Míngeda taan jed'an gaali beeta ol gam (gaali ol gam) gaali kun duub futt'e jed'e ol cee, laf keesa.

'We are Gabbra now. We are now in the land of the Boran[43] custom, in the land of camels.' Then the camels, you know, now they were standing at that place called Míngeda [where one can hear camels underground], the camels struggled to get upwards, you know, struggled to get upwards, these camels then said, 'Hopp!' and jumped out, out of the ground.

Yo gaali kan ol bae, duub 'ee Míngeda', gurban kan 'ee Míngeda, atin nu hoo, fula nu aada iti-si-tolcin, dibbayu si buuf, ati laf sorioo, sí-muudana.''

When these camels came out, 'Yes Míngeda', the boy said, 'Yes Míngeda, we are yours, [this is] the place where we hold a ritual for you, we shall pour libations for you, one will go on pilgrimage to you.'

After the appearance of the camels the two wanderers stayed three days in the area. Then suddenly – hopp! – a young female sheep (*karso*) appeared out of the ground, which meant that they could hold a sacrifice. It was a white sheep with a black head and neck (the pattern is called *gordíti*, masculine: *gordic*). This was the first time that blood was smeared on the camels.[44] To commemorate this event, a similarly marked female sheep is sacrificed periodically in the same place.

The two then moved on, driving their camels and followed by their rocks, until they came to Dakha Qaqalla where the father died. The rocks have remained there up to today.[45]

While the camels were grazing the boy used to disappear into the hole of a termite mound. To his embarrassment, a girl appeared in the area apparently looking for him.

Intalti taan gurba kan ímmarti. Gurbaan kan yo intal taan argu bol seene. Gaali kaan arma iyyáu armum bula asum oromaté, armum tae.

The girl searched around for the boy. When the boy saw the girl he went into the cave. The camels did not roam far from there, they sat down near the cave, stayed there.

Gaali kaan armum bula armum oromate, halkan bola bae, gaal kan elmate bola deebie.

The camels sat down for the night right there, [the boy] came out of the cave at night-time, milked the camels for himself [and] went back into the cave.

Intalti taaan guyyá sadii wolinole, guyya abresa intal taani gurbaan kaan wolti-d'ufan. Gaadé gurba kan yo ini bola bae, gaadum gaade, yo ini bola ol bae gubbat, gurbá-lle bocol gugurda kana gurbaan, intaltí-lleen guddo ya harm baafte. Wolti-d'ufan.

This girl now stayed around for three days,[46] on the fourth day the girl and the boy came together. She hid when the boy came out of the cave, she remained under cover until the boy came up out of the cave, and the boy was a big young-ster, also the girl was grown, she had breasts already. They came together.

Nagaa wolfuud'an. Yo nagaa wolfuud'ani: 'at gos tam?' 'An Kárbayu.' 'Kárbayu man kam?' 'Worr Ali Afata.'

They greeted each other. When they had greeted each other [the girl asked the boy], 'Which tribe[47] are you?' 'I am Kárbayu.' 'Which house[48] of Kárbayu?' 'The people of Ali Afat.'

'Atin intalti worr kam?' "Ule.' "Ule man kam?' 'Orkor.' 'Ammatan duub ati-lleen mal barbat?' 'An korm barbadd'a, d'iir barbadd'a.' [snaps] Ínqabate. Yo isiin jete, garac yabae.

"Of which people are you a daughter?' "Ule.' 'Which house of 'Ule?' 'Orkora.' 'So, and now, what are you looking for?" 'I am looking for a bull,[49] for a man.' [Informant snaps his fingers to indicate the rapidity of the following course of events.] He got hold of her. After a while her belly became big.

Guyyá lacu gaal wolinqabat kan. Yo intalti taan hagum teeti teete d'alte.

That was the day both of them together took possession of the camels. When the girl had stayed as long as she had stayed she gave birth.

Worri kaan gann sadíi obase gann sadeeso inobasín yo worri kaan bule lafa kae, maqumaan lafá, at agarte. . . . 'At eesá galte?' 'Nu Kárbayu, Kárbayu min Gumí taan.' Gabbra iti-gabae. 'At eesa galte?' 'An Safara ga-gale.' 'An Korré ga-gale.' 'An Rendilla ga-gale.' 'An Turkana.'

They stayed three years and before the third year was over when they got up in the morning the whole country [was full of people] as far as you can see.

'Where have you come from?' 'We are Kárbayu, this house of Gumi of Kár-bayu.' The Gabbra had come to them. 'Where have you come from?' 'I have come from the Somali.' 'I have come from the Samburu.' 'I have come from the Rendille.' 'I am Turkana.'

It is obvious that the process of formation of the Gaar phratry is tele-scoped here to fit into one sunny morning. When we examine the history of the different lineages, all informants, including the present one, will state that the different parts of Gaar joined the phratry at different times. But this is not the point here. This account stresses the earlier arrival and ritual superiority of Ali Afat and the composite nature of Gaar. Both points are illustrated in this vivid scene of people coming from all direc-tions and asking each other about their origins.

To my knowledge there is today no lineage in Gaar claiming Turkana origin. This, however, does not mean that Gaar has not incorporated Turkana at any time in its history. We have to remember that people who are adopted into a lineage will normally take the name of that lineage, accept gifts or inherit property from the lineage and behave in all respects, including exogamy, as members of the lineage. The vast majority of trans-ethnic life histories, be they captured children or poor people who look for benefactors, has certainly not resulted in separate lineage identities and recognisable inter-ethnic clan relationships of the type we examine in this book. People were fully adopted and their different origin was forgotten within a few generations. The biological composition of the groups studied thus may be much more heterogeneous than is reflected by their lineage structure. A partial adoption with the preservation of a separate identity will only obtain under specific conditions. There must be a reason for not assimilating the migrants fully. Either they come as a coherent group or, if the migration involves single persons or households, they come with their own camels with different, inheritable brands, a fact that needs to be pre-served in the public memory because it involves rights in camels. One may therefore say that the descent reckoning of camels is more rigid and has a conservative influence on the lineage structure of people. We shall come across a number of illustrations of this below. Now, however, let us return to the story of Ali Afat.

Aki nami Kárbayú biyye durrat argan akan. An amma sorio yo qallan, yo an gorrau, sorio taan hariradd'e, yo jede, 'Kárbayu, na tolc, Kárbayú ten, Kárbayú, worr Ali Afata, ka Afate rafu, umam worr kena na it-tis.' Aki Kárbayu argan akan.

That is how the people of Kárbayu appeared before the [rest of the] population. Now, when a sacrifice is held, when I cut its throat, when I have wiped its back, I say, 'Kárbayu, make us, our Kárbayu, Kárbayu, the settlement of Ali Afat [and] where [someone of] Afat sleeps, origin of our people, herd us.' That is how Kárbayu first appeared.

The sociological aspect of this account is, I think, obvious: it explains the relationships between people by describing how these people joined each other to form a society. If we re-examine this origin tale of Gār against the background of what we have heard about the camel complex (chapter 4) we shall, however, notice soon that it is also a story about camels. It mentions Míngeda as the origin of the camels and describes the mythical first performance of camel-related rituals. In this context we might add that Míngeda remains a sacred site to other Gabbra as well. When one passes near there, one should always deposit a small symbolic sacrifice, be it a toothstick, a lump of camel dung or some other minor item. Apart from being a story about people and a story about camels, thirdly, and most importantly, we are dealing here with a story about the relationship between the two. The major theme is the legitimacy of the *qallu* lineage Ali Afat as owners, keepers and protectors of camels. As we have heard above that Ali Afat originated from a cattle country, this legitimacy needs to be stressed because it could be doubted. As this lineage obtained their camels by supernatural means, however, these camels are not only *alál*, i.e. full property,[50] but also the visible sign of the divine sanction of camel keeping by this lineage. The supernatural relationship with camels is underlined by the claim that things like incense (*qumbi*), camel dung and *baarad* (R: *harcha*, a shrub on which camels like to browse), which are closely associated with camels or camel rituals, grew out of the body of the young man of Ali Afat, between his shoulders.

This legitimacy as a priest of the camels is an important point because, in addition to all the functions he shares with the *qallu* of other phratries, the *qallu* of Kárbayu, as the *qallu* of the senior phratry, has to initiate the age-set promotions for the whole of Gabbra society. In one age set in which another phratry, Galbo in 1951, initiated their *dabela* before Gār did so in 1957, these *dabela* are said to have died en masse within a short span.

Interestingly, the informant denies that the lineage Ali Afat, in spite of its name, has ever been Somali or Muslim. Former Muslims, he says, can only be found among the *galtu*, 'those who have entered', the latecomers. Contrary to other ritual specialists who tend towards more reconciliatory interpretations,[51] he sees his function as *qallu* as something alien to Islam.

These *galtu* within Gār are numerous. In relation to Ali Afat and Orkor who are mentioned in the origin tale, all others can be called *galtu* because they joined the nucleus later.[52] We cannot examine the history of all lineages; even smaller subunits of Ali Afat (Waaqaba, Wódabre) are said to be adopted and are attributed foreign origins. Among the other lineages Warabdér, Eidamole (like their Odoola namesakes) and Okadawa are said to come from the 'Somali' and Isaako from the *Korre* (Samburu).[53] According to one informant, Galabloye came from the 'Somali', according to another from the Samburu. We have no way of deciding from these sparse testimonies whether 'Somali' (*safara*) here means PRS or later immigrations by Muslim Somali. Of interest are the lineages Qoshobe and

Borqosho, which are said to have split from Galbo phratry, the former from its namesake, the latter from Massa. This seems to indicate that the phratry boundaries at some time have been rather permeable and are younger than many elements of the lineage structure. Even between the major groupings of Gār, re-identification of subunits seems to have been possible. Barre, Geedi and Gidalle are said to have belonged to Gasarán in Rerwalán before they joined Kárbayu. Whenever they have disagreements with other parts of Kárbayu, they threaten to go back to Rerwalán, with whom they have to settle on ritual occasions in any case.

The lineage Gasarán deserves closer attention. They are also called Fur and, by Rendille, Teilan. The bulk of them is believed to have joined Gār 'after Ḥaara had been killed',[54] but a part of them came later. As in the case of Usmalo/Ḥarrau, we have here an example of a lineage which has been represented both in Rendille and Gabbra societies and which has repeatedly been the channel of trans-ethnic reaffiliation.

The later arrivals are also referred to as the Fur of Maado. Their most prominent representative is the ex-chief Wario Yaatani. Yaatani was, according to his own account, the son of Qanacho s/o Adano s/o Maado s/o Kotte. Maado came from the Rendille lineage brothers. Taking into account the age of the informant and counting 40 years per generation, we arrive at 1780 as the approximate date of Maado's arrival. Chief Wario thinks that at that time the other Fur had already been with the Gabbra for two or three generations. This is independent confirmation that the historical events which underlie the Ḥaara story must have taken place in the seventeenth century. There is fairly general agreement that even this earlier Fur migration – which is connected to Sakuye ethnogenesis, as we have seen above (chapter 4) – took place after the tiriso, the allocation of the Gabbra to Boran clans. Fur tiriso inqábu ('Fur do not have tiriso'). We shall see also in other cases that the lack of a tiriso affiliation is taken by Gabbra as an indication that the lineage concerned arrived in the area after the process of allocation had already been finished. The fact that Maado joined other Fur who had already established themselves in Gabbra society is also expressed by the proverb Fur Maado gale, gaalu guban diide ('Maado joined Fur and refused to brand the camels'). (Instead of a camel brand Fur uses a scar as a property mark.)

The most recent migration from Rendille Fur to Gabbra Fur is that of Karchawa, the father of the trader and county councillor Elema Karchawa. This recent migration shows that this inter-ethnic clan relationship still provides a usable link. In succession to Ḥaara, both Wario Yaatani and Elema Karchawa demonstrate that Fur continues to produce strong leaders, as does Sharamo Ali, who was a country councillor. From anecdotes quoted in chapter 4 we have learned that Fur's strength is also believed to be of a crude physical kind.

For our reconstruction of the chronology of the first Fur migrations it is a fortunate circumstance that, apart from the Rendille, Gabbra and Sakuye, there is a Fur group among the Waso Boran, where they are also called Jaaro. With our genealogical reckoning we here arrive at 1630 as the approximate date of migration. Various independent sources thus point to the middle of the seventeeth century.

Our only informant[55] of this lineage was Gollo, age 41, s/o Bonaia s/o Happ'i s/o Taaro s/o Halakke s/o Jilo s/o Fiqayu s/o Korondille. Korondille was a Rendille and said to be the ancestor of all of Jaaro. According to Rendille naming habits, it is reasonable to assume that Korondille had been born at Korondille, a mountain and water point north of Buna and well to the north-east of the area which Rendille have grazed in recent generations. Gollo describes the separation from the Rendille Fur as an act of ecological specialisation. Korondille, who was rich in cattle, exchanged his few camels for cattle and joined a cattle people in a cattle area, while his clan brothers specialised in camels and remained in the lowlands. Obviously Korondille could not join the Waso Boran because there were no Boran on the Waso at that time.[56] He went to Dirre in the Ethiopian highlands and joined the Gon moiety of the Boran. Some of his descendants remain there to this day. The Fitawrari[57] Halakke Guyyó is said to be a Jaaro and thus can be added to the impressive list of chiefs of Fur extraction. The Kenyan branch of Jaaro also produced a chief. Waako Happ'i, a FaBr of our informant, was a chief of the Waso Boran until the mid 1950s when he roused the anger of the British,[58] who believed that he obstructed their recruitment of schoolchildren and detained him in Marsabit. He did not fare much better with subsequent Kenyan governments because he now lives in exile in Somalia where he is believed to receive a pension.

The Boran Jaaro are aware that certain lineages of the Gabbra and Sakuye are their clan brothers and avoid intermarriage with them.

In spite of their earlier specialisation in cattle, the lineage later, in the lowlands, invested part of their vast surpluses of cattle and smallstock in camels. Gollo himself was a camel herder in his youth. He admitted that he did not always keep the complicated rules about good and bad days of the week for various camel-related activities. He is, however, aware that traditional camel herders in the neighbourhood, Sakuye and Gabbra Malbe migrants, did keep such rules. His family, like other rich Boran who diversified into camels, kept these in a rather unceremonial way except that they performed *sorio* and *almado*, as do Samburu Ariaal, Hofte Boran and other cattle people who have taken to camel breeding. When the Waso bonanza came to a brutal end in the *shifta* emergency the practice of *sorio* and *almado* disappeared with the machine-gunning of the camel herds.

FUR NAMES AND PROPERTY MARKS

A-fura (R) means 'I open' and *fur* is an 'opening', i.e. a notch in the ear. All camels of the clan D'ubsañai have such a notch in the right ear. In the case of the subclans Wambíle, Bulyárre, Gudére, Migichán, Dókhle and Asurua, this notch is small, *fur ti nugul* ('the small *fur*') (Diagram 19). In the case of the Teilán subclan, the people who are also known as Fur in the narrow sense, the notch is shallower and wider, *fur ti balladan* ('the wide *fur*') (Diagram 20).

The larger lineages of this subclan are Arandiide, Höso, Kiráb and Orguile.

All subclans of D'ubsañai share the brand on the right side of the neck, and in addition Mirgichán has a longitudinal brand on the left fore-leg. Another peculiarity on the subclan level is that white (the preferred colour) and whitish (*boróg*) camels of the Wambíle subclan (*Kulalioorat* – 'the first campfire place') are branded with a spot on the right cheek (Diagram 21).

We have heard above that Maado, when he joined the Gaar, refused to brand his camels. The camels of Gasarán in Gaar share the earnotch with the Teilán subclan of D'ubsañai but do not have a brand. Instead they make an incision in the skin of the neck to leave a strip of skin dangling down. This mark is called *quuca* (B), which is reminiscent of the Rendille word *khuujo*, meaning the natural pockets of skin which dangle from the necks of some camels and sheep and most goats.

All Fur (Gasarán) of the Gabbra are Fur Gudda ($\triangleq$ R: *fur ti balladan*), i.e. Fur in the narrow sense, and thus correspond to the Rendille subclan Teilán.

The Sakuye distinguish between Fur Gudda and Fur Diqa ('the small *fur*' $\triangleq$ R: *fur ti nugul*). The latter may derive from all or any of the D'ubsañai subclans (if these had become differentiated from each other at the time of the Rendille – Sakuye split) with the exception of Teilán ('Fur Gudda') and Asurua, which has also preserved a separate identity among the Sakuye.

Diagram 19   The 'small *fur*' earclipping

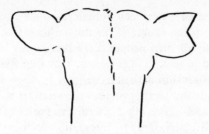

Diagram 20   The 'wide *fur*' earclipping

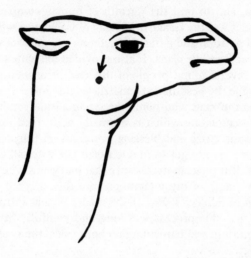

Diagram 21   The *dakar* ('camel fly') brand for white and whitish camels of D'ubsañai Kulalioorat

GAALORRA/GAAL HORRA, GAALDEILAN AND RENGUMO

Writing a book about clan affiliation, reaffiliation and adoption means that one is not only dealing with evidence for historical reconstruction but with an important element of public life on the borderline between law and politics. Citizenship, if this term from our own more bureaucratic culture is permitted here, cannot be acquired simply by saying that one wants to become a Rendille, a Gabbra, or whatever. One has to associate oneself with a household which is part of a lineage which is part of a subclan which is part of a clan, and only by belonging to a clan can one also claim to belong to one or more ethnic groups.

The anthropologist among the Rendille is in the same position as any other stranger, be he a northern Somali livestock trader or a Gabbra ex-militiaman who, in the course of his duty, shot a Gabbra raider and now cannot go back to his own people. Like these other individual strangers, he is well advised to seek to fit as best he may into Rendille society and to develop a pseudo-kinship with one friend or another, who slowly becomes a brother and thus indirectly provides the stranger with mothers, uncles, sisters, cousins and many other useful categories of people, and, most importantly, with a clan. Only by integration such as this will the stranger be able to survive in an area outside efficient government control, to do his job, be it trade or poaching or, in our case, participant observation and interviewing, and to find the warmth of human companionship.

In my case it was the Gaalorra subclan of Gaaldeilan which provided me with a social position and a frame of reference to interact with people from the nine other Rendille clans. It also provided me with a home which was located wherever I found people of this clan or of their adoptive brother clans. I became the best man at a marriage and took part in a circumcision ceremony as the man who holds the circumcision candidate around the waist.[59] In a ceremony which is normally performed on small children, the clan-specific curse and blessing powers were transferred to me. The only thing one cannot get from one's clan is a wife; all the daughters are one's sisters. But the clan makes sure that one gets a wife from elsewhere.

The early stages of my integration into this clan are described in the introduction to Schlee (1979). If the reader of that introduction gets the impression that this process was long and painful, with many setbacks and much bluffing and bargaining on both sides, the reader would be just about correct.

While Gaalorra, being the most numerous and ritually most important subclan of Gaaldeilan, is often simply referred to as 'Gaaldeilan', it is only fourth in the order of seniority. The 'first-born' subclan is Keele, which only comprises a few houses. It is followed by Búrcha, a subclan of 'Boranto' (Gabbra?) origin, which is equally small. Elémo is an eighteenth-century war spoil, acquired when a Gabbra camel herd was stolen along with the 'people belonging to it'. I return to them below. Madácho is a subclan which stems from Gaalorra through a female link: a girl with 'bent legs' (lüñlo made) could not find a husband and was therefore 'married' all alone: she was circumcised and given a house so that she could live like a married woman. A man of the clan Tubcha begot a son with her. As the Tubcha man had not paid brideprice, this boy did not belong to him, and as he did not stem from a Gaalorra father, he did not belong to Gaalorra either. Having no patriline at all, he therefore became the founding ancestor of a subclan of his own: Madácho.

Keele, Búrcha, Elémo and Madácho are *wakhkamur*[60] and culturally represent the 'Standard Average Rendille', if there is such a thing in this highly differentiated society. Elémo, although they were captured eight generations ago and still occasionally go to see their Gabbra relatives, have not the slightest trace of non-Rendille customs or peculiarities. Gaalorra, on the other hand, is very different from the others and may, along with Odoola, be culturally the most divergent Rendille clan. This perhaps was a fortunate circumstance because it opened my eyes to the importance of clanship and led my attention to inter-ethnic clan relationships; until then I had accepted the ethnic group, the habitual subject of anthropological monographs, as a natural unit of investigation.

Divergent does not mean marginal nor by any means weak. The *iibire* curse of Gaalorra is one fo the most dreaded, and Gaalorra is linked – by an adoptive brotherhood and by mutual participation in the ceremonies of transmitting the curse of the newborn[61] – to Nebei, the ritually most important clan of Belesi Berri, the eastern moiety. It is their deviance that makes Gaalorra strong.

Gaalorra is sometimes referred to a *Marle ti af guudan* ('Marle [Arbore] with the red mouth') and we shall see below that Gaalorra is indeed represented among the Arbore on the shores of Lake Stefanie (Chew Bahir) in Ethiopia. A Gaalorra woman, of Saale origin, who was angry with her husband, in the course of her lamentation complained to me that the Gaalorra are *chii* ('enemies') and that they suffer no negative ritual consequences in killing (other) Rendille – 'they do not have blood from the Rendille' (*Rendille d'iig makakhabto*). 'Blood' here stands for the stains on a murderer's social and ritual person. This definitely is not so, but their behaviour suggests that Gaalorra, and, under their protection, the rest of Gaaldeilan, do not mind spilling Rendille blood quite as much as other clans do. When Libaale were warriors (1937–51), young men of Gaaldeilan once killed a warrior of Rengumo[62] in a fight over precedence at a wall[63] and badly wounded a dozen more. Apart from the cleansing ceremony, the killer went unpunished because neither compensation nor vengeance is customary in such cases. The ideology seems to be that one is punished enough by having reduced one's own tribe.

The impression of a low degree of loyalty to the Rendille cause is increased by an incident in 1966 when a Gaaldeilan settlement was purportedly warned by Gabbra/Boran raiders of impending raids. It was said that Gaaldeilan people should not visit other settlements because these would be raided. Instead of warning the other Rendille, Gaaldeilan, conscious of the feeling of relatedness to and the trust shown towards them by the Gabbra, remained silent. On the subsequent night about 70 people were massacred around Kargi. Gaaldeilan informants insist that this account is untrue.

Gaaldeilan's proclivity to violence is proverbial and often ridiculed. In the years I spent with them I had occasion to watch many a good beating with herding sticks even among respected elders who should normally carry on their disputes by verbal means. (I did not know about their reputation when I first settled with them.)

This combination of features – being 'strangers' or 'enemies' and being 'hot' or violent – is instrumentalised, so to say socialised or domesticated, in the public ritual function with which they are entrusted. Being 'enemies', they are believed to have power over enemies. It is they – and Harrau, as we have seen above – who 'blow' in the direction whence enemies are expected so as to blind or confuse them.

While enemies can be the object of Gaalorra's curse they can also be its agency. In the same way as someone cursed by Saale is expected to be run over by a rhino and someone cursed by Rengumo to be bitten by a snake, Gaalorra have the horse as their curse. This may sound surprising because horses rarely attack people and do not have poisonous bites, but 'horse', as in Boran, stands here for cavalry. The traditional enemies of the Rendille – Boran and Gabbra – used to have horses until these were classified as arms and forbidden by the British. To say that other Rendille who are cursed by Gaalorra succumb to the horse is thus equivalent to saying that they fall victim to attacks by non-Rendille.

Apart from the ritual powers ascribed to them, Gaalorra have a number of other cultural features which clearly set them apart from other Rendille.

In Rendille-land we find three types of houses. While the Odoola house and the Standard Rendille house are mirror images of each other, the houses of Gaalorra are built according to a different structural principle. In the case of Rendille and Odoola houses the scaffold to which the mats are tied is made of two semicircular frames bridging the entire width of the house, and the subordinate ribs are attached to them (Diagram 22). The Gaalorra house has only one such frame (Diagram 23). To increase the depth of the construction so that it encloses the same area as the Standard Rendille house, the struts forming the back of the house are made up of two sections: a shorter section, which is driven into the ground, and a longer, curved section, which is tied to the first one and connected to the frame, thus forming part of the roof.[64]

A small feature of the house is attributed enough significance to be used as another name for Gaalorra: *amomísa*. The *amomísa* is a small narrow mat of palm fibres, maybe two spans long, which is occasionally smeared with the brains – something a Rendille would never eat – or blood of a slaughtered animal. At a new settlement site, while the woman – the owner and mistress of the house – is busy arranging the interior of her abode, the *amomísa* is placed in a conspicuous position on the roof matting above the door. This is a sign that no male, including her husband, is yet allowed to enter. When the woman is in a more receptive mood, she tucks the

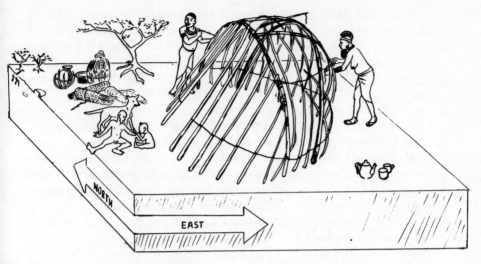

Diagram 22   Frame of a standard Rendille house

amomísa out of sight between the mats and sticks of the house. Women of other clans do not have such practical signals. Apart from this, the *amomísa* does not appear to have a practical or ritual function, although, of course, it serves as a visual symbol of group identity. The same name is used by the Gabbra for the ordinary mat above the entrance.

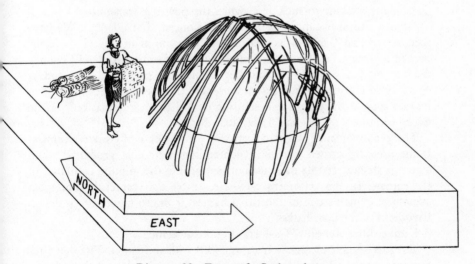

Diagram 23   Frame of a Gaalorra house

Unmarried daughters and wives of Gaalorra are also recognisable by their personal attire. Unmarried girls wear strings of perforated ostrich shell discs (*ntorénye*) dangling from their belts. This has been copied 'long ago' by girls of Tubcha, an adoptive brother clan.

Gaalorra girls do not become *sabade*, whereas other Rendille declare the daughters of one age set of the generation cycle of three to be *sabade* and delay their marriage by one initiation cycle of 14 years.[65]

In their fertile years Gaalorra women wear sheepskins around their waist and shoulders rather than the usual goatskins, although the former are thicker and take more effort to scrape thin and smooth. In attaching the skirt to the bodies, which involves making tucks in appropriate places and securing them with decorative seams sewn with narrow skin strips, they are, however, no less skilful than their sisters elsewhere.

In their childbearing years married women grow their hair long, shaving only the forehead, temples and nape, while the top hair is worn, Boran style, in dozens of well-greased tresses. As Odoola women have the same style, women with a reputation for hairdressing are in high demand among both clans. Other Rendille women shave their heads or, if their first born is a boy, retain a central longitudinal crest stiffened with mud, the *doko*.

The hairstyle of babies also differs: while other Rendille shave their children's heads for the first time a week after the birth, the Gaalorra delay this until weaning.

Men wear the *ħaad'i Gaaldeilan* ('the brass [ring] of Gaaldeilan) around their right wrist. In spite of its name this ring is only worn by Gaalorra and has to do with their *iibir* power: the first ring is given to a child when 'his tongue is made to suck', i.e. when the power is transmitted.

Other cultural peculiarities of Gaalorra consist of avoidances. We have seen above that Gaalorra women do not dress in goatskins. This forms part of a more general goat avoidance. In earlier times people of Gaalorra did not eat goats at all; nor did they drink their milk, and even today, contrary to all other Rendille, they use sheep for certain sacrificial ceremonies such as the end of the seclusion period after circumcision[66] or the *naabo* ceremony (see Schlee 1979: 405–24).

The goat avoidance is particularly acute in the case of Gaalorra camels. Items used for camels are never contaminated by goat products; when a goat is slaughtered its meat cannot be put into the milking container of the camels. In this, Gaalorra camels resemble *dorr* camels.[67] This goat avoidance explains one of the ritual names or praise names of Gaalorra: Riyodiido – 'the goat haters'.

Unlike other Rendille, Gaalorra do not eat game.

They have their own customs connected with the moon. The day after the new moon, all other Rendille smear their foreheads and the ridge of their noses with white chalk, while in the case of Gaalorra the mixture is red: it contains chalk and an extract of the *ħiiyi Gaaldeilan* ('the root of Gāldeilan').

Gaalorra men only pour milk libations (*sadaka*, ex Arabic via Swahili) on Sundays, i.e. the Day of the Camel, on new moon, on full moon (*goban*) and on the day preceding it (*haugd'eer*), while other Rendille, who do not enjoy the same special relationship with God, have to perform these sacrifices every day.

If, after hearing about a clan culture so divergent from the general picture, we surmise that Gaalorra must be a recent addition to the Rendille clan spectrum, oral tradition will contradict us. Other subclans which are culturally completely assimilated can be shown to be recent immigrants, whereas Gaalorra, be they 'red-mouthed Marle' or not, must have been part and parcel of Rendille society for centuries, since they are also represented among the Sakuye who split from the Rendille around 1650.

The clan origin myths about Gaalorra are given in Rendille and German in Schlee (1979: 253–68). I therefore only give a summary version in English here.

When Gaalorra had come out [emerged, appeared], he came from the Lake [Turkana, Rudolph]. They were two men. One followed the *qallu* [R: *khallu*]. The *qallu* were his brothers. The other one came towards the side of the Rendille. He met Fofén with the Black Camels [the ancestor of the Nebei subclan of Saale]. (Barowa Ad'icharreh)

In another version *qallu* is not used as the name of a lateral branch but of the original group:

Even me, about *qallu*, from our people who stem from there, a long time ago, we only hear the tale and the tale we hear goes like this:
When *qallu* emerged,[68] two men were born as brothers. When they separated, one came via Mount Kulal and married a Rendille girl. The one who passed that side joined the Boran and married a Boran girl. (Urri Tarwen)

[These two people] were like Muslims. They do not drink goat milk. [They only drink] milk of sheep and camels and cattle. They also do not eat goat meat. Nor do they eat the wild animals which normally are in the bush. So they are holy. (Barowa Ad'icharreħ)

The informant knows very well that Muslims do not avoid goat products and also do not abstain from game if the throat is cut while the animal is living. 'Muslim' here stands for people who keep strict avoidances and so are 'holy' (*lagan*), the same term that is used for a number of Rendille categories of people of special ritual status and for *dorr* camels (see Schlee 1979: 354–57).

When [the brother who had come to the Rendille] met Fofén, he asked Fofén for a camel bull. He was given the bull. Fofén [said] to his sons, 'I have given a bull to that man, then, when the camels walk over there, when I shout "Yui!" do not turn around!' Then he shouted, 'Yui!' Gaalorra turned around. He looked that way, stood like a tree and died on the spot.

Fofén had not liked to give his bull to Gaalorra. [But Gaalorra] was feared for his *iibire*. So he gave him the bull, but cursed, killed him. If [Gaalorra] was given a bull, it was only because one was afraid of his *iibire*-power. (Barowa)

A Nebei ('Fofén') informant describes the same episode in the following way:

Gaaldeilan was only this one man, and his wife was already old and barren. The man could not be overpowered. He could not be overpowered by curse. He and Fofén were equal. He came to ask for a camel bull. 'Go and drive it!' he was told. When the camels had gone a certain distance he remained there standing on the ground. He died upright. The wife came running and entered the house. No birth, she had never given birth. 'Go and get your house!' [Fofén] said to her. So she joined the clan settlement. 'Go and enter the house of this woman!' [Fofén said to his sons, thus telling or allowing them to make the woman their concubine]. The woman gave birth to a boy. A brass bracelet was taken out [of a bag]. It was put on the child['s wrist]. His tongue was suckled.[69] Gaaldeilan that day became part of this clan. There they got each other. So they are brothers, and the boy is just of this clan [Nebei]. (Eisimbasele)

If we recall what we learned in chapter 2 about *patres* and *genitores*, it becomes clear that by begetting a boy and giving him a brass ring – their clan insignia – they did not establish a valid claim to him. The 'owner', i.e. the nearest senior patrilineal relative, of the boy was living among the Boran. Only he could establish such a claim. But he was busy founding a clan in another country.

[...] he married the Boran girl. He slept in the house. When the woman had became pregnant, he called the Boran. 'Do not enter my house!' he said to them. 'I [go and] look for a brother of mine, do not enter this house!'

[...] When people got up in the morning, a puff adder was sleeping on the woman; the woman had no way of getting up, the thing was on here [her breast].

A cow was milked, it is said, [the milk container] was tied to a stick, was stretched out towards it. When it sipped the milk, a little bit of the milk got spilled, it licked the milk, one poured out more, it drank it, came down, rolled up ['sat down'] here, so, it had left her.

When in the evening the livestock came back, they just milked milk, poured it out [for the snake], it drank it, so the woman adopted the snake and [every evening] put it back into its place [= bag or basket]. [...]

[Her husband, in the meantime] came walking towards here. In a land to that side, when he came there, he collected a [stray] loading camel. The loading camel had a hide ring [from a sacrificial animal] around its neck.

When he came to the Rendille – his brother before had married and a man of Nebei had killed him by curse – [he asked], 'What have you seen of that man [his brother]?' 'At first he had married, and a man whom he had asked for a bull, a bull to serve his camels, that man cursed and killed him.' In the time of origin the Rendille were full of dangerous people. (Urri Tarwén)

'Show me the man who has killed my brother!' 'It is Fofén,' he was told.

'You have killed my brother, look, wait for me!' 'Brother, do not kill me, do not curse me, let us adopt each other!' This is how he implored him. (Barowa Ad'icharreñ)

The other side, Nebei, describes the behaviour of Gaalorra as not so aggressive and that of Fofén as much less submissive:

The wife of Gaalorra whose husband had been killed went into the house of the man of Fofén. He stayed with her until he begot a child by her. Then Gaaldeilan came. The men were sitting outside [the settlement] and Gaaldeilan came and entered the house. 'Go!' he said to the boy to whom the woman of Gaaldeilan had given birth [and who] normally said 'Father' to the man [Fofén], 'go, say, "Father's Younger Brother" to him, Father's Younger Brother, my mother is calling you.' Gaaldeilan was sitting in the house.

The boy came, normally he said, 'Father' to the gentleman, [but now] he said, 'Father's Younger Brother.' 'Hai!' the other one turned around, 'ai, this boy, who made him become like this and told him to say such a thing?' The woman came running and held Fofén around the waist. 'O my Fofén, do not kill my son!' So she was told, 'All right, go away!' [And to Gaalorra Fofén said,] 'I shall hold one hand, hold you the other!' So it was like this and Gaaldeilan took the boy. This was [the story of] the boy of Gaaldeilan. This is how they [Nebei and Gaalorra] found each other. When he had been born, the boy's tongue was suckled and the brass ring was put around his arm. The brass ring which they now give to each other and the tongue they suckle each other stems from there. (Eisimmirdana)

They fear each other very much. They do not marry each other's daughters. They do not have concubinage with each other. So they are brothers. When God made these people emerge, they thus emerged together. (Barowa Ad'icharreñ)

While the hostile interpretation of Fofén's behaviour would have been that, after killing the Gaalorra man, he took his wife as spoil, the diplomatic way of seeing this is that he behaved like a brother towards Gaalorra by caring for his widow and begetting children in his name. This latter view was adopted and consequently Gaalorra and Nebei became brother clans with all that implies, such as extending the exogamy rule and granting each other access to each other's wives, which is the present state of affairs.

So much for the Rendille branch of Gaalorra. Let us now return to the pregnant woman we left among the Boran.

That woman lived on, and when she gave birth, she gave birth to a boy. When she had given birth to the boy, she sat down on a stone and did not give birth afterwards.

That boy now goes and marries people, marries women. The cattle with whom the man had come are not mixed with other cattle. They graze alone. They do not multiply. Other cattle procreate and become many. But these are just one herd. Only this boy inherits them, nobody else. When they go out to pasture, the gate [in the thornbush fence] is shut.

If someone stands at that gate and says, 'I am Gaaldeilan, I am Katebo,' then it is said, 'Open the gate!' He comes through the gate. If he has cheated, the gate does not open.

Now, people who come from there, who do not drink camel milk nor that of goats, for whom only sheep are milked,[70] are plenty among the Boran.

Yesterday when I was born, I did not eat goats, I did not eat camel meat, I did drink camel milk but not that of goats, until some later day I just started somehow to eat those types of livestock.

These people now, when they come to visit us, when someone comes here and says, 'I do not eat that,' [then we reply,] 'Oh! you are Katebo, people of Katebo!'

They keep cattle, smallstock, horses, these three.

The ideas of elaborate and rigid avoidances are linked to that of curse power. The Sakuye Gaalorra, after centuries of separation and numerous Oromo and Somali influences, still show the same combination of traits. *Gaaloraan nam jabba; gaalálle ingórratu* ('Gaalorra are strong people; they do not even slaughter camels') was the spontaneous reaction of a Sakuye Matarbá elder when I mentioned that clan.

[...] Only that one boy is born, he [in his turn] marries a whole settlement, they give birth and give birth, and then again, when the place of the grand-father comes around,[71] again a girl of that clan is married. That girl again does not fail: she only gives birth to one boy.

[...] Only this child is born. When she has given birth one does not talk about her any more. She does not give birth to another child.

[...] My eye has not seen it, but the ear of it I have heard: among the Ethio-pians [or 'Sidamo' – the Rendille do not distinguish here] even somebody with a gun does not enter that settlement, nobody goes in there. Yesterday when the Ethiopians mistreated people, when they defecated inside the houses, they did not go there. These [*qallu*] when they pray [= curse] they just finish people.

Now the Gabbra, Alganna, stay until they have passed some years and then they sort out young entire camel bulls, drive them, drive them, until they take them there. If they do not take them, and the proper time has passed, then the camels which are brought in [in the evening] and are fenced in break through in the night and get lost.

These camels, all the time, camels get lost from Alganna. 'We perish, what shall we do?' 'This tribe, their span has elapsed now the camels do not enter the settlement site,' in the evening and in the forenoon Alganna keeps on run-ning [after their stray camels] while the other Gabbra prosper in comfort, until then some young camel bulls are selected, driven and taken there. When the bulls have been driven and brought [to the *qallu*] he cuts a stick for the people. The ones for whom he cuts such a stick breed their herds in a proper way. That is how it is.

[...]These Alganna, who are called Alganna, they are just this tribe ['*qallu*'] . I have never seen a people who are more numerous. [Urri Tarwen)

There are many more tales about the *qallu*: he is not buried but his body vanishes; as he does not really die, people do not mourn him but dance, etc. (see Schlee 1979: 264ff.).

The reader, of course, will have recognised the *qallu* institution of the

Boran behind this, although from the Rendille perspective tribal names and ritual functions are somewhat confused and the picture is slightly blurred. *Qallu* is used as a tribal or clan name, while the clan which is meant can be easily identified as Karrayyu, because, as I have mentioned in chapter 4, it is the *qallu* of Karrayyu to whom Alganna take camels. 'Katebo', as we have heard above, is used among the Oromo as a name of a strain of cattle, not of a human group.

As the Rendille have never belonged to the Worr Libin alliance one might dismiss the claim of a Rendille clan to be related to the *qallu* lineage of Karrayyu, with their resounding name and far-reaching power, as being rather pretentious. It would be interesting to know whether Boran informants would acknowledge this claim.

Waako D'iriba, who is already familiar to us, confirms that Gaalorra and Alganna both originate from the *qallu* lineage of Karrayyu and he volunteered the information that originally both abstained from camel flesh but that later the *qallu* 'spat' for them so that now they can eat it.[72] He also confirms much other information about the *qallu* which we have heard from Rendille, like their practice of castrating cattle by magical means simply by touching their backs with a stick, etc. (see chapter 3 above), whatever may be the empirical reality behind this. This shows that the Rendille accounts are not fairy tales which spring from geographical and social distance but are shared by the Boran themselves.

Waako D'iriba modifies what Urri Tarwen has told us about the restrictions on the fertility of the *qalliti*, the wife of the *qallu*, and thus confirms it in principle: she only has one son but may, in addition, have two daughters. He had not heard about the stone, which, according to Tarwen, is responsible for blocking the fertility of the woman who sits down on it.

If we were in a position to conclude, from this high degree of mutual confirmation, that Gaalorra indeed, like the nucleus of Gabbra Alganna, has split from Karrayyu Worr Qallu, we would find a quick end for this chapter. But there seems to be more to it.

According to our Rendille traditions, Gaalorra did not split from Worr Qallu but both lineages were founded by one man, one in his own name and one in his dead brother's; and originally the two brothers did not come from the Boran but from the 'Lake'. And we may add that this is an origin they share with others, namely with the Rendille clan Rengumo, and that the relationship between Gaalorra and Rengumo continues to be a very special one. This other cycle of traditions now points, if it points to any living people at all, to the Arbore, and by logical extension one might therefore ask whether the *qallu* lineage of Karrayyu, if indeed they are of identical origin, are, after all, Boran.

All Rendille informants agree that both Gaalorra and Rengumo were separated from their original people, sometimes identified as the Geleba (Dasanech), by a lake, which suddenly widened and deepened and thus cut a caravan in two. This, of course, reminds us of the Iris tradition of the Gabbra, but the peoples and context are not identical. One informant[73] gives the names of the two boys who, according to him, ended up on their own to the east of the water as Gaalorra and Gaalorle, of whom the latter was to be the founding ancestor of Rengumo. Gaaldeilan then went to Mount Kulal, saying *a kulal-ena* ('it is our sleeping place'), using the word for the fenced open-air resting place in a camel camp. The young man of Rengumo stayed in the area of North Horr and there, apparently, asked the lineage Gaalñaile of Uyám for a mad girl to marry as he had only smallstock and no camels, which he would have needed to marry a healthy girl. This mad girl, through her three sons, Arbele, Adisomo and Aicha, became the ancestress of all of Rengumo.

More details about this clan are given above and elsewhere.[74] Here we are only interested in Rengumo history in so far as it overlaps with that of Gaalorra, and in this context we should mention one contemporary custom which is often attributed to the common migrational history of the two clans.

At the marriage of a Gaalorra man, smallstock is slaughtered and eaten exclusively by Gaalorra and any Rengumo people who happen to be there, but by no other clans.

This applies to two ritual slaughters, both of which differ from the marriage rituals of the other Rendille and may therefore be added to our list of rituals peculiar to the Gaalorra. While other brides can be circumcised (clitoridectomised) at various times during the marriage process, in the case of daughters of Gaalorra and brides of Gaalorra only the morning of the second day, *maanti min labañcho* ('the day when the [new] house is assembled'), is used for this purpose. Before circumcision, the head of the young woman is shaved and at the same time a young ewe is slaughtered. The intestinal fat (*moor*) is used to cover the girl's shaved head as a symbol of a new start.[75] This sheep is called *suben ti inám lakamooricho* ('the young ewe with which the girl is intestinal-fattened'). While other Rendille dispense with the sheep unless the girl is an eldest daughter, the custom is indispensable for the daughters and brides of Gaalorra. The meat and intestines of the sheep are wrapped in the skin until evening. Then, when the new house has been built and the first fire is drilled there, another young female sheep, *suben ti dab lakabiro* ('the sheep with which the fire is drilled'), is slaughtered. Other Rendille would use a male camel calf as *birnán* ('drilling'). (None of these slaughters can be called a sacrifice [*sorio*] because the consecration phase [*d'ikhnán* = 'washing', *harirnán*[76]] is omitted. All slaughters at the occasion of a marriage are not carried out for God but for human beings.) Only then is the meat of both animals cooked, using the traditional earthen pot (*diri*), in the new house. The right side of the animals will be eaten by men of Gaaldeilan, including the other subclans, and Rengumo, the left side by wives of Gaaldeilan, daughters of Gaaldeilan and daughters of Rengumo. The latter cannot take any meat home because their husbands and children belong to other clans (unless, of course, these daughters of Rengumo happen to be wives of Gaaldeilan).

Another animal, the *ħelenki gurrot* ('the ram of the marriage song'), is killed by a man of Rengumo, if such a person is available, and its blood is stirred (to remove the fibrine) in a half gourd held under the cut throat by a daughter of Rengumo. For the equivalent ritual at a marriage of Rengumo, Gaalorra people are called on to perform these tasks. The stirring of the blood is done with a fresh green *gaer*[77] twig, not a dry stick, by a woman who has never had to lament the death of a child. The freshness of the stick and the luck of the woman are obvious expressions of the desire for marital bliss.

Apart from the common geographical origin of Gaalorra and Gaalorle to the west or north-west of Lake Turkana and their common fate of being separated from their homeland by the widening lake, there is another link betweem Gaaldeilan and Rengumo. Keele, the eponymous ancestor of the first subclan in the seniority order of Galdeilan, is said to have been the orphan son of a stranger who was married to a Rengumo girl. As he was 'alone' (*kelei*, an etymology of his name suggested by the informant[78]), his maternal grandfather raised him and gave him livestock. His smallstock has the same cut in the right ear as that of Rengumo and his camel brand is similar to that of Rengumo but has an additional distinctive mark. Keele was the first subclan to adopt the name Gaaldeilan and he later gathered the other subclans around him.[79] *Gaal d'eilan* or, with a finite verb, *gaal ad'eilama* means 'the camels walk [back to the enclosures] in the evening' and is interpreted as an indicator of Keele's original wealth.[80] Búrcha, the next subclan to join Gaaldeilan, is said to have come from the north and to have consisted of many (*buur*) people. After this, Keele met Gaalorra and asked him his name. The answer was 'Marle'. Keele responded: *Marle d'ud'um kaelani, magaħin a Gaaldeilan* ('Let us regard Marle as a pejorative name, your (pl.) name is Gaaldeilan.' As Keele retained his first position in the seniority order of the emergent clan, instead of telling the newcomers to pitch their houses in front of his own, as would have been customary and propitious, his subclan has never multiplied and even today consists of only a few houses (Barowa Ad'icharreħ). (There are, however, also other stories explaining this lack of growth, which involve a curse of some kind.)

When asked, how this tradition about the Rengumo connection fits chronologically with the above account of the link to the Boran Karrayyu, the same informant gave the following order of events. (This order may spring from my desire for consistency as it was not information offered spontaneously. It shows, however, that, logically, the two strains of tradition are not mutually exclusive and that they can be combined.)

1 Gaalorra and Gaalorle came from the west of the lake.
2 Gaalorra split in two: one brother went to join the Boran while the other stayed at Mount Kulal. Gaalorle got married and the clan Rengumo started to grow.
3 Generations later, Keele, a lineage founded by a daughter's son of Rengumo, adopted Búrcha and later the Kulal branch of Gaalorra and combined them under the name Gaaldeilan.
4 A man of this southern branch of Gaalorra asked a man of Nebei for a camel bull and was killed by miraculous means in the process.
5 A man from the Boran branch of Gaalorra came to avenge his clan brother but was persuaded to accept Nebei as a brother clan instead.

While the mythical version quoted above personalises clan history and speaks of single men who met and interacted, this attempt to fit events into a plausible chronological frame allows some generations to elapse before Keele, who could not have existed when Gaalorra and Gaalorle came from the west, adopted the other subclans of Gaaldeilan. 'Gaalorra', 'Nebei', 'Rengumo' etc., here stand for descent groups, while the myth telescopes the lineages into single personalities.

This version also allows the migration from the west, the emergence of the Worr Qallu Karrayyu among the Boran and the final integration of a part of Gaalorra into Rendille society to be seen as gradual processes with intermediate phases.

Barowa claims that, at an unspecified period in the past, Gaalorra did not participate in the *gaalgulamme* age-set ritual of the Rendille but held a sacrifice of a bovine calf. Instead of the Rendille preparations for the marriage of an age set,[81] they used to kill and burn on ox. Even now they drive a herd of sheep rather than camels to the settlement of the bride on the first day of the marriage ceremonies. All this points to an ultimate origin outside the PRS camel culture in a cattle-raising area, although by 1650, when the Sakuye split from the Rendille, Gaalorra was represented among the PRS people with some degree of cultural assimilation.

All this seems to suggest that the claim of the Rendille Gaalorra to have originally been 'Marle' has to be taken seriously. 'Marle' today is largely synonymous with Arbore, the name of a small cattle-raising people from the western shore of Lake Stephanie. Similar names (Marile, Merille, etc.) seem to be widespread in the area and also to refer to Nilotic populations. To equate the 'Marle' of the Rendille traditions with the Arbore of today and to regard the present Arbore territory as the Gaalorra cradleland would, of course, mean neglecting everything we have learned from our historical study of more southernly areas: namely, that ethnic boundaries are fluent and that people migrate. In fact there are traditions that some or all of the present-day Arbore once lived farther west, to the west of the Omo river, i.e. north-west of Lake Turkana.[82] Other traditions point to an earlier intermingled residence with the Dasanech who live around the northern end of Lake Turkana and the lower Omo.[83] We can therefore only point to the general area and the general cluster of peoples.

There is, in fact, a clan group called Gaalorra among the Arbore. The information about them, which I regard as reasonably safe because it is mutually confirmed by independent informants, is somewhat sparse and general:

1   They are highest in the seniority order of the Arbore (Joore, Irile).
2   They are 'qallu', i.e. ritual specialists (Joore, Irile).
3   They observe a number of food avoidances (Joore, Irile). They do not eat goat, game or camel but only mutton and beef (Joore). They only sacrifice sheep, not goats, and a ritual specialist in their midst, Kiriyom by name, abstains from goat meat (Irile).
4   They have magical means of finding out and killing illegitimate sons (Joore, Irile).

Points 2 and 3 are highly reminiscent of the traditions and the ritual practice of the Rendille Gaalorra.

If we take these traditions at face value, they also imply that these same 'Marle' Gaalorra are not only brothers of the Rendille Gaalorra but also of the Worr Qallu of the Karrayyu Boran, the clan of one of the ritual heads of the once mighty Worr Libin alliance. Although this may sound like a fantastic imposition, what Haberland (1963: 126–9) has to say about Karrayyu and the Sabbo moiety of the Boran in general makes it at least possible that the origin of the Worr Qallu has to be sought outside Boran territory to the west. Haberland tentatively reconstructs an earlier moiety structure of the Boran which consisted only of the present-day Gona moiety – itself divided into Haroresa and Fullele – and the nucleus of Karrayyu, which had a central position between Haroresa and Fullele. Such a moiety structure, plus an additional element which does not belong to either moiety, is, according to Haberland, not unusual among the Oromo. This old structure is still reflected in the seating arrangement at the big gada ceremonies (Haberland 1963: 127). Karrayyu later co-opted many stranger groups and Maṭṭari (literally, 'the bundle'), similarly emerged as a new synthetic unit. All these then formed the Sabbo moiety, which was structurally mirrored by Gona, the internal binary division of which lost importance in the same measure as the emergent major unit – of which Gona was to be a division – gained importance.

The evidence adduced by Haberland to support this historical model consists of structural as well as behavioural observations.

The Sabbo[84] moiety has one major and three minor *qallu*, although from the general Oromo pattern, in which there is only one *qallu* for the whole society, one would have expected Sabbo to have no *qallu* at all, because there is a more senior *qallu*, the one of Odítu, who belongs to the other moiety, Gona. This suggests that Sabbo is composed of formerly independent groups who were allowed to keep their *qallu* (1963: 128).

Karrayyu and Mattari (Matt'arri in our spelling) are synthetic supra-clans and structurally different from Dígalu or the 14 clans of Gona (1963: 127, 131, 132).

The Sabbo moiety is associated with the left side in certain rituals, which marks them as junior, while Gona is associated with the right-hand side (1963: 127).

Unlike Gona and groups outside Boran society who are considered original Oromo, the Sabbo are allowed to eat forelegs (1963: 127).

Although today the *qallu* of Karrayyu (Sabbo) is richer and more influential than the one of Odítu (Gona), he is regarded as junior and has only recently assumed functions in the *gada* system (1963: 154).

The *qallu* of Sabbo is restricted to the western part of Boranland and is not allowed to cross the Dawa river in the east (1963: 129).

The external origin of the Worr Qallu of Karrayyu is also supported by the traditions collected by Baxter (personal communication). Boran society was already well established with *aadafi sera*, but the *qallu* gave these 'customs and laws' the impress of *Waaqa* – 'God' (see also Baxter 1965: 69ff.).

GAALORRA AMONG THE GABBRA

While the semi-mythical clan relationship of the Rendille Gaalorra to their putative Arbore brethren and the Worr Qallu of Karrayyu must be regarded as very old, if we accept it at all as historically real, most of the Gaalorra among the Gabbra trace their origin to comparatively recent emigrations from the Rendille.

Among the Gabbra, Gaalorra is represented by only seven elders and their dependants. Of these seven, five descend from a man called Diido, two in the first, two in the second and one in the third generation. Diido is said to have been the grandson of a certain Dibis, who came from the Rendille. This must have been early in the nineteenth century. I have contradictory information about the other two elders. While some claim that these can also be traced to recent Rendille immigrants, others say that they are 'original' Gabbra and have not entered Gabbra society via the Rendille but from the north.

Gaalorra does not have much lineage identity of its own among the Gabbra. In Sharbana they maintain close relationships to Konte, in Alganna to Diisa and Halano. Their prominent position in the age-set rituals of Sharbana, however, makes it appear possible that at least some of them have a long-established position in this phratry.

Customs associated with their powers to bless and curse are very similar to those of the Rendille Gaalorra, which would not be surprising in the case of recent immigrants.

SOMALI LINKS

Somali traders from the Gelible subgroup of the Degodia who live in Rendille-land claim to be 'Gaaldeilan' in Rendille terms. This claim is supported by statements by pastoral Degodia that there are Gelible among the Rendille, etc. Apart from such claims, no cultural or historical evidence has been found, other than a certain marginality of Gelible among the Degodia,[85] of a common origin of the two groups. The evidence quoted by Schlee (1979: 278–81) was fabricated by the interpreter, who was a Gelible and had a position to defend among the Rendille. (My comprehension of Somali was rather poor then.) On the sociological level, this clan relationship by now does exist, because its existence has been claimed so often.

MASSA/ELÉMO/BORQOSHO

The lineage Massa is the *qallu* lineage of the Yiblo moiety of the Galbo phratry of the Gabbra. They are the seniormost segment of this senior moiety. Within Yiblo they form a close unit with their brother lineage Chaaqo and observe the same exogamy rules. Chaaqo is also represented in the Sharbana and Alganna phratries. This circumstance is explained by reference to the back-migration from Iris, when some married women remained with their fathers because their husbands were cut off from them by the water.[86] All these parts of Chaaqo, including Massa, respect each other as brothers and sisters and do not intermarry.

Massa itself, apart from Galbo, is represented in the pseudo-lineage Borqosho in the Gaar phratry of the Gabbra and in the Gaaldeilan clan of the Rendille, of which they form the Elémo subclan. The presence of Massa among the Rendille and in Gār is attributed to the same chain of events.

> *Et lama eñenet. Walal. Gaal d'ele, chii large, lafird'e. Kan lakatabe, Dooma katabte, Rendille khaate, goobis khabai.*

> They were two men. Brothers. The camels gave birth, enemies were seen, everybody fled. One of them was abandoned, Dooma[87] abandoned him, the Rendille took him, along with his homestead.[88]

Other Rendille and Gabbra versions agree with this one, which I have chosen for its laconic brevity. Repeatedly it is stressed that the man who was captured along with his dependants and livestock was rich in camels and that many of these had just calved, so that it was difficult for him to escape. His camels were fenced on Buurgabo,[89] an outcrop south of Turbi, surrounded by the wide, undulating, treeless Diida Galgallo, an obvious place for making camp since – at least today – it is the only place far and wide which has thornbushes for fencing. (There is also a defunct borehole which is shown on some maps.) Like the rest of Galbo, and like Elémo until today, this man also only selected white bulls for breeding with the result that most of his camels were white. People of Elémo refer to this in an exclamation which, almost like a ritual name, is used for swearing or as expression of anger or astonishment: *Gaal d'akhan Buurgaabo ogooge!* ('White camels covered Buurgaabo!').

The brother of the man who was left behind received some help from Gār neighbours and thus managed to escape from the Rendille. He started to ask the Galbo, who should have tried harder to help their clansmen to move, embarrassing questions: *Ebel me, goob ebel me?* ('Where is So-and-so, where is So-and-so's settlement group?'). He only got an answer *raas on kijira* ('He is on the abandoned site').

> *Maanti lanokhti, Rendille khaate, Gaaldeilan khaate. Khaaaté, gaal khabai, goobis khabai guuriche. Mad'iñin lakka.*

When they returned, the Rendille had taken him, Gaaldeilan had taken him. Taken him along with his camels, his family, they had made him move. They had not even raided him.

> *Kuus goorat laokhiche, Gār minye gargare, khaate. Dooma katabte. Kuus Gār makhaatina? Kī Gār khaate la 'an m'atin isoonokhd'i,' yidañ, 'Dooma. Maso-onokhd'i, ikatabtene, walalei chii khaate, anná ikatabtene, ani yaaf ti goorat chii ikasookhaate, iche raaña.' Dooma diide.*

That one had been lifted up, Gār had helped him, taken him, isn't it? Galbo had abandoned him. Didn't Gār take him? The one whom Gār had taken said, 'I shall not go back to you, Galbo. I shall not go back. You had abandoned me, the enemies have taken my brother, also myself you had left behind, I shall follow the tribe who has helped me to get away from the enemies.' He rejected Galbo.

> *'Nyaama, gooben ki goorat chii to khaate, sookhata, walalei sookhata!' 'Chirrinka inti nañ kasookhaano makhabno, kale, nañ isoonokho!' Diide. Diin waite.*

'Go and bring back our family which has been taken by an enemy tribe, bring back my brother!' 'Right now we do not know from where to bring him back [= there is no means of bringing him back], come, return to us!' He declined. They did not let him.

> *'Baria, wañari ween atin ikhalla, de sañata ch'il bariye, indo walañ kaagartan.' Sundun dab goya gesse, ibeen sundume dab kabariite, uranti gaal dab kabolkhiche; ch'il bariye, eti miigenye inta kijiro tuuman weñe, gaal goya gesse.*

'Go to sleep, I shall slaughter a big billy goat for you, tomorrow morning you shall see something with your eyes.' He put the branding iron into the fire, the

Diagram 24 Kóbola (Gār, Gabbra) including Borqosho and Massa/Elémo (Gabbra Galbo and Rendille Gaaldeilan)

branding iron stayed in the fire the whole night, he had made the fire inside the camel yard; when. it had become morning, he called all able-bodied people who were around and led them to the midst of the camel herd.

... *Gaal batarr chiire. 'Kalea,' yid'añ, 'atin tusa,' gaal batarr chiire.*

He branded his camels on the thigh. He said, 'Come, I shall show you something,' and branded the camels on the thigh.

While Massa and Elémo mark their camels by a cross on the crupper, this renegade changed his camel brand to the one of his new adoptive brothers of the lineage Borqosho of Gār, who mark their camels by a bent line on the right thigh (Diagram 24). By making Galbo look on, he derived pleasure from the pain they felt when seeing their clan and clan herd being diminished.

Elders of Massa in Galbo – who understandably remain silent about the disappointment expressed by this renegade – describe the capture of Elémo-to-be by the Rendille as a fairly recent event. Although they cannot name any ancestors common to themselves and Rendille Elémo, they claim that they know Elémo's place in the seniority order of Massa and thus their settlement position if they ever came back to join their original clan.

The order goes like this (present-day elders are listed with their remembered patrilineal ancestors to show their genealogical distance from each other):

1   Abudo Guyyo Qarqaba Barile Guyyo Utala Guyyo Ali Abudo[90]
2   Abudo Ibrai Ali Abudo Guyyo Utala, etc., like 1
3   Yara Haama Guyyo Utala, etc., like 1
4   Elemo subclan of the Rendille
5   Duub Jilo Guyyo
6   ...
...

This claim may be vain or not. If any Rendille Elémo decided to join Massa, he might end up in position 4 because Abudo Guyyo believes him to belong there, irrespective of whether this corresponds to genealogical reality or not. And if the Elémo ever died out, Yara Haama or his descendants would inherit from them, and this would be acknowledged by the Rendille, because camels which are unlawfully inherited are called *ood* and are believed to be unpropitious.[91] If Yara Haama had the slightest doubt that he was the rightful heir he would reject the camels, because the Gabbra share this belief. Luckily Elémo does not show the slightest tendency to die out.

In less serious matters one may find *ad hoc* arrangements. I once had to function as an interpreter in a discussion between Abudo Guyyo and a young man of Elémo who had come with me because he had been bitten by a snake and wanted to try Gabbra medicine.[92] Abudo asked the younger man whether he was his 'brother', his 'brother's son' or whatever his generational position was. The conclusion reached was that Abudo was the 'father's brother' of the younger man, i.e. a clansman of the parental generation. No genealogical evidence was given for this, and the arrangement rested solely on Abudo's apparently superior knowledge of which, apart from the firmness of his voice, no proof was given. It might have been somewhat awkward if the younger man had turned out to be the older man's 'grandfather', although, taking into account the long generation spans of the Rendille, this would have been perfectly possible. To regard each other as paternal uncle and fraternal nephew, however, may have been compatible with similar arrangements with earlier generations of Elémo, about whom Abudo Guyyo was well informed from mutual visits and from grazing in their neighbourhood in times of peace.

Some people, like Abudo Guyyo, talk about the split between Massa and Elémo as if it was a recent affair, two or three generations removed from the living elders. If we followed Godaana Ali Abudo, whom we have quoted above, then we would have to place this split in the late nineteenth century. Godaana states that the eponymous ancestor of Elémo was a certain Elimma,[93] s/o Mamo s/o Bagawo, while the brother who joined Gār was Gorei Mamo Bagawo, father of Guyyo, an old man who is still alive. This chronology is definitely telescoped. There are Elémo elders who are still remembered, not only by name but visually, who have been born by Rendille women of known clans and who have lived as Rendille among the Rendille at a time when, according to this chronology, they should still have been Gabbra.

Other people treat the above events as part of the mythical past. This other extreme is represented by Ildirim Toord'eer, a Gaalorra elder,[94] who says that Elemo appeared at the time when God created man clan by clan. He starts with the foundation of the Gaaldeilan clan by the mutual adoption of Keele and Gaalorra and places the incorporation of Elémo in the same chain of events:

Aranki Gaalorra Bei soomañe, koban khaba, kobanki D'eñes. Ch' us Kulal sarche sookore, khure to ñaad'et khaba.

The man of Gaalorra crossed the lake to this side, he had a boat, an El Molo boat.[95] When he came up Mount Kulal, he had a brass cup.[96]

Nyirakhó la akhaba, gududan. Nañ Gaal Khol nad'eñ. Gaal Khol maanta ulubba dubis akhabna, gaal Wario akijira, ulubba lakka. Goob Elémo lakka khaba.

He also had a camelcalf, a red one. We call it [the strain] Khol Camels. We still have the progeny of the Khol Camels today, there are some among Wario's[97] camels even now. Also the Elémo subclan has got some.[98]

Keele chirriye makhabala soosöñti, Gaalorra ladeñ, Keele ch'u ye-e-ka, 'ko Waakh isii,'[99] Keele yid'añ.

When the gentleman called Gaalorra came walking towards Keele and Keele looked at him, he said, 'God gave me one.'

Kan Gaalorra la iyeye: 'an a ki is-khab-on. Ínam Gaalorra.' A gedöñ, inenyet, derka? [lama] Derka lama on minya? Gaalorra derka a kan on minya? Kan kaldach on minya añanai. Lamacho iska-furate. Ibeen ko.

And this one, Gaalorra, said, 'I am one who owns himself.[100] Son of Gaalorra. 'So, how many human beings were there? [Answer by the author: Two.] So there were just two, isn't it? Gaalorra was just this one, isn't it? He was only this one alone. The two of them settled together. For one night.

Sañaka sooguurte. Worran ch'at Gelgel, at Moyale jitat ña tabto, buuri booran Gelgel d'añcho katolo magarati, Buurgaabo lad'eñ? [Aa, arge.]

The next day they moved towards here. If you pass through the Gelgel[101] on these roads[102] towards Moyale, don't you know the grey hill standing in the middle of the Gelgel, called Buurgaabo? [Answer: Yes, I have seen it.]

Elemoñiye gaal kad'ele inta yaalon liisoobeñe, Keele on usu icho Gaalorra iskhaban. 'Ko Waakh isii torro,' us yid'añ.

Elemo whose camels had given birth and who just stayed there, they met, just Keele and Gaalorra were together. 'Again God has given me one,' he [Keele] said.

Elémo la iyeye: 'An a ki kulman, is-khab-on.'

And Elémo said, 'I am complete, just by myself.'

A maantöñ? A maanti inenyet d'akhamba Waakh takkai kasoobabañche. Inenyeta nooole Rendille dulo at agarto, eba la etó on soobeñe, derka kharkharad'e.

When was that? It was when God created [literally: 'made come out' (see Schlee 1978b)] all people one by one. All these people of Rendille whom you see walking about, were only created as one man each [one man per clan], then they split.

Goob Elémo, maantas derka, a kan on. Ko ad'an torro yombo il d'añka lañele melle.

The clan Elémo, then, was only this one. Another one who was acquired later, some time in between, does not exist.

By all means, Toord'eer adds, has the subclan Elémo already been among the Rendille at the time of Irale, a devastating famine which occurred when the fathers of D'ismaala were warriors. The age-set D'ismaala was circumcised in 1881 and that of their fathers, if we assume a regular unrolling of the system, in 1839. At that time the drought had forced the Rendille to the north, where they had to pay levy to some enemy tribe, probably the Boran.

> 'As Elémo was small, he was told to pay his share together with some other clan. He was offended by this proposal and responded *yaaftenyo yaaf to malikakhayo* ('our tribe cannot be added to some other tribe'), and paid a full share of the levy alone, with the help of the in-laws of Gaaldeilan. By this statement, which has become proverbial, the name of Elémo is linked to the time of Irale. (Barowa Ad'icharreñ)

Toord'eer's account has a similar shape to other Rendille clan origin myths: it treats clans as single persons, it orders them in time and thus in seniority, it describes their relative status. In other words, it is a political charter and not a historical account. Nevertheless we can recognise the same event and the same place: the Elémo being immobilised by many newly born camel calves on Buurgaabo. The question which still remains open is when did this occur. Before I investigated this matter in detail I tended to believe that the Elémo were a fairly recent, say mid-nineteenth-century, addition to Rendille society. In minor quarrels even Gaalorra, who are themselves called 'Boranto' by other Rendille, refer to the Elémo as 'Boranto',

Table 14 A genealogy of Elémo

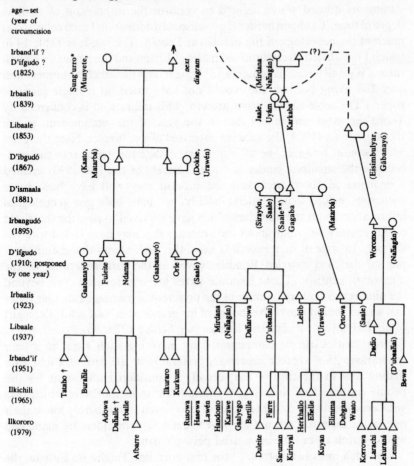

age — set
(year of
circumcision)

Irband'if ?
D'ifgudo ?
(1825)

Irbaalis
(1839)

Libaale
(1853)

D'ibgudó
(1867)

D'ismaala
(1881)

Irbangudó
(1895)

D'ifgudo
(1910; postponed
by one year)

Irbaalis
(1923)

Libaale
(1937)

Irband'if
(1951)

Ilkichili
(1965)

Ilkororo
(1979)

* A Rendille personal name. Sung'urro is also used as a name of the sublineage that descends from this woman.
** Sororate marriage as a replacement for a deceased elder sister (*mingessi*). This woman is the *mingessi* of the first houes and therefore senior to her co-wife from Matarbá, although she married later.
Note: Only those persons have been marked as dead who had reached adulthood and who, as they belong to the younger age sets, would have been expected to be still alive. The clans of origin of the wives of Elémo, which are used for sublineage identification, have been given in brackets. The names of killers (*meerát*) have been underlined.
   Age-set affiliations of people who lived in the earlier part of the nineteenth century are based on extrapolations. I have assumed two intervening age-sets between fathers and sons, although there can be more than two.

which can mean Gabbra or any other Boran-speaking people. The Gabbra statements quoted above seemed to confirm the impression of shallow depth of time. To obtain harder chronological information I then collected as much of the genealogy of the subclan as I could. The result is Table 14 in which I have listed all circumcised males of Elémo and the females who link them. (With all wives, daughters and younger boys the subclan numbers well over 100 living persons and would not have fitted on a single piece of paper.) The table shows recent growth. This impression is confirmed by Toord'eer, who remembers that in the year of the circumcision of the Irbaalis age set (1923) the subclan consisted of five houses. Now there are 30. It would, however, be wrong to extrapolate this trend into the past, because the smallpox epidemic (*sugeri charreñ*) of the late 1890s created a demographic bottleneck and the subclan may well have been more numerous before that. Understandably, we have only got genealogical information about the branches which have survived to pass the threshold of this century and none about the branches that may have ended with the last one. In spite of such probable gaps, this table shows that members of the subclan had married Rendille wives in the earlier decades of the nineteenth century. These Rendille wives are remembered even beyond the nineteenth century because of the preferential marriage rule that states that a man should marry the 'bones of his grandfather' (*laf achi*), i.e. a girl of his FaFaMo's subclan and lineage (see Schlee 1979: 96–7)

Irregularities can be compensated by marrying such a girl in a later generation. As a 'correct' marriage, preferably in the case of a first wife (failing that in the case of the second) is considered important for the people and livestock to thrive, it is important to memorise of which clan your ancestors were daughters' sons (*eisim*) even if you barely know their names, because you are not allowed to refer to your elders by name and would shrink from uttering a dead person's name.

One such line of ancestors,[103] the first-born line Tataho s/o Fuleite, the last four generations of which are included in the above table, goes back well into the eighteenth century (Diagram 25). I have extrapolated the circumcision years of the respective generation sets from the present working of the system. Readers who do not believe in the time stability of such systems are free to take these numbers as mere approximations. The lineages and clans of origin of the females are given in brackets.

This genealogy fits well with Rusowa's[104] statement that his subclan has been among the Rendille for four *achi* ('grandfathers'), i.e. double genera-tions. Indeed, Rusowa himself is seven generations remote from Elimma, his small children eight. If we accepted this genealogy as correct, it would mean that Elimma ('Elémo'), who according to all traditions was an elder with his own herd when he was captured by Gaaldeilan, must have joined Rendille society around 1700, that is, not much later than the Rendille–

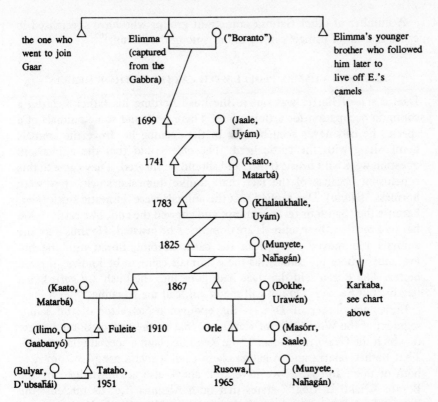

Diagram 25   Genealogy of a part of the Elémo subclan showing circumcision years and approximate time-depth of this subclan among the Rendille

Sakuye split (*c.* 1650). The fact that they are still referred to as 'Boranto' shows how long it takes to become Rendille. That in practice they defend the Rendille cause is shown by the number of underlined names in the Ilkichili column of Table 14 above. All these people bear killer beads around their necks for having killed Gabbra/Boran raiders.

MASSA AMONG THE BORAN

Among the Waso Boran there is a Massa group who are thought of as 'Gabbra'. Since the Boran presence in Isiolo District is of recent origin, this Massa group probably joined the Boran in some more northerly location. The existence of Massa among the Boran is known to their Gabbra and Rendille clan brothers.[105]

The Massa of the Boran are associated with the Odítu clan of the Gona moiety, which corresponds to the *tiriso* affiliation of their Gabbra counterparts.[106]

A number of other Gabbra immigrant groups who have specialised in cattle instead of camels can be found among the Boran.[107]

ALGANNA – CAMEL PEOPLE WITH CATTLE IN THEIR HEARTS

Dáe, a son of Berre, was out in the bush herding his father's cattle, a common occupation for a Boran boy. There he found some animals of a species he had never seen before. In the evening he drove the animals home along with the cattle herd. The elders said that the animals in question were wild beasts (*bines*) and should be speared. They came to this conclusion because of the fact that, unlike domestic stock, they were hornless (*qullulu*). Dáe replied that the animals were domestic stock (*hori*) because they had four teats, a hump, and chewed the cud, like cattle. 'God has told me that these animals are domestic,' he insisted. He thus kept the animals and moved away from the cattle-keeping Boran into the hot lowlands, where his camels, as these animals came to be known, thrived better. The Boran said that Dáe had 'gone into the bush' (*al gal*), like a bandit, but he said 'Do not call me *al gal*, call me Alganna.'[108]

Berre, the father of Dáe, is the eponymous ancestor of the senior segment of the Worr Qallu of Karrayyu, that is, the part of Boran society to which the Gaalorra subclan of the Rendille claim a special relationship. That both Gaalorra and Alganna claim such a relationship is known to both of them and is, as we have seen above also acknowledged by the Boran. Waako D'iriba[109] states that both Alganna (i.e. its nucleus: the Boruga lineage) and Gaalorra derive from the Worr Qallu Karrayyu and that originally none of them used to eat camel meat; later the *qallu* prayed ('spat') for them so that now they can eat camels.

While the Rendille Gaalorra only have vague memories of the former ceremonial importance of cattle for their age-set promotions, the ritual life of Alganna is still very much that of a cattle people, although in their economy camels figure no less prominently than they do in other phratries. The *jila* journey they undertake for their promotion ceremonies makes this ritual fixation on cattle evident.[110] Another peculiarity in connection with the *jila* is that the Alganna are the only Gabbra phratry which does not install its own *hayyu* but lets the Boran *qallu* of Karrayyu, from whose lineage their original nucleus is said to derive, do this. Ritually and according to their traditions of origin, they are therefore much more an appendage to Boran society than alien allies as is the case with the other Gabbra and Worr Libin. While in the two latter we can distinguish an older layer of PRS culture and a younger layer (younger to them!) of Boran culture, in Alganna both these cultural roots go back deep in time and are closely interwined.

The holy drum of Alganna, unlike the wooden drums of other phratries, is made of metal. It is said to have been cut from the drum of Karrayyu which was originally longer. According to Haberland, the fact that the Worr Qallu of Karrayyu possess a drum is untypical for Boran. He postulates a foreign origin for the object (1963: 154) and for its holder (*ibid.*: 127ff. and 131ff.).[111] The ultimate origin of this drum may remain obscure.

A different version from the usual claim that the Alganna drum comes from the Boran has been offered by Ali Ramata.[112] He says that Boruga got the drum from the *qallu* of the Arbore. When I pointed out that other people recall this differently, he explained that at that time the Arbore and Boran were just one people with one *qallu* and that therefore there is no contradiction between the two versions. Anyhow, the *qallu* in question was of the clan Karrayyu and even today, he says, the *qallu* of the Arbore is of Karrayyu. If indeed at that time level there was no ethnic division line between the Arbore and the Boran (or the future Sabbo moiety of the latter), then the Gaalorra traditions described above,[113] which claim 'Marle' (Arbore) and Boran connections in the same breath, can be regarded as confirmed.

Boruga later incorporated other people who had split from the Boran, or whichever pre- or proto-Boran group is meant by that term. Other lineages of Alganna are of various PRS origins, some older, with vaguely claimed 'Somali' connections, others more recent nineteenth- and twentieth-century Rendille immigrants. All Rendille immigrants who do not have a known clan equivalent to some other Gabbra lineage and phratry are counted as Alganna. Alganna thus is a residual category. The existence of such a residual category demonstrates the sociological importance of inter-ethnic clan relationships: they are so useful that where they do not exist people have to make them up. The mythical justification for this is that, after the return from Iris,[114] a part of Alganna split from the main body and went south, where they developed into the Rendille,[115] so that in fact the Rendille are Alganna. As this tradition does not tie in with any other traditions, we can reject it as a historical truth and instead accept it as a sociological truth.

The Alganna of 'Boran' origin, with the exception of the Boruga themselves, are still distinguishable from the others by the *gutu*, the pigtail on the back of the head, into which the men plait their hair like the Boran of certain age grades do. Among the Alganna the *gutu* is worn by those men whose fathers have reached the *dabela* grade. It is shaved off, as the Boran do in their *gadamooji*[116] ceremony, when the men reach the *dabela* grade themselves.

The relationship of Alganna to camels is still ambivalent. When a camel is slaughtered, it is not allowed to face the house but is turned to face the open range. As the Alganna economy relies heavily on camels (which some of the immigrants from the Boran have acquired in raids against the Rendille), there must, however, be some whose ritual service are better suited to promote the wellbeing of camels than those of the cattle-minded former-Boran nucleus.

Among the Alganna this role is performed by Garawaĥle, the senior lineage of the senior clan Nebei of the Belesi Berri moiety of the Rendille. An immigrant group from that clan has to hold a sacrifice of a young female sheep (*karso*) on Kallés, one of the western foothills of the Hurri highlands (Badda Hurri, Hurri Hills on the maps, Halimuralle in Rendille). On this occasion the other Alganna settle in order of seniority (direction of the arrows: high to low) around the hill in the formation shown in Diagram 26.

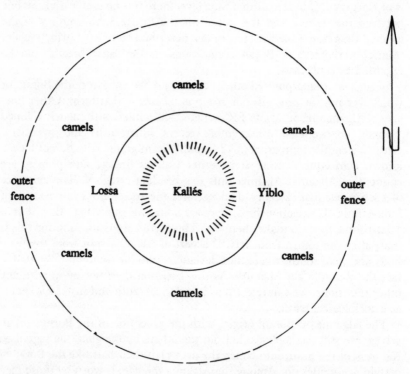

Diagram 26 Spatial arrangements around the hill Kallés on the occasion of Garawaĥle's sacrifice.

Note that the Yiblo moiety, equated with the 'Eastern Moiety' of the Rendille, indeed settles in the east and the 'western' Lossa in the west. Contrary to comparable Rendille arrangements (e.g. *gaalgulamme*) and in accordance with the general Gabbra practice, the settlement order does not form a full clockwise circle but makes two chains from north to south.

After the sacrifice, milk from camels of Garawaĥle and Rengumo, another Rendille immigrant group, is given to all children in large hemispherical milking vessels (*gorfa*).[117] This ceremony, of course, takes place in a *sorio* month.

A ritual for all Alganna camels is thus performed by a segment who are camel keepers of old and to whom camels were given by God as their legitimate heirloom. While the *qallu* and *hayyu* lineages dominate in the management of people, Garawaĥle and Rengumo are indispensable for the management of camels.

Garawaĥle, Rengumo and others refer to themselves as 'Gabbra' and 'Alganna' when asked for their tribe (*gos*) and as 'Rendille' or by their respective Rendille clan names when asked for their section (*balbal* – 'gate'). 'Rendille' in this context is a part of Alganna. Other Rendille Gabbra and earlier PRS immigrants are not given such general labels but are known either by specific names or integrated into named lineages which existed before their arrival. Yaabar is believed to have come from Sharbana.[118] The founder of this lineage, who lived about six generations ago, is said to have left his paternal clan as a boy because he did not get the camels he demanded. In Alganna he associated himself to Noles. Dolio stems from the Gabbra Miigo. According to some informants[119] – Rendille not among them – the eponymous ancestor Dolio is also the founder of the Rendille clan Urawén.[120] He is said to have left children among the Gabbra before moving on and marrying again among the Rendille. Eilo stems from the Chaaqo lineage of Galbo. Strangely, Eilo never acquired a clear moiety affiliation in Alganna. I have described the putative background to this change of phratry in connection with the tale of the return from Iris in chapter 4.

My informants disagree on the origin of Koyot and Gádara. Not only PRS but also Oromo groups and individuals joined Alganna in the course of time. From these descend the Jalle (from Arsi), Noles (Boran), Diisa (Boran), and a part of Helmale. As we cannot trace and examine all these putative or real inter-ethnic clan relationships in equal detail, I want to have a closer look at the latter group, Helmale, and leave the others aside.

Helmale is an example of a composite lineage or pseudo-lineage which historically and ritually has four different components.[121] The subunit Lucho provides the Yiblo moiety with their *qallu*. The first such *qallu* was found near Goobso, a site on the south-western edge of the Ethiopian escarpment where even today the Alganna go to hold their age-set promotion ceremonies. The *qallu* of Lucho is believed to be a were-lion, to grow fur in certain ritual circumstances and to rub cheeks and shoulders with lions and pythons.

Later the Baabo Doyo sublineage, who are of Boran origin, joined Helmale (Abudo).

Guuto Boi is said to have come out of the lake. He was an El Molo, a Cushitic-speaking fisherman (Abudo).

The last group to join Helmale are Rendille from Saale-Gaabana(*yó*). According to one of them (Abudo Mamo), this migration took place not longer than five generations ago (counted from a senior living elder) and to have involved a whole settlement group including women, children and camels. Although recent in comparison to the other parts of Helmale, these Gaabana can look back on a longer presence in Alganna than many other Rendille immigrants who only joined the Gabbra during the famine of the 1890s. This is reflected, as we have seen, in their name – they are 'Helmale', not 'Rendille' – and in a few other characteristics. Helmale Gaabana have changed their moiety affiliation from Belesi Berri (≙ Yiblo) to Lossa – a rather rare event. They also have changed the fireplace from the right (northern) half of the house to the left, where the Gabbra have their hearth stones. Yet later Rendille immigrants have retained their original moiety affiliation and the spatial arrangement of the interior of their houses, as well as their camel brands: they have kept the brand of their Rendille clan Saale Gaabanayó and have not adopted the *gólole*, the

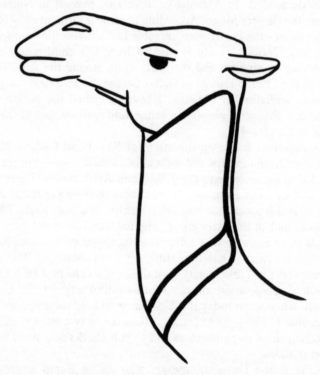

Diagram 27   Helmale (*gólole*). For the brand of Gaabanayó, see Diagram 31 below.

elaborate brand of Helmale, on the left side of the neck (Diagram 27).

Alganna thus is a microcosm in which we can observe in miniature all the processes of clanship and ethnic dynamics to which this book is dedicated: we find a nucleus of association (Boruga) and around it ethnically completely integrated old associates (the bulk of Alganna), other groups which have kept fresh memories of their Rendille origin (Gaabana in Helmale) and yet others who are even today referred to as 'Rendille'. We might add all other Rendille, though they may be hostile strangers, as potential members of this phratry, because Rendille immigrants would automatically be identified as 'Alganna' unless they have another Gabbra clan affiliation. The widest of the concentric circles of which Alganna is composed thus comprises, from their point of view, the entire Rendille society.

MATARBÁ

Segments by the name of Matarbá exist in the Belesi Baħai moiety of the Rendille and the corresponding Lossa moieties of the Sakuye and of the Sharbana phratry of the Gabbra.

From the Matarbá lineage of Sharbana one of the three *hayyu* of this phratry is chosen, and also among the Sakuye one of the eight *hayyu* offices belonged to this clan until this institution declined. This shared feature cannot, however, be attributed to the common origin of the three branches of Matarbá, because the Rendille do not have such an institution and probably the PRS did not have it either. The Matarbá of Sharbana and Sakuye are therefore likely to have acquired these offices after they split from their Rendille equivalent and, as we shall see, independently of each other. Though Matarbá did not inherit its *hayyu*ship from its PRS origins, one of the prerequisites of *hayyu*ship may derive from its PRS clan identity: the absence of an *iibire* (R) or *qallu, eebiftu* (B) power to curse and bless, a weakness which is also a strength in so far as it is associated with propitiousness and purity.[122]

One of our Sakuye sources (Sakuye 3) describes the first *hayyu* installations in an episode which directly follows the foundation of Sakuye society by the combining of Rendille and Miigo elements under Boran patronage.

Also our Sharbana source[123] states that the Matarbá segment of that phratry acquired its *hayyu*ship only after it had become a part of Sharbana. Here is the full story:

Niitin tokko ala tokko qabti̠, gurba tokko qabti̠, gaaf beela Rendille irra-badde̠.

A woman had one she-camel and one boy; during a time of hunger she got lost from the Rendille.

The fact that this woman, who was driven away from the Rendille by hunger, had a she-camel of her own is possibly the main reason why the separate lineage identity of her son's heirs is still remembered. If it had not been for the separate strain of camels, the boy might have been adopted into some other lineage and his Rendille origin would have been forgotten.[124]

Worrí Quchaburí oró qallate, foon quubse. Gurban diqa wolinqubsifate, mata haate.

A settlement of Quchabúr[125] had slaughtered male camels, they were satiated with meat. They allowed the small boy [and his mother] to make camp with them and shaved his head [as a sign of adoption, symbolising a new start].

Ini guba isá ingube, guba Quchabura gubi jenán diide.

He [later] continued to mark [the camels] with his brand and rejected to use the brand of Quchabúr.[126]

This summary names the main elements of the adoption of the future Quchabúr into Matarbá: hunger, the feast of meat, the formal adoption, the refusal to give up the original camel brand. Another account[127] establishes the logical links between these elements. As I could not tape it, I reproduce it here in a free version from my notes:

At a time when Rendilleland was hit by drought, and the Rendille ventured far north, beyond Mount Deemo, a woman of the clan Matarbá who had a small son joined Quchabúr. She had a she-camel for the transport of her belongings.[128] Quchabúr had slaughtered a fattened camel ox and she offered him her son for a leg. So Quchabúr bought the boy. Quchabúr had a number of daughters, the eldest of whom was blind. As nobody wanted to marry her and as her father insisted that her younger sisters could not be married before, none of the girls was married. When the young boy grew up he insisted on branding his camels, the progeny of his mother's beast of burden, with the Matarbá brand instead of the Quchabúr brand. Quchabúr was in a position to reject this demand because he had bought the boy, who thus, together with his possessions, had become Quchabúr. But he gave in under one condition: that the boy marry the blind girl who, once a different camel brand was accepted and a different identity recognised, would no longer be his adoptive sister and would thus become marriageable again.[129]

According to his original moiety affiliation among the Rendille, the boy and his progeny were counted at Lossa, while Quchabúr[130] is Yiblo (≙ Belesi Berri). At some later time this lineage, Matarbá of Sharbana, inherited the *hayyu*ship from another lineage of Lossa which had died out. Thereupon the lineage Quchabúr, once having been brothers of Matarbá and still maintaining a close relationship with them, agreed that they themselves should no longer become *hayyu*.[131] Since then members of two sublineages of Bahae, Bahae Diimtu and Konte in Bahae Gurratti, alternate in the *hayyu* office of Lossa. The other part of Bahae Gurratti, Matabálle, cannot become *hayyu* because they are *qallu*.

MATARBÁ'S *HAYYU*SHIP AND ITS GIFT FOR DIVINATION

Worri haggum Gabbrat gagale yuub. Quchaburi ku-llen durri ínqaba, amm inqábu. Duuba waan isá iti-dabbarse jejed'ani: hayyumá-lle iti-dabbarse, yuubomá-lle iti-dabbarse jed'ani.

These people were diviners already when they joined the Gabbra. Also Quchabúr formerly had [the gift of divination], now they do not have it. Now, it is said that they [Quchabúr] passed on the following things to them [Matarbá]: they passed on the *hayyu*ship and the gift of divination.

As the Matarbá of the Rendille do not claim any gift of divination, we might question the statement that the Matarbá of Sharbana were already in possession of this gift when they joined the Gabbra, especially as the sentence directly following this statement explains that Matarbá acquired the gift of divination from Quchabúr. (This is, however, not necessarily a logical contradiction, since the gift bestowed by Quchabúr might have been added to a similar gift which already existed.)

Duub worri waan d'arrá inqábne, objú-lleni, falfallá-lleni imbéeku, duumesi Waaqa beek.

Now, these people are not liars, they do not know [have] inspired dreams and sorcery, they know the clouds of God [Sky].

Waan wolfakata: isáf Helmalét wolfakata; bines lafá ka nam nyaatu beek. Helmalén hanan ati d'uttu si keesa beek; worri-lle akum sun waan gara Waaqa beek.

What is similar to each other: they and Helmale[132] are similar to each other; they know [the whereabouts of] the animals of the land which eat human beings. Helmale even knows [sees] the milk you drink inside you; and the people [Matarbá] know in the same way the belly of God [i.e. the sky].

Ini duuba aki atin karatasi tas somtu, worrí-lle waan gara Waaqa sin iti-dawu beeka:

Like you [know how to] read those papers, these people know what the belly of God tells them:

woni kun halkan hamot wo d'ofti, halkan dansát wo d'ofti, ka mogá-lle, ka robá-lle.

[they know] what foretells a bad night, what foretells a good night [in English one would say 'day'], be it one of fear of enemies or one of rain.

Nu maqá waan chinaan baasan malle; ayaani torba, nu-lle maqán yo baasani: torb. Ayaan torba kan kees worrí akasuman beek, halkan Waaqi wo dawu.

For us names are not something which we pull out of our ribs ['which we get from anywhere'; compare the German idiom *sich aus den Rippen schneiden*]; there are seven days of the week and we, when we name [a child], have seven names. Among these seven names they [Matarbá] thus know, in which night God tells something.

Starting from common knowledge, namely the seven days of the week and their prognostic functions, some of which have been discussed in chapter 4, the informant here explains the principles of divination which have the calendar as their base. The names referred to are those listed in chapter 4, like Mamo (for boys) and Midín (for girls) for children born on a Monday, Isaako and Talaso respectively for children born on a Tuesday, etc.

Nam gudda gurrá ka lafan himan, woni sun waan artíti akanumán beeka. Akanumán beekani, fin tolfate, akanumán gul deema, worri Matarbá mal jed'a?

If many people of the land are called [just] by the name [literally: 'the ear'] they know things about them just like this. Just like this they know things, if a custom is to be performed, [the others] follow [their advice] just like this, [they ask:] what do the people of Matarbá say?

Inini guddo nama himu diida, yo si-la si barsise, yo hag worrá-lle gaiubat duumes jaala ímbarata.

They do not like to tell something [about their professional methods] to somebody, if they would teach you, you would learn about the clouds even if you would not reach their level.

Duub waan sun kan duumes kan ka gaalá-lle (duula), ka ree, ka looni, ka duul deemu ímbeek. (Mamo Wario)

Now, they know these things, the clouds, be it of the camels, or of the smallstock, or of the cattle, or of going to war.

Duul wayák ka deebu qubu, ka beel qabu, duumes horí ka deeme lafit wúqate[133] *lafit gabbatu ímbeek.*

They know whether a war expedition will suffer thirst or hunger, the clouds [which tell] in which region the livestock will slim down and in which region they will become fat if they go there.

Thus at least divination is partly an acquired skill, not a gift, and may be exercised by one clan while being unknown to their brother clan.

What the Matarbá of Rendille and those of Sharbana actually share, apart from their name and their *wakhkamur* status, is their moiety affiliation (Belesi Baħai ≙ Lossa), and their camel brand on the upper part of the left foreleg (R, B: *togoog*) (Diagram 28). Rendille and Gabbra agree that Matarbá of Sharbana corresponds to Baltor (Feecha), not to Kaato (Gaalgidele), among the segments of the corresponding Rendille clan.[134]

The Matarbá of the Sakuye are also Feecha and use the same camel brand, which is peculiar to Feecha and distinct from that of Gaalgidele. They too are Lossa. They too do not possess an innate power to curse. They differ from their Gabbra and Rendille counterparts in that they are considered the first-born (*angafa*) of their moiety.

The pattern that emerges from this comparison is that certain elements, like the name, the property marks, the moiety affiliation and presumably innate ritual powers, are constant over time, while roles which have to do with political power (*hayyu*, *angafa*, diviner) are adapted to the demands made and the possibilities offered by the respective society.

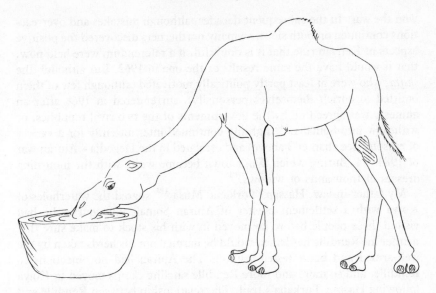

Diagram 28   The *togoog* brand of Matarbá

SAALE AND AJURAN

In May 1984 my father-in-law, a Somali trader in Rendille country, decided to move 400 head of cattle to Koiya, a cluster of waterholes some 25 km south-east of Laisamis. This country today is considered the fringe of Rendille and Ariaal grazing and to be in dangerous proximity to the Somali of Wajir District, although earlier, in the colonial period, Rendille grazing extended even farther east, to Arba Jahan on the 'Somali line', which is now the district and provincial boundary.[135] These migrations of Rendille camel camps occurred after the initial period of opportunist readjustments to pressures (see Chapter 3 above) had been overcome and the British had succeeded in establishing a firm and sometimes harsh rule, which guaranteed a safer, more widespread and therefore more conservationist use of the grazing resources than in certain later periods. The year 1956 is, in Rendille, even called *Arbaĥ ti Ajuran*, 'the Wednesday year of the Ajuran', because it was in that year that the Rendille camels were peacefully grazed in the proximity of the Ajuran. But after this relatively successful later phase of colonialism everything was spoiled by the extremely clumsy procedure of decolonisation, during which the British made about every political mistake which could be made. We have already described the disastrous effects of their 1962 referendum (chapter 3 above). The blame for the terrors of the subsequent guerrilla war thus does not fall on the Kenyan government or on the Somali, but squarely on the shoulders of the British, who by then were thousands of miles away in safety. Kenya won the war. In the subsequent decades, although mistakes and overreactions continued on both sides, so many northerners discovered the positive aspects of Kenyan rule that it is doubtful, if a referendum were held now, that it would have the same results as the one in 1962. But although the *shifta*, who were at least partly politically motivated (although few of them omitted to enrich themselves personally), surrendered in 1968 after an amnesty was agreed on by the governments of the two rival republics, or withdrew into Somalia,[136] fighting continued intermittently for a variety of reasons (see chapter 3 above) and escalated in the Degodia – Ajuran war of 1983–84, during which Wajir town became white with the mourning dresses of thousands of widows.[137]

My father-in-law, Hassan 'Turkana' Musa,[138] shared the waterholes of Koiya with a settlement cluster of Ajuran Somali. Of course, he had visited these people before he moved in with his stock to make sure that neither his Rendille herdsmen would be harmed nor his herds taken by the well-armed and battle-tested Ajuran. The Ajuran had no objections to Rendille, and so more and more Rendille satellite camps moved to Koiya following Hassan Turkana's trail. The relationship between Rendille and Somali is traditionally good. As we have seen above (chapter 4), they regard each other as lost brothers. But, in contradiction to the apparent syllogism that the brothers of one's brothers are one's brothers, some of them are not. The Ariaal are 'brothers' of the Rendille but their relationship with the Ajuran and all other Somali is cool, to say the least. The Rendille, for all practical matters except age-set promotions and certain marriage customs, make no distinction between themselves and the Samburuised Ariaal, who, in turn, regard themselves as Samburu whenever it is convenient to do so. Samburu and Somali are traditional enemies. When they meet in the bush they often try to kill each other on sight. As the Rendille make no distinction between the Ariaal and themselves, the Ariaal can go and graze wherever the Rendille go, although for many monolingual Rendille communication with the Ariaal, many of whom only have a rudimentary mastery of the Rendille language, is difficult and control of the Ariaal warriors is impossible – not only for linguistic reasons. Concubinage is even more important and desirable among the Ariaal and Samburu warriors (see Spencer 1973: 99) than among the Rendille (Schlee 1979: 145) and therefore the young Ariaal are even keener than the Rendille to kill and to sing boasting songs about it in front of the girls. Therefore the Ajuran were soon forced to distinguish between 'good' and 'bad' Rendille, or, as they put it, between 'white' or 'original' (*'asil*) Rendille and 'those who speak Samburu'. On the other hand, the Rendille had difficulties in deciding which of the high-handed gunmen who invited themselves to eat the Rendille smallstock was to be regarded as a guest and which was a robber, and whether there was any difference between the two. But Rendilleland was overgrazed and dried out because the spring rains had failed, and there was no pasture within reach comparable to that around Koiya. So one had to try to get along with one's neighbours. In September this precarious balance broke down in a sudden escalation of violence. Many lives were lost and much stock was stolen on both sides; more stock was lost because the herds stampeded during the raids; and yet more stock starved because they had to be moved to safer but poorer pastures. As in other wars, there were only losers.

But back to May. In one of the many misunderstandings between Rendille and Ajuran over the wells of Koiya some shots were fired and a group of Rendille youngsters who had come to fetch water fled in one direction while their donkeys stampeded in another. Hassan Turkana, not only out of personal interest but also in his role as a local political leader, tried to resolve matters. The Somali were willing to return the donkeys, but these had got lost again and first had to be found. The donkey affair was to be lengthy and inconclusive. At one stage my father-in-law took a Rendille warrior, one of those who had taken the donkeys to the well, with him to the centre of the cluster of Somali hamlets to introduce him to Mu'allim Ibrahim and Kosar Muḥammed[139] and other Ajuran elders. He had told the boy to identify himself as Saale when asked for his clan, and this the boy did. Kosar reacted in a speech, the gist of which was, 'I am Bedán Ajuran and you are Sánle Ajuran. We are brothers, sons of the same father. There should never be fighting between us. We did not want your donkeys; they just came running towards us. Although I have more important things to do than worry about donkeys, I shall do my best to find them, so that you can see our good intentions, etc.' The Ajuran believe that Saale, the largest of all Rendille clans,[140] is derived from an eponymous ancestor Sanle s/o Ajuran, while the Waqle section of the Ajuran, to which Kosar and most of the others present belonged, derives itself from Bedán s/o Ajuran (see below, Diagram 30). Saale, and in a vaguer sense all Rendille, are therefore regarded as brothers of, or 'the same' as, the Ajuran. Ajuran traders in Rendilleland are therefore regarded as some sort of Saale even though the Sanle subsection of the Ajuran is not very numerous and even though all of the few Ajuran in Rendilleland stem from other subsections. But as there is no clan 'Ajuran' in Rendille society, 'Saale' is *faute de mieux* accepted as the nearest equivalent. As a person known to have Rendille connections, I was repeatedly greeted enthusiastically in a remote part of north-eastern Kenya by people unknown to me who identified themselves as Saale. 'You know I am Saale, Ajuran, Saale! That is the same thing. Saale, Sanle, Ajuran!'

Once, in the course of a lengthy discussion,[141] Kosar tried to explain to his rather immature and pugnacious sons how to distinguish between friend and foe in the Rendille–Ariaal cluster. In this discussion Kosar presented an idealised picture of the Rendille clan Saale. Saale, he said, were taller and lighter-skinned than other Rendille and were handsome, just like the Ajuran. This, of course, is ideology in its purest state, without any link to reality. Due to clan exogamy Saale can be expected to exhibit, and according to superficial observation do exhibit, exactly the same mix of genes as all other Rendille. Nor are Ajuran especially tall or light-skinned or handsome. I saw many people of very slight build among them and I noticed a high incidence of squints and similar eye distortions. I am not a physical anthropologist, so I want to leave the question open whether or not this may be due to the homozygotic combination of undesirable recessive genes through close endogamy. Although what Kosar said is not true, I have quoted it here because it shows the extent to which the belief that Saale and Ajuran are related influences ethnic and racial stereotypes.

At Koiya this belief, whether true or false, was very useful for maintaining an uneasy peace. Hassan Turkana, whose father was Somali but whose mother is a Rendille from Saale Kimogól, well knew how to appeal to this belief and use it for his aims.

But let us now consider the cultural and oral-historical evidence for this assumed inter-ethnic clan relationship. The former is slender. Certain sections of Ajuran show slightly more PRS features in their way of dealing with camels than recent central and northern Somali immigrants, which points to a longer presence in the area and makes them more Rendille-like. But all these similarities are reminiscent of the Rendille in general; there are no specific Saale features in Ajuran camel culture.

The part of the Ajuran which shares these PRS elements is Walemügge, which comprises the subsections Garen, Gelbaris and Gashe, but not Sanle (see below, Diagram 30). The scattered Sanle elements among the Kenyan Ajuran, some of whom have lived for generations among the Garre, cannot be expected to exhibit any features of camel culture which are specific to them and common among them. Waqle, the other major Ajuran section beside Walemügge, does not share many of the PRS customs of the latter.

Like the other groups culturally derived from the PRS, Walemügge camel herders[142] have restricted the access of women to lactating camels within living memory. Unlike the Rendille and Gabbra, who keep this restriction for the whole lactation period, the Walemügge allowed their womenfolk to approach the camels and even to milk them when the calf was one month old. It was a custom which protected the newly born calves from the danger of contamination by the women.

Indoran. Nadd'een huggum-ki qabtu̱ fa kan irra-doran. Nadd'een huggum-ki qubtu [gaal] iti-indíatu. Indoot. Ijjes.

They set them apart [literally: make them *doro*[143]]. They set them [the camel calves] apart from women who have menstruation [*huggum-ki*, a Somaloid word of Arabic origin]. Menstruating women do not approach [the camels]. They [the calves would] die. They [would] kill [them]. (Moħammed 'Ummar[144])

By 'menstruating women' Moħammed 'Ummar does not mean women who are actually menstruating but women in the fertile span of their lives (although actual menstruation may be an aggravating circumstance). He explains that camels were normally milked by young boys and confirms that in all cases the milker had to be a chaste man, preferably a bachelor (*nam qerot*). The danger for camel calves comes from human sexuality as such, not from any specific menstrual or other secretions.[145] In all tthis the Walemügge agree with the Rendille and the Gabbra of today and the Garre and the Sakuye of the recent past.[146]

Maalim D'iiso 'Ummar, Garen,[147] remembers a form of camel loan which he calls *irmans* (B: *irmaan*, R: *irban* means 'colostrum' and also the animal that has it). The custom is equivalent to R: *maal* B: *dabarre*, and not to *kalaksimé*, as the name seems to suggest, while most Somali, including Waqle Ajuran, know only *kalaksimé*-like customs or outright gifts.[148] This is confirmed by Waqle informants[149] with reference to Garen and Gashe (both Walemügge), while Moħammed 'Ummar (Gelbaris in Walemügge) only remembers forms of loan which did not involve any rights in the progeny of the shared beast.

For our present purpose suffice it to say that such similarities neither support nor contradict the claim of a special relationship between Saale and Ajuran, because they are shared with all other Rendille, with the Gabbra and with many others too. The cultural evidence for the historicity of this inter-ethnic clan relationship is inconclusive.

We therefore turn to the evidence provided by oral tradition. The claim of the Ajuran and of Saale to be related, nay, virtually identical, is mutual and, on the level of belief, unshakable. But how exactly has this relationship come to be? We shall see that the traditions about this are contradictory and as inconclusive as the cultural evidence. We start with the origin of the Ajuran and then examine how and when Saale is believed to have split from them.

Ajuran oral tradition is full of surprises. Once, when I introduced myself to a local government official, an Ajuran who was the chief of a small township, and explained the nature of my research to him, he said that it was a very good thing to spread the knowledge of Ajuran history because too few people appreciate that the Ajuran are not Somali but Arabs. By this he meant that Ajuran do not derive themselves from Samal or Somal, the eponymous ancestor of the Somali, but directly from Abu Ṭālib, the uncle (FaBr) of the Prophet. (In this narrow sense neither the large Darood clan family nor the Sab are Somali either.) Just how Ajuran, the eponymous ancestor of his people, descends from Abu Ṭālib is left to the imagination of the genealogical specialists. I never found two identical

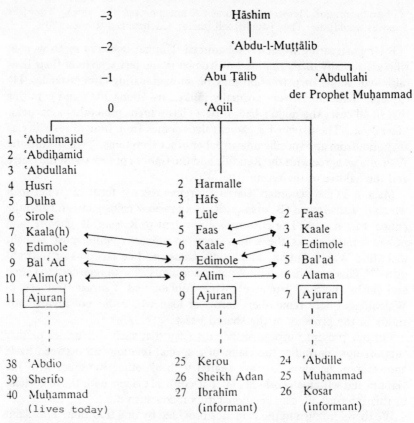

Diagram 29 Alternative explications of the 'Aqiiliyy origin of Ajuran. O stands for the generation of the Prophet, the arrows point out correspondences between names. The symbol ⌐¬ stands for two different things. In the −1 generation it signifies that Abi Ṭālib and 'Abdullahi are brothers; farther down, in the +1 generation, it links three conflicting names for the ancestor through which Ajuran is believed to descend from 'Aqiil.

accounts and just quote three versions which are as good as any other (Diagram 29).

As a father can have many sons but every son only one father, it is clear that these versions contradict each other. Furthermore, none of the three variant names corresponds to any of the ten sons of 'Aqiil recognised by Arab tradition, according to Wüstenfeld's *Genealogische Tabellen* (1853), namely Abu Sa'īd, 'Abdallah, 'Abdu-1-Raḥmān, Muslim, Hamza, 'Ali, Muḥammad, 'Uthmān, Ja'afar and Obeidallah. The value of these Ajuran genealogies is sociological and ideological rather than historical, except for the four or five ascending generations from Ajuran, which, as the arrows indicate, show a high degree of consistency. The consistency may be due to the fact that in this portion of the chart the genealogy reflects historical facts or that mutual agreement has been reached because of the importance of these descent relationships as a social charter. But how these ancestors, all of whom have non-Muslim names, are linked to the Quraish, the tribe of the Prophet, is left to the discretion of every individual Ajuran, as long as he gets to 'Aqiil bin Abu Ṭālib somehow. The Prophet, to whom these pedigrees seek to establish a relationship, ironically has discouraged exaggerated interest in genealogies because it is hardly compatible with the egalitarian ideals of Islam.

It is obvious that, because of these genealogical beliefs, any inquiry into the history of the Islamisation of the Ajuran cannot use direct questions. To ask 'When and how did the Ajuran become Muslims and to which beliefs did they adhere before that?' does not make sense to an Ajuran. His eponymous ancestor is believed to have always been a Muslim and to have descended from people who had been converted to Islam at the time of the Prophet.

All traditions agree that Sanle is the first-born of Ajuran. The sons of Ajuran are always given in a fixed order, in three alliterating or rhyming pairs which are followed by Walemügge.[150] Walemügge is not accompanied by a brother whose name starts with W, nor by a brother whose name ends in -ügge; he has no partner, he stands alone. He is also said to be born by a different mother from the other six: a threefold isolation. This list of brothers goes:

Ajuran todoba rux as dhaley, dhuq Ajuran aah: Sanle iyo Saalemüggaa, Dhaqse iyo Dhaqsóro, Bedaan iyo Bedbedaan, líxdan isku báh waye. Walemügga oo bacadiged keligiis bah gar yara u eh.

Ajuran begot seven children, the old man Ajuran: Sanle and Saalemüggaa,[151] Dhaqse and Dhaqsóro,[152] Beddan and Bedbedaanm,[153] these six are by one mother. Walemügge alone was born later by a different mother.[154]

There is a tradition how Sanle lost his primogeniture to Walemügge. This tradition, of course, belongs to the Walemügge. I heard it from Maħad 'Ali Mamo Cirresa, a Garen:[155]

[Ajuran] yo beeni godaanu eeget hafe. Sorori bisaan fuul teefan deebian. Akanum fuul kedeebian. Jennaani, intal Garjeltu jed'ani, gos tokko, ta ree kejirt, intal guddo, fordo, hartu irre-ga-bae.

[The old man Ajuran once] stayed behind, when the people moved on. People had left a wooden bottle full of water next to him and left him. They were out of sight. In this situation, a girl from a tribe called Garjeltu, who was with the smallstock, a big, clever, skilful girl, met him.

'Abo, nagaa?' jed. 'Nagaa.' 'Godaan tokko arm yaate?' jennaan, 'hi-yaate.' 'Díatu?' jed', 'd'aqaba?' jed'.

'Daughter,[156] peace be upon you?'[157] He said. 'Peace.' 'Has a caravan[158] passed here?' 'It has.' 'Is it close?' he said, 'can I catch up with it?'

Yo sadeen rrá-rrá-haftu olfuud'atu, sí d'aqabta, ínarga. Yo sadeen tan ol in-fuud'atín, in-d'áqabtu," jet. 'Aabo, sadeen maan?' jed'.

She said, 'If you lift up three things which you are dragging along, you can catch up, I can see that. If you do not lift up these three things, you cannot catch up.' 'Child, what are these three things?' he said.

'Dirot bisanit arma rra-rra, diro arma deefat, waya mata buufat, korbo hidd'at akan hidd'an kan, jabbesitu. Ule at amma laf d'ad'abat tan, laf irra-buqis, umul irr keyat!'

[If you] take the dangling water container from here [= out of your hand] and put it back here [= suspend it from your elbow], take the cloth from your head and tie it around your waist, the way it is tied, tightly. This stick with which you prop yourself up from the soil, pluck it out of the soil, put it across your shoulders!'

'Hagám? [Sadíi.] Sadeen rrarra tan, yo at ol-fuud'atu, ín-d'aqabt, deebis!, yo at ol in-fuud'atín, in-d'áqabtu,' jet.

'How many? [Three.] These three dragged-along things, if you lift them up, you can catch up, put them in order! If you do not lift them up, you will not catch up,' she said.

Jennáan, irra-hiiqé, arti jeté, gam sun tae, laf hare, ule worrane, fincaae. Akan laalt, intalti furdo, akan laalt.

After this, he left, went over there, sat down there, swept the ground with his stick, stuck the stick into the soil, and urinated. She looked on, the girl is clever, she looked on like this, [furtively].

Irra-hiiqé, aci jeté, waya mid'aafaté, old'eefate. Jennaan d'ufte, fincaan kan irrejj-ate.

He left, went some distance away, put his cloth on properly, and turned around. Then she came and looked at that urine.

'Orr, yo sila golol fa mid'aasan tokko keesat hafe. Tokko d'ala. Maqaa ya-oobaafate, muca tokko keesat hafe." Homaccum kan laalt.

'Wow, if one gives him proper food and so, there is one more in there. He will beget one more [son]. His name is [nearly] complete [= almost all his sons are born already, just] one more remains in there.' She just looked at that foam.

Ini ín-d'aqa, mar deefaté, worr ammo qubaté. Warran fuud'até, ka ufum sila mukh jal taa, 'an intal tan fuuud'a, aabo, fuul ké-deem,' jennaan yad'ufe. Jarsi kan lad'ufe.

He heard it, tied his sheet, the migrating group now had made camp. He took his spear, and sat down under a tree. 'I shall marry that girl, son,[159] be aware of that,' he said when he came. That old man came.

Íntae. 'Diir kaa, "intal sun na kadadd'a!" jed'. D'iir jahan taan ínjed'a beekh. Intal tam?' 'Tan na kadadd'a!' jed'. Jennaan, yo ini d'ufe, aki dubr guyyá kan ka uf-im-béene, beeni kan diide.

He sat down' 'Men, get up and ask for that girl for me!' he said to his six sons. 'Which girl?' 'Ask for that one for me!' he said. When that was said, they disagreed like the undisciplined children of these days[?].

Sanle kan, ka worra gudda, 'ínkad'anna, kaa!'' jed'. Beeni kan diid. Sanle kan jars kan intal tan kad'at.

This Sanle, who was the big man of the group, said 'We shall ask for her, get up!' The others did not agree. Sanle asked for this girl [as a bride] for this old man.

Jennan intal tan biyy yaamt. 'Yo waan isan na gololcisan isan na keenitan, an jars kan ín-fuud'a̲' jet, 'yo waan an isan gololcu isan na-t in-kéenitan, infúud'u.'

Then the girl called a meeting. 'If you give me my sustenance, I shall marry this old man,' she said, 'if you do not give me my sustenance, I shall not marry him.'

'Maal?' jed'an. 'Goromí lam. Ta reefu d'alte, ta gaala, yo mukh armá na hidd'an. Goromi looni lam. Yo arma akasi na hidd'an. Chufu maan ammum tan d'ad'alt.

'What is it?'' they asked. 'Two heifers. Which have already calved, of the camels, if they are tied for me here to the tree. Two cattle heifers. If they are tied for me here likewise. All of them should just have given birth.

'Yo holiye tirsú lam arma na hidd'an. Korbeyi lam armat hidd'an. Yo itille lam na keenan. Ta gaaf t'unalle baaft arma na hidd'a. Tokko itille, goga gaala, itille sunit na keenan. Welki kun lama kun ka welki hodd'a ka hanan qabbanesu, kun ka hanan isa inqábbanoftu, welki akana yo na keenan, an jars kan ínfuud'a.

'If they tie two young sheep here for me. If they tie two goats here. If they bring me two sleeping skins. If they bring me [a kind of] honey. If they bring me one camel hide. If they bring me one milk container which is plaited [of plant fibres] and cools the milk, and one which does not cool the milk, if they bring me such containers, I shall marry the old man.

'Ilm d'ira an d'alu, yo angaf tolcan, an jars ínfuud'. Yo ilm an d'alu maanda tolcan, angaf intolcín, an jars kan infúud'u̲.'

'The male child to whom I shall give birth, if it is made the first-born, I shall marry the old man. If the son to which I shall give birth is made a later-born and not made a first-born, I shall not marry the old man.'

Sanle kan 'chuf sí tolc' jed'. 'Yo at ilmitu̲ ilmi keen-lle angaf,' jed'. 'Waan at feed'u chuf sí tolc, jed'. 'Jars durres!'

(This) Sanle said, 'I shall do all that for you. If you have a child, that child [of ours (the general "ours" for people of the same tribe)] will be the first- born.' He said, 'I shall do for you everything you want. Put the old man ahead [= love and respect him as your husband]!'

Waan isiin himatu̲ chuf qiteese iti-keene̲. Iti-dae. Mamulumaan keesa jarsi kan gabbaté, mooraé, fuul jiraate, halkum kan d'uub d'iir tae. Isí-lle reefu reefu naf d'iqaté, ga-baat.

Everything she had named he made ready for her. He gave it to her. The old man was taken care of and fattened, he got a full belly, his face became smooth, and very soon, one night, he became a man. She had had a bath and came.

Worri halkan kan wol-d'ae. Wolti-barrate. Halkum kan, halkan kan, barrate?, ilman gará seent. Ilm kun maan? Walemügge, barrad'! Kaná gará seene.

That night they clashed. They came to know each other [carnally]. That very night, you understand?, that night the child entered the belly. Who was that child? Walemügge, know that! That one entered the belly.

Jars kan ya-due. Yo halkan dukan geetu, qub akan diibsite, garac qabdi, qub kanat isi iibse, ak feed'u sagal tani keesa qub kan. Intalti tan. In-d'álle, beek. Diib-seensi qub kan.

The old man died. When the dark phase of the moon came, she knew that she was pregnant and felt sick, she was pregnant and from the time she knew it she had troubles, all through the nine months. This girl. She did not [yet] give birth, you know. [But] her troubles started from the time she knew [she was pregnant].

Dir tan barracum barratté, ilman yo gara jirtu akan taat. Gaaf d'alte gedó addesite, 'inijjefna,' wolinjed'an. Jennaan Sanlen kan diid. Ka kale darre kaan. Angaf isá Sanle kan. Oboleyi 'Ín-ijjefna,' jet.

She came to know the men better and better, this happened while she was pregnant. When she was about to give birth they plotted to kill the child. When that was said, Sanle disagreed. The one who had brought her, the first-born. His brothers said, 'We shall kill him.'

Oboleyi 'inijjefnu' jennaani, nami kale iti-darre kanáaniti, jennaan gar teefat, d'ala.

So the brothers said, 'let us kill him,' and here was the man who had brought her [and objected to this plan], so they sat apart from each other [and then the young woman] wanted to give birth.

Hag qubé abbá fa d'ufaní, harki d'alacu diide. Harki kan ga-bau diide. Hark kan qaban, qube kan ké-kayan. Harki kan ga-bae.

Before they brought the finger ring of his father, the arm refused to the born. The arm did not come out. They got hold of the hand and put the finger ring on it. [Then] the arm came out.[160]

Hagi sure abbá fa gafuud'ani, sure matá maran kan, gafuud'anif, mata ga-bahu diide.

Until the turban of the father was brought, the turban to be wound around the head, [until] it was brought, the head refused to come out.

Hinnaan jennaan hagi barcuma abbá ka durri kan gafuud'aní, jal kayan malle ga-d'alcu diide.

When it was tied, [the rest of him] did not want to be born until the old stool of his father was brought and held under [the woman].

Qube kaani, sure taani, barcuma (kaan) jarsa kaani, jarsí-lle ya-due, waan kan chuf argate. Walemügge banantun kan.

This finger ring, this turban, this stool of the old man, who had died already, he got all this. This is the story of Walemügge.

Worri kan, ka abban habaare, Sanle kaani eebisa, Sanle ín-eebisa, wan kan abaare,

Sanle tun Waqle tan, Sanlen sun. Tan Walemügge, nami angafa jed'an namic kan,
Walemügge kan. Akam?

Among those people, whom their father had cursed [= reduced to junior status], Sanle prayed and had the power to curse and Sanle, that Sanle belongs to Waqle [in the widest sense in which every non-Walemügge is a Waqle]. Walemügge [now] is the one referred to as first-born, this Walemügge. How [was that possible]?

Waqle angaf kaan, maand'a taan tolcan, duub Walemügge durr taa. Yo beeni bun
nagga Walemügge durr yaman. Yo durri duulani Walemügge wol durr yahan.
Angaf, angaf.

This first-born Waqle was made the last-born, so Walemügge sits ahead of him. If people pour out coffee, they call Walemügge first. If in earlier times they went to war, Walemügge went ahead of the others. He is the first-born, first-born.

Walemügge durr hagam? Garén, Gelbariś fa Gashe, Riiba. Abraan tan. Yo duulan
kaan tanuma wol durr deem. Yo bun naggan tanuma durr deem. Baratté?

How many used to be Walemügge? Garen, Gelbaris, Gashe and Riiba. These four. When they went to war they went in this order. When they have coffee they precede each other in this order. Do you understand?

Waqlen durri angaf kan, ka Sanle kan. Sun ya maand'owe, eebi, jarsa fa. Worri
kan ka gari eegi jars Walemügge kan gasoobadde, Rendille fa kéjir. Ka Garri amm
kuuno Darawa fa kéjir. Fula injírre inqábu. Leisam kéjir. Baratté? Gari chuf gar ufi
gargar badde, gargar.

Waqle used to be the first-born, this Sanle. That one became the later-born, with respect to [the sequence of] the prayers of the elders and so on. Later, after the time of the man Walemügge, a part of these people got lost. They are [now] among the Rendille. The ones of the Garre are among those Darawa. There is no place where they are not. They are among the Leisam [in the Jubaland]. Do you understand? All these parts separated and dispersed, now they are separated.

This text is very instructive: it shows us on which grounds one section of the Ajuran claims a position senior to that of another section; it tells us of a family drama of rivalry and jealousy and it depicts to us something which is rare in local oral tradition – a strong female main character. The social values attached to wealth and procreation and attitudes towards sex are also illustrated.

It is not only instructive but also beautiful. It appears to me to consist of three episodes, of which the first and the last mirror each other, while the central episode – the marriage – is the turning point or, to use the same metaphor, the mirror itself. The three episodes thus can metaphorically be equated to (a) the original image, (b) the mirror and (c) the image which appears to be behind the mirror and which differs from the original by being inverted. The structural categories by which I arrive at such a conclusion may appear somewhat Lévi-Straussian and accordingly arbi-

trary. Any reader who has enough leisure can make an alternative structuralist analysis of this tale which is as good as mine. But although the
interpretations may differ, I think that most readers will share the general
impression that this tale is well told and highly structured. My own
'structuralist' reading goes like this:

Episode (a): The encounter between the old man and the girl in the bush   This
episode itself has a tripartite division because the flow of information
between the man and the girl is reversed twice. It first flows from the girl
to the man, then from the man to the girl, and finally again from the girl to
the man. Asked by the old man whether, having been left behind as
useless and burdensome, he has a chance of keeping up with his migrating
group, the girl responds by explaining to him the conditions for faster
travel. Three personal items need to be arranged properly: the waterbottle, the stick and the cloth. Here we find a sequence of three embedded in
a sequence of three which again is embedded in a sequence of three. The
flow of information is now inverted and for a short time follows the flow of
urine which springs from the man. The girl reads from the man's urine
that, if fed properly, he is able to have another child. Again the flow of
information is reversed. The man overhears the girl and concludes that she
is a remarkable girl and deserves to be married.

Episode (b): The negotiations leading to the marriage   First the old man
convinces his son, who may be better suited to travelling than he is, to go
as a suitor in his stead. He goes, reaches agreement with the elders of the
girl as a matter of course (it is not even mentioned in the tale), but gets
involved in lengthy bargaining with the girl herself, who by her skill and
tenacity confirms our impression that she is indeed remarkable. In an
order which may reflect the order of values in the female mind, she
procures the promise of capital assets ('capital' in the original sense of
'cattle'), a number of household items, and the primogeniture for her
future son. The account of the marriage ends with its consummation
which is made possible by the excellent care which is taken of the old
man's dwindling resources. The consummation results in immediate preg-
nancy. The prediction that this would be the last act of begetting by the
old man is confirmed by his subsequent death.

Episode (c): The birth   In spite of envy and murderous thoughts on the
part of his elder half-brothers, by the very circumstances of the birth the
child secures primogeniture by obtaining the status insignia of his late
father. Again, as in the first episode, three personal items of the old man
are the focus of the tale: this time the finger ring, the turban and the stool.
While the number is identical, their direction of movement is reversed: in

Episode (a) the old man pulled the waterbottle, the stick and the cloth closer to his body by lifting them up and by tying the cloth properly; now the ring, the turban and the stool are moved away from him. He posthumously passes them on to his son; he bequeathes them.

The epilogue, in which the consequences of these events for the social structure and spatial distribution of Ajuran are described, does not fit structurally into this scheme and is not really a part of the tale. I think that Maħad 'Ali just repeats a couple of things which have been said already and explains for the benefit of a poor foreigner what must in any case be evident to an Ajuran.

The number three (three things to be lifted up, three things to be passed on) of course, is a regular feature in European and African folk tales. I hope that my little exercise in mock structuralism has suceeded in demonstrating that this tale invites structuralist interpretation (along the lines followed here and possibly along many other lines) as a true folk tale does, and this is what it is: an artistic, well-told, enjoyable folk tale. With reference to history, to which we now return, we may therefore conclude its analysis with the suspicion that this tale is not necessarily closer to historical reality than other folk tales. Real life is not normally nearly as well structured.

Concerning the relationship between Sanle and the Saale of the Rendille, we learn in the epilogue that Sanle later dispersed and joined many peoples, among them the Rendille. We do not hear how or why, but that is explained in another tale, which we have in two versions by Ajuran informants, one a Boran speaker and the other a Somali speaker. I give the Somali version[161] in full and quote the Boran version[162] only where it differs.

> *Maalintas tarikh-da ma aqanné lakini maalinti Ajuran la hawariye wadaad-ka as hawariye, Sheekha Burale la yidhado; intu soo qabtey Ajuran-ka marka wadaad kan falfalou weye intu subax walba waxa la arka guudkiis qooyó.*

I do not know the date, but when Ajuran was scattered, the sheikh who scattered them is called Sheikh Burale. The Ajuran got hold of this religious personality, who was gifted with an evil power to curse, because it was seen that his hair was wet every morning.

> *Wadaadkan wa nin ouliace oo timo weyn le. Mar kasta timihiisa waa qooyanyihin. Habeen iyou dararba.*

The sheikh was a holy man with much hair. His hair was always wet. Night and day.[163]

Holy men often have long hair, especially among non-Muslims of northeast Africa and among the less orthodox representatives of Islam. Examples for the former are numerous *qallu* of the Oromo and for the latter the sons of Abba Ganna,[164] who serve as mediums in the possession seances of the *oulia* adherents among the Sakuye. On the other hand, I have never met an orthodox sheikh, somebody who was literate in Arabic and well versed in the *shari'a*, who had the hairstyle known as the Afro look in Europe. There seems to be a close correlation between certain hairstyles and certain religious persuasions.

Markasa la yidhi: wadaadkan woxus guudkiis qooyan yeho nagahan (bacada) habeenki as kudaqda. Subax walba wa qabeisaneya. Wadaadkan waa nin ouliace.

Then it was said: this sheikh, the reason for his hair being wet is that he sleeps with women at night. He washes himself every morning. This man is a holy man.[165]

Wadaadka walasooqabtoo xoog loguxirey. Markas Ajuranka lafiigey. Markasas (bacadi) Sanle soofakadey.

So they got hold of the sheikh and he was shaved by force. Then Ajuran was scattered. At that time Sanle escaped towards here [Marsabit District].

Wahabaarey.

He cursed [the Ajuran].

The other version specifies the kind of curse. It is an analogous or sympathetic one. The Ajuran are to be scattered as the hair of the sheikh has been scattered.

Ajuran kabil kasta (inti Soomaali-eh) waa gelen. Ki gaale galay ki Soomaali galay. Ajuran ku wei kalafiigeen.

The Ajuran joined all tribes (as far as they are Somali). Some joined non-believers, some joined Somali. The Ajuran were scattered.

The other version specifies:

Ajurani fula chuf gargar-bae. Laf qubatu, Islan laf jíru, ka ini kees in-jírre in-árgan. Ka ini keesat gudda taaté-lle in-jíru.

The Ajuran separated [and went] everywhere. One cannot find a settled country where Muslims live and where there are no Ajuran among them. And [on the other hand] there is no country where they have become numerous.

These accounts refer to the Ajuran in general and hardly contain specific reference to Sanle or to other clans. Only when specifically asked, did Mu'allim Muḥammad explain that Sheikh Burale was a Garen and that the Sanle migration to the future Rendille did not consist of a single man but of a whole group with their livestock.

Apart from these traditions the Ajuran also share the even more general Reer Diid story already familiar to us from chapter 4, namely that the ancestors of the Rendille lived far apart from the settlements of their Somali tribesmen, that they were separated from them by warlike events, that they were forced to give up Islam in order to be allowed to marry Samburu girls, etc.[166]

The historical evidence is rather vague and does not allow us to ascribe a historical basis to the inter-ethnic clan relationship between Sanle (Ajuran) and Saale (Rendille). As the cultural evidence, as I have said earlier, is nonexistent, we can conclude that the result of our inquiry is negative: we have no evidence that the two clans are related by origin (and, of course, we have no evidence that they are not related). But this does not disturb the Rendille or the Ajuran. Sociologically this relationship is valid, no matter how and when it has come to exist.

There is even a Rendille who has gone 'back' to the Ajuran and who, as a matter of course, has been accepted by them as a tribesman. He is the son of Raage Torruga, a colonial chief, who (very much to the dismay of the English, who wanted to keep ethnic and religious groups neatly separated) was the first Rendille to convert to Islam. He shared and propagated the Reer Diid tradition of a Muslim Somali origin for the Rendille and, stemming from Nebei, a subclan of Saale, he looked for relatives among the Ajuran. As Nebei (Schlee 1979: 227–32) is the most powerful *iibire* clan[167] and has prayer and peacekeeping as its foremost ritual duties, Raage Torruga believed he had found his relatives in the Faq Shinni section of the Ajuran Sanle. Faq Shinni is a group with priestly functions. Raage Torruga thus employed the same method of cultural comparison as the cultural historian, but less rigidly. The criterion of form (*Formkriterium*, as defined by Graebner, [1911]) prevents us from describing the ritual functions of Faq Shinni and Nebei as evidence for a historical relationship between the two, because all they share is their ritual states, and this may be a response to a universal functional need or to a universal experience of God, in either case to something general rather than specific to any particular culture on clan or ethnic level. Only if ritual specialists of the two groups employed similar ritual instruments in similar ways, might some earlier contact between them, either by common origin or early interaction, be suspected. I have therefore abstained, in my cultural comparison above, from describing the ritual characteristics of Faq Shinni, preferring to do it here, on the level of belief. These characteristics may explain how somebody like Raage Torruga came to believe that Faq Shinni are related to Nebei because of their religious importance. We describe them in the words of Mu'allim Ibrahim, who belongs to this group himself.[168]

He first explains the meaning of *Faq* (which is probably derived from Arabic *faqīh* – 'somebody well versed in law and divinity'):

Wexey habaarán waa la arki jirey, wexey uduceyan waa la arki jirey, Faq nimáda saas ee Faq u ahayeen'. Maqi um beina gutahay.

It has been seen what they curse, it has been seen for what they pray. That is how the Faq are Faq. We just know it from hearing.

This somewhat Rendille-like explanation of what a religious specialist is –
somebody with a powerful curse and prayer – reminds us that the Somali
have been Cushites for longer than they have been Muslims.

One example of a Faq group are the Faq Rooble, who, like the Faq
Shinni, the Faq Yuunis and the Faq Maħad, also belong to the Ajuran:

*Faq Rooble maxaa loyidhi, iido [= iyódo] ladhiboodi sidan oo kale abar ay tahay
aa la yidhi – alxamdulillahi – 'adigi Ilaahi kacabsanaa bacadiga mar walba waa
dhorsanae (ilaahi kacabsana)' – waa tan as leedahai-ee – 'roob udawa' liyidhi.*

About Faq Rooble one says that people got into trouble, that there was a
drought like now, he was told – praise be to God – 'You who fear God, you who
always pray' – that was his way – 'bring us rain,' he was told.

*Roob doona bacadigeda maalinko as oome (maalin) saddax maalin roob a dadki
kifaari waae. [. . .] Sababti asagana Faq Rooble loyidhi roob kas ehed (de) roobki
as lahelley – Allahu akbar – Faq Rooble ad noqtey. Faq Rooble sabab tas laguyidhi
an maqley.*

A *roob doon* [a rainmaking ceremony was performed], then only one [more] day
people remained thirsty [and then for] three days the rain did not give people a
break. That rain was the reason why he was called Faq Rooble, because of the
rain that was obtained – God is great – he became Faq Rooble. I heard that he
was called Faq Rooble for that reason.

Roob, of course, means 'rain' and *rooble* (like the father of Ido Rooble
[Robleh][169] is somebody who brings rain or is otherwise associated with
rain (normally the name is given to a child who is born in the rainy
season). Faq Shinni, his own group, has such an association with *shinni*
('bees').

*Hadi an maqley, habaar kooda wax as qabanaye, duco-doda-na waa-lo-aqbaley,
sasaa Faq loyidhi.*

According to what I heard, their curse sticks and their prayer gets accepted, that
is why they are called Faq.

*Waa-dhorsanayeen' – alxamdulillahi – oo niman Iláahi kacabsanaye (oo bacadi
dhorsanayeen') nin Ilaahi udowa; Faq hadá layidhi saasa loyidhi.*

They became holy – praise be to God – they were people who feared God, people
who were close to God; if one says Faq one says it because of that.

*Faq Shinni-ga, markas ey Faq Shinni loguyidhi cèel oo shínnida biyyo cèel kacabey-
sey as Ilaahi kutugaayey marki ladhiboodoba meeshi shinnidi macan sababta
logudarey waa un kadhasheen'.*

When Faq Shinni were called Faq Shinni, they prayed to God at a well where
bees used to drink water and [literally, 'when'] caused trouble because just
sweet bees [= honey bees] multiplied at that place.

No section of Saale has ever freed a well from bees and thus made access
to it possible again, nor has that Rendille clan any other association with

bees. The cultural features and the oral traditions of Saale and Ajuran (or parts thereof) are too general where they are congruent and too incongruent where they are specific to allow any historical conclusions about the nature and origin of their interrelationship to be drawn. The only thing we can state with certainty is that Saale and Ajuran claim to be related – a fact which the groups concerned and everybody who has bothered to ask them know anyhow.

While the factual history of remote periods is sometimes difficult to reconstruct, the process of making up or modifying historical traditions is easier to describe because we can observe it today. Such observations allow us to discern ideological tendencies and permit statements about the direction in which history has been distorted, if indeed it has been distorted. Using the Ajuran and others as examples, I have discussed such tendencies elsewhere under the title 'The Islamisation of the past'.[170] Here I want to limit myself to a brief summary of the main argument.

All Somali claim Quraishitic descent, some through Samaal, their eponymous ancestor, others independently through Isaaq, Darood, Ajuran or others who were or have been reinterpreted as Arab sheikhs. From a demographic viewpoint it is indeed possible that the Somali do descend from immigrant Arabs. Such wealthy and respected immigrants may have had many children by numerous Somali wives and, by the repeated intermarriage of their descendants with the rest of the population, may have found their place among the ancestors of the entire Somali nation in the same way that tens of thousands of present-day Upper Saxons and Poles may descend from Augustus the Strong. But it is not in this way that the Somali claim to descend from immigrant holy men but agnatically, i.e. exclusively in the male line. This implies that at the time of the arrival of the first such immigrant there were no Somali. According to the internal logic of this view, the wives of the early immigrants must therefore not have been Somali either. A simple solution would be to postulate that the sheikhs brought Arab wives from Arabia. Oral tradition, however, does not opt for this choice, apparently because it would not explain the obvious physical differences between Arabs and Somali. Rather it is claimed that the Arabs took African, most often Abyssinian (Habash), wives. The fact that the Somali have a language which is very different from both Amharic and Arabic, a fact which is obvious also to non-linguists, remains unexplained by this emic theory. One is not worried about how it was possible that Semitic-speaking (Arab) forefathers took Semitic (Abyssinian) wives and begot with them a nation of Cushitic speakers. In Somalia, just like in the rest of the world, criticism and curious questions stop at the threshold of ideology.

Apart from this claim to Arab Muslim ancestry, the Ajuran claim to have been the original inhabitants of the Wajir area and to have been there

even before the Warra Daaya. The implications of both claims have
already been briefly mentioned in chapter 3: the first serves Islamic legitimacy, the second legitimate occupation of a territory. These two elements
have to be reconciled. This is done by maintaining that the Ajuran
immigrated into Kenya very early and, of course, as Muslims. Any
tradition of descent from Somaloid pagans would be incompatible with
such a theory. Any such Somaloids, of whom the relatedness cannot be
negated because of similar speech, habits and (maybe) overlapping clan
structures, therefore have to descend from the Ajuran because the Ajuran
could not tolerate the idea of descending from them. By a procedure
similar to the genealogical parasitism by which they have attached themselves to the Quraish, they now have to incorporate others into their own
genealogy. Two Somaloid peoples have been dealt with in this way. The
first are the Madinle, Madale or Madanle, semi-mythical well diggers,
about whom we have heard some rather fantastic traditions (chapter 4):
that they were also called ben Izraeli, that they were giants with enormous
noses for the detection of underground water, etc. Apart from this we only
know about them from what I. M. Lewis (1955: 47) says in connection
with events of the fifteenth century without revealing his source:

> The region between the Shebelle and Isha Baidoa was left in the hands of the
> Madinle, a tribe of whom little more is known than that they were allied to the
> Ajuran. The Ajuran influence was considerable and the pressure which they
> exerted to the south-east contributed to the collapse of the Muzaffar dynasty of
> Mogadishu.
>
> [...] by the first quarter of the 17th century a new tribal family made their
> appearance. The Rahanwein [...] defeated the Madinle and moved into the
> Baidoa plateau [...].

While in chapter 4 the Madinle appear to have preceded the Ajuran, even
as their enemies, in any case as non-Muslims as their cognomen ben Izraeli
suggests, Lewis depicts them as their allies.

The Ajuran genealogies of today deal quite differently with the Madinle:
they make them Ajuran. There is only some disagreement as to whether
Madinle is identical with or the son of Madale s/o Beidan s/o Ajuran (in
Diagram 30 I incorporate both versions synoptically). The conspicuous

---

This chart combines the views of Kosar s/o Muḥammad, Diiso s/o ʿUmmar and
Muḥammad s/o Maḥmud about their own genealogies. The genealogy of
Muḥammad Sherifo, with 40 generations between the Prophet (FaBrSo of Aqiil)
and his namesake, is the longest of all. It was the only written genealogy. It was
kept by a relative of Muḥammad Sherifo between the pages of a Qurʾan (facsimile
in Schlee (1979: 285); see also Schlee (1988). A causal connection between the
length of this genealogy and its written form is entirely possible. To the right we
find Ido Roble(h) with his son, grandson and ancestry (see chapter 3 above). This
part of the genealogy is based on information by Moḥammed ʿUmmar.

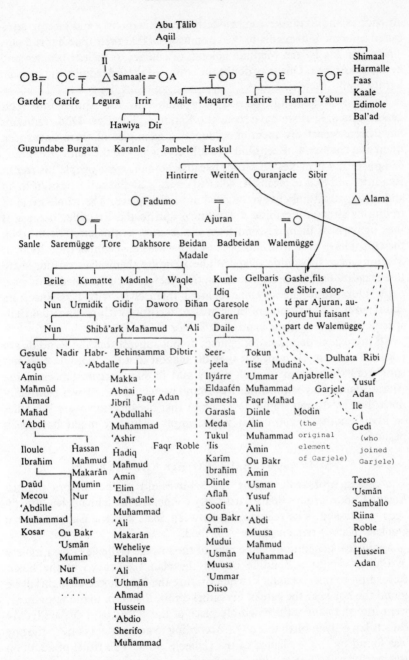

Diagram 30   Genealogical ideas of some Kenya Ajuran

absence of the Madinle from modern Kenya is piously and simply attributed by some informants to the circumstance that their time has run out.
The wells dug by the Madinle belong, of course, to their tribesmen and
heirs, the Ajuran. One may doubt the reality of these Madinle, but one can
hardly doubt their usefulness.

The second Somaloid people incorporated by the Ajuran into their
genealogies are, as we have seen, the Rendille. The Reer Diid traditions
have been repeatedly mentioned and two examples of them have been
quoted in chapter 4. 'Reer Diid' is a folk etymology of the name 'Rendille'.
Linguistically it makes no sense, because Somali: *reer* ('people') is *reer* in
Rendille, and S: *diid* means R: *diid* ('to reject'). Sound shifts from /r/ to /n/
and other such unlikely events have not taken place. The whole cycle of
traditions aims at ascribing a Muslim origin to the Rendille, because if
they or parts of them descend from the Ajuran, as the latter claim, then
they must have been Muslims because otherwise the claim of the Ajuran to
Muslim ancestry would collapse. The Rendille themselves do not share
these traditions. Not being Muslims, they feel no need for Muslim or even
noble Quraishitic ancestry and content themselves with clan ancestors
coming out of the ground of their present territory with pagan ritual clan-
specific artefacts in their hands (cf. Schlee 1979: 238ff.).

All these considerations, of course, do not suggest that the Rendille are
not related to the Ajuran, but they do suggest that the Rendille have not
split from the Ajuran in such a way and in such circumstances as the
Ajuran claim. Maybe the other way round we would meet fewer contradictions. But an Ajuran would never admit that his ancestors were Rendille,
or like Rendille, because that would imply that they might have been
pagans.

A NOTE ABOUT SAALE IN OTHER ETHNIC GROUPS

The presence of Saale among the Sakuye and in the Gabbra phratry
Alganna, some groups being particulary connected to Helmale, has already
been mentioned. The relationship between Saale and the Gabbra lineage
Odolale (Galbo) remains to be described.

About five generations ago a man of the lineage Galleole (Lossa moiety
of Galbo) caught a Rendille boy of the clan Gaabanayó in the bush.
According to one version,[171] when driving the herd home at nightfall he
found the boy near the gate of his camel camp, took him to the settlement,
went into the *naabo*, the assembly place of the elders, and declared, 'My
camels have given birth to a boy.' According to another version,[172] the boy
was found by the herdsmen of the Galleole elder. The ritual of adoption
was performed. The motive for adoption is sometimes considered to be
childlessness.[173] The Galleole man had to withdraw into dirre in what is
now the Sidamo province of Ethiopia to prevent the Rendille of the clan

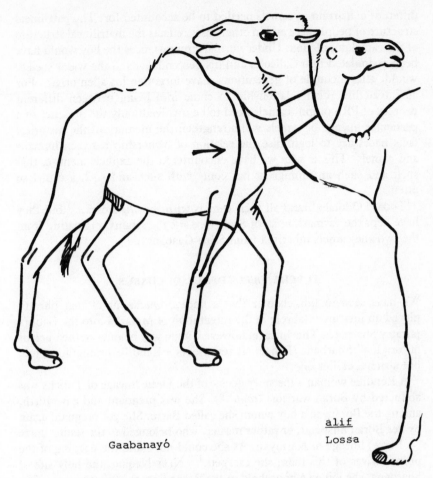

Gaabanayó

<u>alif</u>
Lossa

Diagram 31   The Gaabanayó's brand and the Galleole *alif* Lossa brand

Gaabanayó from claiming the boy back. For Gaabanayó the loss must have been particularily acute since the boy was the only son of his father.[174] Decades later the Rendille man found his son and joined him among the Gabbra. He had two she-camels. These were later inherited by his son, who also inherited camels from his adoptive father. He thus had two *alál* strains of camels: those of Gaabanayó, which kept the brand of that clan through the generations, and Galleole camels, which had the *alif* Lossa brand (Diagram 31).

This circumstance may have caused the continued existence of the descendants of the man as a separate lineage, known as Odolale and even today not considered part of Galleole, in spite of the formal adoption. The different *alál* strain of camels needed to be accounted for. The patrilineal structure of people here and in other cases reflects the matrilineal structure of the camel population. Under normal circumstances the boy would have been assimilated into Galleole, and his descendants and the wider society would, after a couple of generations, have forgotten his alien origin. For an inter-ethnic clan relationship to come into being between different peoples of PRS origin, camels need to be involved: only the presence of a particular lineage of camels will strengthen the memory of the historical facts necessary to legitimise the relation of ownership between humans and camels. This is why we have encountered the explicit mention that such and such an immigrant has come with such and such a camel so often.

Today, Odolale brand all their camels with the *alif* Lossa,[175] but they have kept the earmark *nebei* of Saale to mark the strains originating from the two she-camels inherited from Saale Gaabanayó.

TUBCHA, DEELE/DENLE, QUCHABÚR

We have seen in this chapter that a lineage Quchabúr of that phratry played an instrumental role in the integration of Matarbá into the Gabbra phratry Sharbana. This lineage, however, in no way belongs to the nucleus of 'original' Sharbana (Bahae). It represents a Rendille immigration too, but a much earlier one.

A Rendille woman – the story goes – of the Deele lineage of Tubcha was abducted by Boran warriors (*raab*[176]). She was pregnant and gave birth, among the Boran, to a boy whom she called Barre. She got pregnant again by her Boran husband, or rather master, who belonged to the senior Barre (= Berre) lineage of Karrayyu. As she could not stand the nagging of the proper wives of this man, she escaped.[177] Near Naqaio, the holy site of Sharbana, she joined a household of the Bahae lineage of that phratry. She delivered Barre's son, whom she called Haldér, and was impregnated again, this time by a man of the Konte sublineage of Bahae. The son who issued from this union was called Korólle (see Diagram 32). These three are believed to be the founders of the homonymous sublineages of Quchabúr. Between these a cultural division separates Barre from the other two. Haldér and Korólle (who apparently have become partly assimilated to Haldér) exhibit certain Boran features. They do not sacrifice camels, and if they have to slaughter a camel for food, they do so somewhat ignominiously, turning it northwards to face the bush[178] rather than turning it eastwards to face the house.

For pouring libations (*sadakha*) these people prefer cow milk to camel milk.

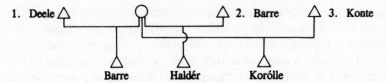

1. Deele   ⚪   2. Barre   3. Konte

Barre   Haldér   Korólle

Diagram 32   Genealogical relationships between the ancestors of Quchabúr

The camel brands of the three sublineages of Quchabúr are the same, and identical to the one of Deele (Rendille, Tubcha) on the back of the right hindquarter (B: *udu gubat*, R: *dube chirta* – 'they mark the buttock') with a diacritical sign in the kidney (*kalle*) region. This is not surprising. Legally, according to both Rendille and Gabbra custom, all the sons of the abducted woman belong to her first husband because he paid the bride-price for her which had never been refunded. Her Boran abductor and his heirs may also have a claim to her progeny because war spoils are regarded as full property. But such considerations do not benefit Sharbana, among whom she lived, because no man of Sharbana had bought or captured her and free association with a stray woman does not establish a claim on her or her progeny. In this way the whole lineage of Quchabúr would – at least as far as the legal fiction is concerned – belong to Tubcha even if none of their ancestors had been begotten by a man of Tubcha.

Contrary to the brand, the ear notches of Haldér and Korólle differ from those of Barre's camels. Barre has a notch in the lower fringe of the right ear (*bong'korsa*); Haldér and Korólle slit the tip of the right ear (*surre*).

Quchabúr intermarry with all other lineages of Sharbana, even with Matarbá, for the reasons discussed above.[179] In fact, the immigrant boy of Matarbá was given a daughter of Quchabúr as a first wife and a girl of Gār as a second. Haldér and the Boran lineage Barre in Karrayyu do not intermarry. They regard each other as brothers because of the historical tradition described above.[180]

Like all other Rendille clans (with the possible exceptions of Nañagán and Rengumo), Tubcha, namely the subclan Deele, is represented among the Sakuye.

Deele of the Sakuye have a clan-specific healing power: they 'spit' on burns and cuts. If they brand camels, this is said to hurt the camels less than the same action performed by other people. Deele have 'cool hands'.[181]

As I have described elsewhere at some length (Schlee 1979: 243ff.), Tubcha is the circumciser clan of the Rendille. (Among the Sakuye this task is not performed by a particular clan.) The Deele and Bolo subclans, but not Gaalálle,[182] are the circumcisers of the entire Rendille society. In

Deele's Rendille origin myth their clan ancestor makes his appearance with a curcumcision knife (*mindila* – 'small, sharp knife', 'razor', etc.), a bleeding arrow (*ganjo*) and an axe (*gidíb*): cutting instruments (*ibid.*: 244). They have a close association with the endogamous caste of black-smiths who fashion such instruments and have ritual power over them (*ibid.*: 245).

Like their Sakuye counterparts, they have 'cool hands'. No Rendille clan other than Tubcha would be entrusted with circumcising the boys.

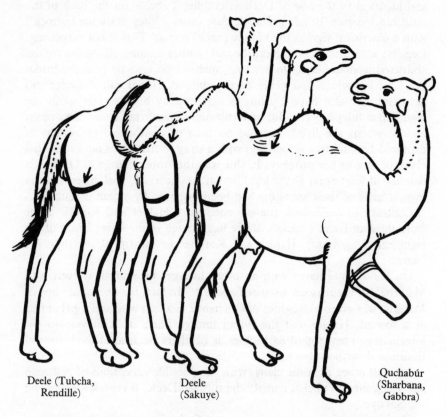

Deele (Tubcha,   Deele   Quchabúr
Rendille)   (Sakuye)   (Sharbana,
                                                  Gabbra)

Diagram 33   The Tubcha brand and its modifications by diacritical marks

They can use this monopoly for political pressure, especially when a circumcision year is approaching. The conflict between Tubcha and D'ubsañai, the early stages of which (up to 1977) I have described else-where (Schlee 1979: ch. 4) led the circumcisers of Tubcha to consider boycotting D'ubsañai by leaving their boys uncircumcised, thus practically leaving D'ubsañai without a warrior age set. This idea was abandoned and the conflict escalated in a different way: all warriors were circumcised and later massacred each other.[183]

Also the practice of Rendille Deele of spitting on a camel which has been bled to prevent complications conforms with the Sakuye idea about the soothing, cooling powers of this clan in connection with iron, fire and heat.

Like the camel brand of Quchabúr (Gabbra), that of the Sakuye Deele consists of the basic, simply Rendille version plus a diacritical element (Diagram 33).[184]

The foregoing comparison of the clans and clan histories suggests that Deele of Rendille and Sakuye share much of their clan physiognomy, while Quchabúr is linked to them only by a rather farfetched and legalistic view of descent.

CHAPTER 6

CONCLUSION

We all have multiple identities. At any given time we select one or a limited number of them as a guideline for our social behaviour. Different identities become relevant in different situations. In some situations we want to mark a difference; in others we are looking for a shared characteristic or a common affiliation. A Rendille who meets a Gabbra can either underline his different ethnicity, especially in a hostile context, or he can point to a clan affiliation which he or one of his relatives shares with the Gabbra in question to establish an in-group relationship.

The existence of such inter-ethnic clan relationships is the result of historical processes. In northern Kenya and southern Ethiopia ethnicity has been rather fluid while clanship is a comparatively conservative principle. Groups can therefore, under certain conditions which have been discussed, preserve their clan identity after an ethnic reaffiliation. If the same clan identity is preserved by other bearers who have not undergone the ethnic reaffiliation process, an inter-ethnic clan identity comes into being. The multitude of the relationships points to the composite nature of the ethnic groups. These relationships are traces left by the ethnogenetic processes of fission and recombination on the social maps of today's populations. They are a matter of the past and the present at the same time. The way they have come to be influences the forms of use to which they can be put. They have a diachronic and a synchronic dimension and can therefore only be studied by a combination of historical and sociological methods.

Diagram 34 summarises some of the more conspicuous inter-ethnic clan

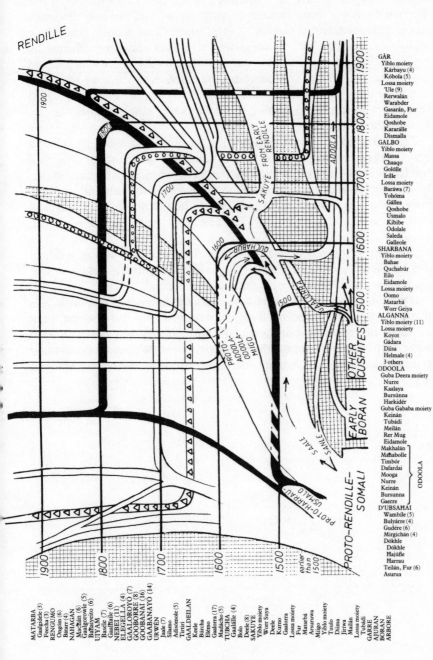

Diagram 34 The emergence of inter-ethnic clan relationships

relationships which have been discussed in this book. As we move in this diagram from one time horizon to another, we can see how emergent ethnic groups exchange parts with each other. Clans acquire new ethnic affiliations, and the ethnic categories themselves constantly change by having different compositions at different time levels. Those who join and those who are joined will never be the same again, but as some old identities are preserved in addition to the newly acquired ones, the numbers of options for self-definition and definition of others becomes larger, identity more complex.

That clanship is a more conservative principle than ethnicity is not a universal law but an empirical finding valid only for the study area until similar evidence for other regions has been adduced. In parts of the interlacustrine area clanship seems to be much more transient, as Newbury (1980) has shown for Rwanda, where he did not find any identical clans in groups that split only 200 years ago (see also Schlee 1985a: 19–20).

The long preservation of cross-ethnic clan links may be the result of their strategic usefulness in the economical and political field – a synchronic factor influencing a diachronic development.

If we can draw a general conclusion from the findings of this book, it is that we should free ourselves from the schools to which we belong, be it sociologically or historically oriented anthropology, and poach in each other's territories to combine the two perspectives. We cannot understand systems unless we watch them mate and reproduce and move through time.

APPENDIX

INTERVIEWS AND THEIR LOCATIONS

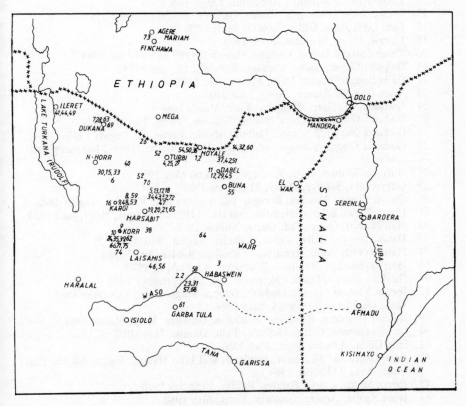

Map 2 Interview locations

Key: Name in alphabetical order, group, subgroup, place (short reference if any), date

1 'Abba Qenca' Maḥmuud 'Abei, Garre, Kuranyó, Banna, Odda, 31 September 1984
2 'Abba Ree', Gabbra Miigo, Odda, 1 October 1984
3 'Abdi Daqani, Degodia, near Habaswein, January 1979
4 Abudo Guyyo, Galbo, Massa, Bubisa, 1979–80, Turbi 1984
5 Abudo Mamo, Galbo, Odolale, Bubisa, December 1979
6 Abudo Mamo, Alganna, Helmale, south-east of Kalacha, May 1980
7 Ali Ramata, Alganna, Diisa, Dukana, May 1980
8 Ballo, Rendille, Odoola, Hammaleite near Kargi, July 1979
9 Barowa Adicharreñ, Rendille, Gaaldeilan, Gaalorra, various locations around Korr and Kargi, 1975–84
10 Barowa D'ogo, Rendille, D'ubsañai, Korr, June 1984
11 Boku Sora, Sakuye, Worr Suya, Dabel (Sakuye 1), February and March 1979
12 Boku Sora and Bidu Happi, Sakuye, Dabel, March 1979
13 Boru Galgallo, Gabbra, Odoola, Bubisa, September, 1979 (Odoola)
14 Boru Sora Suura, Gabbra Miigo, Gurar (Miigo), August 1979
15 Chief Dibba Wario, Gaar, Kalacha, May 1980
16 Dadio Arbele, Rendille, Rengumo, Kargi, July 1980
17 D'enge Guyyo 'Korinya', Galbo, Galleole, Bubisa, 15 June 1984
18 Doti Qalla Rasa, Galbo, Bubisa, April 1980
19 Ducale, Isaaq, Marsabit, April 1979
20 Duub Gadafo, Galbo, Usmalo, Marsabit, 1980 and 14 June 1984
21 Galgallo Diima, Galbo, Usmalo, Marsabit, 14 June 1984
22 Gallo Bonaio, Boran, Jaaro, Merti, June 1980
23 'Gara Gudda', Ajuran, Merti, June 1980
24 Godaana Ali, Gaar, Waaqaba, Korr, March 1984
25 Godaana Guyyo 'Korinya', Galbo, Galleole, Turbi, January 1979
26 Godaana Guyyo 'Korinya', Galbo, Galleole, Farole, 24 August 1984
27 Godaana Guyyo 'Korinya' and Jirima Mollu, Galbo, Turbi, February 1980 (Gabbra)
28 Gurracca D'ibbo, Gaar, Karbayu, Dukana, May 1980
29 Guyyo Cito, Sakuye, Dabel, 31 August 1984
30 Guyyo Waato, Alganna, Boruga, Yaa Alganna near Kalacha, August 1980
31 Haato Wario, Sakuye, Matarbá, and Haato Halake, Sakuye, Merti, June 1980
32 Ḥaji Ḥassan, Garre, Tuf, Gurar, August 1979
33 Halake Guyyo, Galbo, Burot, Kalacha, August 1980 (Galbo 2)
34 Ḥarrau (with *duub*), Rendille, D'ubsañai, Bubisa, April 1980
35 Ḥarrau (harelip), Rendille, D'ubsañai, Korr, April 1979
36 Ibrahiim Isaako, Gabbra Miigo, Butiye, 31 September 1984
37 Ibreen Yaatani ('Ibreen Gudda'), Gabbra Miigo, Bute, 9 October 1984
38 Idris, Gaal Jecel, Logologo, May 1984
39 Ildirim Toordeer, Rendille, Gaaldeilan, Gaalorra, Korr, March 1984
40 Int'allo Gababa, Galbo, Galleole, Tullu Diimtu, May 1980
41 Irile Diida, Arbore, Ileret, May 1980
42 Isaaq Gurracca 'Ali, Garre, Sabdawa, and Edin Hassan, Garre, Adoola, Rer Mug, Bute, 9 October 1984
43 Jirima Mollu, Galbo, Barawa, Bubisa, February 1980
44 Joore Agalle, Arbore, Gaalorra, Ileret, May 1980
45 Katelo Goa, Sakuye Miigo, Dabel, 30 August 1984

46 Kosar Muḥammad, Ajuran, Waqle, Koiya, May 1984
47 Kossich Roba, Sharbana, Bahae, Goof Mude, 31 March 1985
48 Lago Ogom and Silamo, Rendille, Urawén, Kargi, April 1979
49 Lote, Dassanech (Denle), Ileret, May 1980
50 Maalim Diiso 'Ummar, Ajuran, Garen, Butiye, September 1984
51 Maḥad Ali Mamo Cirresa and Tuulich Abba Kiyyo, Ajuran, Garen, Bute, 10
    October 1984
52 Mamo Wario, Sharbana, Bahae, Bubisa, April 1980; near Turbi, August
    1984; near Maikona, March 1985
53 Masur Gaalḥai, Rendille, D'ubsaḥai, Kargi, April 1979
54 Moḥammed Maḥmuud Muusa ('Karo), Ajuran, Garen, Butiye, September
    1984
55 Moḥammed 'Ummar Ḥussein, Ajuran, Gelbaris, Garjele, Buna, March 1980
    and 6 October 1984
56 Mu'allim Ibraḥim, Ajuran, Sanle, Faq Shinni, Koiya, May 1984
57 Mu'allim Mukhtar 'Usmān, Garre, Tuf, June 1980
58 'Okolla' Ado Abdi Bakur and Jilo Sora Jilo, Sakuye, Malka Daka (Sakuye 3),
    June 1980
59 Ortowa 'Ilkomele' Rendille, Elémo, Bagasi, 1979
60 Osman Golija and Sheikh Aḥmad Kanoo Mahad, Ajuran, Gurar (Ajuran),
    August 1979
61 Rooba Kurawa, Sakuye, Fur, Gafars, June 1980; Garba Tula (Sakuye 2),
    October 1984
62 Rusowa s/o Orle Elemo, Korr, 1984
63 Sambura Aneita, Gaar, Gasaran, Dukana, May 1980
64 Sheikh Isma'il Abdille, Degodia, Arba Jahan, 1979
65 Sheikh Muḥammad Ḥassan, Marsabit, May 1985
66 Urri Tarwen, Rendille, Gaalorra, Korr, 1976
67 Waako D'iriba, Boran, Marsabit (Boran), April 1980
68 Waako Huqa, Boran, Matt'arri, Merti, June 1980
69 Waato Katelo, Gaar, Dukana May 1980
70 Wario Yaatani, Gaar, Gasaran, Lag Segel, April 1980
71 Weris Ḥassan, Isaaq, Korr, 1984
72 Yaatani Boru Huqa, Galbo, Usmalo, Bubisa, 15 June 1984

Additions

73 Dolio, Miigo, Agere Mariam, 11 January 1986
74 Eisimbasele, Ilim, 1976
75 Eisimmirdana, Korr, 1976

NOTES

CHAPTER ONE

1 As this book had to be cut down to two-thirds of its original length, the preliminaries are extremely brief. Some of the methodological problems of field research in more than one ethnic group are described by Schlee (1985c). The 'monographic approach' and some of its implications as well as the differences between continental and British research traditions have been discussed by Schlee (1984c: 22–3; 1985b: 19–20).

2 There are classical exceptions. Among the more recent works which overcome the ethnic perspective and give due attention to clan history and the constant shifts in territorial and ethnic units, Lamphear's study of Jie history (1976) stands out. He also makes use of clan-specific cultural features.

3 The numbers of Kenyan Gabbra Malbe and that of the Miigo both fluctuate greatly from year to year. In 1985 and 1986 many of Gabbra Malbe went to the Sidamo and Arero districts of southern Ethiopia, as they had done on a cyclical basis in former decades, to hold their age-set promotion ceremonies (Schlee 1978b; 1987c and in preparation).

On 11 January 1986 I met Gabbra Miigo as far north as Agere Mariam, i.e. some 250 km inside Ethiopia, north-west of the main body of Boran whose south-eastern neighbours they normally are. A man from the clan Dolio, whose group were selling milk there, explained to me that the lowlands, which are suitable for camels, reach as far as Finchawa. He was well acquainted with northern Wajir (Kenya), where he had formerly lived. In 1984 the Miigo had held age-set promotions at Mt Hees in Sidamo.

P. T. W. Baxter (personal communication) believes that the Miigo mainly lived in Ethiopia in the 1950s. In Kenya he only met an occasional traveller.

4 The sketch map in this chapter does not show geographical features. Names

of towns, rivers, etc., can be found on the map on p. 237, which shows the locations of interviews.

5 P. T. W. Baxter's impression is 'that in the 1950s very few, if any, Sakuye on the Waso were even token Muslims; Boran there derided them for this' (personal communication).

6 The census numbers for single Somali groups may be on the low side because the census categories comprise units of different hierarchical status. 'Hawiyah' may comprise Ajuran (who perceive themselves as a subgroup of the Hawiyah), and 'Somali so stated' comprises any Somali who refused to identify himself as a member of any particular Somali 'tribe' (Republic of Kenya, 1981).

7 The most conspicuous among the Somali traders are the Isaaq, who originate from northern Somaliland and whose ancestors came to Kenya as recruits of the British armed forces.

8 All languages in question belong to the Lowland branch of Eastern Cushitic but are nevertheless mutually unintelligible. The Somaloid languages (Rendille and Somali) are closer to each other than both are to Oromo, but even between these two successful communication between monolinguals is rudimentary and difficult.

9 This boundary is largely identical with that between Eastern and North-Eastern Province of present-day Kenya.

10 On the problem of ethnic identity in other parts of Kenya and its assumed stability over time, see Ogot 1970, Janmohamed 1976, and Ochieng' 1976.

11 We here leave aside the American culture area studies, which would have to be discussed separately and which are neither historical nor sociological.

CHAPTER TWO

1 The Ariaal and the Rendille/Samburu relationships are the subject of Spencer (1973). The Ariaal are a highly interesting symbiotic association of Rendille and Samburu elements, which to describe *in extenso* would, however, transgress the frame of the present work, as they are a phenomenon of transition between a Cushitic and a non-Cushitic (Nilo-'Hamitic') group. The estimate of their number is based on the 1962 census and the rate of increase assumed by Spencer, and is correspondingly crude.

2 Schlee 1979: 98–128, and pp. 63–73 below.

3 This is a *leitmotiv* of Schlee (1979) and is richly exemplified there.

4 All this is extensively described in Schlee 1979, pp. 181ff. and 365ff., especially 386ff.

4 A fuller version of this list, which includes the praise-names of the camels of each group and a number of ritual functions can be found in Schlee 1979: 173–180, along with a diagram which delineates boundaries of exogamy and endogamy.

5 Without qualification meaning the Gabbra Malbe of Marsabit as distinct from the Gabbra Miigo of Wajir District.

6 See below, pp. 63–4.

7 The binary distinction between *iibire* and *wakhkamur* or their Gabbra equivalents is reminiscent of what I. M. Lewis (1963) has called 'dualism in Somali notions of power'. The *iibire* of the Rendille, however, are the core of Rendille society and by no means an endogamous caste of paupers like the *yibir* among the Somali. The Somali idea that God's blessing compensates for the lack of secular power can therefore not be applied to the Rendille and the Gabbra. *Iibire* and *wakhkamur* are both integrated parts of a balanced system of power; neither of them is marginal.

  8 One such example is given below, p. 194.

  9 See below pp. 26–9.

 10 See below, pp. 115–22 and 161.

 11 Kenya National Archives, PC/NFD 1/4/2, microfilm reel no. 45.

 12 The following description heavily borrows from Haberland 1963: 115ff.

 13 See below, pp. 73–90.

 14 See below, p. 225.

 15 See chapter 3.

 16 I. M. Lewis writes *sheegad* while most others write *sheegat* or even *shegat*. *Sheegad* seems to be the most correct.

 17 Kenya National Archives, Wajir Political Record Book II; Kenya National Archives, Isiolo Political Record Book.

 18 See chapter 3.

 19 A term borrowed from I. M. Lewis (1982).

 20 P. 227.

CHAPTER THREE

  1 Including features which have been changed and those which have been preserved by the forces of history.

  2 The traditional hunt carried out by specialised tribal and caste groups has recently received a fatal blow from the modern laws on wildlife preservation, although no species of animals was ever threatened by traditional hunters.

  3 It is also spelled *almhato*.

  4 See below.

  5 For a comparison of social structures and historical missions of Galla and Amhara, see Levine (1974).

  6 The ritual journeys or pilgrimages to the *qallu* are called *muuda* ('anointment') because during their course the visitors anoint the *qallu* (see Goto 1972: 37–8).

  7 In the Cushitic substratum of Ethiopia snakes are a common symbol of God and the ritual power derived from God (see Levine 1974: 60). P. T. W. Baxter has seen the *katello lemani* in which the young pythons are kept, but not the snakes themselves (personal communication).

  8 To the present-day Somali the origin of the very narrow and very deep wells of Wajir is a riddle. They attribute this technical miracle to the legendary giants.

  9 Another aspect, of course, is that in 1916 local British forces were diverted into Tanganyika to fight the Schutztruppe.

 10 Pronounced 'Roobleñ' in Somali and 'Roble' in Boran. The name means 'with rain' and refers to the season of birth.

11 Kenya National Archive, Wajir Political Record Book, Ref. Gedid, compiled 1950.

12 There are two exceptions to this. One is the immediate surroundings of new boreholes and townships, the other those stretches of land where for lack of security nobody has dared to graze his animals for a long time and where bush encroachment with all its negative effects has taken place. This latter form of pasture degradation, however, is due to undergrazing and not to overgrazing. Ecological and development problems have been discussed more fully by Schlee (1981 and 1982b).

13 Kenya National Archive, OC Northern Frontier to Chief Secretary, 15 March 1925, PC NFD 4/1/7, quoted by Dalleo (1975: 261).

14 The final version of this line is still recognisable in the modern boundary between the eastern and north-eastern provinces of Kenya.

15 Kenya National Archive, DC Marsabit to Commissioner of Police, 29 May 1928, PC NFD 4/1/4.

16 Kenya National Archive, Garissa Political Record Book, 1932. This Mr Sharpe is the man after whom the 'Gei Bwana Shaaf', the 'Tree of Master Shaaf', in the Yel valley of Rendille country is named, where he used to spend the hot hours of the day when passing there on his journeys. I have not found what type of 'material' the Rendille believed him to be.

17 See below, pp. 56–8.

18 Pp. 147–62, 199.

19 All societies in question also keep smallstock. As this is not a distinctive feature and therefore irrelevant to the explanation of inter-society differences, it is not relevant here.

20 See pp. 200–5.

21 The abbreviation is still in use although no longer corresponding to any administrative unit of independent Kenya.

22 See below, pp. 60–1, 89, and Schlee (1979: 343ff.).

23 The mistakes of the colonial past, such as pedigree mania and narrow, rigid restrictions, should, of course, be avoided, while other practices of the colonial government, like providing migrant settlement groups and satellite camps with armed escorts, mounted on camels, to enable them to graze the areas which might otherwise be unsafe should, I think, be revived because they increase spatial mobility and thus further a balanced use of resources.

Such escorts should also help to overcome the present imbalances in the security system which result from the fact that the police have only been able to enforce restrictions on the possession of arms in the case of groups closer to the centre, while the borderland populations practise gun-running, cattle rustling and booty trading across the Ethiopian and Sudanese borders. The better these groups are armed, the lower the morale of the police whose duty it is to disarm them, a pattern which reminds us of the failure of early attempts by the British to control the Somali.

Another problem in fighting warfare and stock theft is the low motivation of the central Kenyans in the forces to risk their lives for other people's animals. This shortcoming is currently being corrected by giving out registered guns to responsible elements among the local populations.

CHAPTER FOUR

1   Those readers who are interested in a closer understanding of the quotations and texts given here in the original languages, may consult the following books and articles: for Rendille, Schlee (1978a), Oomen (1977a); for Boran, Andrzejewski (1957, 1960), Tucker and Bryan (1956), Church of the Province of Kenya (CPK) Language School (n.d., but *c.* 1978), Venturino (1973, 1978). For Somali, the reader should refer to numerous works by Andrzejewski, Cerulli and a growing literature by Somali in Somalia.

For reading in Boran there are numerous texts of a scholarly or ecclesiastical nature. The New Testament of the Bible Sociey of Kenya (1978), translated by the Rev. S. Houghton and others, seems to be of a high standard. For original texts the writings of Andrzejewski. The most recent bibliography on languages spoken in Kenya can be found in Heine and Möhlig (1980).

As I do not wish to go too deeply into linguistics here, the reader should also consult these works for phonemic systems and principles of transcription. Here I simply want to point out that the conventions used in this book for Somali and for Boran/Rendille are different. The post-alveolar *d* is marked *dh* in Somali – this corresponds to the official Somali orthography and therefore has been retained here although it is an unfortunate choice: in many orthographies and transcriptions of other languages this combined grapheme stands for a quite different sound, namely a dental stop or a dental fricative. In both Rendille and Boran this sound has approximate equivalents in the respective phonemic systems. (The Boran sound has occasionally been called 'emphatic', which the Rendille sound is not, but both are post-alveolar retroflexes.) Both have been marked *d'*, which corresponds to the established Boran convention.

Long vowels have been marked by reduplication (*aa*) or (if corrections were applied after typing or in cases in which I did not want to alter a familiar word shape) by a lengthening mark (ā). These two conventions are used interchangeably.

2   The Boran, who do not form part of this camel culture, also have a different system of time reckoning and divination involving a cycle of twenty-seven days (*ayaana*) instead of seven. The Boran-speaking camel herders, Gabbra and Sakuye, however, have the seven-day week and the seven-year cycle with the corresponding terminology.

For a fuller discussion of the Rendille system of reckoning months and weeks, which is common to all groups sharing this 'camel complex', see Schlee (1979: 82–6).

3   Rendille version of an explanatory myth linking species of animals with days of the week is given in Schlee (1979: 239–40).

4   Days are counted, as in the Bible, from sunset to sunset. Thus 'Sunday night' is the night from Saturday to Sunday.

5   'R' stands for the Rendille language, 'B' for the Boran language.

6   These transactions can theoretically also take place on Tuesdays (Rendille, Gabbra, Garre, Sakuye), Thursdays (Rendille, Garre) or Fridays (Rendille, Gabbra, Sakuye). All groups, however, have a very strong preference for Monday.

7   In the case of the Garre this applies to the more traditional areas (Malka Marra, Woiyam); other parts of Garre have been acculturated to modern Somality.

8 Only males who abstain from sexual intercourse are allowed to milk camels.

9 The wide symbolic use of this tree is discussed in Schlee (1979: 440ff.).

10 Collecting a camel which has been given for ritual services such as being the best man at a marriage or godfather at circumcision is done in the same way.

11 By payment of the brideprice a woman becomes *alál* in the sense that her progeny belongs to her husband. A woman who lives with another man would remain *alál*, i.e. her husband would benefit from the brideprice for her daughters and her sons would be counted as his legal descendants.

12 The Rendille version of this story is given in Schlee (1979: 355–6).

13 As opposed to the satellite camp, where there are no cooking utensils.

14 To refrain from intercourse is considered essential for building up and conserving strength. Convalescents will postpone resuming relations for long periods of time for fear of a relapse. Gabbra fathers warn their sons that premature intercourse will deprive them of the necesssary endurance to deflower their infibulated virgin brides, so that age-set mates or, as a last resort, an old woman with a razor will be called to help. Rendille elders often point to their children and say, 'That is where all my strength has gone.' The fear of women who pollute camels and weaken men is, I hope to demonstrate, deeply rooted.

15 Interview, June 1980, Merti.

16 Mu'allim Mukhtar describes the past, because for much of Garre such customs have been abandoned in favour of standard Somali culture. However, he says there are still more traditional areas like Malka Marra and Woiyam. We have to reserve the problem of the distribution of cultural traits for later.

17 Part 3.3. of Schlee, 1979, is on the *mērát* institution of Rendille, i.e. the killer status, pp. 343–49.

18 In former times women and girls of a raided settlement were often kidnapped. Nowadays government control makes it impossible to keep captured women, so they are usually killed.

19 The gift of a *sarma* is common to the cultures deriving from proto–Rendille–Somali but not limited to them. The Boran have a similar custom involving cattle (Baxter, personal communication).

20 This is a feature of warriorhood which is cultivated among the Gabbra and especially the Rendille. The latter use the verb *a-kima*, *a-kinta* for 'to rave' or to have a reduced state of control in which one needs to be held by several people so as not to destroy whatever is in one's way and to end up bleeding in a thorn fence. These states of mind frequently occur during dances or for example, after a shock, being stepped on accidentally while sleeping, especially after a long period on a high-protein diet and sexual deprivation in the camel camp. As these states are associated positively with strength, wildness and warriorhood, they sometimes seem feigned. As the ideal of Rendille warriorhood (not manhood as it might apply to married elders!) is to be in a state of mind just below an aggressive outburst, i.e. in a state of permanent alarm, it is very likely that these attacks of raving can also be a sort of automatic response in 'neutral gear' to a false alarm, unless, of course, they are theatre to impress the girls. The inclination to *kim* is furthered by the intake of drugs such as *dolo* (*Euphorbia* sp.).

The Gabbra and the Boran (Baxter, personal communication) share these ideas in a less pronounced form. Their term *onne* can also mean 'heart' or 'wantonness'

($\hat{=}$ R: *tibichau*, 'being overfed', 'wanton', 'kidding').

The whole complex of ideas belongs to the outside, to warriorhood, the bush, the wilderness, and not to the settlement, the law, good behaviour, etc. This binary distinction reminds us of themes discussed by Duerr (1978).

21   Compare above the rules about milking camels and their link to women and sexuality.

22   A Nilotic custom, in my sample limited to the Rendille.

23   The concept of *mar* ('to come around') is shared by Boran and Rendille speakers. It is a very central idea in the perception of time, involving explanation of history as well as divination (Schlee 1978a: 162–70).

24   See above, p. 11 (Rendille) and 16f. (Gabbra).

25   *Talishi* is the water into which one has spat after every line when reading the Qur'an. This water thus contains those verses of the Qur'an and is then sprinkled as a blessing over livestock and people. Kenya Somali do so on Maulid. Cushitic ideas about spit and its association with curse and blessing seem to play a role here (Schlee 1979: 81).

26   *Ergams*, which the Rendille call *ergeg*, is a fibre made from *Asparagus* sp. roots. For the many practical and ritual uses of this fibre see Schlee (1979: 96).

27   For a description of the ritual details of a Rendille *sorio* see Schlee (1979: 98–107).

28   Belesi Bahai and Belesi Berri in the case of Rendille and Lossa and Yiblo in the case of the others. See above, chapter 2.

29   In so far as they still own camels after the heavy raiding and machine-gunning of the herds during the *shifta* period.

30   I.e. the more traditional part of Garre, as explained above.

31   There is no evidence for this from Garre.

32   The evidence for Garre and Sakuye is exclusively oral.

33   The tree which these sticks are taken is called *eijér* (R) or *ejjers* (B), which is what the stick itself is called by the Gabbra. More ritual uses of the *gumo* and of *eijér* are discussed in Schlee (1979: 438–40).

34   There is great variation as to where and how this is done. While Rendille and Gabbra perform all actions described so far in front, i.e. west, of the house, with the animal facing the northern doorpost, looking east, Sakuye and Garre hold the sacrifice inside the camel enclosure. The cardinal points to which the animals are oriented while slaughtered are discussed on pp. 149–50.

While a Muslim would slit the throat with a single cut, Rendille usually try not to cut the oesophagus so that the blood, which may be (in the case of a *sorio* animal only partly) drunk or used for cooking, does not become contaminated by the contents of the stomach. They thus cut around the oesophagus, pierce the neck behind it, and then cut through the trachea and the arteries with one slit up to the ears.

35   It is very clear to the Rendille that *sorio* has nothing to do with Islam. I once observed how one of the few Muslim town-dwelling Rendille, who had come to perform *sorio* with his clan, was reminded by bystanders not to say *bismillahi Allahu akbar* while cutting the throat. Some of the Christian preachers in the area reject this form of *sorio* because Jesus was the true *sorio* (sacrifice).

36   Generally *haugdéer* is held to make up for a *sorio* which for some reason

cannot be performed on the proper day.

37 When I accompanied the Galbo phratry of the Gabbra to their age-set promotion sites in Ethiopia in 1986 the camels were not watered for seventeen days at the peak of the dry season and grazing was severely restricted during this period: on five days for ritual reasons and on three days because of migrations (Schlee 1987b).

38 The purported reluctance of the Rengumo clan to marry in the month Dibial stated by Spencer, (1973: 63) is due to his misunderstanding the Rendille calendar. He assumes a link between the cycle of twelve months and the solar year. In reality there is no such link. William Torry, in his description of the Gabbra (1973), falls into the same trap. See Schlee (1979: 84–5).

39 From Arabic صوم.

40 Hunt (1951) equates *dab-shid* with the 'old Persian New Year (perhaps dating from the Persian occupation of Zeila)'. As we shall see, the distribution of this and related customs makes them appear to be a proto–Rendille–Somali element and does not particularily point to Zeila as the centre. On the other hand, such foreign influences are difficult to refute with certainty.

41 Schlee (1979: 108–9) demonstrates how the Rendille rules work if applied strictly.

42 There are various other occasions in connection with festivals and cosmic events which make an *ulukh* necessary (Schlee 1979: 128). There are also natural features like rocks or groups of trees which are regarded as gates and are passed on journeys by migrating Rendille herds or settlements. Tablino also mentions two cairns, called *uluqo*, near Farole mountain on the Ethiopian border where the Galbo phratry of Gabbra has to pass on a ritual journey (Tablino 1974: 55).

43 This would be *huulúqo* and *uulúqo* respectively in our spelling.

44 Boku Sora, Sakuye, March 1979, and Mu'allim Mukhtar, Garre, Tuf.

45 I have never heard this or a similar story from Rendille.

46 Waato Katelo, Gabbra, Gār, Dukana, May 1980.

47 Chief Dibba Wario, Gabbra, Gaar, Dukana, May 1980.

48 Jirima Mollu, Gabbra, Galbo, Bubisa, February 1980.

49 See Schlee (1979: 120–21).

50 To avoid terminological confusion, it needs to be said that in this context 'generation sets' are not meant to comprise entire generations without subdivisions, although the term is used in that sense by some authors. In this book generation sets are sets whose recruitment is primarily determined by the generational principle, while the age of the potential initiate comes in as a secondary consideration if at all. The number of sets per generation, i.e. whether a son would be recruited into the first, second or *n*th set after that of the father, does not suggest to me a binary classification which categorises systems with one set per generation as separate from all others.

In presenting his material Stewart (1977) distinguishes 'generation group systems' from 'Gada systems', but, in the course of his analysis, he goes on to say that both are subtypes of one major type (the unique paternal linking system), only distinguished by the number of sets per generation (1 or > 1) (p. 88). About the Jie, whose system he treats as one of generation groups, he says: 'Each Jie g-group is made up of a number of sub-groups (Gulliver calls them "age-sets")' (p. 214).

Similarily, Tornay, talking about the '*Classes générationelles*' of the related Toposa, states '*en réalité, j'ai compris sur le terrain que les Toposa conçoivent chaque génération comme constituée de deux subdivisions majeures, et ce sont les noms de ces subdivisions que nous voyons apparaître dans les modèles indigènes* . . .' (1982: 145). The number of sets per generation might therefore be open to discussion even in some of those systems generally treated as having sets comprising entire generations. As the number of sets per generation is, as Stewart himself has shown, typologically not a very basic feature, I therefore hesitate to adopt his terminological distinction between 'generation group systems' and 'Gada systems' which is based on that feature.

In the course of our analysis we shall find closely related systems of neighbouring groups which even have promotion ceremonies which take into account each others' timing, but which differ in the number of sets per generation.

A more basic and historically more distinctive difference between the Paranilotic and Nilotic systems, which are generally referred to as 'generation-set systems', and the Cushitic *gada* systems is the one stressed by Haberland (see below): the latter are characterised by the 'exact number', i.e. intervals expressed by fixed numbers of years, the former not. Stewart speaks repeatedly of 'pressure' being 'built up' to force the inauguration of a new set among the Nilotes. Cushitic *gada* systems, on the other hand, follow a rigid calendar and can adjust to social pressure only within the narrow options that remain.

51   Spencer's assumption that the Rendille have to wait for a cue from the Samburu to start such cycles (1973: 33, 45) is erroneous. Their own reckoning is clear enough for them. (See also Schlee 1979: 156).

52   See p. 9 above and Schlee 1979: 161–2.

53   See below, pp. 162–6.

54   This is a case of 'adjacent linking' which, according to Stewart, is very rare. 'There are one or two instances, but it is decidedly uncommon' (1977: 127).

55   See Schlee 1979: sections 1.2.4 and 1.2.5 on *Sabade* and clitoridectomy.

56   This age-graded agnatic terminology is used if no relationships through female links are counted. On the other hand, a real or classificatory mother's sister's son, for example, would be referred to as such irrespective of his age-set position.

57   See p. 160 below.

58   No enrolment into a junior age set and subsequent 'climbing' is necessary if the candidate is the appropriate age for circumcision already. Stewart (1977: 111) who bases his account on Spencer, is mistaken in this detail.

'Climbing' is described by Stewart as follows: 'If the son no longer is an infant, but has not reached the minimum enrolment age, then he cannot, like most of its members, enrol in F-3 [the third age set after his father's] when it is inaugurated. He is, however, allowed to take part when F-3 perform the Galgulumi [*gaalgulamme*] ceremony, ideally the year after it is inaugurated, in practice sometimes rather later. After having participated in the Galgulumi, the boy does not act as a member of an age group until the time comes when F-4 is inaugurated. By then he has passed the minimum enrolment age, and he is initiated – a process involving circumcision – together with those for whom initiation is simply the means by which they enrol in F-4' (1977: 109).

Contrary to this account it needs to be said that uncircumcised boys are not allowed anywhere near the *gaalgulamme* ceremony. What happens is that on the eve of a ritual bath which is part of the ceremony, the participants throw their headgear (*tadeyó*) of ostrich feathers (*rukumba*) into an acacia tree and leave them there. The headgear of a boy who will later 'climb' into that age set will be taken along and left there too, as will be the ones of potential participants who have been prevented from taking part by disease, jail, school, army or for other reasons. For the system to work, of course, it makes no difference whether the prospective 'climber' joins the *gaalgulamme* in person or is represented by ostrich feathers.

The Rendille have an elaborate calendar and never perform any ceremonies at unspecified times 'rather later'. *Gaalgulamme* is carried out in a *sondéer* month of the Saturday year following the Friday year of circumcision. If this is prevented for some reason, it can be postponed to the Saturday year of the following seven-year cycle (The only know example is the 1938 one which was postponed to 1945.)

There is also another, much less ceremonious way of climbing an age set than the one described by Stewart and Spencer. A junior son who has not been circumcised with his elder brother because he had not reached the enrolment age or because there are not enough camels for the simultaneous marriage of two brothers can be individually circumcised at the death of his elder brother and marry as soon as the age set to which his elder brother belonged does so or at any convenient later time. Nobody would even ask questions about ostrich feathers in such a case.

Incidentally, *eido*, which Stewart (1977: 110), quoting Spencer, thinks to be a mutual form of address for age-set mates and to have no other meaning, is indeed an affinal kinship term referring to wife's sister's husband or concubine's sister's lover in the case of unmarried warriors. (The girlfriends of one age set are all 'sisters' in the wider sense of tribe-wide generalisations of the agnatic model.) As a term of address for age-set mates it contains a jocular connotation and a slight sexual allusion.

59   See chapters 3 and 4 and pp. 209–28.

60   The Margudo initiations were therefore to be expected in 1984. In the meantime (interview Dolio, Agere Mariam, 11 January 1986) I ascertained that promotion ceremonies actually took place that year.

61   See p. 160 below.

62   Younger sons enrol in any age set junior to the second one after their father's. Contrary to the Rendille, there is no way that their descendants can rejoin their original age-set line.

63   Tablino (1980) and interviews with Jirima Mollu and Elema Rooba about Galbo, interviews with Mamo Wario and Kossich Rooba about Sharbana and Alganna, with Godaana Ali Sori about Gār and Alganna. Not all these sources are consistent which each other and I made a number of conjectures. I hope I have correctly described the basic patterns; the details are subject to later correction.

64   For Afar, see I. M. Lewis (1955: 166); for Samburu, see Spencer (1973: 88); for Maasai and Nandi, see Huntingford (1969: 84, 116).

65   The major and combined cycles of these Oromo systems have not even been discussed here. Their complexity is indeed remarkable (see Legesse 1973).

66   See p. 212f.

67   Chapter 5.

68   See, for example, pp. 141–3 below on the Gabbra–Boran relationship.

69   Interview Haro Katto Ratolle, Sakuye, Deele, in Merti, June 1980.

70   Interview Guyyo Cito, Dabel, 31 August 1984. Guyyo explains that chief Ali Sora successfully refused to pay taxes to the colonial administration, arguing that the Sakuye did not have a country of their own. If they had to pay taxes, the Sakuye would simply cross into Ethiopia. Finally the Sakuye were given the wells of Dabel which until then had belonged to the Boran, and the wells of Ajao, which had belonged to the Ajuran. The Ajuran then read the Qur'ān and cursed Ali, thus causing his accident. When Boku succeeded, he renounced any further territorial claims, much to the dismay of his tribe. He arbitrarily arrested and beat people and exacted gifts. This entirely negative view of Boku's personality is, however, not typical of Sakuye public opinion.

71   See above.

72   See above.

73   Compare chapter 3 above.

74   Interview Mohammed 'Ummar Hussein, Ajuran, Garjele, in Buna, 1979. For more information by and about this man see pp. 212f., 263, n.141, n.142 below.

75   For Somali who link their genealogies to that of the Prophet it is logically necessary to claim to have come from the north, whether this is justified or not.

76   See pp. 9f., 14 above and chapter 5 below.

77   The crossing of a large body of water is also a common feature of Oromo separation myths.

78   Oromo warriors are often known by the names of their horses which are used in praise. Bali is the name of a province in southern Ethiopia.

79   *Aki Gorei*: A comment by a Gabbra. Gorei is a holy place of the Gabbra, north of the Ethiopian border, where it is believed that mystical camels can be heard under the ground.

80   Baxter (personal communication) points out an association between the ideas of darkness, fresh green pasture (which is darker than dry grass) and female lubricity among the Oromo.

81   Anglicised plural of a Swahili word meaning 'field' or 'garden'.

82   *Moile agugaña* = 'Moile thunders'. The earthquake-like noises occasionally emitted by Mount Moile are said to be forebodings of war and distress and seen in connection with this tradition.

83   A tradition shared by some Gabbra and other Boran speakers, and also, as Baxter (personal communication) points out, the Tana Orma.

84   Dadio Arbele, Rendille, Kargi, July 1980, quotes the above traditions about the Boran expansion as an explanation of this. He gives Somali as his source. Dadio Arbele is a Muslim, a former soldier in Burma during the Second World War and a former member of the County Council.

85   'Isir Schlee d/o Hassan Turkana Musa, Somali, Isaaq, from a family of traders who have been living in Rendille country for three generations, Bayreuth, November 1981.

86   The transcription of the following Rendille texts differs from Schlee (1978a and 1979) in so far as it distinguishes /h/ and /ħ/ (emphatic) and /d/ and /d'/ (dental

versus post-alveolar). (Lamberti [1983: 379ff.] discusses the intricacies of this latter distinction and concludes that there are no regular correspondences between /d/ and /d'/ in Rendille and similar distinctions in related languages. The problem is further complicated by idiolectal variation. Acoustically, this difference is less marked in Rendille than, say, in Oromo. This gives rise to a rather confused picture in the literature.) It differs from all analyses by others (Heine, Oomen, Sim) in so far as it recognizes 18 vowel phonemes instead of five or ten. I shall mark -ATR (or +open, whatever we name this feature) as a, e, etc., at least in stressed syllables. (In unstressed syllables vowels tend to be semi-mute and/or subject to harmonic tendencies so that such distinctions become difficult to make.)

In my Boran texts, underlined vowel graphemes have a different meaning: they refer to mute vowels, also called vowel-coloured breaths.

87 Dadio Arbele, interview cited above. Here he gives the late chief Chudugle, a Rendille with Muslim connections, as his source. In another place the reason for not marrying the girl is phrased as: 'We are fewer than these people, [...] they might destroy us [literally: "make us get lost" – *Doda inno nuchule*, [...] *de inno baabicha*].'

88 Dadio Arbele.

89 A fuller version of this text can be found in Schlee 1988.

90 Many of these are given verbatim in Schlee (1979: ch. 2).

91 As in the case of the Gabbra, although less so, Islamic contacts or origins of the ancestors of the Rendille, or of some of them, have to be taken into account and may be the basis of some present customs. This element of their culture, however, apparently tends to be overstressed to match up to prestigious Muslim neighbours. Rendille converts to Islam do not hesitate to claim identity with certain Somali clans, thus obscuring possible real historical connections by overlaying them with a veneer of ideology.

92 This clan Miigo is not to be confused with the Gabbra Miigo.

93 The following texts are rendered in the original Boran or Rendille with a close, annotated translation in Schlee (1987a: 274–92). I give a slightly freer and more readable translation here.

94 *Reer* is Somali for Boran: *worr* = 'people', 'lineage'. *Rug* is the smaller, *Fur* the larger unit.

95 More precisely, Fur is a part of the Gār phratry of the Gabbra (and of the D'ubsaħai clan of the Rendille). I elaborate on this clan relationship on pp. 166–74.

96 See pp. 60f. above. The Rendille expression for *sarma* is *aiti magaħ*.

97 In this version the *sarma* belongs to a member of Ħaara's (Aara's) mother's clan, in the Rendille version (below) to another section of his own clan.

98 According to Rendille folklore, after such a feast Hāra slept not just a day but a week, with his metabolism so active that when on one occasion a crow came to inspect his anus for leftovers he killed it with a fart.

99 Interview Ħarrau (with *duub*), Bubisa, April 1980. As I quote two different members of the lineage Ħarrau on the following pages, I distinguish them, as the Rendille do, by visible features since referring to senior Rendille men by their first names is generally avoided. One of them has got a *duub* (a ritual headdress) and the other a harelip.

100 The incident ise said to have happened at Korolle, 150 km east of the lake.

101 Interview Harrau (harelip), Korr, April 1979.

102 Can *Fur* and *Haara* be variants of the same word?

103 Meaning my car, which has occasionally used for such purposes.

104 Interview Harrau (harelip).

105 Harrau (with *duub*), Bubisa, April 1980 (Rendille). The same belief is found among the Sakuye, who told me an anecdote of a man of Fur who was locked up in a prison cell by the British and walked out of it through the opposite wall.

106 The Harrau lineage in Du'bsahai, Rendille, claims descent from Garre. The coincidence of names may thus not be accidental, especially since names of camel matrilineages and those of the patrilineages of their owners can often be interchanged.

107 Interview Waako Huqa, aged 87, Boran, Mat'arri, in Merti, June 1980.

108 The camel nomads who cover their houses (tents) with mats, as distinct from the Boran.

109 'The bull Maddo' is the starless spot surrounded by the Great Magellanic cloud nebula, which is thought by all groups of camel herders discussed here to resemble a camel in shape.

110 According to Mu'allim Mukhtar (Garre), this was the camel colour preferred by the Garre before the introduction of northern Somali strains changed the breeds in many areas.

111 The Hofte were an association of Lowland Boran and Gabbra and form a transitory group, as do the Ariaal between the Rendille and the Samburu.

112 Boran high priest (see pp. 24f. above).

113 The informant here anticipates the name that, according to all versions, was given to them only later.

114 The name of the cattle belonging to the *qallu* of Karrayyu (see chapter 3).

115 See p. 99 above.

116 In this part of the world camels have a tendency to get lost towards the east, i.e. against the wind. The distance involved can be covered at a leisurely speed by a peripatetic camel bull in a single night.

117 The two languages are, with some effort, mutually intelligible and may have been more so in the past.

118 "I remember Waako Diriba very well. . . . Very sharp tempered, knowledgeable and a bit cantankerous. He was already a respected *jarsa* or a *jalabba* in 1951' (Baxter, personal communication).

119 Rendered above as 'migration of the many' or, more loosely, 'the long trek'. The expression *Kedi Guure*, however, is less common among the Gabbra Malbe than among the Sakuye, the Garre, the Miigo and the Ajuran.

120 The *mbao* game (Diagram 14) offers an opportunity to hear short genres of oral literature like praise verses, elaborate insults, etc., full of historical allusions, with which the competitors incite each other. Taking the stones of the adversary is playfully treated like raiding his camels, and winning is celebrated much like a victory in war with killers' songs or insultingly described in terms of a sexual exploit. The playful context, however, grants complete verbal licence, so that no one ever gets seriously angry.

121   The idea of the cyclicity of history is common to all the groups discussed here. The Rendille view of the 'coming around' of events is discussed in Schlee (1978b and 1979: ch. 0.6.5). While the Rendille view is linked in a quite straight-forward fashion to their age-set system and the ideal generation span, among the Gabbra and Boran we find cycles of different lengths and these can either separately exercise their own determining force on history directly or combine to form a major cycle which recurs every x number of years where x represents the smallest common multiple of the constituent cycles. Legesse (1973: 193) illustrates this point with the two cycles of the *gada* system: there are 5 *gada* classes (8 years each) per ideal generation (40 years) on the one hand and a set of 7 recurrent names (*maqabasa*) on the other. These combine to form a major cycle of $7 \times 40 = 280$ years ($\hat{=} 7 \times 5 = 35$ *gada* classes), after which the same name again is given to the same *gada* line in genealogical terms. Among the Gabbra I found *daji* explained as referring to events that recur in the 9th cycle of seven years, while *marar* recurs in the 8th cycle, *koltomát* in the 10th and *adál* in the 12th.

122   Hees or Ees is a mountain in Dirre in Sidamo Province of Ethiopia.

123   This does not agree with the meaning of *adál* given in the preceding note.

124   This informant likes to refer to the Gabbra as Boran, stressing the wider political affiliation instead of the ethnicity. To avoid confusion we shall translate this as 'Gabbra' unless the Boran in the common understanding of the term are meant.

125   See pp. 162–6.

126   These three lineages all belong to Galbo phratry.

127   Galbo 2 states that the daughter of Kibibe was milked into the lake to enable the Gabbra to go to Iris, not at the time of their return.

128   See pp. 56–9.

129   Informants: Harrau (harelip), Koor, April 1979, and Masur Gaalhai, Kargi, April 1979.

130   Like the one at *almodo*, see pp. 69, 247n.42 above, and Schlee (1979: 0.6.7.2.4 and 0.6.9).

131   A textile sheet of ritual importance. Among the Gabbra it is an insignia of the *hayyu*, among the Rendille it is owned by certain lineages (see Schlee 1979: 231). Among the Boran it is a ritual attribute of the village head (*abba worra*). The first *qallu* of the Boran was found wrapped in such a sheet (Baxter, personal communication).

132   This means that after losing her husband, of Chaaqo lineage in Galbo phratry, she went back to her father in the phratry Alganna. The descendants of this girl are called by the lineage name Eilo, which interestingly enough has no moiety affiliation in Alganna, because strictly, by the original brideprice for their foremother, which was never paid back, they belong to Galbo (see Gabbra clan list, pp. 18–20 above).

133   The Odoola 'clan' of Rendille is very small. An examination of the Rendille social organisation and their historical traditions would suggest that Odoola is a relatively recent arrival among the Rendille and that this Gabbra tradition is a simplification in so far as it attributes the same migrational history to all Rendille.

134   Such inter-ethnic clan identities are discussed in chapter 5.

135   According to Galbo 1, Odoola settled at Karhola, north of Turbi.

136   'Here' is used since Bubisa, where the interview took place, is closer to Rendille country than to the ritual home areas of the Gabbra enumerated above.

137   In this context of listing the central ritual sites of various political units, the *gaalgulamme* ceremony of the Rendille is paralleled to the *jila* journeys of the Gabbra undertaken to the holy places of their phratries scattered across the Ethiopian border.

Ideally, the *gaalgulamme* should be held on the shores of Lake Turkana (Rudolph). The last one, in 1980, however, was held uphill, east of Kargi because the shores of Lake Turkana were not considered safe because of the Turkana. The main participants – i.e. all the young warriors – are not allowed to take any weapons with them when they go to the *gaalgulamme*; they carry their ritual sticks (*gumo*) instead (see Schlee 1979: 1.3.5).

138   The salty waterholes of Korolle or *worr ti magade* are situated north-east of Kargi and just south of Meidahad (R), Meidatte (B), where the Gabbra of Bubisa, among them the informant, water their camels (Meidatte: 2° 46′ N, 37° 45′ E; Korolle 2° 37′ N, 37° 40′ E).

139   'Grey' Boran, i.e. real Boran, as distinct from peoples allied to the Boran. At least the Rendille translation of the term (*Boranto ti booran*) interprets *bor* as *booran* ('grey'). Haberland (1963: 24) translates *Borāna bōru* as *die Borana aus dem Osten* (*boru* ≙ 'morning', 'dawn').

As there is no doubt that the Samburu are basically Eastern Nilotic, this tradition has to be understood as relating to one or the other agnatic unit of the Samburu.

In fact, a part of Lorogushu, the lineage Kukuto, claim descent from Dambítu.

140   As the Dambítu even today are a substantial clan among the Boran, this can only refer to a part of that clan.

141   Using the same word as for the Boran high priests.

142   This implies that the diverse Gabbra phratries sent delegations to their respective places of origin in Garre country and that Makkamedina (derived from Makka and Medina like Hawadan from Hawa and Adan, the Somali form of Adam) is such a place in Garre country. By this cavalier treatment of geographical terms we see that the Islamic varnish is rather thin while the traditional belief system underlying this rudimentary Islam is elaborate and coherent.

143   We would say seven. The age-set cycle is linked to the seven-year 'week'. The difference arises from the fact that the unit taken as a starting point is not counted as 0 but as 1. Also, in German common usage 'Friday in eight days' means Friday in a week and not the following Saturday. Alternatively, this may be a reference to the age-set cycle of the neighbouring Boran which consists of eight years.

144   There is a story about how Sharbana got the primogeniture from Odoola by cunning: a test was agreed on to solve the conflict of claims and each phratry tied a sheep to a tree outside its settlement to see which would be eaten by wild animals and which would survive. Sharbana secretly brought their animal in to safety at night and tied it to the tree again at daybreak, while the Odoola's sheep was devoured.

In practice, at least as far as the sequence of age-set promotions is concerned, Gār today has the most senior position among the Gabbra phratries.

145   Pp. 54–92.

146   Chapter 5.

147   Here an episode is inserted which does not fit into the present discussion but which I do not want to withhold. It is an etiological account of the division of labour in child care and has a strange similarity to the judgement of Solomon. I leave the reader to decide whether it can also be seen as a piece of evidence for the higher status of women in an earlier period.

Yo isiin harka qabtu sun, nadd'een ijolle (isiin) im-báátu, d'iraa baat. (D'iraa maan?) Gaaf ijjesu gayan kana, yamallate, dirtí-llen, ya ijjeca isii mallate. 'Ijolle tante na rrá-fuud'!' jete. 'In-fúúd'u, badád!' 'Koot, gargar kútana,' jete, billá fuud'ate, d'ufe. 'Ah ijolle tiyy in-ǵorrain, ken!' Aki ijolle durri d'irti baat, isiin baat deebiten, akás.

When they had [the power] in their hands, the women did not carry the children, the men carried [them]. (What did the men?) When the time of [Banoiye's] killing had come near, they had a meeting, the men also, they decided to kill her [Banoiye. At that time the men said to the women (here both treated as singular),] 'Take your child from me!' [The woman answered,] 'I do not take it, carry it!' [Man,] 'Come, let us cut it apart,' he took the sword and came. 'Ah, do not slaughter my child, give it to me!' [the woman said.] That is how before the men carried the children and how the women came to carry them.

148   See pp. 125f. above.

149   If such a rule ever existed.

150   To Baxter (personal communication) this explanation seems speculative. It seems to him unlikely that Boran ever raided Gabbra because there was no one else to hand. Even during the *pax britannica* Boran from Marsabit, and even a few from Waso, went to Ethiopia to raid Dassanech and Guji; Somali in the east and Samburu and Maasai in the south were also potential victims at different times.

151   Similar, i.e. not identical.

152   Waako Huqa, Merti, June 1980.

153   Godaana Guyyó and Jirima Mollu, Turbi, February 1980.

154   Waako Huqa.

155   See chapter 3 above.

156   Unwritten, of course.

157   'Which for Boran to kill Boran it certainly is – and cannot be settled by compensation' (Baxter, personal communication) The Rendille deal with murder by purification and not by compensation because they regard it as self-inflicted harm to one's own group.

158   Using the Swahili word *tofauti*.

159   This spatial distribution has led to strange misinterpretations by historical linguists (see Schlee 1987a).

CHAPTER FIVE

1   An example of the historical misconceptions to which certain types of historical linguistics can lead are Bernd Heine's theories about the migrations of the peoples he calls Sam (1978, 1981). Both the general model underlying Heine's theory and his treatment of linguistic facts have been analysed critically by Schlee (1987a).

2   See Möhlig (1976, 1981c); also discussed in Schlee (1987a).

3   See pp. 9f. and 248n.58 above and Schlee (1979: 161–2).

4   Schlee (1979: 3.1) discusses extensively the partly esoteric beliefs and practices connected with this drum. For texts about the drum, see Schlee (1978a: 61–106).

5   See pp. 162–6 below.

6   See pp. 68–73 above and Schlee (1979: 108–27).

7   But why do Americans call a left-handed baseball player or boxer a 'south-paw'? Is it because the sun, going west, leaves the south to the left, the north to the right and the east behind?

8   See p. 67 above.

9   See pp. 68–71 above.

10   See p. 123 above.

11   *gose* ≙ R: *kulal* is the fenced sleeping place for herdsmen between the stock enclosures.

12   Cursing oneself by cursing one's father is a common form of expression of surprise or anger by women which does not usually have much importance attributed to it. Thus Rendille women might say: *Eñen inno korre* ('our father has mounted us'), *eñén bakate* ('our father has kicked the bucket'), or the like.

13   *Acacia mellifera* (R: *bilhil*), a thornbush used for fencing. The branch of *Acacia mellifera* cut here for the entrance to the enclosure is meant to make it impossible to get out.

14   As both accounts of this myth involve father-daughter incest, we may pause here to remember that the complementary constellation, mother–son incest, al-legedly looms large in our own collective subconsciousness, particularly in the consciousness of the psychoanalysts, who even propose the Oedipus complex as a type of human universal. Much has been written about this, as well as about incest in general – whether it is universally regarded as a sin, whether its biological disadvantages, which need neither be immediate nor conspicuous, are a sufficient explanation of its widespread moral denunciation, etc. Without wishing to get too involved in this debate, I just want to stress that incest, first of all, is a cultural fact, since the forbidden-kin categories and the boundaries of exogamous groups are culturally defined. Coming back to East African pastoralists, I wish to make a point in favour of alliance theory. I have discussed elsewhere (Schlee 1981 and 1982b) the emphasis on human reproduction and widespread alliances among nomads (for labour needs, fighting strength, jural protection, risk balancing and as a measure of happiness and success). Exogamous marriage serves all these needs. One acquires people (a) in form of a bride, (b) in form of her future children and (c) in form of a new group of affines. A bride from the in-group would provide (a) and (b), but not (c). The widespread avoidances concerning affines should not be seen as indicators of a negative relationship but as a means of avoiding strain and thus as an instrument of protection of the valuable and precarious in-law relationship. That our myth focuses on father-daughter incest may be significant, since it is the patriarch who manages herds and people and takes care that his daughter is strategically married instead of wasting her alliance potential antisocially and

unpolitically in the in-group. Whether incest is a sin or not, it is definitely social nonsense, since, if generally practised, it would lead to the collapse of kin-based social structures. These would become smaller and more redundant as kin categories coincide. Whatever the biologists or psychologists have to say, we as social scientists should not forget this aspect of the matter.

That incest is a theme in the cultures studied in this book is not only illustrated by this myth but also by abusive language. 'We have put them onto their girls/ daughters' means we have killed them. 'May he fuck their own girl/daughter/ sister' is a widespread abuse. The American English equivalent 'motherfucker' interestingly enough refers to the complementary Oedipal constellation. Perhaps in the end not only Freud had a mother problem somewhere in his heart. In our area of study, however, the daughter problem seems to be more deeply rooted. The inverse curses, those of daughters involving their fathers, have been quoted in note 12 above. There incest also alludes to death.

15 Spencer (1973: 44) discusses more ideas and practices concerning uneven scars (*bajo*).

16 See p. 134 above.

17 See pp. 131, 253 n. 131 above and Schlee (1979: 231).

18 See pp. 15–17 above.

19 We have come across the name Harrau above in chapter 4, p. 118. There it referred to the camels of Hassan Buro who was expelled from the Garre and was to play a part in Sakuye ethnogenesis. In the D'ubsahai clan of Rendille there is a lineage Harrau. We shall see below, pp. 162–6, that a historical connection between the groups who use Harrau as their own name or as the name of their strain of camels is more than likely.

20 See chapter 3 above.

21 The historicity of the place Iris and the fabulous circumstances of the return from there are of very little concern here. Whatever might have happened in reality, we can safely assume that there was *some* migrational event that imprinted itself deeply into folklore, and that this event took place before the establishment of the Gabbra public ritual. In the above line of argument, 'Iris' means this point in time, irrespective of the details of the events.

22 Ballo, Odoola, Rendille, Hammaleite near Kargi, July 1979, and 'Abdi Daqani, Degodia, near Habaswein, January 1979.

23 The Sakuye do not use this term.

24 Boku Sora and Bidu Abi, Sakuye, in Dabel, March 1979.

25 See p. 118 above.

26 As note 24 above.

27 Waako Huqa (Boran), Sakuye 1, Sakuye 3.

28 Another clan of Sakuye Miigo is Jiriwa; I cannot determine whether they are derived from Hassan Buro or from elsewhere. It is interesting to note that 'Jirua' has also been reported as one of the moieties of Gabbra Miigo together with a Gabbra Miigo tradition that the Sakuye Miigo derive from them (Kenya National Archive, Mandera District Annual Report, 1921).

29 Occasionally one wonders at how these factors are naively omitted by historians who want to compute chronologies on the basis of genealogies. European royal dynasties or similar data are taken to determine generation length as if such units of measurement were universally constant, but '... as A. H. Jacobs has pointed out, [they] must always be tested against sociological facts of each society in which they are used to determine accurately their length. In the case of the Pastoral Maasai, for example, Jacobs found the mean length of a gene- ration to be of the order of forty years, whereas both Oliver and Ogot found a mean length of about twenty-seven years for dynastic generations among the Ankole and Luo' (Lamphear 1976: 33). Lamphear himself reckons with 40 years for the Jie and this number seems to be typical for East African pastoralists.

Most confusion seems to arise from the lack of distinction between the age difference between a father and his first son (which is often relevant in a dynastic context) and that between him and his (statistically) medium son (average age difference between a father and his sons), which tends to be much higher, esp- ecially in the case of old polygynists who continue to have young children at an advanced age.

30 See pp. 20, 22.

31 Unpublished census.

32 The largest clans of Rendille are D'ubsañai (542 houses) and Sāle (619 houses).

33 I have discussed the *dorr* camels of this lineage in chapter, pp. 59f.

34 The fabrication of this holy drum is described in Schlee, (1979: 321–3), where the first three cuts are erroneously ascribed to Harrau instead of Hajufle. Instead of repeating the description of this complex process here, suffice it to say that Jibanjib contains the most frightening symbols of power such as the teeth of many carnivores. The complete set of rules for handling this drum clearly marks it as a seat of power.

35 Interview Ballo, Odoola, Rendille, July 1979.

36 Here quoted in inverted commas because we do not know what their exact relationship with the Garre of today may be, which proportion they form of the ancestors of today's Garre and which proportion of their descendants today might be counted as Garre.

37 This is a rare case of presentation of the sky (= God) as female, since obviously here the sky gives birth. Among Kenyan Cushites, as in many other parts of the world, Earth is usually the female counterpart of a male Sky.

38 The half-brothers Guyyo and Rooba Huqa, who have a low opinion of each other, in two separate interviews in Bubisa, March 1980.

39 Conversely, the Rendille name for 'Boran' may also include the Gabbra. This terminology may have its root in the reciprocal attitudes of the two neigh- bouring peoples who count each other among their enemies.

40 Harrau (with *duub*).

40 Gurracca Dibbo, Ali Afat, Dukana, May 1980.

41 Afat is also one of the recurrent age-set names.

42 This trait is shared with the nucleus of Alganna. We shall see that the adoption of a ritual complex sympathetic to and propitious for the camels is given mythological importance by both phratries.

43 Here taken in the wider sense to include the Gabbra. The Boran proper do not have a ritual association with camels.

44 See p. 65 above.

45 In a variant of this tale one of the rocks marks the grave of the ancestor of Ali Afat and the other one the grave of the ancestor of Orkor of 'Ule, the most senior segment of the Lossa moiety of Gār. One of them died when he heard about the death of the other. There is disagreement as to who died first. In this variant the two rocks stand for the two moieties, not for a father and his son. Again we find the association with rain: when the two rocks moved onto the graves they were hidden by dense rain. The son of Ali Afat is believed to have performed the burial rites.

46 Literally: 'Girl this [emphatic] day three together-passed-the-daytime'.

47 Or 'clan', 'lineage', etc.

48 'Lineage' in our usage.

49 Or 'buck', 'stallion', 'ram', etc. *Korm* means an entire male of any species of animal.

50 See pp. 57f. above.

51 Like Boru Galgallo, Odoola, whom we have quoted repeatedly on pp. 126–37 and 150–61.

52 The only segments which have ever challenged Ali Afat's anteriority are believed to be 'Ule and Rerwalan. These two sections are said to have accepted Ali Afat's claim to be the 'first born' when one day their camels refused to sit down at a sacrificial site while Ali Afat's camel did not hesitate to do so.

53 Unconfirmed information by single informants.

54 See pp. 115–17 above.

55 What he said about chiefs and politics, however, is common knowledge and could be confirmed by people of other origins.

56 See chapter 3.

57 Amharic title.

58 To do justice to the British I have to admit that all my information stems from the other side and thus necessarily is partial.

59 For details of circumcision rituals see Schlee (1982b: 118ff.) and for age-set ceremonies in general see chapter 4 above.

60 See pp. 10f. above and Schlee (1979: 181ff.).

61 See Schlee (1979: 181–2).

62 Although their relationship to Rengumo is closer than to other Rendille, as we shall see below.

63 Under the surface there was also another reason for this fight. Earlier a Gaaldeilan warrior had beaten an age-set mate from Rengumo and, to add insult to injury, taken his club. The D'ubsahai girlfriend of another Rengumo warrior thereupon pronounced *kurunkei ki d'aayan tumbo matinkasiicho, ch'atin Gaaldeilan ijehin* ('From my black snuffbox I shall not give you tobacco unless you beat Gaaldeilan'). Unluckily for her, the resulting fight had the wrong outcome. Fittingly, the nickname of the girl was Kurund'aaye. ('Tobacco' is often used as a euphemism for sexual favours, and to refuse it implies withholding these latter favours as well.) Later she was married by a Gaaldeilan, as a punishment as some people jokingly claim, and is now the mother of a bunch of Keele warriors who do show no more docility than the age set of their fathers.

64 For more details of house construction, see Grum (1978a).

65 See Schlee (1979: 95–7) and pp. 89f. above.

66 *Idem.*

67 See pp. 59–61 above and Schlee (1979: 354ff.).

68 'Come out [of the ground]', see Schlee (1978b) for the mythological references to this concept.

69 This is the usual way to refer to the ceremony of transmitting the *iibire*
power (see Schlee 1979: 181–2).

70 I.e. if they are in the lowland where there are no cattle.

71 See the cyclic idea of history described in Schlee (1979: 89ff.) and the
practice of preferential marriage connected therewith (*ibid.*: 96ff.), namely marrying 'the bones of one's grandfather', i.e. a girl of one's FaFaMo's clan, so as to
produce a son who is like one's grandfather. (See also pp. 78f. above.)

72 In the same way the avoidance was lifted for some Boran of Karrayyu Berre
(Baxter, personal communication).

73 Dadio Arbele, Kargi, 1980.

74 Above, and Schlee (1979: 235ff.).

75 See Schlee (1979: ch. 5)

76 See above and Schlee (1979: 102, 104). See also Mauss and Hubert (1899),
who beautifully describe the recurrent features of sacrifices, many of which we also
find in the *sorio.*

77 *Cordia sinensis Lam.* See Schlee (1979: 440ff.) for other uses.

78 Barowa Adicharreñ, Gaalorra, Korr, March 1984.

79 I here use 'he' and 'himself' because the origin tales do not make the
distinction between 'he' and 'they' but always refer to clan groups as individual
personalities. As I do not want to impose an artificial distinction on my material, I
want to leave it open, too, whether in a given place reference is made to a person or
a group.

80 Note, however, /d/ versus /d'/!

81 See Schlee (1979: ch. 4).

82 Interview Irile Diida, Ileret, May 1980.

83 Interview Lote, Dasanech, Denle, Ileret, May 1980, and interview Joore
Agalle, Arbore, Gaalorra, Ileret, May 1980.

84 Haberland points to the similarity of this name to Sab, one of the binary
divisions of the Somali, the other being Samal. Apart from the similarity of names,
there is no evidence of a relationship between Sabbo and Sab.

85 See chapter 3 above.

86 See p. 132 above.

87 The Rendille name for Galbo.

88 Interview Godaana Ali 'Sori' Abudo, Gaar, Gabbra, Korr, March 1984.
Language: Rendille, text slightly rearranged.

89 The Short Hill.

90 The informant.

91 See pp. 130f. above.

92 Like the Rendille medicine, this consists mainly of a luxurious meat and
blood diet to speed up recovery. Herbal medicine is added to the meat soup.
According to Baxter (personal communication), Boran do the opposite: they
restrict the diet of such patients.

93 An entirely plausible derivation of the name which is also supported by some Rendille informants.

94 Interview Korr, March 1984.

95 This boat is an innovation in comparison to other versions of this story. El Molo, called D'eñes by the Rendille, are a group of fishermen on the shores of Lake Turkana.

96 This cup was used instead of the usual piece of ivory for the transmission of *iibir* power until it was taken by enemies some time long ago (Barowa Ad'icharreñ).

97 Wario Eisimfeecha, Gaalorra, a common acquaintance.

98 Transferred to them as *alál* when they joined the clan (according to Barowa Ad'icharreñ).

99 Elliptic for *isiiche*.

100 This formula expresses the fact that Gaalorra regarded himself as an independent unit.

101 *Gelgel* or *dowñi Gelgelet* is the Rendille name for the Diid Galgallo, the Galgallo plain.

102 He means the Isiolo–Addis Ababa all-weather road.

103 The informant is Rusowa s/o Orle. Cross-checked with other Gaaldeilan elders.

104 Third person in the bottom line.

105 Gallo Bonaio, Boran, Jaaro, Merti, June 1980; Abudo Guyyo, Gabbra, Massa; Ortowa 'Ilkomele' Elémo, Rendille.

106 Gallo Bonaio, Merti, June 1980; Godaana Guyyo and Jirima Mollu, Gabbra, Galbo, Turbi, February 1980.

107 See, for example, p. 173 above.

108 Interview Guyyo Waato, Boruga, Yaa Alganna, August 1980, and Godaana Ali, Waaqaba, Gaar, Korr, March 1984. Goto (1972: 31–2) quotes a similar tradition.

109 Whom I have cited with the short reference '(Boran)' in chapter 4 above. Another Boran informant, Waako Huka (Merti, June 1980), confirms that Alganna stems from Karrayyu, and in particular from the lineage of the *qallu*, the 'king' (*kinki*), itself.

110 I hope to deal with these pilgrimages in a separate publication.

111 See also pp. 189f. above.

112 Alganna, Diisa, Dukana, May 1980.

113 See pp. 181–90.

114 See pp. 122–33 above.

115 Interview Boru Galgallo, Odoola, Bubisa, September 1979.

116 For *gadamoji* see Tablino (1980: 61ff. – Venturino's eyewitness account of one full ceremony), Haberland (1963: 220ff.) and Legesse (1973: 99ff.).

117 Mamo Wario, Sharbana, Chalbi, May 1980; Abudo Mamo, Helmale, Alganna, and Chief Dibba Wario, Gār, near Kalacha, May 1980.

118 Interview Guyyo Waato, Boruga, Yaa Alganna 9 August 1980, and interview Waato Katelo, Yaabar, Dukana, May 1980.

119 Waato Katelo, same interview; Abudo Mamo, Helmale, near Kalacha, May 1980, and others.

120 The Rendille, however, use *Dolía* as a praise name for the camels of Urawén!

121 The following account is based on the interviews with Abudo Mamo (see note 114 above) and Ali Ramata, Alganna (Diisa), Dukana, May 1980, and on information from my guide, Godaana Umuro.

122 A divergent view put forward by Spencer could not be confirmed (Spencer 1973: 64; Schlee 1979: 237).

123 Interview Mamo Wario, Bahae, Sharbana, April and May 1980, in Bubisa and elsewhere; language: Boran.

124 See p. 228 below and Schlee (1985b).

125 A Sharbana lineage (see pp. 230–3 below).

126 Otherwise his descendants today would be counted as a part of Quchabúr and their separate lineage identity would not have been maintained.

127 By the *qallu* Kossich Rooba, Sharbana, Bahae, near Wangure (Goof Mude), 31 March 1985.

128 This is unusual. Loading camels are normally castrated males. Probably the loading camels of this woman had succumbed to the drought.

129 Mamo Wario also mentions that the adopted Rendille boy married a daughter of Quchabúr but does not explain this.

130 Like Tubcha (see pp. 230–3 below).

131 Power is always carefully balanced in Gabbra society. It can be concentrated, but always at least in two places, never in one.

132 A section of Alganna (see pp. 203–5 above).

133 Equals *húqate*; 1st pers.: *húqad'e*.

134 The names of these influential lineages are here used as synonyms of those of their respective subclans.

135 Between Marsabit District of Eastern Province and Wajir District of North-eastern Province.

136 The last group of those who had lived in exile in Mogadishu were pardoned by President D. arap Moi in 1984 and taken to public meetings in the border districts as a demonstration of national reconciliation.

137 White is the Muslim colour of mourning.

138 The spelling of Somali names in the following is rather inconsistent. I here write 'Musa' instead of the better 'Muusa' because it is used in this form by my father-in-law in writing, on his car and his shop and in many documents. This is a case of established usage. In other cases I try to write names the way I heard them. The pronunciation is influenced by many factors, not least by the language of the interview. The same informant may refer to himself or some other person as Moħammed, Ma'ammed or even Mamo in Boran, Moħammed in Somali or Muħammad if he wishes to demonstrate his knowledge of the 'correct' Arabic form. In one instance, when I did not immediately understand 'Ou Bakr', the informant repeated the name in Arabic for my benefit: 'Abu Bakr'. The spelling thus does not reflect a standard but given realisations in given situations.

139 As these two will be quoted repeatedly, I want to introduce them briefly. Both are around 50 years of age and accepted as informal leaders. Mu'allim Ibrahim, who derives his title from his literacy in Arabic and his knowledge of the Qur'ān, is a former policeman. He is wealthy, corpulent and influential, and wears some conspicuous scars, the result of one of the many recent 'misunderstandings' with Rendille. Prior to independence Kosar Muħammad was the NPPP chairman of the now defunct Moyale District. The abbreviation stands for the Northern People's Progressive Party, which fought for the unification of the north with Somalia. Later he was a 'corporal' among the *shifta*.

140 See p. 14 above.

141 Koiya, May 1984.

142 Most Gelbaris and many Gashe are cattle people. Camels, however, seem to predominate in the Garen economy.

143 See pp. 59f. above.

144 Mohammed 'Ummar Hussein, Ajuran (Garjele), interview in Buna, 6 October 1984, language: Boran. Mohammed 'Ummar was born in 1893. He is extremely knowledgeable because of his experience of nearly a century and because of his association with the later 'King' Ido Robleh, who was his close agnate.

145 This was also clearly seen by Elliot Fratkin, who explained to me in 1974 that 'the smell of sex is bad for the calves', a phrase he may have heard from his Ariaal informants (personal communication). Mohammed 'Ummar's memory of this avoidance between fertile women and lactating camels is confirmed by Sheikh Muhammad Hassan (May 1985, Marsabit) with reference to the Walemügge, not to his own section, Waqle. He explains that there was an avoidance of any contact between women and lactating camels. Women were not even allowed to walk through the camel enclosure. If a woman dared to break this rule, any subsequent indisposition of the camels would be blamed on her. Walemügge informants (apart from Mohammed 'Ummar, who is above such considerations) tend to deny that such an avoidance ever existed and ascribe such customs only to the Garre (Mahad 'Ali Mammo Cirresa and Tuulich Abba Kiyyo, Garen, Bute, 10 October 1984; Maalim D'iiso 'Ummar, Garen, Butiye, September 1984). This fits in with the general tendency of Muslim Somali to deny ever having possessed PRS customs themselves and to ascribe them to their neighbours.

146 See p. 59 above.

147 Interview, Butiye, near Moyale, September 1984.

148 See pp. 56–8 above.

149 Mu'allim Muhammad, Koiya, May 1984, and Sheikh Muhammad Hassan, Marsabit, May 1984.

150 Stefan Reichmuth (personal communication) points out that this corresponds to folk patterns he found among Sudan Arabs.

151 Another version is Saremügge.

152 Another version is Tóre and Dhaqsóre.

153 Also Beidan and Badbeidan or similar.

154 Interview Mu'allim Ibrahim Sheikh Adan Kerou, Sanle, Koiya, May 1984. Language: dialectal Somali. The herdsman and religious teacher Ibrahim Sheikh Adan is the only representative of Sanle I have ever met. He grew up among the Garre and joined his fellow Ajuran in 1987. He speaks a Rahanweyn dialect with his womenfolk, but used the common northern Kenyan form of Somali during the interview.

155 Bute, 8 October 1984. Language: Boran.

156 This form of address is mutual and thus can either mean 'father' or 'child', 'son' or 'daughter'. The Boran *abo* is often also used in the vaguer sense of 'Hey man!', while the Somali *Aabo(u)!* has kept the original meaning.

157 In Boran, this greeting is phrased as a question: 'Peace?' The answer is 'Peace.'

158 'People on the move' (*godaan*).

159 A reciprocal address: 'father'/'son'.

160 'Arm' and 'hand' are the same word in Boran, *hark*. The hand (in the narrow sense) had come out, but the 'hand' (in the wider sense) remained in the birth channel until the finger ring was put on.

161 Mu'allim Muḥammad, Waqle, Koiya, 18 May 1984.

162 Moḥammed 'Ummar Hussein, Gelbaris, Buna, 6 October 1984.

163 Here the tale has been rearranged. This section comes later on the tape.

164 See p. 20 above.

165 In order to purify himself for prayer, a Muslim who has had sexual contact since the last prayer, in addition to the usual ablutions, has to bathe his entire body, including the head. Wet hair may thus be a way of identifying somebody who has slept with a woman. It seems that, in this case, Sheikh Burale was suspected of having slept with women other than his own wives and rightful captives. (In Islam general sexual abstinence is not demanded even from the most pious and legitimate intercourse therefore provides no ground for offence. In the Old Testament and in Islam adultery is a property offence because it infringes on the rights of the owners or guardians of the women involved. It has nothing to do with sex as such being good or bad. In Christianity the heavy emphasis on sexual morality, with total abstinence as its purportedly highest form, seems to go back to St Paul rather than Jesus.) How his enemies have come to the conclusion that the wet hair of Sheikh Burale indicates adulterous intercourse, and why they punish him, as we shall see, by shaving his head, thus destroying the outward sign of the purported offence rather than preventing a repetition of the offence itself, remain open questions and have to be counted among the logical weaknesses of this version, although the shaving – fighting the symptom rather than the cause – may be psychologically understandable and reminiscent of certain traditional and modern types of magic and medicine.

The version by Moḥammed 'Ummar does not venture into these intricacies. He explains the shaving thus: *Maagi, waan dibbi in-háan: kibir-ki* – 'Molestation, they did not shave him for any other reason: conceit.' (*Kibir-ki* is Somali, the rest of the phrase Boran.)

166 Interview Mu'allim Ibrahim, Ajuran, Faq Shinni, Sanle, Koiya, May 1984.

167 See pp. 10f. above.

168 Koiya, May 1984. Language: dialectal Somali.

169 See chapter 3 above.

170 Schlee (1988), which contains an appendix with Rendille and Somali texts which are not or not fully rendered in the present volume, and which should therefore be consulted by those who desire fuller documentation. Translation and comments are in French and German.

171 Interview with the *hayyic* Abudo Mamo, Odolale, Bubisa, December 1979.

172 Godaana Guyyo 'Korinya', Galleole, Farole, 24 August 1984.

173 Interview with the *hayyic* Abudo Mamo Odolale, Bubisa, December 1979.

174   Jirima Mollu, Bubisa, December 1979.

175   See p. 131 below.

176   See pp. 125f.

177   Mamo Wario, Sharbana, Bubisa, April 1980. According to another informant, Kossich Rooba, Sharbana, near Goof Mude, 31 March 1985, the woman did not escape but was installed with her children as a satellite household in the plains because her master could not keep the camels which he had taken as war spoils in the cool highlands of the Boran heartland.

178   This is a different motivation from that of the Muslim practice. Muslims turn the animals to be slaughtered into the *qibla*, towards Mecca, which in Kenya happens to be north. This superficial similarity should not lead us to confuse the two customs.

179   P. 206.

180   Interview Mamo Wario, Sharbana (Bahae), Bubisa, April 1980.

181   Interview Haro Katto Ratolle, Deele Sakuye, in Merti, June 1980, and interview Haato ('mother of') Wario, Matarbá Sakuye, and Haato Halake, Sakuye, in Merti, June 1980.

182   See p. 13.

183   The central theme of Schlee (1979) is that ritual specialisation among the Rendille enforces co-operation and thus unity – unity through difference, through the balance and interconnection of diverse powers – a somewhat functionalist view. Now, in view of the increasing internal violence of Rendille society, I have to add that this mechanism, if indeed it exists, sometimes does not work.

184   In the case of Quchabúr the reason for adding such a diacritical element to the original brand is, according to Kossich, Goof Mude (March 1985), to prevent their camels being confused with enemy (Rendille) camels.

BIBLIOGRAPHY

ABBADIE, Antoine d'(1880) 'Sur les Oromo, grande nation africaine', *Annales de la Société Scientifique de Bruxelles*, 4: 167–92.

ABIR, Mordechai (1968) *Ethiopia: the era of the princes*. London: Longman.

ABRAHAM, R. C. (1964) *Somali–English Dictionary*. London: University of London Press.

ALMAGOR, Uri (1978) *Pastoral Partners*. Manchester: Manchester University Press.

ANDRZEJEWSKI, B. W. (1957) 'Some preliminary observations on the Borana dialect of Galla', *Bulletin of the School of Oriental and African Studies*, 19 (2): 354–74.

—— (1960) 'The categories of number in noun forms in the Borana dialect of Galla', *Africa*, 30: 62–75.

—— (1962) 'Ideas about warfare in Borana Galla stories and fables', *African Language Studies*, 3: 116–36.

—— (1964a) *The Declensions of Somali Nouns*. London: SOAS, University of London. Agents: Luzac & Co. Ltd, 46 Gt Russell St, London, WC1.

—— (1964b) 'The position of Galla in the Cushitic language group', *Journal of Semitic Studies*, 9: 135–8.

—— (1968) 'Inflectional characteristics of the so-called weak verbs in Somali', *African Language Studies*, 9: 1–51.

—— (1972) 'Allusive diction in Galla hymns in praise of Sheikh Hussein of Bale', *African Language Studies*, 13: 1–31.

—— (1975) 'A genealogical note relevant to the dating of Sheikh Hussein of Bale', *Bulletin of the School of Oriental and African Studies*, 38, 1: 139–40.

AVANCHERS, P, Léon des (1859) 'Esquisse géographique des pays Oromo ou Galla, des pays Soomali, et de la côte orientale d'Afrique', *Bulletin de la Société de Géographie*, Mars: 153–70.

AYLMER, L. (1911) 'The country between the Juba river and Lake Rudolf', *Geographical Journal*, 38: 289–96.

BARTELS, Lambert (1983) *Oromo Religion*. Berlin: Reimer.

BARTON, Juxon (1924) 'The origins of the Galla and Somali tribes', *Journal of the East African Natural History Society*, 19 (September): 6–11.

BAUMANN, Hermann, Richard THURNWALD and Diedrich WESTER-MANN (eds.) (1940) *Völkerkunde von Afrika*. Essen.

BAXTER, P. T. W. (1965) 'Repetition in Certain Boran Ceremonies, in M. Fortes and G. Dieterlen (eds.), *African Systems of Thought*, pp. 64–78. London: Oxford University Press for the International African Institute.

—— (1966a) 'Stock management and diffusion of property rights among the Boran), *Proceedings of the Third Conference of Ethiopian Studies*. Addis Ababa. 116–27.

—— (1966b) 'Acceptance and rejection of Islam among the Boran of the Northern Frontier District of Kenya, in I. M. Lewis (ed.), *Islam in Tropical Africa*, pp. 233–50. Oxford: Oxford University Press.

—— (1979) 'Boran age-sets and warfare', *Senri Ethnological Studies*, 3: 69–95.

—— and Uri ALMAGOR (eds.) (1978) *Age, Generation and Time: some features of East African age organisations*, London: C. Hurst.

BIASUTTI, Renato (1933) 'I resultati della spedizione Cerulli nell' Etiopia dell' sud-ovest', *Rivista Geografica Italiana* (Firenze), 40: 184–9.

BIBLE SOCIETY OF KENYA (1978) *Wold'aqisa Haraa* (New Testament in Borana). United Bible Societies Code Number 263 3m.

BOHANNAN, L. and P. (1953) *The Tiv of Central Nigeria*. (Reprinted 1962) London: International African Institute.

BONTE, Pierre (1979) 'Segmentarité et pouvoir chez les éleveurs nomades sahariens, éléments d'une problematique', in *Equipe écologie et anthropologie des sociétés pastorales*, pp. 171–99. (*Pastoral Production and Society*). Paris and Cambridge: Maison des Sciences de l'Homme and Cambridge University Press.

—— (1981) 'Les éleveurs d'Afrique de l'est sont-ils égalitaires? A propos de travaux recents', *Production pastorale et société*, 9: 23–37.

BRAUKÄMPER, Ulrich (1978) 'The ethnogenesis of the Sidama', *Abbay* 9: 123–30.

—— (1980a) 'The Sanctuary of Shaykh Husayn and the Oromo-Somali Connections in Bale', paper presented to the first International Congress of Somali Studies, Mogadishu, 6–13 July.

—— (1980b) 'Oromo Country of Origin: a reconsideration of hypotheses', paper presented to the Conference on Ethiopian Studies, Tel Aviv.

—— (1980c) *Die Geschichte der Hadiya Süd-Äthiopiens*. Wiesbaden: Steiner.

—— (1983) *Die Kambata*. Wiesbaden: Steiner.

—— (1984) 'On food avoidances in southern Ethiopia', in: Sven Rubenson (ed.): *Proceedings of the Seventh International Conference of Ethiopian Studies*. Lund. 429–45.

CARR, Claudia (1977) *Pastoralism in Crisis: the Dassanech and their Ethiopian lands*. Chicago: University of Chicago.

CERULLI, Enrico (1926) 'Iscrizioni e documenti Arabi per la storia della Somalia', *Rivista degli Studi Orientali*, 11: 1–24.

—— (1933) *Etiopia Occidentale*. vol. II, Rome. Sindicato Italiano Arti Grafiche.

—— (1938) *Studi etiopici*, vol. II: *La lingua e la storia dei Sidamo*. Rome: Istituto per l'Oriente.

—— (1957) *Somalia: scritti vario editi ed inediti*, vols. I–III. Rome.

CHURCH OF THE PROVINCE OF KENYA (CPK) LANGUAGE SCHOOL (n.d., but *c.* 1978) Boraana Basic Course, Nairobi (hectographed).

DAHL, Gudrun (1979) *Suffering Grass: subsistence and society of Waso Borana*, Stockholm Studies in Social Anthropology, Department of Social Anthropology, University of Stockholm.

DALLEO, Peter T. (1975) 'Trade and pastoralism: economic factors in the history of the Somali of northeastern Kenya', Ph.D. Thesis, Syracuse University.

DOUGLAS, Mary, and Phyllis M. KABERRY (eds.) (1972 [1976]) *Man in Africa*. London: Tavistock.

DUERR, H. P. (1978) *Traumzeit*. Frankfurt: Syndikat.

DYEN, Isidore. (1956) 'Language distribution and migration theory', *Language*, 32 (4): 611–26.

EHRET, Christopher (1971) *Southern Nilotic History*. Evanston: Northwestern University Press.

–––––– (1974) *Ethiopians and East Africans: the problem of contacts*. Nairobi: Historical Studies 3, Nairobi: East African Publishing House.

EVANS-PRITCHARD, E. E. (1940a) *The Nuer*. Oxford: Clarendon Press.

–––––– (1940b) 'The Nuer of the southern Sudan', in M. Fortes and E. E. Evans-Pritchard, *African Political Systems*. London: Oxford University Press for the International African Institute, pp. 272–96.

FAGE, J. D. (ed.) (1970) *Africa Discovers Her Past*. London.

FERENC, Aleksander (1980) 'Le peuple Oromo dans les écrits et l'historiographie éthiopiens', *Africana Bulletin* (Warsaw). 29: 81–95.

FLEMING, Harold C. (1964) 'Basio and Rendille: Somali outliers', *Rassegna di Studi Etiopici*, 20: 35–96.

FROBENIUS, Leo. (1910) 'Kulturtypen aus dem Westsudan', *Petermanns Mitteilungen*, Ergänzungsband 35 (Heft 166).

FUKUI, Katsuyoshi, and D. TURTON (eds.) (1979) *Warfare among East African Herders*. Osaka: Senri Ethnological Studies.

GOTO, Paul S. G. (1972) 'The Boran of Northern Kenya: origin, migrations and settlements in the 19th century', BA thesis, University of Nairobi.

GRAEBNER, Fritz. (1911) *Methode der Ethnologie*. Heidelberg: C. Winter.

GRUM, Anders (1978a) 'Rendille Habitation, vol. 1: A preliminary report' (unpublished).

–––––– (1978b) 'Rendille Calendar' (MS).

–––––– (n.d. but *c.* 1978) 'Census of Rendille houses' (unpublished).

GUIDI, I. (1907) 'Historia gentis Galla', in C. Conti Rossini (ed.), *Historia Regis Sarsa Dengel*. Louvain (reprinted 1955).

HABERLAND, Eike (1963) *Galla Süd-Äthiopiens*. Stuttgart: Kohlhammer.

HEINE, Bernd (1976) 'Notes on the Rendille language (Kenya)', *Africa und Übersee*, 59 (3): 176–223.

–––––– (1978) 'The Sam languages: a history of Rendille, Boni and Somali', *Afroasiatic Linguistics*, 6(2).

–––––– (1979?) 'Linguistic evidence on the early history of the Somali people', undated revised version of a paper prepared for a symposium on the tenth anniversary of the Somali Revolution, Mogadishu, 15–20 October 1979.

–––––– (1980) *Language and Dialect Atlas of Kenya*, vol. II: *The Non-Bantu Languages of Kenya*. Berlin: Reimer.

–––––– (1981) 'Some cultural evidence on the early Sam-speaking people of Eastern Africa', *Sprache und Geschichte in Africa*, 3: 169–200.

–––––– (1982) *Language and Dialect Atlas of Kenya*, vol. X: Boni Dialects. Berlin: Reimer.

––––––, H. HOFF and R. VOSSEN (1977) 'Neuere Ergebnisse zur Territorialgeschichte der Bantu (Juli 1975)', in W. Möhlig, F. Rottland and B. Heine (eds), *Zur Sprachgeschichte und Ethnohistorie in Afrika*, pp. 57–125. Berlin:

Reimer.

——— and Wilhelm J. G. MÖHLIG (1980) *Language and Dialect Atlas of Kenya*, vol. I: *Geographical and Historical Introduction*. Berlin: Reimer.

HENIGE, David P. (1974) *The Chronology of Oral Tradition: quest for a chimera*. Oxford: Clarendon Press.

HJORT, Anders (1981) 'A critique of "ecological" models of pastoral land use', *Ethnos* (Stockholm), 46: 171–89.

HOGG, Richard (1980) 'Pastoralism and impoverishment: the case of the Isiolo Boran of northern Kenya', *Disasters*, 4 (3): 299–310.

HUNT, J. A. (1951) *A General Survey of the Somaliland Protectorate 1944–1950*, Colonial Development and Welfare Scheme, D.484. London: The Crown Agents for the Colonies.

HUNTINGFORD, G. W. B. (1955) *The Galla of Ethiopia: the kingdoms of Kafa and Janjero*, Ethnographic Survey of Africa, North-Eastern Africa, part 2. London: International African Institute.

——— (1963) 'The peopling of the interior of East Africa by its modern inhabitants', in R. Oliver and Gervase Mathew (eds.), *History of East Africa*, pp. 58–93. Oxford: Oxford University Press.

——— (1969) *The Southern Nilo-Hamites*, Ethnographic Survey of Africa, East Central Africa, part 8. London: International African Institute.

JACOBS, Allan H. (1968) 'A chronology of the Pastoral Maasai', in B.A. Ogot (ed.), *Hadith*, 1. Nairobi: Kenya Literature Bureau.

JAENEN, Cornelius J. (1956) 'The Galla or Oromo of East Africa', *Southwestern Journal of Anthropology* 12: 171–91.

JANMOHAMED, Karim K. (1976) 'Ethnicity in an urban setting: a case study of Mombasa', in Bethwell A. Ogot (ed.) *History and Social Change in East Africa*, *Hadith*, 6. Nairobi: Kenya Literature Bureau.

JENSEN, A. E. (1936) *Im Lande des Gada*. Stuttgart: Strecker & Schröder.

——— (1942) 'Neuere Notizen über das *gada* System', *Paideuma*, 2. (Leipzig): 84–94.

——— (ed.) (1959) *Altvölker Süd-Äthiopiens*. Stuttgart: Kohlhammer.

——— (1960) 'Beziehungen zwischen dem Alten Testament und der Nilotischen Kultur in Afrika', in *Cultural in History: essays in honour of Paul Radin*. New York.

JUNGRAITHMAYR, H. (ed.) (1978) *Struktur und Wandel afrikanischer Sprachen*. Berlin: Reimer.

KEENE, A., and H. SPITTLER (1976) *English–Somali Dictionary*. Pasadena, Ca.

KELLY, Hilarie (1979) 'The Orma of Tana River District', a preliminary report for Dr Mbithi, Sociology, 7 February, Nairobi (hectographed): Department of Sociology, University of Nairobi.

KENYAN NATIONAL ARCHIVES (KMA) (detailed references in footnotes).

——— NFD records.

——— Wajir Political Record Book 1, 2.

——— Garissa Political Record Book.

——— Isiolo Political Record Book.

——— Moyale Station Reports.

——— Moyale District Annual Reports.

——— Gurreh Annual Reports.

——— Mandera District Annual Reports.

——— Wajir District Annual Reports.

KLUCKHOHN, Clyde (1936) 'Some reflections on the method and theory of the Kulturkreislehre', *American Anthropologist*, 36: 157–96.

LAMBERTI, Marcello (1983) 'Die Somali-Dialekte: eine vergleichende Untersuchung', PhD thesis, Cologne.

LAMPHEAR, John (1976) *The Traditional History of the Jie*. Oxford: Oxford University Press.

LEACH, Edmund (1954) *Political Systems of Highland Burma*. London: The Athlone Press.

LEGESSE, Asmarom (1973) *Gada: three approaches to the study of African society*. New York: Free Press.

LEVINE, Donald N. (1974) *Greater Ethiopia*. Chicago: University of Chicago Press.

LEWIS, Herbert S. (1966) 'The origins of the Galla and Somali', *Journal of African History*, 7 (1): 27–46.

LEWIS, Ioan M. (1955, 1969) *Peoples of the Horn of Africa: Somali, Afar and Saho*, Ethnographic Survey of Africa, North-Eastern Africa, part 1. London: International African Institute.

―――― (1959) 'Clanship and contract in northern Somaliland', *Africa*, 29: 274–93.

―――― (1961a) 'Force and fission in northern Somali lineage structure', *American Anthropologist*, 63: 94–112.

―――― (1961b) *A Pastoral Democracy: a study of pastoralism and politics among the northern Somali of the Horn of Africa*. London: Oxford University Press.

―――― (1963) 'Dualism in Somali notions of power', *Journal of the Royal Anthropological Institute*, 93: 109–16.

―――― (1972 [1969]) 'From nomadism to cultivation: the expansion of political solidarity in southern Somalia', in Mary Douglas and P. M. Kaberry (eds.), *Man in Africa*: 59–77.

―――― (ed.) (1966) *Islam in Tropical Africa*. Oxford: Oxford University Press.

―――― (1980 [1965]) *A Modern History of Somaliland: from nation to state*. London & New York: Longman.

―――― (1982) *The Somali Lineage System and the Total Genealogy*. Ann Arbor: University Microprints (reproduction of a typed report prepared in 1957).

LOW, D. A. (1963) 'The Northern Interior, 1840–84', in R. Oliver and G. Mathew (eds.), *History of East Africa*, vol. I. Oxford: Oxford University Press.

MARKAKIS, John (1974) *Ethiopia: anatomy of a traditional polity*. Oxford: Clarendon Press.

MAUD, Philip (1904) 'Exploration of the southern borderland of Abyssinia', *Geographical Journal*, 5: 552–79.

MAUSS, Marcel, and Henri HUBERT (1899) 'Essai sur la nature et fonction du sacrifice', *L'Année sociologioque*, 2.

MERKER, M. (1910 [1904]) *Die Massai: eine ethnographische Monographie eines ostafrikanischen Semitenvolkes*. Berlin, reprinted 1968. New York: Johnson Repr. Corp.

MIDDLETON, J., and D. TAIT (eds.) (1958) *Tribes without Rulers: studies in African segmentary systems*. London: Routledge & Kegan Paul.

MÖHLIG, Wilhelm J. G. (1976). 'Guthries Beitrag zur Bantuistik aus heutiger Sicht', *Anthropos*, 71: 673–715.

―――― (1977a) 'Zur frühen Siedlungsgeschichte der Savannen-Bantu aus lauthistorischer Sicht', in W. Möhlig, F. Rottland and B. Heine (eds.), *Zur Spracheschichte und Ethnohistorie in Afrika*, pp. 166–85. Berlin: Reimer.

―――― (1977b) 'Dialektgrenzen und Dialektkontinua im Bantu-Sprachgebiet von Kenia: zum Problem der Grenzfindung und Grenzgewichtung', in J. Göschel, P. Ivić and K. Kehr (eds.), *Dialekt und Dialektologie*: 291–306. Wiesbaden:

Steiner.

————— (1977c) 'Synchrone Faktoren des Sprachwandels im Savannen-Bantu', in H. Jungraithmayr (ed.), *Struktur und Wandel afrikanischer Sprachen*, pp. 132–50. Berlin: Reimer.

————— (1979) 'The Bantu nucleus: its conditional nature and its pre-historical significance', *Sprache und Geschichte in Africa*, 1: 109–41.

————— (1980) 'Lehnwortforschung und Ethnohistorie', *Paideuma*, 26: 7–20.

————— (1981a) 'Stratification in the History of the Bantu Languages', *Sprache und Geschichte in Africa*, 3: 251–316.

————— (1981b) 'Die Bantusprachen im engeren Sinne', in B. Heine, T. C. Schadeberg and E. Wolf (eds.), *Die Sprachen Afrikas*, pp. 77–116. Hamburg: Buske.

————— (1981c) 'Lineare und hybride Lautverschiebungen im Bantu', in H. Jungraithmayr (ed.), *Berliner afrikanistische Vorträge*, pp. 83–101. Berlin: Reimer.

MOL, Frans (1978) *Maa: a dictionary of the Maasai language and folklore*. Nairobi: Marketing and Publishing Ltd.

MONOD, Théodore (ed.) (1975) *Pastoralism in Tropical Africa*. London: Oxford University Press for the International African Institute.

MÜHLMANN, Wilhelm E. (1964) *Rassen, Ethnien, Kulturen*. Neuwied & Berlin: Luchterhand.

NEWBURY, David S. (1980) 'The clans of Rwanda: an historical hypothesis', *Africa*, 50 (4): 389–403.

OCHIENG', William R. (1976) 'The transformation of a Bantu settlement into a Luo Ruothdom: a case study of the Yimbo community in Nyanza up to AD 1900', in B. A. Ogot (ed.), *History and Social Change in East Africa* (*Hadith*, 6), pp. 44–64, Nairobi: Kenya Literature Bureau.

OOMEN, Antoinette J. G. (1977a) 'Aspects of Rendille Grammar with Special Reference to Focus Structure', MA thesis, Nairobi.

————— (1977b) 'The Adequacy of the Features Tongue Root Position, High, Low and Back in a Comparison of Aspects of Rendille and Somali Phonology' (MS) Nairobi.

————— (1978) 'Focus in the Rendille clause', *Studies in African Linguistics*, 9: 36–65.

————— (1981) 'Gender and plurality in Rendille', *Afroasiatic Linguistics*, 8 (1): 33–75.

OGOT, B. A. (1970) 'Historians and East Africa', in J. D. Fage (ed.), *Africa Discovers Her Past*. London.

PANKHURST, Richard (1965) 'The trade of southern and western Ethiopia and the Indian Ocean ports in the nineteenth and early twentieth centuries', *Journal of Ethiopian Studies*, 3 (2): 37–74.

PAULITSCHKE, P. (1889) 'Die Wanderungen der Oromo oder Galla Ostafrikas', *Mitteilungen der Anthropologischen Gesellschaft in Wien*, 19: 165–78.

————— (1983) *Ethnographie Nordost-Afrikas*, vol. I: *Die materielle Kultur der Danakil, Galla und Somali*. Berlin: Reimer.

PHILIPSON, J. H. (1916) 'Notes on the Galla', *Man*, 16 (107): 177–81.

PIRONE, Michele (1954) 'Leggende e tradizioni storiche dei Somali Ogaden', *Archivio per l'Antropologia e l'Etnologia*, 84: 119–43.

PLOWMAN, Clifford H. F. (1918) 'Notes on the Gedamoch ceremonies among the Boran', *Journal of the African Society*, 18: 114–21.

PRATT, D. J., and M. D. GWYNNE (1977) *Rangeland Management in East Africa*. London: Hodder & Stoughton.

RAVENSTEIN, E. G. (1884) 'Somal and Galla Land; embodying information collected by the Rev. Thomas Wakefield', *Proceedings of the Royal Geographical*

Society, 6: 255–73.

REPUBLIC OF KENYA (1981) *Kenya Population Census 1979*, vol. I. Central Bureau of Statistics. Ministry of Economic Planning and Development.

ROTTLAND, Franz (1982) *Die südnilotischen Sprachen*. Berlin: Reimer.

SAHLINS, Marshal (1961) 'The segmentary lineage: an organization of predatory expansion', *American Anthropologist*, 63: 322–45.

—— (1985) *Islands of History*. Chicago: University of Chicago Press.

SAVOIA, Luigi Amadeo di (1932.) *La esplorazione dello Uabi-Uebi Scebeli*. Milano: Mondadori.

SCHLEE, Günther (1978a) *Sprachliche Studien zum Rendille: Grammatik, Texte, Glossar, with English Summary of Rendille Grammar*. Hamburg: Buske.

—— (1978b) 'Soziale, kosmologische und mythologische Bezüge der Verben "herauskommen" und "sich drehen" im Rendille', in H. Jungraithmayr (ed.), *Struktur und Wandel afrikanischer Sprachen*, pp. 162–70. Berlin: Reimer.

—— (1979) *Das Glaubens- und Sozialsystem der Rendille: kamelnomaden Nordkenias*. Berlin: Reimer.

—— (1981) 'The Orientation of Progress: conflicting aims and strategies of pastoral nomads and development agents in East Africa, a problem survey', paper for the conference on Cultural identity and Development in Africa, Bayreuth, 11–13 June.

—— (1982a) 'Annahme und Ablehnung von Christentum und Islam bei den Rendille in Nord-Kenia', *Ostafrikanische Völker zwischen Mission und Regierung*, pp. 101–30. D-8520 Erlangen: Lehrstuhl für Missionswissenschaften, University of Erlamgen, Jordanweg 2.

—— (1982b) 'Zielkonflikte und Zielvereinheitlichung zwischen Entwicklungsplanung und Wanderhirten in Ostafrika', in Fred Scholz und J. Janzen (eds.), *Nomadismus – ein Entwicklungsproblem?*, pp. 96–109. Berlin: Reimer.

—— (1983) 'The Causative in Rendille', paper presented at the XXII Deutscher Orientalistentag, Tübingen, March.

—— (1984a) 'Nomaden und Staat: das Beispiel Nordkenia', *Sociologus*, 34 (2): 140–61.

—— (1984b) 'Intra- und interethnische Beziehungsnetze nordkenianischer Wanderhirten', *Paideuma*, 30: 69–80.

—— (1984c) 'Une société pastorale pluriethnique: Oromo et Somalis au Nord du Kenya', *Production pastorale et société*, 15 (Autumn): 21–39.

—— (1984d) 'Oromo Expansion and its Impact on Ethnogenesis in Northern Kenya', paper presented at the Eighth International Conference on Ethiopian Studies, Addis Ababa, November.

—— (1985a) 'Les Nomades et l'Etat au Nord du Kénia', paper presented at the European colloquium 'Perspectives Anthropologiques sur l'Histoire Africaine: Pouvoirs et Etat', Paris, 20–23 November.

—— (1985b) 'Inter-ethnic clan identities among Cushitic-speaking pastoralists', *Africa*, 55 (1): 17–38.

—— (1985c) 'Mobile Forschung bei mehreren Ethnien: kamelnomaden Nordkenias', in Hans Fischer (ed.), *Feldforschungen*, pp. 203–18. Berlin: Reimer.

—— (1987a) 'Somaloid history: oral tradition, *Kulturgeschichte* and historical linguistics in an area of Oromo/Somaloid interaction', in H. Jungraithmayr and W. W. Müller (eds.), *Proceedings of the Fourth International Hamito-Semitic Congress*, Marburg, September 1983. Amsterdam & Philadelphia: John Benjamins. (Vol. XLIV of the series *Current Issues in Linguistic Theory*.)

—— (1987b) 'Camel Management Strategies and Attitudes towards Camels in the Horn', paper presented at a workshop on 'The Exploitation of Animals in

Africa', Aberdeen, March. (*Proceedings* in preparation by J. Stone. Aberdeen University African Studies group.)

—— (1987c) 'Holy Grounds', paper presented at a workshop on 'Property Rights and Problems of Pastoral Development in the Sahel', Manchester, April. (*Proceedings* in preparation by P. T. W. Baxter.)

—— (1988) 'L'islamisation du passé: à propos de l'effet réactif de la conversion de groupes somalis et somaloïdes á l'islam sur la représentation de l'histoire dans leurs traditions orales', in W. Möhlig and H. Jungraithmayr (eds.), *La littérature orale en Afrique comme source pour la découverte des cultures traditionelles*. Collectanea Instituti Anthropos, 36. Berlin: Reimer. .

—— (forthcoming.) 'Who are the Tana Orma? The problem of their identification in a wider Oromo framework', in W. Möhlig and C. J. Winter (eds.), *Peoples of the Lower Tana River: contributions to their languages, cultures and history*. Berlin: Reimer.

—— (in preparation) *Heilige Berge und Pilgerfahrten im kenianisch-äthiopischen Grenzgebiet.*

SCHLEICHER, A. W. (1893) *Geschichte der Galla*. Berlin: Th. Fröhlich.

SCHNEIDER, Harold K. (1979) *Livestock and Equality in East Africa: the economic basis for social structures*. Bloomington: Indiana University Press.

SPENCER, Paul. (1973) *Nomads in Alliance*. London: Oxford University Press.

STATISTISCHES BUNDESAMT WIESBADEN (1982) *Statistik des Auslandes: Länderbericht Kenia:* Stuttgart & Mainz: Kohlhammer.

STEWART, Frank Henderson (1977) *Fundamentals of Age-Group Systems*. New York: Academic Press.

STRECK, Bernhard (1982) 'Beharrung und Wandel in der Religion der Maassai', *Ostafrikanische Völker zwischen Mission und Regierung*, pp. 83–100. D-8580 Erlangen: Lehrstuhl für Missionswissenschaften, Jordanweg 2, University of Erlangen.

TABLINO, Paolo (1974) *Note sui Gabbra del Kenya*. Marsabit: Catholic Mission, P. O. Marsabit, Kenya.

—— (1975) 'The Calculation of Time among the Gabbra of Kenya' (MS.), Marsabit.

—— (1980) *I Gabbra del Kenya*. Bologna: EMI.

—— (1980–81.) 'Nomi personali usati dai Gabbra del Kenya', *Rassegna di Studi Etiopici*, 28: 77–91.

TALBOT, Lee M. (1971) 'Ecological aspects of aid programs in East Africa, with particular reference to rangelands', in B. Lundholm (ed.), *Ecology and the Less Developed Countries* (Bulletins from the Ecological Research Committee, 13), pp. 21–51. Stockholm.

TATE, H. R. (1904) 'Journey to the Rendille country, British East Africa', *Geographical Journal*, 23 (2): 220–28.

THOMSON, J. (1968 [1885]) *Through Masailand*. London: F. Cass.

TORNAY, Serge (1982) 'Archéologie, ethno-histoire, ethnographie: trois façons de reconstruire le temps', in J. Mack and P. Robertshaw (eds.), *Culture History in the Southern Sudan*, pp. 131–48. Nairobi: BIEA.

TORRY, William J. (1973) 'Subsistence Ecology among the Gabra, Nomads of the Kenya/Ethiopia Frontier', PhD thesis, Columbia University.

—— (1978) 'Gabra age organisation and ecology', in P. T. W. Baxter and U. Almagor, *Age, Generation and Time*, pp. 183–206. London: Hurst & Co.

TRIMINGHAM, J. S. (1976 [1952]) *Islam in Ethiopia*. London: F. Cass.

TUCKER, A. N., and M. A. BRYAN (1956) *Handbook of African Languages*, Part III: *The Non-Bantu Languages of North-Eastern Africa*. Oxford: Oxford University Press for the International African Institute.

The Non-Bantu Languages of North-Eastern Africa. Oxford: Oxford University Press for the International African Institute.

TURNBULL, R. G. (1955) *The Darod Invasion*. Privately published.

TURTON, E. R. (1974) 'Bantu, Galla and Somali migrations in the Horn of Africa: a reassessment of the Juba/Tana area', *Journal of African History*, 16 (4): 459–537.

TUTSCHEK, Karl. (1844) *Dictionary of the Galla Language* (Galla–English–German). München.

ULLENDORF, Edward. (1973) *The Ethiopians*. London: Oxford University Press.

VENTURINO, Bartolomeo. (1973) *Dizionario Borana–Italiano*. Bologna: Editrice Missionaria Italiana.

—— (1978) *Dizionario Italiano–Borana*. Marsabit: Catholic Mission.

VOSSEN, Rainer. (1982) *The Eastern Nilotes*. Berlin: Reimer.

WERNER, Alice. (1914) 'The Galla of the East African Protectorate', *Journal of the African Society*, 13 (50); January: 121–42, and April: 262–87.

—— (1915) 'Some Galla notes', *Man*, 15: 17–22.

WESTERN, David. (1974) 'The Environment and Ecology of Pastoralists in Arid Savannahs', paper presented at the Social Science Research Council symposium on 'The Future of Traditional "primitive" societies', Cambridge, December.

WINTER J. C. (1981) 'Bantu prehistory in Eastern and Southern Africa: an evaluation of D. W. Phillipson's archeological synthesis in the light of ethnological and linguistic evidence', *Sprache und Geschichte in Afrika*, 3: 317–56.

WÜSTENFELD, Ferdinand (1853) *Genealogische Tabellen der Arabischen Stämme und Familien*. Osnabrück: Otto Zeiler.

INDEX